A HISTORY OF
THE CHURCH IN ENGLAND

A HISTORY OF
THE CHURCH IN ENGLAND

JOHN R. H. MOORMAN
D.D., Litt.D

THIRD EDITION

MOREHOUSE PUBLISHING
Harrisburg, PA

Copyright © 1963, 1967, 1973, 1976, 1980
by John Richard Humpidge Moorman

First published in Great Britain by A & C Black, Ltd

Published in the United States by

Morehouse Publishing
P.O. Box 1321
Harrisburg, PA 17105

Morehouse Publishing is a division of The Morehouse Group.

Moorman, John R. H. (John Richard Humpidge), 1905-
   A history of the Church in England / John R. H. Moorman.—3rd ed.
      p.   cm.
Originally published: 3rd ed. London : A. and C. Black, 1973.
Includes bibliographical references (p. xxx-xxx) and Index.
ISBN 0-8192-1406-X
   1. Great Britain—Church history.   I. Title.
BR743.2.M6   1994   94-6111
274.2—dc20   CIP

Printed in the United States of America

03 02 01 00   10 9

PREFACE TO THE THIRD EDITION

In preparing a third edition of this book, I have tried to correct any errors in previous editions and to add, especially in the bibliographies, what seem to me to be the more important works which have been published in recent years. I have also added a new chapter to tell the story of the Church during the last twenty-five years or so. In doing all this I am much indebted to the Rev. J. G. Bishop and to the Rev. Dr. G. R. Selby for their help and advice.

JOHN R. H. MOORMAN
(Bishop of Ripon)

Ripon,
1972

PREFACE TO THE FIRST EDITION

IT is notoriously difficult to pour a gallon of water into a pint pot. It is almost as difficult to compress the history of 1750 years into 400 pages. This book, therefore, can be no more than an introduction, a guide to such as are interested in the history of the Christian Church in England and wish to know more about it.

In drawing up this account I have tried to tell it as a story, a narrative of events (based, like other events, on cause and effect) from the first preaching of the Word in England down to the present day. In so doing, a careful selection of facts has had to be made; and I cannot suppose that any other historian would have made the same selection or that my selection will satisfy every reader. That is inevitable. All history that is worthy of the name is biased, because every writer who is a true historian and not a mere annalist, must have a point of view which will inevitably reveal itself in his pages.

In writing a history of the Church in England the historian has to handle subjects of great controversy and diversity of opinion, subjects which are bound up with the deepest emotions and strongest convictions of mankind. What, for example, are we to make of the Reformation? To some the breach with Rome cannot appear otherwise than as a great disaster. Yet to others it may wear the aspect of a providential deliverance, a real sign of progress under the power of the Holy Spirit. So it must be with any kind of history, and especially the history of religion.

v

I therefore make no claim to be impartial. Indeed, I hope I am not; for impartial history would be very dull.

Historical text-books are almost certain to contain a large number of sweeping statements for which little evidence can be produced simply because there is no space for it. This book contains many such generalizations. But in order to help the reader to follow up any subject in which he is interested I have given references to what I regard as the most useful, reliable and accessible books. These represent, of course, only a small fraction of the literature available; but there are about 800 of them mentioned in the following pages, and most of the 800 will give further references and bibliographies for those who desire them.

I should like to thank the Rev. J. C. Dickinson of Cambridge and Canon Lowther Clarke of Chichester for having read parts of the manuscript, and for their criticisms and suggestions.

JOHN R. H. MOORMAN

Chichester,
1952.

CONTENTS

vii

PART I

THE ROMAN AND ANGLO-SAXON PERIOD

CHAPTER I

THE CHURCH IN BRITAIN BEFORE 597

i. *The Coming of the Faith*

THE exact date when the Christian message first came to England is unknown. At the time when the Christian Church was gradually extending its influence in the countries on both sides of the Mediterranean, England was in process of being colonized by Rome. Roman legionaries were marching along their own well-made roads, Roman officers were bringing the old British tribes to heel, Roman law was being administered, and one more province was in process of being absorbed into the great Roman Empire which now dominated the known world.

Among those who came from Rome, whether soldiers, administrators, traders or camp-followers, there may well have been some who had heard and accepted the message of the Christian Church and who secretly prayed to the Christians' God while their fellows did homage to the old gods of the State, or to Mithras or Isis or one of the gods of the mystery religions. But of this we have no certain knowledge. If there were such, they have left no record behind them. But where history is silent, legend and tradition have produced strange and wonderful stories of journeys to this island made by S. Paul or S. Philip or S. Joseph of Arimathea and of the founding of a Christian church at Glastonbury.[1]

The first mention of any Christians in Britain is in Tertullian's tract against the Jews, written about 200, in which he speaks of parts of Britain, inaccessible to the Romans, which had yet been conquered by Christ; while Origen, writing about forty years later, includes Britain among the places where Christians are to be found.[2] It seems clear, then, that about the year 200 the Christian world was becoming aware of the fact that there were believers in Britain, and it has been suggested that, when the savage persecutions broke out

---

[1] The earliest written record of S. Joseph of Arimathea is in an addition of *c*. 1250 to the Chronicle of William of Malmesbury. See J. Armitage Robinson, *Two Glastonbury Legends* (1926), for a critical study of the tradition.

[2] A. W. Haddan and W. Stubbs, *Councils and Ecclesiastical Documents* (1871), i, pp. 3-4. But see W. H. C. Frend in *Christianity in Britain, 300–700*, ed. M. W. Barley and R. P. C. Hanson (1968), p. 37.

in Gaul in 177, a number of Christians fled northwards and that some may have found their way to these shores.

For the next century or so little is known of these Christians in Britain. The third century was, on the whole, a time of great advance for the Church for, apart from the persecutions of Decius and Valerian (249–60), it was an age of comparative peace and security when books were written, churches built and schools founded. In Britain some organization was being set up, for, by the year 314, there were several bishops in the country, three of whom —Eborius of York, Restitutus of London and Adelphius probably of Colchester[1]—attended the Council of Arles. This shows a considerable advance in the establishment of the Church on a diocesan basis, and implies that the scattered Christians of the third century had by now organized themselves into a definite Church. No British bishops are known to have answered the Emperor's summons to Nicaea in 325, but Athanasius expressly states that the British Church accepted the decisions of that Council.[2]

The first Christian in Britain whose name is recorded was Alban who, according to Bede, was a layman of the Roman city of Verulamium who gave shelter to a Christian priest fleeing from his persecutors. While the priest lay hid, Alban learnt of the Christian faith and was converted; and when the soldiers came to arrest the fugitive, Alban, dressed in the priest's cloak, gave himself up, was condemned to death, and martyred on the hill where the abbey church of S. Alban's now stands. The date is generally assumed to have been 304, during the persecutions of Diocletian.[3]

With the passing of the Edict of Milan in 312 the Christian Church entered upon a new phase of its history. For three centuries the Christian faith had been classed among the 'illicit religions'; it had always been to some extent unpopular; and the shadow of persecution had lain over it. By this decree Constantine removed the ban, and for the first time in history the Christian was free to declare his faith openly without fear of a cruel death. From this time onwards a great and rapid advance was made.

[1] The third bishop is styled of the *civitas colonia Londinensium*, but no name is given. Various suggestions have been made, *e.g.* Caerleon-on-Usk in Haddan and Stubbs, *Councils*, i, p. 7; but it is now thought that Colchester is the most likely; M. Deanesly, *The Pre-Conquest Church in England* (1961), p. 7.

[2] *Ibid.* pp. 7–8.

[3] Bede, *Ecc. Hist.* i, 7; cf. C. Plummer, *Baedae Opera Historica* (1896), ii, pp. 17–20. The account, which presents a number of difficulties, also mentions the martyrdom of two Christians, Aaron and Julius, at Caerleon-on-Usk. Bede is here using Gildas; see J. A. Giles, *Old English Chronicles*, p. 303.

Such an advance must have been made in Britain, but still our evidence is very scant. In 359 some British bishops again attended one of the great councils of the Church, the Council of Rimini; but they were so poor that three of them were driven to accept the imperial offer of money to pay their expenses, though all the other bishops present had refused to do so in order to preserve their independence.[1] This would suggest that the Church in Britain, though becoming more organized, was as yet poor, and no doubt many of its members were drawn from among the semi-Romanized natives who were far from being the most prosperous members of the community. Yet that there were Christians among the richer Romans is proved by the appearance of Christian symbols, such as the *Chi-Rho* sign, among the mosaic pavements which adorned their villas.[2]

Apart from such decorations the Christians of the period of the Roman occupation have left little trace of their handiwork. The chief exceptions are the little Christian chapel at Lullingstone in Kent, built about 360 and decorated with mural paintings, and the chapels at Silchester and Hinton St. Mary of about the same period. The chapel at Silchester was a small building, only about 42 feet in length, with an apse at the western end of the nave, aisles, transepts and narthex. The altar appears to have been of wood and the priest celebrated facing west with his back to the congregation. Outside the church was a stone trough where the faithful washed before entering the church.[3] No doubt there were other churches in different parts of the country, but few traces of them have so far been found.

ii. *Pelagius, Germanus, Ninian*

Although the Christian Church by the end of the fourth century had existed in Britain for close on two hundred years, our knowledge of any individual Christians (with the exception of S. Alban) is extremely limited. From this point onwards Church History takes on a new aspect. We leave the mists of conjecture and anonymity and enter into the clearer light in which real personalities can be distinguished.

The first of these was a heretic—Pelagius—the man who roused

[1] Haddan and Stubbs, *Councils*, i, pp. 9-10.
[2] See Jocelyn Toynbee's article in *Christianity in Britain, 300-700*, pp. 177-92.
[3] A. W. Clapham, *English Romanesque Architecture* (1930), i, pp. 12-13, and M. Deanesly, *Sidelights on the Anglo-Saxon Church* (1962), pp. 13-14.

the fiercest passions of S. Augustine and who has given us the heresy which to this day holds so strong an attraction for the British people. Pelagius was a Romanized Briton and a monk, well-educated, urbane, highly civilized. About the year 380, when he was quite a young man, he left Britain never to return. For the rest of his life he travelled about the Mediterranean world, 'an elusive and gracious figure, beloved and respected wherever he goes ... silent, smiling, reserved', and he appears to have ended his days in Syria.[1] Pelagius, like some other Christians, had been shocked by the hard and rigid doctrines of S. Augustine, which seemed to him to deny the moral courage and dignity of man. He found it difficult to believe in Original Sin, and so great was his faith in man that he believed it possible for man to reach perfection without the intervention of supernatural grace. It was this which aroused the indignant fervour of Augustine and led to his condemnation.[2]

Pelagius never taught in Britain, but his doctrines found a footing here through the teaching of one Agricola early in the fifth century. To counteract this the bishops in Gaul invited two bishops to come to Britain—Germanus, Bishop of Auxerre (418–48) and Lupus, Bishop of Troyes (427–79). These two arrived in Britain in 429 and immediately made their presence felt. Germanus had been a soldier and man of action before becoming a bishop, and was obviously a man of great force of character. Finding the British timid and lacking in self-confidence he organized them as a fighting force and, with wild yells of 'Alleluia', led them to victory against a marauding army of Picts, probably near Mold in Flintshire. Wherever Germanus went, he encouraged and strengthened the British against their opponents, whether pagan Picts or Pelagian heretics. Striding through the country with a bag of relics round his neck Germanus, by his preaching and by his miracles, convinced all gainsayers and put new life and courage into the British Christians.[3]

Meanwhile, further north, a more gentle apostle of Christ was at work in the valleys of Cumberland and southern Scotland. This was Ninian who, after studying the monasticism of S. Martin at Marmoutier, came to Britain, apparently as a solitary missionary, perhaps as early as the year 397. At Whithorn in Galloway he founded a

[1] Collingwood and Myres, *Roman Britain*, pp.308-9.
[2] See J. F. Bethune Baker, *Early History of Christian Doctrine* (2nd ed. 1920), pp. 301-20.   [3] Bede, *Ecc. Hist.* i, 17-21.

monastery built of stone and whitewashed so that it might be the most conspicuous object in the district. This came to be known as the White House, or *Candida Casa*, and became the base from which Ninian and his monks set out on their evangelistic journeys. These seem to have taken them not only among the savage Pictish tribes in the neighbourhood of the Roman Wall but also up the east coast of Scotland.[1] Whithorn continued to act as a centre of evangelistic enterprise for some time, one of its most famous members being S. Kentigern who worked in Scotland, northern England and Wales early in the sixth century.[2]

iii. *S. Patrick*

While Ninian was at work in Galloway there was growing up in the west of England a small boy who was soon to make his mark on the history of the expansion of the Church. This was Patrick, the son of a British 'decurion' or local administrator called Calpornius who was a deacon and the son of a priest. The family, who lived somewhere near the sea,[3] were one day attacked by a gang of pirates young men into slavery, among them Patrick now about fifteen years of age. He was taken to Ireland, where he was kept in captivity as a swineherd; but after six years he escaped, and perhaps spent some time in Gaul where he may have come into contact with the monastic movement under the leadership of S. Martin of Tours. While he was undergoing his training he conceived a desire to return to the scenes of his captivity in order that he might preach the Gospel to the men among whom he had lived and suffered. After visiting his old home in Britain he was, in the year 432, consecrated as bishop for work in Ireland and immediately returned there as the apostle of Christ.

For the next thirty years Patrick fought a hard battle against the

---

[1] See W. D. Simpson, *St. Ninian and the Origins of the Christian Church in Scotland* (1940), and J. MacQueen, *St. Ninia; a Study of literary and linguistic evidence* (1961).

[2] For Kentigern see K. H. Jackson 'The Sources for the Life of St. Kentigern' in *Studies in the Early British Church*, ed. N. K. Chadwick (1958).

[3] Attempts to locate the place of Patrick's birth and childhood have all ended in failure; see R. P. C. Hanson, *Saint Patrick* (1968), pp. 113-6.

he Irish tribes, and his life was often in danger. He
ly in Ireland and made many converts, baptizing them
by the same and and ordaining clergy everywhere. He attempted to
introduce the diocesan system which he had studied in Gaul, but it
failed chiefly through lack of any cities which could form the centres
of government. The only diocese which had any kind of permanence
was that of Armagh where Patrick himself ruled. But if the diocesan
system failed, the monasteries which Patrick founded became the
chief feature of the Irish Church. The Irish monasteries were quite
unlike those of the rest of Europe, as was also the relationship between
a bishop and an abbot. Whereas in the usual system the bishop had
general oversight of the monasteries in his diocese, in the Celtic plan
the abbot ruled supreme and often had a number of bishops among
his choir-monks. The monastery, in fact, was little more than 'an
ecclesiastical replica of the tribe'.[1] The bishop generally had no territorial jurisdiction: he was raised to the episcopate because of the
sanctity of his life and was invested with the powers of ordination,
confirmation and consecration; but he had no administrative function. That belonged to the abbot.

As Patrick travelled about, monasteries sprang up everywhere, some
of them so large as to include several thousand monks. There was no
one rule which all obeyed, for each monastery had its own. Many
of them were very harsh, for the Christianity of some of the monks
had not yet gone very deep and nothing less than a rigorous and
strict discipline could control the large numbers of recently converted
pagans. But the monasteries were much the most important element
in the early life of the Irish Church, and it was from them that the
missionaries went out with the message of Christ.[2]

iv. *The Anglo-Saxon Invasions*

While in Ireland Christianity was advancing, in England it had
been forced to retreat. Early in the fifth century the Romans abandoned their hold on England and the country was rapidly overrun
by the invading armies of the Jutes, Angles and Saxons. The British
were either conquered and absorbed into the new society or they fled

[1] A. Hamilton Thompson in *Bede; his Life, Times and Writings* (1935), p. 62.
[2] See *The Tripartite Life of S. Patrick* in the Rolls Series, J. B. Bury, *Life of S. Patrick* and R. P. C. Hanson, *Saint Patrick* (1968).

westwards and settled in the mountains of Wales or among the Cornish tors. The invaders largely destroyed the Christian Church in the parts which they conquered, and for 150 years the faith was practically extinct in England. Its place was taken by a form of Teutonic heathenism which the conquerors brought with them.

In the strongholds of the West, however, the Church continued to exist. Our knowledge of it comes chiefly from Gildas who wrote in Wales about 535. He is severely critical of the British clergy whom he describes as 'unworthy wretches, wallowing, after the fashion of swine, in their old and unhappy puddle of intolerable wickedness'.[1] But though Gildas has little that is good to say of the British Church, and though it may well have deteriorated in its isolation, his picture is not one of chaos. There is organization. There are bishops holding synods to which their clergy are summoned. There are monasteries where some kind of rule is kept.

The British Church also had its saints, among whom the most famous was S. David, the only one of the four patron saints of these islands who was a native of the country which he represents. David (c. 520–88) was a typical Celtic abbot-bishop, an evangelist and founder of monasteries, and he was ably supported by other saints —S. Illtyd his teacher, S. Deiniol and others.

Thus while, in England, Wodin and Thor had usurped the place of Christ, in Wales the Christian Church kept the light of the faith burning. Cut off though it tended to be from the rest of Christendom it still managed to hold out against the pressure of paganism both from within and from without. But it paid the penalty of isolation. It tended to become insular and self-absorbed; and, as Bede complained, it made no attempt to convert the Saxons. For missionary zeal in the sixth century we must look mainly not to Wales but to Ireland.

v. S. Columba

After the death of S. Patrick about 461 church life continued to develop in Ireland, the monastery being still the centre of organization and activity. It is in the school attached to one of these monasteries, Moville, that we first meet Columba, son of Phelim, of the royal house of Niall of the Nine Hostages. The boy, who had been

[1] J. A. Giles, Old English Chronicles, p. 345; cf. Haddan and Stubbs, Councils, i, pp. 44-107.

born in 521, was known as Colum the dove, but his character had more of the eagle than the dove about it. Tall, broad, vigorous, tempestuous, with a voice of thunder, he could strike terror into the heart of any who opposed him. He has been described as 'a typical Irishman, vehement, irresistible: hear him curse a niggardly rich man or bless the heifers of a poor peasant; see him follow a robber who had plundered a friend, cursing the wretch to his destruction, following him to the water's edge, wading up to the knees in the clear, green sea-water, with both hands raised to heaven'.[1]

So violent a nature, especially in one of royal blood, was almost bound to be implicated sooner or later in Irish tribal politics and feuds. About the year 560 a petty dispute over the ownership of a manuscript developed into a quarrel in which whole tribes were involved and led to the battle of Culdreihmne in which Columba led his forces to an overwhelming victory, leaving three thousand of the enemy dead upon the field. But Columba had gone too far. The Church turned against him, and he was obliged to leave the country.

In 563 Columba left Ireland with twelve companions in an open boat and sailed northwards, landing finally at Hy or Ioua, now called Iona, a small island off the west coast of Scotland. Having discovered that they were out of sight of Ireland, and therefore less likely to be tempted to return, they buried their boat and decided to make this island their home. On the eastern shore of the island, immediately opposite Mull, they built a monastery of the usual Celtic pattern— a church and refectory of wood, a group of bee-hive huts, and an encircling wall protecting the whole enclosure. The life which they lived was that to which they had been accustomed in Ireland. It was hard, simple and austere. Much time was spent in tilling the soil of the island, fishing in its waters, copying manuscripts and in performing the daily round of prayer and praise. Nor was their work confined to the cloister. Iona soon became a centre from which missionary journeys were undertaken both to the mainland of Scotland and to the islands of the Hebrides.

For over thirty years Columba laboured here. Much of his time was spent as father of his family of monks, a family which soon became very large, for the fame of Columba spread far and wide. To Iona also came many who were sick in body or troubled in spirit, for the abbot's powers were held in high repute and many stories of

[1] R. H. Hodgkin, *History of the Anglo-Saxons* (1935), i, p. 254.

miraculous healings and blessings were current. But Columba was also often engaged in missionary journeys. Southern Scotland seems to have already accepted some form of Christianity, so that it was to the unconverted Northern Picts that Columba directed his energies. We find him at Aberdeen and in the Orkneys, but his greatest triumph was in the conversion of King Brude at Inverness. As Columba went on his travels he found the powers of the druids strongly entrenched, but with the cry of 'Christ is my Druid' he beat them at their own game as a wonder-worker and brought them to contempt. Then he began to build on the sure faith of Christ, and the pagan clans were gradually brought within the fold of the Christian Church.

In his later years Columba spent more and more of his time at Iona. In spite of his homesickness for Ireland,[1] and his occasional visits there, the island of Iona was now his home, and he divided his time between the communal life of the monastery and the more solitary life of a hermit. He died at Iona on June 9, 597 at the age of seventy-six.[2]

By this time Augustine had landed in Kent and the conversion of England had begun.

[1] See the poem 'Columcille fecit' in Trenholme, *The Story of Iona*, pp. 155-6.
[2] For the life of S. Columba see Adamnan, *Vita S. Columbae*, ed. W. Reeves (1857 and translation by J. T. Fowler (1895). Also E. C. Trenholme, *The Story of Iona* (1909), and Lucy Menzies, *St. Columba of Iona* (1949).

NOTE ON BOOKS

FOR general history see R. G. Collingwood and J. N. L. Myres, *Roman Britain* in the *Oxford History of England*, vol. i (1936), and *Cambridge Medieval History*, vol. ii. The chief sources for the history of the Church in this period are Bede's *Ecclesiastical History*, Book I, and the documents in Haddan and Stubbs, *Councils and Ecclesiastical Documents*, vol. i (1871). The best modern history of the period is that by M. Deanesly, *The Pre-Conquest Church in England* (1961). See also her *Sidelights on the Anglo-Saxon Church* (1962). For the Celtic Church reference may be made to L. Gougaud, *Christianity in Celtic Lands* (1932), J. A. Duke, *The Columban Church* (1932), J. F. Kenney, *Sources for the Early History of Ireland*, vol. i (1929), J. Ryan, *Irish Monasticism* (1931), F. E. Warren, *Liturgy and Ritual of the Celtic Church* (1881), and N. K. Chadwick, *Studies in the Early British Church* (1958). See also *Christianity in Britain, 300-700*, ed. M. W. Barley and R. P. C. Hanson (1968).

CHAPTER II

THE CONVERSION OF ENGLAND
(597–664)

i. *S. Augustine of Canterbury*

THE initiative for the conversion of England belongs to S. Gregory the Great. This Roman monk was deeply concerned with the state both of the Empire and of the Church. Not only was the Empire being overrun by barbarians, but countries which had been Christian were being lost to paganism, and neither Church nor State seemed able to deal with the problem. Among the lands which had suffered in this way was England, where the Germanic gods reigned supreme. It was with these anxieties on his mind that Gregory encountered the Anglian boys in the forum at Rome and was inspired to take action. We need not take the whole story of the punning conversation between the saint and the slave-master exactly as it has come down to us, but it may well be based upon fact. This warm-hearted and far-seeing monk was deeply moved by the spectacle of these helpless little pagans, and decided that, sooner or later, missionaries must be sent to their distant land. 'The episode', says Hodgkin, 'marks something more than the birth of an idea in the mind of one of the world's great men. It is a turning-point in the history of Latin Christianity.'[1] For the first time for many years the Roman Church had shown signs of a missionary concern.

The story of the 'angelic Angles' belongs probably to about the year 586, and during the next few years Gregory made a number of attempts to arrange a mission to England. Once he set out himself, but after three days was recalled to Rome, so great was his popularity. But in spite of constant procrastination the idea of a mission never left him, and when he became pope in 590 he devoted part of the revenue of the papacy to buying up Anglian slave-boys in order that they might be educated in the Christian faith and eventually sent back to their own land as ambassadors of Christ. This, however,

---

[1] R. H. Hodgkin, *History of the Anglo-Saxons*, i, p. 259.

would take many years, and the need was urgent. Appeals from England for Christian teachers were already reaching Rome.[1] There was no time to lose.

Thus, a few years later, in 596, Gregory selected one of his own monks, Augustine, prior of his own monastery on the Coelian Hill, and laid upon him the charge of leading an expedition to England. Augustine probably had no particular desire to undertake such a mission; he gives no impression of being an ardent evangelist; but he was a man under obedience. Gregory was not only his immediate superior in the monastery, he was also the successor of S. Peter and must be obeyed. Augustine, therefore, accepted the charge 'on obedience' and set off with a small party of his fellow-monks. But, travelling through Gaul, such terrible tales were told him of the savagery of the English people that both his courage and his obedience failed him, and he returned to Rome. Gregory, however, was not the sort of man to allow of failure, and Augustine was told to take heart and go forward.

The small band of evangelists landed in Kent early in 597 and soon discovered that their fears were totally unfounded. Ethelbert, King of Kent, who came out to meet them, was a civilized ruler with considerable sympathy for the Christian faith, and a Christian wife, Bertha, daughter of a Frankish king. Augustine was not, therefore, martyred on arrival. On the contrary, he was received kindly by the king who, though so cautious that he refused to meet him under cover for fear of magic and demanded a conference in the open air, willingly listened to what he had to say. Within a few weeks Augustine had made rapid progress and many baptisms had taken place. Of any serious opposition there was none.

The victory was certainly surprisingly easy, but there were reasons for this. Chief of these was the presence of the Christian queen, Bertha, and of her chaplains who had already done something to prepare the way for the message which Augustine came to deliver. Then again, Ethelbert was not a savage barbarian, but a comparatively cultured man and a ruler strong enough to carry his people with him in a change so drastic as the adoption of a new religion. Moreover the old Teutonic heathenism of the Angles was becoming out of date, and had little to offer to an age becoming more and

[1] In one of his letters Gregory says that news has reached him that the English were anxious to become Christians (*Epist. Gregorii*, i, p. 431).

more civilized. The ground was thus well prepared. Augustine had only to go in and reap the harvest.

Conversions followed so rapidly that Augustine and his monks were hard put to keep pace with them. In the autumn of 597 Augustine went over to Gaul to be consecrated as bishop, and on Christmas Day of that year he is said to have baptized over ten thousand converts in and around Canterbury.[1] No one could deny that the mission had been an outstanding success.

Gregory rejoiced to hear such good news of his protégé and watched over the little mission with the closest attention. He sent books, relics and ornaments for the churches which Augustine was building, and was always ready to give advice on the problems with which the missionaries were faced. About 601 Augustine wrote to the pope, sending a number of questions upon which he needed advice, and Gregory replied at some length.[2] The first question concerned the allocation of church money, Gregory laying down the principle, which was maintained throughout the Middle Ages, that the income of the Church should be divided into four parts—one for the bishop, one for the priest, one for the relief of the poor, and one for the upkeep of the church. On liturgical questions Augustine was advised to make his own rite, choosing what he found to be most 'pious, religious and correct' in the customs of other churches and adapting them to the needs of the English. Many of the problems were matrimonial or concerned with ceremonial purifications. Shortly afterwards Gregory sent a further letter in which he set out a plan for the division of England into two provinces each with an archbishop and twelve suffragans.

Gregory's only unwise step was in giving Augustine authority over the British bishops who had kept the flame burning during the years when the rest of England had reverted to heathenism. It was perhaps natural that the pope should ignore the rights of these rather dim and remote prelates, and that he should expect them to give way to his own nominee. But it was a mistake, for the British bishops bitterly resented the complete disregard of their position and refused to co-operate with the Roman mission or to attempt to reach agree-

---

[1] So said Gregory in a letter to the Patriarch of Alexandria (Haddan and Stubbs, *Councils*, iii, p. 12).

[2] Bede, *Ecc. Hist.* i, 27; H. Gee and W. J. Hardy, *Documents Illustrative of the History of the English Church* (1896), pp. 3–9; M. Deanesly, *Augustine of Canterbury* (1964), pp. 60–75.

ment on such matters as the date of Easter, baptismal customs, and so forth. The British Church may have lacked many graces, but it had some right to consideration. This right was ignored, and 'the chance of a united Church in Britain was lost for centuries'.[1]

With Gregory's death in 604 Augustine lost his best friend and most powerful supporter; nor did he himself survive much longer. But the mission was doing well. In the Kingdom of Kent many thousands had accepted the Christian faith and the Church quickly became firmly established. Not only was a new see at Rochester founded in 604, but an attempt was made to start a new diocese for the East Saxons with its centre at London. At Canterbury a number of churches had been built. The old church of S. Martin which probably went back to Roman times, and which had been used by Queen Bertha before the coming of Augustine, was restored. The archbishop set up his own see at Christ Church where he lived, probably on communal rather than strictly monastic lines, surrounded by his clerks. Near by he founded a monastery dedicated to S. Peter and S. Paul,[2] where the Rule of S. Benedict could be kept; and churches sprang up in many parts of the Kingdom of Kent. English workers having had little or no practice in building in anything but wood, builders were brought from Gaul or Italy who proceeded according to the designs with which they were familiar—a nave and semi-circular or polygonal apse and a number of projecting rooms, known as 'porticus', to north and south.[3]

Augustine died in the year 604 and his ministry to the English lasted therefore only about seven years; but during that time much was done. Augustine himself has not come down to us as a very forcible or original character. He was sent to do a job of work and he did it to the best of his ability. But he showed little enthusiasm, and a certain lack of courage. In Kent the way was made comparatively easy for him under a friendly and sympathetic king, and Augustine was content to stay in that kingdom and made no attempt to venture further afield. Nevertheless he led his expedition to victory and success, and if the way was made light for him that was not his fault but his good fortune. At his death the Church in Kent was living and active, but its roots did not go very deep and it

[1] R. H. Hodgkin, *History of the Anglo-Saxons*, i, p. 268.
[2] The dedication was later changed to S. Augustine's.
[3] A. W. Clapham, *English Romanesque Architecture* (1930), i, pp. 25-33.

nearly expired in 616 when a heathen succeeded to the throne.

ii. *The Roman Mission to Northumbria*

When S. Augustine had been at work in England for about four years he was joined by another Italian monk called Paulinus. After spending twenty-four years at work in the south of England he was consecrated bishop in 625 in order that he might accompany a Kentish princess called Ethelburga on her way north to marry Edwin, King of Northumbria.

On arriving at York Paulinus found himself very much as Augustine had been when he first came to Canterbury. He had a strong supporter in the queen, and a heathen king who was at least interested in the faith of the Christians. Paulinus began at once to preach the Gospel to the king and his nobles, and, like Augustine, his success appears to have been rapid. Coifi, the high priest of the old religion, was immediately converted and the witan meekly followed the lead given by the king. Edwin was baptized on Easter Eve, 627, at York in a wooden church which had been specially erected for the occasion.

Paulinus, 'a tall figure, slightly bent, with black hair, a thin hooked nose and an emaciated face',[1] worked indefatigably in Northumbria as Bishop of York. He travelled over much of Yorkshire, Nottinghamshire and north Lincolnshire preaching the Gospel in the villages and baptizing the people in the clear waters of their becks and rivers. So great was his success that in 634 he was made archbishop, and the *pallium* was sent to him from Rome. But before it reached him the whole situation in the north had changed: Edwin was dead, Paulinus had fled to the south, and the Christian Church had practically disappeared. Possibly the work had been done too quickly and was consequently superficial. Anyhow, there remained but one faithful soul, James the Deacon, 'the one heroic figure in the Roman mission',[2] who lived on near Catterick, in imminent danger of death, quietly ministering to the needs of the faithful.

---

[1] Bede, *Ecc. Hist.* ii, 16. This description was given by one of his converts.
[2] F. M. Stenton, *Anglo-Saxon England* (1943), p. 116.

iii. *East Anglia and Wessex*

The only attempt which S. Augustine had made to extend the Church beyond the borders of Kent had been the establishment of the bishopric of London in 604 in the territory of the East Saxons. The experiment failed, and it was not until about 630 that an opportunity for evangelistic work arose in that kingdom. In that year the king, Sigbert, who had lived in Gaul and had accepted the Christian faith there, invited a Burgundian bishop called Felix to come over to East Anglia. Felix arrived, set up his see at Dunwich, established the Church in the kingdom and founded a school. About the same time a wandering Irish monk called Fursa settled down as a hermit, probably at Brough in Suffolk, where he recorded a number of strange apocalyptic visions. But neither the bishop nor the hermit was able to do much, and the final conversion of the country belongs to a later age.

The apostle of Wessex was a Roman called Birinus who reached England about 633 with a strong desire to preach to the West Saxons. For a time he acted as a 'regionary bishop' without a definite see, though in time he settled at Dorchester where he worked until about 650. His work was good, for he was a holy man. But he was not a great administrator, nor were his labours crowned with immediate success.[1]

iv. *The Scottish Mission to the North*

Edwin, the Christian King of Northumbria, was killed by Cadwallon, at the battle of Heathfield in 633, and, except for the heroic work of James the Deacon, the Christian Church in the north collapsed altogether. For a year—the *annus infaustus*, or 'disastrous year' of Bede—there was chaos, and it seemed as if all the good work done by Paulinus would be destroyed. But in 634 the remaining Christians began to take heart again. Far away in Iona was a young man called Oswald who had been sent there as a child on the death of his father in 617 and who had been brought up and educated by the monks. Shortly after the death of Edwin, he succeeded to the combined kingdoms of Deira and Bernicia, and immediately raised an army to drive out the heathen usurpers. The

---

[1] M. Deanesly, *The Pre-Conquest Church in England* (1961), pp. 77–8.

forces met near Rowley Burn, south of Hexham, in 633; Oswald set up a wooden cross and called his soldiers to prayer before the battle. Cadwallon was defeated, and Oswald became undisputed King of Northumbria.

He immediately set himself to restore the damage which had been done to the cause of the Christian faith in the 'disastrous year', and sent to Iona for a bishop to evangelize his people and restore the waste places. The first who came fled in despair; 'The people are hopeless', he said. But the second was Aidan, one of the most saintly and gifted of the monks of Iona, and it was he who restored the Christianity of the north.

Aidan was a typical Celt, more monk than bishop, who fixed the centre of his work on the rocky promontory of Lindisfarne, near to Oswald's castle at Bamburgh. Here he founded a monastery and filled it with monks from Iona. But Aidan himself was often away from his monastery. Bishop of the whole of Northumbria, he travelled on foot over a large part of his diocese, preaching the Word, baptizing, confirming, ordaining. Often he went with the king, who acted as his interpreter, since Aidan was unfamiliar with the speech of the Northumbrians. Abstemious, ascetic, industrious, fervent, Aidan was constantly on the move, accompanied by a handful of monks as his companions. Even as they walked they said the Psalms or meditated on the Scriptures in order that no time might be lost.

The partnership of Aidan and Oswald, so perfect a symbol of what the alliance between Church and State should be, ended with Oswald's being killed at Maserfelth near Oswestry in 642, when he was succeeded by his brother Oswy. Aidan lived on until 651, and remains by far the greatest figure in the early history of the Northumbrian Church. His monastery at Lindisfarne sent out missions all over England even as far as the estuary of the Thames. As these missionaries went, they built rough wooden churches in which the people might worship, nor was it long before monasteries began to appear. Some of these were for men, some for women, while some were double monasteries for both men and women, though always under the authority of an abbess. The most famous of these monasteries was at Whitby, where S. Hilda ruled over a large community of both monks and nuns from 657 to her death in 680.

In spite, therefore, of the collapse of the Roman mission to Northumbria in 633 the Church was soon re-established, though according to a different tradition. For the Scottish missionaries had been trained in the customs of the Celtic Church which varied in some ways from that of Rome. The most important was concerned with the date of Easter, the Celts fixing their Easter according to a different reckoning from the Romans,[1] so that Easter in the north of England might fall some weeks before or after Easter in the south. On the cut of the tonsure the two Churches also differed, the Celtic monks apparently shaving the front of the head while the Romans wore only a circlet of hair. There were differences also in ceremonial, such as the wearing of crowns by bishops, the introduction of the *pedilavium* or feet-washing at a baptism, the strict penitential system, and even such things as the 'joint consecration' of the Eucharist by two priests which was carried out at Iona.[2]

The points at issue were not in themselves of great importance, though the double Easter could be most inconvenient. The question was whether the Northumbrian Church was to take its orders from Rome or from Iona. Until that question had been settled there could be no hope of religious amity in England.

v. *The Conversion of the Midlands*

The Gospel was late in entering the great Kingdom of Mercia owing to the power of Penda, the heathen king. But in 653 he allowed four Christian priests to enter his territory. Most of them were Irish, and all looked to Lindisfarne, not Canterbury, as their spiritual home.

One of these four, Cedd, who had been brought up as a monk at Lindisfarne, was shortly afterwards transferred further south to Essex, among the East Anglians, where he became a bishop, though without a see. He worked there for some years building a number of churches, of which one, at Bradwell-on-Sea, remains to this day. He also founded there at least two monasteries according to the Celtic plan.

Like all Celtic bishops, Cedd was a great founder of monasteries, and on one of his periodic visits to Northumbria he founded a religious house at Lastingham in the heart of the Yorkshire moors. He

---

[1] They are sometimes described as 'Quartodecimans', but this is not strictly accurate; see Plummer, *Baedae Opera*, ii, pp. 348-53.

[2] On all this see F. E. Warren, *The Liturgy and Ritual of the Celtic Church* (1881).

brought with him some East Anglian monks, but in 664 a pestilence swept the district and carried off all the inmates of this house except one boy.

Cedd was succeeded as Abbot of Lastingham by his brother Chad, who shortly afterwards became Bishop of York and later of Lichfield, the see of the Kingdom of Mercia. But he still held his abbacy and so kept up the monastic-episcopal tradition of the Celtic Church.

vi. *The Synod of Whitby and after*

By the middle of the seventh century ecclesiastical affairs were getting more and more chaotic in England, especially in the north. Two cultures had met, one from Rome and the other from Ireland, and there were various points in which they differed. In Northumbria the work begun by Paulinus and carried on by James the Deacon had been Roman in origin but had been largely superseded by the Scottish mission from Iona. This had now sent missionaries into Mercia and East Anglia, men who were naturally accustomed to the Celtic traditions. Now, in the north of England, there was growing up a generation of younger men (of whom the most prominent was S. Wilfrid), who had lived abroad and had no patience with the old conservative ways of the Scottish Church. It was becoming increasingly clear that some settlement of these differences must be made.

The matter became urgent in 663 when the King of Northumbria, Oswy, was made aware that he would be observing Easter at a time when his wife, who was of the Roman persuasion, would still be keeping her Lenten fast. The problem clearly demanded a solution, and an assembly was therefore called together at Whitby, under the supervision of the great abbess Hilda.[1]

Among those who attended on the Celtic side were Cedd and Colman, Bishop of Lindisfarne. On the Roman side were James the Deacon and Wilfrid. The king presided.

The discussion turned mainly on the date of Easter, Colman defending the Celtic custom by reference to the Fourth Gospel and to S. Columba. Wilfrid appealed to the authority of Rome and S. Peter.

---

[1] On the date of the Synod of Whitby see F. M. Stenton, *Anglo-Saxon England*, p. 130 and W. Levison, *England and the Continent in the Eighth Century* (1946), pp. 265-79.

After some discussion the king gave his judgment in favour of S. Peter on the grounds that he would rather be on good terms with the Keeper of Heaven's gate than with S. Columba. His verdict was given 'with a smile' (*subridens*), which suggests that he had really made up his mind before the discussion took place.

The verdict was a triumph for the Romans and a bitter blow to the Celts. But there can be little doubt that the king was wise in his judgment. The point at issue was a comparatively small one, but the principle behind it was a big one. Either the English Church was to be brought into line with Western Christendom, or it was to struggle on in its independence. Had the Synod of Whitby chosen the latter course nothing but stagnation could have ensued. But by choosing in favour of Rome, the Church in England brought herself in touch with the blood-stream of the Catholic Church and could henceforth play her full part in the life of Christendom.

After his defeat at Whitby Colman retired, with many of the Irish monks, first to Iona and then to Ireland, and the work of the Scottish mission came to an end. But it had done its work and done it well. Missionaries from Lindisfarne had penetrated far afield and had influenced the course of church history in the south as well as in the north. 'The strands of Irish and continental influence were interwoven in every Kingdom and at every stage of the process by which England became Christian.'[1] From now onwards Lindisfarne must give place to the greater uniformity of Canterbury and Rome; but the holiness, simplicity and devotion of the northern saints and missionaries left their mark on the Church, which they continued to influence for many years.

Among those who represent the period of transition none has left a sweeter memory than S. Cuthbert. Born about 634, and brought up as a shepherd-boy on the hills of Lammermuir, at the age of sixteen he was admitted as a novice in the monastery of Old Melrose where he received the Celtic tonsure. Soon afterwards he went with a party of monks to Ripon where, coming under the influence of S. Wilfrid, they changed their tonsures to the Roman pattern. In 661 he was made prior of Old Melrose and in 664 abbot of Lindisfarne. For two years, 684–86, he was Bishop of Lindisfarne, but he finally retired to his tiny cell on the island of Farne where he died on March 20, 687.

<hr />

[1] F. M. Stenton, *Anglo-Saxon England*, p. 125.

S. Cuthbert has all the marks of that kind of sanctity which we associate with the Celtic Church. He was by choice a monk rather than a bishop, and a hermit rather than a monk. The accounts of his night-long vigils, of his standing knee-keep in the sea while he prayed, of the sea-otters following him up the beach to lick his feet, of his battles against demons in his island home, and of his last days in his cell nibbling his dried onions to support life in his frail body, are all in keeping with the highest flights of Celtic sanctity. But Cuthbert was also a supporter of the new movement towards Rome. 'Have no communion', he cried, 'with those who depart from the unity of the catholic peace, either in not celebrating Easter at the proper time or in evil living', and as a bishop he won the praise of his biographer for maintaining the dignity of his office.[1] For the sake of peace and progress Cuthbert knew that the Church in England would have to come into line with the rest of western Christendom, but he was nonetheless a child of the Celtic Church which had moulded his life and laid its sweet influence upon him.

[1] B. Colgrave, *Two Lives of St. Cuthbert* (1940), pp. 111, 285.

NOTE ON BOOKS

There are two general histories of the Anglo-Saxons in England, R. H. Hodgkin, *A History of the Anglo-Saxons*, 2 vols. (1935) dealing with the earlier period, and F. M. Stenton, *Anglo-Saxon England* in the *Oxford Histories*, vol. ii (1943). For S. Augustine see M. Deanesly, *Augustine of Canterbury* (1964). A. Hamilton Thompson's essay on 'Northumbrian Monasticism' in *Bede: his Life, Times and Writings* (1935) is most important. Other books as in Chapter I.

CHAPTER III

CONSOLIDATION AND ADVANCE
(664–793)

i. *Theodore and the Reorganization of the Church*

THE Synod of Whitby may have achieved unity but it failed to achieve stability, and for the next five years the Church came near to shipwreck. Pestilence swept the land and wholly disorganized the Church. Deusdedit, the Archbishop of Canterbury, died in 664 and no successor was appointed for five years. The pope tried various men, but each of his nominees, for one reason or another, refused. Decimated by plague and distracted through lack of leadership, the Church in England fell on evil days.

The man who pulled it together and gave it new life and inspiration was an elderly monk of Asia Minor, Theodore of Tarsus, who, at the age of sixty-six, boldly set out for these shores accompanied by two monks, one a learned North African called Hadrian, and the other of English extraction called Benedict Biscop. This party, which amounted to a second Roman mission, reached Canterbury in May 669 and their leader lost no time in learning what the situation was. He made an immediate and thorough visitation of his province, only to find that south of the Humber there was but one bishop in office, and in the north only two—Chad at York and Wilfrid at Ripon. Theodore immediately sent Chad to Lichfield, made Wilfrid bishop of the whole of Northumbria, and consecrated bishops for Rochester, Dunwich and Winchester.

The wisdom and strength of this vigorous old man soon made themselves felt, and reforms were immediately put in hand. Realizing the necessity of corporate action Theodore summoned all the bishops to a synod which was held at Hertford in 672. There, having quickly won their confidence and support, he proposed a set of canons which they gladly accepted. These included regulations for uniformity in the observance of Easter, for the relationship of bishops with the religious houses in their territory, for the administration of the marriage

23

laws, and for a regular synod to be held each year at Clofeshoh.[1]

Whether such an annual synod was, in fact, held with any regularity is doubtful. The next occasion on which we know of a council being held was at Hatfield in 680. The Council of Hertford had been concerned mainly with domestic affairs, with the establishment of order and uniformity throughout the country. At Hatfield the bishops were asked to concern themselves in a matter of oecumenical importance. That there was trouble with heretics in Constantinople might seem a matter of but small interest to a bishop trying to deal with pagans in Cumberland: to Theodore it was a source of the deepest concern. He saw it not only as, himself, a native of Asia Minor but also as a great Churchman. The faith of the Church was threatened: all Christians must rise to defend it. At Hatfield the archbishop explained what was happening and invited his suffragans to attest their orthodoxy. The Church in England was beginning to play its part in the Church universal.[2] By means of such synods Theodore achieved a unity in the country which has never been equalled.[3] As Bede says, he was the first archbishop whom the whole English Church obeyed,[4] and this at a time when the country was still politically divided into a number of separate kingdoms.

His profound learning, wisdom and experience set the archbishop head and shoulders above everyone else in the country, and his counsel was often sought, especially on the subject of what penance should be imposed upon sinners who sought reconciliation with the Church. A collection of Theodore's judgments was made, known as the *Penitentiale*, which deals with a variety of problems. Many are concerned with the grosser sins—drunkenness, fornication, theft and homicide; others deal with moral and matrimonial questions, with breaches of ecclesiastical discipline, or with lapses into paganism. Everywhere his judgments, based mainly on the older customs of the Celtic Church, are set down with confidence and finality. The *Penitentiale* opens with these words: 'If anyone who is a bishop or an ordained man shall be an habitual drunkard, let him either cease to be so or be deposed. If a monk make himself sick through drinking let him do penance for thirty days.' Great was the range of the subjects upon which Theodore's judgment was sought. Many were con-

---

[1] Gee and Hardy, *Documents*, pp. 10-12. Clofeshoh has not been identified.
[2] *Ibid.* pp. 13-15.
[3] In 734 the Province of York was separated from Canterbury.
[4] Bede, *Ecc. Hist.*, iv, 2.

cerned with marriage customs, e.g. 'At the time of a marriage the priest ought to say Mass and bless the couple, after which they shall keep away from church for thirty days. At the end of this time, they shall do penance for forty days and give themselves to prayer, and then they may communicate with an offering.' Others dealt with divorce, the archbishop declaring that 'if a woman leave her husband, despising him, and will not return nor be reconciled to him, after five years and with the bishop's consent it shall be lawful for him to take another wife'.

Other decrees dealt with the relations between the Roman and Celtic Churches, Theodore maintaining that 'those ordained by the Scottish or British bishops, who are not catholics in the keeping of Easter and in the matter of the tonsure, are not united to the Church but must be confirmed by the laying-on of hands by a catholic bishop'. Superstition is condemned in such sayings as: 'Anyone burning corn where there is a dead man, for the benefit of the living and of the house, shall do penance for five years'. Other decrees are purely practical, such as: 'It is lawful to eat hare which is good for dysentery. Its gall should be mixed with pepper for those in pain.'[1]

Theodore died in 690 at the age of eighty-seven. During his twenty-one years as Archbishop of Canterbury he had done more for the Church in England than any of his predecessors. He found it confused and drifting: he left it well organized and self-confident. Like Augustine, he kept in close touch with Rome and did much to implement the decision reached at Whitby five years before his arrival. His wise leadership gave great strength to the Church and inaugurated what may be regarded as one of the most brilliant centuries in its history.

ii. S. Wilfrid

Theodore seems to have had little difficulty in enforcing his will on the bishops; the one problem was S. Wilfrid who caused the archbishop considerable trouble. Born in 634 of northern parentage Wilfrid became a determined Romanizer. After studying abroad for some years he returned to England as Abbot of Ripon shortly before the Synod of Whitby, at which he scandalized some of his northern friends by his vehement advocacy of the Roman tradition. Being made Bishop of Northumbria, with his see at York, in the same year

[1] The *Penitentiale* is printed in Haddan and Stubbs, *Councils*, iii, pp. 173-213.

as the conference, he showed his distrust of the whole bench of English bishops by going to Gaul for his consecration. But he stayed there so long that the people of Northumbria despaired of his return-ing to them and appointed S. Chad as their bishop in his stead. En-raged at this, Wilfrid returned in 666 and set up his see at Ripon. It was not until Archbishop Theodore came to his rescue that he was able to oust S. Chad and so enter upon his office as bishop of the whole of Northumbria.

For eight years Wilfrid ruled his vast diocese with energy and power. Unlike the simple Scottish bishops, he ruled as a prince-bishop, though still technically a monk. His biographer, Eddius, is loud in his praises—of his knowledge (he knew the Psalter and the four Gospels by heart), of his magnificent building at York, Ripon and Hexham,[1] of his asceticism so severe that he washed every night until the pope advised him 'to put an end to this rigour'.[2] But a man so forceful and so violent ('cast in the mould which afterwards pro-duced Becket and Wolsey')[3] could hardly hope to avoid making enemies, nor was it long before he quarrelled with his king and was driven into exile.

While Wilfrid was away, first working as a missionary in Frisia and later pleading his cause at Rome, Theodore took the opportunity of dividing the vast, unwieldy diocese of the north into three—York, Lindisfarne and Lindsey—to the great indignation of Wilfrid who felt himself betrayed on all sides. He ventured to return in 680 but was captured and, after languishing in 'dungeons darkened by foul fog',[4] he escaped and made his way to Sussex, the last remaining stronghold of paganism in England. Except for a small community of Irish monks at Bosham the kingdom of the South Saxons had so far been neglected by Christian missionaries. Wilfrid therefore set up his *cathedra* at Selsey and travelled far over weald and down, and out to the Isle of Wight, preaching the faith of Christ. In 686 he became sufficiently reconciled with Theodore to return north again, this time as Bishop of Ripon and Abbot of Hexham. But after five years his restless and demanding spirit clamoured for more power and again

[1] The 'crypts of wonderfully dressed stone' mentioned by Eddius are still there at Hexham, though the 'dressing' was mainly done by Romans, long before Wilfrid's time.
[2] Eddius Stephanus, *Life of Wilfrid* (ed. B. Colgrave, 1927), pp. 7, 13, 35, 37, 45, 47. This and Bede are the main sources for the life of Wilfrid.
[3] R. H. Hodgkin, *History of the Anglo-Saxons*, i, p. 344.
[4] Eddius, *Life of Wilfrid*, p. 73.

he was banished, this time going to Mercia where he administered the diocese of Leicester and founded a number of monasteries. In 702 further attempts were made to reach a compromise, and at the Synod of Austerfield, in South Yorkshire, Wilfrid was allowed to return to Northumbria but only as a simple monk. Again he appealed to Rome, even going on foot to the holy city to plead his cause; but the only result was that he returned in 705 as Bishop of Hexham. He died at Oundle in 709.

A man of clear vision, who saw the Church in England not as it was but as it might be, Wilfrid laboured with restless energy to attain some, at least, of his ideals. He was proud, domineering, arrogant, and as such he fails to win our love as it is won by the humility and simplicity of Aidan or Cuthbert: yet there was a touch of real greatness about this fiery servant of God, burning with zeal for evangelism and unswerving in his loyalty to the Church.

iii. *Church Life in the Eighth Century*

By the beginning of the eighth century, thanks largely to the work of S. Theodore, the Church in England was making rapid advances in organization and in its hold upon the people. When Theodore arrived in 669 the country was still in the 'missionary' stage, with considerable districts still unevangelized. Bishops ruled over vast territories (totally unlike the compact dioceses of Italy and the south) often conterminous with the kingdom in which their see was placed. For some time the diocese was the only unit of administration which the bishop served from a central cathedral town by means of a group of priests, known as his *familia*, who went out to baptize, teach and visit in the remoter districts.[1]

With dioceses so vast it was sometimes found convenient to divide the territory up, and, while the bishop controlled the whole area, to plant other *familiae* in the more important centres of population. These came to be known as 'minsters' and were the origin of the collegiate churches, served by a group of secular canons, which played an important part in the later Middle Ages.[2]

[1] Gee and Hardy, *Documents*, p. 20.
[2] The 'secular canon' should be distinguished from the 'regular canon' of later years who was a member of a religious community and lived under a rule. See below, p. 69.

The parish, with its church and resident priest, owes its origin almost entirely to the initiative of the local landlords. As the manorial system developed, it was natural that each manor should wish to have its own church and its own minister. The earliest parish churches were, therefore, *private* churches (or *eigenkirchen*, as they are generally called) owned by the local thegns who had built them, endowed them out of their own land, and assumed the right to choose the men who should serve them. The village priest was therefore very much his lord's 'man' and subject to his authority and jurisdiction. But he was not a serf. He was a freeman, exempt from labour-dues, and endowed with his own land. His only duty to the community, apart from his spiritual functions, was that he normally kept the bull and boar which served his parishioners' beasts.

The parish priest was, in fact, a small freeholder living upon his glebe which he normally tilled himself. As a member of the manorial community he owed allegiance to his lord, while as a servant of the Church he also took his oath to the bishop. This latter was often of great service to him. 'No man can serve two masters', but there is something to be said for having two overlords, for the one can often be invoked for protection against any injustice on the part of the other. If the parish priest had been merely the nominee of the lay lord his position would often have been most precarious. As it was, not only did he require nomination by his patron, he needed also the bishop's institution and induction before he could enter upon his benefice. And once he had established himself by this double entry it became extremely difficult to dislodge him.

In addition to his glebe, which was generally reckoned as twice that of the villein, the parish priest could claim from his people certain dues. Among these were the 'soul-scot' which entitled a priest to the second-best animal of anyone dying in his parish (the lord of the manor taking the best as 'heriot'), 'plough-alms' of a penny for each plough-team in his parish, 'church-scot' and 'light-scot' paid in kind, as well as other small dues. But his most important source of revenue apart from the glebe was in tithe, the right to collect one-tenth of all produce whether of the land or of beasts. At first tithe had been a voluntary gift on the part of the faithful, but it was too valuable a source of revenue to be treated so casually, and the Church did its utmost to make it a compulsory tax upon all, though this was not achieved in England until the tenth century.

In the eighth century the parochial system was only struggling into existence, and it must have taken many years to reach completion. But already the principles were being laid down which have governed the life of the Church to this day, and some of the boundaries were being drawn which are still in force after twelve centuries.[1]

Quite apart from the parochial system were the monasteries, many of which owed their origin to the earliest days of the conversion. S. Augustine had himself founded the abbey at Canterbury which now bears his name, while the Celtic Church in the north was almost entirely monastic. Wilfrid, who claimed to have introduced the Benedictine Rule into England, was closely wedded to the monastic life, presiding, at various times, over his two foundations at Ripon and Hexham. Theodore, and the members of his mission in 669 were all monks, one of them, Benedict Biscop, becoming abbot of S. Augustine's, Canterbury, for some years before proceeding north to found a Benedictine abbey at Wearmouth in 674 and a twin house at Jarrow in 685.

As the Roman influence gradually supplanted the Scottish, so the Benedictine Rule replaced the Celtic forms of monasticism in the religious houses, the few scattered communities of Irish monks, as at Glastonbury, being converted to what was the normal rule of life for western monachism. This movement brought English monasticism into line with what was happening on the continent and gave it new life and vigour. S. Benedict Biscop's two foundations in the north-east soon became renowned for their learning, both acquiring fine libraries which Benedict himself brought back from his various journeys to Rome.

Education and learning were making advances also outside the monasteries. In early days the only schools were those connected with the bishop's *familia*, children being sent to the bishop to be instructed by his clerks. Most of these schools were content with the rudiments of education, their object being to teach boys enough Latin to qualify for ordination. Theodore and Hadrian, however, both taught at Canterbury, nor were they content to instruct boys in the elements of Latin grammar but held classes in the liberal arts and in Roman Law. John of Beverley, Bishop of Hexham in 687,

---

[1] See G. W. O. Addleshaw, *The Beginnings of the Parochial System* (St. Anthony's Hall Publications, No. 3, 1953).

kept a school in the north, and there were great schools at York and
Ripon about the same time.[1] The monastic schools catered only for
their own oblates, the children of the cloister.

iv. *The Scholars: Aldhelm, Bede, Alcuin*

The intellectual ability of men like Theodore and Hadrian, and the
impetus to scholarship which they gave, led to a flowering of English
learning in the eighth century which influenced the whole of
western Europe.

The earliest writer to achieve fame was Aldhelm (*c.* 639–709).
Having been taught first by an Irish scholar, he was attracted to
Canterbury, where he sat at the feet of Hadrian for some years. In 675
he became Abbot of Malmesbury and in 705 Bishop of Sherborne
when the great diocese of Wessex was divided. As a bishop he served
his diocese well, and showed a great zeal for evangelism. A pleasant
story tells of his standing on the bridge at Malmesbury, disguised as
a minstrel, and singing to the people in his strong voice until he had
collected a crowd to whom he then preached the Gospel.

But Aldhelm's chief fame is as a writer, though his style has often
attracted more attention than his matter. None of his English writings have survived, but his Latin works show a vast range of learning.
This, however, is set out in a style so strange that it makes stiff reading. Aldhelm was a man who loved words for their own sake. He
collected all manner of strange and uncouth words and revelled in
acrostics, alliteration and word-play. Yet behind all this was sound
learning, and he has been described as 'beyond comparison the most
learned and ingenious western scholar of the late seventh century'.[2]

The Venerable Bede was considerably younger than Aldhelm,
having been born in 673 in the north of England. He entered the
monastery of Wearmouth at the age of seven, but was transferred a
year or two later to Jarrow. In 685 the monastery was devastated by the
plague, which carried off all the monks except the abbot and Bede,
then a boy of twelve, upon whose shoulders then fell the task of keeping the worship of the community alive until new recruits could be

[1] See M. Deanesly in *Camb. Med. Hist.*, vol. v, chap. xxii and A. F. Leach, *Schools of Medieval England* (1915).
[2] F. M. Stenton, *Anglo-Saxon England*, p. 183. See also G. F. Browne, *St. Aldhelm* (1903) and the article by W. Hunt in *D.N.B.*

found. Except for an occasional visit to York or Lindisfarne, Bede never left Jarrow, where he died in 735. Yet, thanks to the industry of Benedict Biscop and his energy in collecting books, Bede was able to read widely and to achieve an international reputation for his writings as historian, theologian, scientist and poet. Altogether he wrote some forty books, which nowadays occupy twelve octavo volumes of print, on a great variety of subjects. As a preliminary to his Biblical exegesis he studied Greek and Hebrew; he took a great interest in matters of chronology, introducing into England the method of dating events B.C. and A.D. which we now employ; he wrote poems and homilies and filled many volumes with Biblical commentaries. Yet today he is known mainly as an historian, his *Ecclesiastical History of the English People* being by far the most important document for the early history of the Church in England. Bede has been rightly called 'the father of English historians' for his work, though written always with a desire to edify as well as to instruct, reaches a high level of accuracy and fair-mindedness. S. Boniface described him as 'a candle of the Church, lit by the Holy Spirit', and certainly his work has illuminated what would otherwise have been a dark passage in our history.[1]

Alcuin, who belonged to a noble family of Northumbria, was born about the time of Bede's death. As a boy he entered the great school at York where he was taught by Egbert, a pupil of Bede. Later, Alcuin himself became a teacher in the school. Unlike Bede, who seldom stirred outside his monastery at Jarrow, Alcuin travelled much. On one of his journeys abroad he met the Emperor Charlemagne, who was looking for a great teacher to preside over his Palace School. Alcuin was appointed to this post and served for a time under the Emperor at Aachen. In 790 he returned to England, but the Danish invasions were just beginning and life was becoming too hazardous and unsettled for scholarship. So Alcuin returned to France, where he was made Abbot of Tours. He died in 796.

In many ways Alcuin belongs more to the continent than to England. Though a Northumbrian by birth and education, he spent most of his time abroad. His writings cover many aspects of church life, but probably his greatest achievement was as a liturgical scholar and

[1] For a full account of Bede see *Bede; his Life, Times and Writings*, ed. A. H. Thompson (1935). The standard edition of his historical works is that edited by C. Plummer in 1896 (*Baedae Opera Historica*). There are many translations (*e.g.* by J. A. Giles in Bohn's Antiquarian Library, 1849).

reformer. In his day the many liturgical uses had been gradually reduced to two—the Roman and the Gallican. Both were known in England, for the Roman missionaries had introduced the Roman rite while the Irish used the Gallican. In the north of England, where Roman and Irish traditions existed side by side, both rites must have been in use, and Alcuin would thus be familiar with each. At Aachen there was considerable liturgical confusion, and Charlemagne was anxious to achieve some kind of uniformity. He procured from the pope a copy of the Roman rite, the *Gregorianum*, but considered it far too rigid and austere. It was at this point that Alcuin was called in to enlarge and enrich the Roman rite by the addition of a supplement. This proved so satisfactory that the new form, devised by Alcuin, gradually ousted the old *Gregorianum* all over Western Christendom. Alcuin has thus left his mark on Christian worship to this day and has been called 'the final begetter of the Western rite'.[1]

v. *Art and Architecture*

The century which followed the Synod of Whitby has sometimes been known as the 'Golden Age' and certainly, both in scholarship and in art, a high level of culture was reached, only to be destroyed in the following century by the Viking invasions. England, and especially the northern part where the Roman and Celtic traditions were in process of assimilation, was at this time considerably in advance of any other country in Europe.

One of the most interesting features of northern art at this time were the stone crosses, so many of which remain in whole or in part to this day.[2] The purpose of these crosses is not altogether clear; they may have been memorials to the dead, or they may have been set up to mark sacred spots before the building of churches. Whatever their purpose, hundreds of exquisitely carved crosses were erected in

---

[1] G. Dix, *The Shape of the Liturgy* (1945), pp. 579–80, 584. Cf. E. Bishop, *Liturgica Historica* (1918), p. 55: 'It is the Englishman, Alcuin, who has been the instrument to settle the structure and tenor henceforth of the liturgy of the Western Church'. Alcuin's works are in Migne, *Patrologia Latina*, vols. c–ci. See also *Monumenta Alcuiniana* in *Bibliotheca Rerum Germanicarum*, vol. vi; C. J. B. Gaskoin, *Alcuin* (1904), and E. S. Duckett, *Alcuin, Friend of Charlemagne, his World and his Work* (New York, 1951).
[2] See W. G. Collingwood, *Northumbrian Crosses of the Pre-Norman Age* (1927); G. Baldwin Brown, *The Arts in Early England* (1903–21), esp. vol. v; and T. D. Kendrick, *Anglo-Saxon Art to 900* (1938).

the north of England and in the lowlands of Scotland. Of these the most famous are the Bewcastle cross in Cumberland and the Ruthwell cross in Dumfriesshire, both of which probably belong to about the year 700. The theme in each is the triumph of Christ over evil, and each cross bears not only a magnificent figure of Christ but also a series of decorations, representing two styles of culture—the interlacing pattern which is essentially Celtic, and the vine-scroll with birds and beasts which is Byzantine in origin. The design and workmanship of these crosses is of a peculiarly high order, and their makers possessed 'a skill and artistry which lifted their works above all other sculpture of the age either in Europe or the Near East'.[1]

Meanwhile similar designs, though far more delicate and elaborate, were being worked out, not with the chisel but with the pen, in a number of magnificent books, some of which have survived through the centuries and may be studied, in all their glory, today. Among these is the *Lindisfarne Gospels*, a superb manuscript of the late seventh or early eighth century, executed at Lindisfarne in honour of S. Cuthbert. Of equal brilliance is the *Codex Amiatinus* written at Jarrow or Wearmouth early in the eighth century. Each of these noble works illustrates the blending of the two cultures, being designed partly on Italian styles copied from manuscripts brought over from abroad, partly on the native traditions of the Celtic Church.[2]

The latter part of the seventh century also saw the rise of a number of great churches. Some of these, such as the church at Abingdon, have since disappeared and are known to us only through the descriptions of chroniclers; but a few have survived in whole or in part. Bradwell-on-Sea (Essex), which was built by S. Cedd about 660 still retains much of its early structure; but the most remarkable survival in the southern province is the church at Brixworth (Northants), a large, basilican structure built about 680, partly of Roman bricks. It is 'perhaps the most imposing architectural memorial of the seventh century yet surviving north of the Alps'.[3]

In the north there are the remains of seventh-century churches at Wearmouth and Jarrow, but the most interesting survival is the small but complete church at Escomb (Co. Durham) which stands

---

[1] R. H. Hodgkin, *History of the Anglo-Saxons*, i, p. 363.
[2] F. G. Kenyon, *Handbook to the Textual Criticism of the New Testament* (1901), pp. 192, 199. The *Lindisfarne Gospels* are now in the British Museum, the *Codex Amiatinus* in the Laurentian Library at Florence.
[3] A. W. Clapham, *Romanesque Architecture in England*, i, p. 33.

3

today very much as it stood when it was built during the childhood of Bede. The northern churches, compared with those of the south, are on the whole ruder and more barbaric in style, due to the fact that the masons who built them were using designs from Gaul, while those in the south were built by Italian masons, though with Byzantine rather than Roman characteristics.

This 'Golden Age' also saw the origins of English religious poetry. According to Bede it was customary, where men were gathered together, for the harp to be passed round while each made his contribution to the general entertainment. It was in this way that Caedmon, the monk of Whitby, having first refused to take part, was directly inspired to lift up his voice and sing the praises of God in creation.[1] From this beginning he went on to sing of the Exodus and of Daniel, so establishing a style of epic religious verse, based upon the secular poetry of the age which told of its great war-lords and heroes, but finding its material in the great narratives of the Bible. If this early religious song found its inspiration in the highly dramatic stories of the Old Testament, it was not long before it attempted a similar interpretation of the Gospels, finding in Christ the hero who had fought the powers of darkness and won through to victory. Thus soon after the unknown sculptors had worked at Bewcastle and Ruthwell to depict the triumph of Christ, Cynewulf and the poets began to sing of His victory in the halls of lords and abbots. Thus the *Dream of the Rood*:

> When the young Hero that was God Almighty
> Stripped Himself, strong and steadfast,
> Bold in the sight of many
> He mounted the high cross when He would redeem mankind.
> I trembled when He clasped me,
> Yet I durst not bow to the ground.[2]

vi. *The Missions to Germany*

The vitality of a Church can largely be measured by its concern for evangelism. No sooner had the Anglo-Saxon Church completed the evangelization of the people of England than it began to turn its thoughts overseas.

---

[1] Bede, *Ecc. Hist.* iv, 24.
[2] See *Cambridge History of English Literature*, i, pp. 41-64.

Much of Europe was now within the fold of the Christian Church, but still large tracts remained pagan, among them Frisia and Saxony which lay nearest to the east coast of England. The first known Englishman to preach the Gospel in Germany was S. Wilfrid who, when driven into exile by his king in 678, spent some months as an evangelist among the Frisians. Twelve years later a more formal mission, under papal guidance, set out under the leadership of S. Willibrord. This mission had considerable success; a cathedral was built at Utrecht, and Willibrord was consecrated as its archbishop in 695.

Meanwhile a young man was growing up in England who was to bring the work of Willibrord to completion. This was Boniface, or Wynfrith, a native of Wessex (possibly Crediton) who was born about 675. He went out to join Willibrord in Frisia in 718 and worked there for many years. Boniface was a man of great courage and determination who went out to fight the powers of paganism as he had perhaps heard the poets sing of Christ battling against the powers of evil. One of his most significant acts was the ceremonial destruction of the Oak of Donar at Geismar, a sacred tree to which many secretly paid reverence. The action symbolized Boniface's contempt for the heathen deities and for the pagan fears and superstitions which lingered in the hearts even of the converted.

Willibrord was a pioneer; it was he who opened up the way. But Boniface was the real Apostle of Germany. In 732 the pope, who strongly supported the mission, made Boniface archbishop, and by 741 eight new dioceses had been formed and the work was going ahead rapidly, though not without difficulty. Boniface, throughout, kept in close touch with England, writing constant letters to his friends at home who supplied him with books, vestments, ornaments, and, above all, recruits. The close contact between the missionaries in Germany and the Church in England was one of the strongest elements in this great enterprise.[1]

As the work proceeded, churches and monasteries sprang up, among the latter the great Benedictine monastery at Fulda. In 742 the first synod was held, and in 745 Boniface became Archbishop of Mainz. All was going well, though at the cost of much labour and

---

[1] Boniface's letters are in *Monumenta Germaniae Historica, Scriptores*, vol. iii, and there is a translation of most of them by Ephraim Emerton (Columbia University, 1940).

anxiety. 'On every hand is struggle and grief,' wrote Boniface to an English abbess, 'fighting without and fear within. Worst of all, the treachery of false brethren surpasses the malice of unbelieving pagans.'[1] Yet it was the 'unbelieving pagans' who killed him. Early in June 754, Boniface had gone to confirm a number of newly baptized converts at Dokkum. There, on June 5, a hostile pagan force appeared and Boniface and most of his companions were martyred. But the work went on. Boniface left behind him a Church well taught and well led, independent yet orthodox, abounding in monasteries and schools. It was one of the greatest achievements of which the Anglo-Saxon Church could boast.[2]

[1] E. Emerton, *The Letters of St. Boniface*, p. 122.
[2] See W. Levison, *England and the Continent in the Eighth Century* (1946), esp. chaps. iii and iv, and C. H. Talbot, *The Anglo-Saxon Missionaries in Germany* (1954)

NOTE ON BOOKS

IN addition to books mentioned in previous bibliographical notes the most important works for this period are W. Levison, *England and the Continent in the Eighth Century* (1946), and P. Hunter Blair, *The World of Bede* (1970). The volume of essays edited by A. Hamilton Thompson as *Bede; his Life, Times and Writings* (1935) contains a number of important contributions. Reference may also be made to vol. ii of the *Cambridge Medieval History*, and to T. Allison's *English Religious Life in the Eighth Century* (1929).

CHAPTER IV

CHAOS AND RECONSTRUCTION
(793–988)

i. *The Rise of Mercia*

ALTHOUGH the century following upon the Synod of Whitby and
the arrival of Theodore of Tarsus was an age of great achievement,
it already contained the germs of deterioration and decay. In 734
Bede wrote a letter to Egbert, his old pupil now Bishop of York,[1]
in which he complains much of the state of the Church as he knew
it in the north. He describes the bishops as shamefully negligent of
their duties, the dioceses far too big to allow of any adequate supervision, the clergy ignorant and worldly, the Eucharist sadly neglected. But his chief attack is upon a type of sham monastery of which
there appear to have been many. Anxious to avoid the military
service to which they were liable many lay lords had founded
communities which could hardly be described as religious houses.
Often they were ruled by laymen and filled with renegade monks.
Many had no priest and consisted only of a motley crowd under no
proper supervision, obedient to no recognized rule and preferring the
company of 'poets, harpers, musicians and buffoons' to the demands
of worship and the discipline of the cloister.[2] Nor was Bede the only
one to complain of the deterioration of the Church in England;
Boniface, writing from Germany, contrasts the loose-living and
negligence of the English with the greater discipline and enthusiasm
of the Germans.[3]

Such complaints and criticisms are, of course, common to every
age, and are a healthy sign, showing that a few, at any rate, are disturbed and dissatisfied and anxious for better things. But in the
second half of the eighth century it was not only a handful of critics

[1] He became archbishop in 732 or 734 (*Handbook of British Chronology*, ed. F. M.
Powicke and E. B. Fryde (1961), p. 263, and York has remained a separate province
ever since.
[2] *Baedae Opera Historica* (ed. C. Plummer), i, pp. 405-23.
[3] E. Emerton, *The Letters of St. Boniface*, pp. 124-8.

who were concerned about these things; the whole Church was aware of its weaknesses and zealous for reform.

For some years councils had been held, either at Clofeshoh or some other place, to correct abuses and consider the well-being of the Church.[1] It was there that a Council was held in 747 at which a number of decrees were passed. Cuthbert, Archbishop of Canterbury, presided over this gathering, and a representative was present from each kingdom except Northumbria which had now become separated from the province of Canterbury. The general tone of the decrees is the need for discipline and reform. Bishops are urged to be more conscientious in visiting their dioceses, to extirpate paganism, to examine candidates for ordination, to promote learning, to enforce uniformity in worship, and to enquire into the morals of the clergy. More especially were they to visit the monasteries and to see how far the rule was being observed. They must see that the hours of worship are properly kept, that monks dress correctly, 'not in the fashionable gartering of their legs', and that nuns do not go about in 'gaudy, gay clothes such as lay girls use'. Above all, they must deal strictly with those sham monasteries, such as Bede describes, which were an offence to religion.[2]

But perhaps even more remarkable than the decrees of the Council is the fact that such a council could be held at all. At least it illustrates the unity and organization of the Church at a time when the country as a whole was still hopelessly divided into a number of separate kingdoms, of which first one and then another rose to pre-eminence and managed to achieve some degree of supremacy over the others.

In the second half of the eighth century it was the turn of Mercia to reach such a position. Under the wise and powerful rule of King Offa (757–96), Mercia rose to such power that its king claimed to be 'King of all the English' though such a claim would, no doubt, have been challenged in many parts of the country. Offa was undoubtedly much the greatest ruler of his generation in England. A man of big ideas, he was one of the few English rulers who had a definite foreign connection, corresponding both with the pope and with Charlemagne. He was also a great benefactor to the Church and the founder of many monasteries.

[1] Councils were certainly held there in 716, 742, 747, 794, 798, 803, 824 and 825 (Haddan and Stubbs, *Councils*, vol. iii).

[2] Haddan and Stubbs, *Councils*, iii, pp. 360–76; Gee and Hardy, *Documents*, pp. 15–32.

Yet his policy with regard to the Church was mistaken. At a time when the Church was the only real unifying force in the country, Offa conceived a plan for separating Mercia from the rest of the province of Canterbury and giving it its own archbishop. Such a desire sprang from patriotism and zeal for his own kingdom; but it was disastrous for the Church. It meant that, at the moment when the Church of the southern province was beginning to act strongly and unitedly in the cause of reform, it was to be split into two. Offa, however, was determined to carry out his project and invited the pope to send to England two legates with power to carry through such a division of the province.

The two legates, George, Cardinal-Bishop of Ostia, and Theophylact, Cardinal-Bishop of Todi, arrived in England in 786, the first of a long series of papal legates who were later to play an important part in the history of England. They made a visitation not only of the southern but also of the northern province and held councils at 'Pincahala' (probably Finchale near Durham) and at Celchyth or Chelsea, both in 787. At both these councils decrees were passed, similar to those promulgated by other reforming councils,[1] and in the same year they succeeded in carrying out the primary purpose of their visit which was to give authority for the division of the southern province into two. Offa thus achieved his ambition; Lichfield became a metropolitan see with its own archbishop and six other dioceses under its jurisdiction—Worcester, Hereford, Leicester, Sherborne, Elmham and Dunwich—leaving only Rochester, London, Winchester and Selsey to the Archbishop of Canterbury. This arrangement lasted until a few years after the death of Offa, but was brought to an end in 803.

ii. The Viking Invasions

By the end of the eighth century the Kingdom of Mercia had gained a supremacy over most of England. Within a few years both it and practically the whole of the country had been completely conquered by Scandinavian invaders, and much of the steady progress which had been made in both Church and State was undone.

[1] Haddan and Stubbs, Councils, iii, pp. 443-62; Gee and Hardy, Documents, pp. 32-44; M. Deanesly, Pre-Conquest Church, pp. 223-7.

The cause of this sudden aggressive move on the part of the tribes living round the Baltic is obscure, but within a century they had forced their way not only into the British Isles but into France and Spain, Italy and Constantinople, Iceland and Russia and even Greenland and North America. Trapped between advancing heathens from the north and Mohammedans in the south, Christendom was called upon to face the greatest menace which had come upon it for many centuries.

The first movement of Viking invaders took place at the very end of the eighth century when marauding parties began to raid the eastern and southern coasts of England, killing and destroying whatever resistance they met, and escaping with their booty to their long ships. In 793 Lindisfarne was raided, the abbey was sacked and its treasures stolen, and such of the monks as escaped with their lives wandered for many years, carrying the bones of S. Cuthbert with them, until they found a permanent home first at Chester-le-Street and then at Durham. Other monasteries shared the same fate, Jarrow being sacked in 794, Iona in 802. In Ireland a deliberate attempt to destroy the Christian Church was made.

As the years went by the attacks became more powerful and more frequent, while from about 850 onwards the invaders changed their tactics from mere plundering raids to systematic conquest. One by one the English kingdoms succumbed, until, by 870, only Wessex remained unconquered, and even that last stronghold of Christendom must have vanished had it not been for the courage and perseverance of its king, Alfred the Great. In face of almost overwhelming odds Alfred fought on, until, by 878, he was able to make a pact with Guthrum the Danish leader whereby the country was divided. All England south and west of a line running roughly from London to Chester was left to Alfred, while everything to the north and east of that line became a Danish kingdom.

The effect on the Church of nearly a century of invasion and conquest had been disastrous. Just at a time when steady progress was being made the Church had been almost completely destroyed over the greater part of the country. Monasteries and churches had been plundered and burnt. Libraries had been destroyed. Monks and priests had been either killed or carried away into slavery. Edmund, the saintly King of East Anglia, had been martyred at Hoxne in Suffolk in 868. Everywhere lay death, desecration and destruction.

The settlement between Alfred and Guthrum in 878, by bringing the war to an end, made it possible for the Church to consider ways and means of building up the waste places. The task was made easier by the apparent readiness of the Danes to accept the Christian message. Guthrum was baptized and many of his followers, and it was not long before churches began to be rebuilt. Once the Danes had been converted, the distinctions between the two races began to grow less, and it is remarkable how quickly some kind of national unity was restored. The saviour of England and of the Church in England in those dark days was King Alfred who, 'alone among the rulers of his time, realized the vital importance of the spiritual issue and devoted no less energy to the recovery of the tradition of Christian culture than to the defence of national existence'.[1]

iii. *King Alfred the Great*

Alfred was by far the greatest ruler in Europe since Charlemagne. Born in 848, at the height of the Viking invasions, he saw his country beaten almost to her knees; yet through his skill and courage the tide was turned, peace was made, and, by the time of his death in 899, the Danish conquerors were being absorbed into the life of the country and gradually converted to the Christian faith, religious life was being once more established, learning was on the increase, everywhere was progress and rehabilitation. The credit for this great victory—spiritual as well as material—belongs almost entirely to King Alfred himself.

When he came to the throne of Wessex in 871 he found the country not only torn by war but impoverished in both religion and learning. 'It has often come into my remembrance', he wrote, 'what wise men there formerly were among the English race, both of the sacred orders and the secular, and what happy times those were throughout the English race, and how the Kings who had the government of the folk in those days obeyed God and His ministers. . . . Also the sacred orders, how zealous they were both in teaching and in learning and in all services which they owed to God; and how foreigners came to this land for wisdom and instruction: and how we now should have to get them from abroad if we were to have

[1] C. Dawson, *Religion and the Rise of Western Culture* (1950), p. 102.

them. So clean was it fallen away in the English race that there were very few on this side Humber who could understand their mass-books in English, or translate a letter from Latin into English; and I ween that there were not many beyond the Humber. So few of them were there that I cannot think of so much as a single one south of the Thames when I came to the throne.'[1]

Alfred, therefore, had two ambitions: to restore peace and to revive religion and learning. The clergy, already growing negligent and worldly in the latter part of the eighth century, had been barbarized by the wars, while the monasteries were practically deserted. Alfred tried hard to restore the monastic life by the creation of new abbeys at Athelney (for men) and Shaftesbury (for women) but the former was not much of a success. So few English religious were available that he was obliged to stock it largely with Gaulish monks under a German abbot, but they quarrelled so much that the place had to be closed down.

More successful were his efforts to found schools. Like Charlemagne, before him, Alfred formed a Palace School to which he attracted a number of scholars, both English and foreign, and in which his own son was enrolled as a student. Alfred was anxious to do two things: to educate the laity as well as the clergy, and to teach the people of England to love their own language. To foster the first of these objectives he encouraged all his nobles to go to school themselves and to see that their sons were properly educated; while, for the second, he himself received instruction in Latin in order that he might translate some of the great classics of the Church into the English language. For years the king himself worked, with his assistants, at his translations, and, by the time of his death, had translated the *Cura Pastoralis* of S. Gregory (a handbook for bishops but containing wise words about the need for education), the *History of Orosius*, Bede's *Ecclesiastical History*, Boethius' *Consolation of Philosophy* and the *Soliloquies* of S. Augustine.

Alfred achieved such distinction as warrior, law-giver, statesman and scholar that later generations have not hesitated to give him the title of 'Great'. In the latter part of the ninth century England sorely needed a great soldier to stem the advance of the Danes and save

---

[1] From the Preface to the *Cura Pastoralis*, quoted in R. H. Hodgkin, *History of the Anglo-Saxons*, ii, pp. 608-9; but F. M. Stenton thinks that Alfred 'heavily overpainted the depression of English learning in 871' (*Anglo-Saxon England*, p. 268).

England from total capitulation. The Church also, demoralized and defeatist, needed a great Christian to give it new hope. In Alfred the country found a leader distinguished alike in the arts of war and of peace, a great scholar-prince from whose zeal and wisdom both Church and State took new courage. In the last quarter of the ninth century Christendom was hard pressed on all sides. There was no one who did more for its salvation than King Alfred.[1]

iv. S. Dunstan and the Monasteries

In almost all his projects Alfred was successful. His chief failure was in the attempt to restore the monastic life among men. Clearly the time for this was not ripe. It needed another century of teaching before the religious houses would rise again out of the ruin caused by the Viking invasions.

The man who did most to refound the monasteries was S. Dunstan. Born about 909, of aristocratic parentage, he was brought up near Glastonbury and was soon drawn into politics. After some years he became a monk though unable to devote much time to the cloister until about 943, when King Edmund made him Abbot of Glastonbury. 'It was a turning-point in the history of religion in England.'[2] Immediately he began to reform the abbey, bringing to the task all his powers of leadership and all his organizing ability. Though, later, he became Bishop of Worcester, Bishop of London and finally Archbishop of Canterbury (960–88) it was at Glastonbury that his greatest work was done.

When Dunstan was a boy the abbey of Glastonbury was a very modest place. As soon as he became abbot it began to grow. Disciples came to him from all parts, attracted by his fame as scholar, musician and artist, among them S. Ethelwold (afterwards Bishop of Winchester) and S. Oswald (afterwards Bishop of Worcester and Archbishop of York). Soon other monasteries began to appear, notably at Abingdon and Westbury-on-Trym, and contacts were made with monasteries overseas.

In all these monasteries the Rule was that of S. Benedict, the

---

[1] The earliest life of Alfred was that by Asser, Bishop of Sherborne who died c. 909. The chief edition of this is by W. H. Stevenson (1904). There is an English translation by J. A. Giles in *Old English Chronicles* (1848).
[2] J. A. Robinson, *The Times of St. Dunstan* (1923), p. 85.

founder of western monachism. The English monasteries were, therefore, fully in line with the monasteries of Europe. But in order to settle the various problems of local usage a meeting was held about 970 at which a 'custumal' was drawn up, known as the *Regularis Concordia* [1] and intended to govern the lives of all English monks. The basis is the Rule of S. Benedict, but a few concessions to English ways of life and to the English climate are made. One of the most significant features of the *Regularis Concordia* are the special prayers for the king which are to be said at each service. This shows how closely the monasteries were connected with the national life. Many monks subsequently became bishops, and England developed the curious custom, elsewhere practically unknown, of the 'cathedral priory', where the cathedral of a diocese was manned not by secular clerks but by professed monks. About half of the great cathedral churches in England were monastic, the prior and monks taking the place of the dean and canons, until the dissolution of the monasteries in the sixteenth century.

Dunstan's greatest work was undoubtedly as a monk, the refounder of English monasticism, and, as such, he has been called 'the patron and father of the monks of medieval England'.[2] But he was also eminent in many other spheres. As scholar, artist and craftsman, musician and organ-builder, he acquired a great reputation, and, besides all this, he was a successful church leader and reformer. Although as a politician he was inevitably involved in controversy and faction and spent some years in exile, yet as archbishop he managed to hold a number of councils at which he pressed for church reform along the lines which obtained on the continent. In many fields—administrative, artistic, scholastic—Dunstan showed such ability that, in spite of the strictures of some historians of the nineteenth century, he must be regarded as one of the most distinguished of English churchmen.

v. *Missions to Scandinavia*

When the Northmen were riding across the shires of England, ruthlessly burning churches, killing priests, and stripping altars, it

---

[1] It is printed in Dugdale's *Monasticon Anglicanum* (ed. Caley, Ellis and Bandinel, 1817-30), vol. i, pp. xxvii-xlv. New edition, ed. T. Symons (1952).
[2] M. D. Knowles, *The Monastic Order in England* (1940), p. 56.

looked, for a time, as if the work of centuries was to be undone and the land relapse into heathenism. Such, indeed, occurred over much of the country; but the religious revival came so quickly that it was not long before the Anglo-Danish Church began to think of sending Christian missionaries to Scandinavia.

The Danes were first converted to the Christian faith early in the tenth century, and by 948 they had their first bishops. But in the latter part of the century a reaction set in. King Sweyn hated the Christians and drove them out of the land. In his later years, however, he became more friendly and we hear of English missionaries, both bishops and priests, working in Denmark about the year 990. Sweyn died a pagan, but his son, Cnut, was a Christian, and, from his time onwards the Church flourished in Denmark.

In Norway the first attempt to introduce Christianity was made by the young King Haakon about the middle of the tenth century. As a boy Haakon had been brought up among Christians in England, much as Oswald, three centuries earlier, had been brought up among Christians at Iona. Haakon returned to Norway in 935 at the age of fifteen, and, as king, he tried to convert his people with the help of teachers and priests from England. Little, however, came of this, and Haakon was killed in 961.

About two years later was born Olaf Tryggvason, the converter of Norway. Olaf was a viking who spent the earlier part of his life as a pirate, raiding the coasts of England or wherever loot was to be obtained. But in the midst of his career he was converted and baptized by a Christian hermit living in the Scilly Isles, and thereupon determined to take the faith back to his own land. In 995, accompanied by English missionaries, he arrived in Norway and began his work. By nature a man of violence, his methods were unconventional, for he offered the Norwegians the choice between baptism and battle. Most of them chose baptism and Olaf marched through the land, a victorious evangelist, until he himself fell in battle in the year 1000.

The English missionaries who took part in these expeditions are shadowy figures of whom little trace remains today. Many were monks and some were probably martyrs. That their work was well done is proved by the high quality of Scandinavian Christianity in later years. Adam of Bremen has nothing but praise for the Churches of the northern kingdoms where devotion abounds, where 'the

bishop is treated as if he were a king' and where priest and people
live together in the bonds of peace and charity.[1]

[1] Cf. C. Dawson, *Religion and the Rise of Western Culture*, pp. 113-14.

NOTE ON BOOKS

SEE the general histories as above, p. 22. J. Armitage Robinson, *The Times
of Saint Dunstan* (1923) is detailed but essential. David Knowles, *The Monastic Order in England* (1940) chapter iii, is important on early English
monasticism. Christopher Dawson's *Religion and the Rise of Western Culture*
(1950) chapter v and K. Latourette's *A History of the Expansion of Christianity*
(1938) vol. ii, chapter ii, should also be read.

THE EVE OF THE CONQUEST
(988–1066)

i. *The State of the Church about 1000*

IN Anglo-Saxon times the boundary between Church and State was far less clearly drawn than it has been in more recent days. The king was regarded not only as head of the Church but as 'the vicar of Christ among a Christian folk'[1] a title which he could never have claimed after the rise of papal power in the eleventh century. Practically all appointments to bishoprics and abbeys were made by the king himself, apparently with little opposition, and many of the king's advisers and servants were ecclesiastics. In the administration of justice the bishop and the earl sat side by side in the shire-court and dealt with all causes spiritual as well as lay.

The revival of church life under S. Dunstan had been most vigorous in the monasteries. In the time of Alfred monasticism had been practically extinct in England, but by the year 1000 there were at least thirty flourishing houses for men and six or seven for women. The north was only just beginning to show a revival of the religious life, but in the southern province there were three main groups of monasteries. One lay in the Fens where Ely, Peterborough and Ramsey had risen to great fame and prosperity; a second group lay in Wessex and included Winchester and Glastonbury for men and Shaftesbury and Romsey for women; while a third group was situated in the Severn valley and included Worcester, Pershore and Evesham. All these houses followed the Rule of S. Benedict as interpreted in the *Regularis Concordia*.

Most of the houses were prosperous and were drawing to themselves not only recruits but also large gifts of property. The very extensive estates upon which the monks lived in later years were already in process of formation. Fine churches were being built and furnished with the best that money could buy or rich friends provide. In many

---

[1] Laws of Ethelred II, quoted in F. M. Stenton, *Anglo-Saxon England*, p. 538.

of the monastic churches the worship was beautifully and reverently performed, some places acquiring fame as centres of music, as is suggested by the old rhyme:

> Merry sungen the monkës of Ely
> When Cnut King rowed thereby.
> Row, cnichts, near the land
> And hear we these monkës sing.

So strong was the monastic life in the period between the death of Dunstan and the Norman conquest that it provided most of the bishops. The great triumvirate—Dunstan, Oswald and Ethelwold—who, having done so much for the revival of monasticism, were appointed to the three most important bishoprics in England—Canterbury, York and Winchester—gave place in their turn to other monks of whom the most distinguished was S. Alphege, now at Winchester but shortly to proceed to Canterbury. Almost every diocese in the country felt the influence of the monasteries and was, for a time, ruled by a monk.[1]

In the year 1000 there were eighteen dioceses in England—in the southern province sixteen and in the north two.[2] Some dioceses were very large, owing to the fact that they had originally been conterminous with a kingdom, and it was therefore impossible for a bishop to keep any very close supervision over his widely scattered clergy. Bishops were, however, constantly urged to visit regularly both their parishes and the monasteries which were under their jurisdiction. To assist them in their work the office of archdeacon had been introduced. The first known holder of such office in England was Wulfstan, Archdeacon of Canterbury in 803,[3] and by the tenth century the archdeacon had acquired a recognized status in ecclesiastical jurisdiction.[4] The further delegation of authority to the rural dean does not seem to have occurred until after the Norman conquest.

In order to make his will known a bishop normally held a synod once a year to which all parish priests were summoned, each with his clerk and servant, and carrying with him provisions for three days and the necessary books and robes. He was also to bring ink and

---

[1] M. D. Knowles, *The Monastic Order in England*, pp. 65-6, 697-701.
[2] The southern province was composed of the sees of Canterbury, Rochester, London, Winchester, Dorchester, Ramsbury, Sherborne, Selsey, Lichfield, Hereford, Worcester, Crediton, Cornwall, Elmham, Lindsey and Wells. In the north were York and Durham.   [3] Haddan and Stubbs, *Councils*, iii, p. 546.
[4] See, for example, the Northumbrian laws in Wilkins, *Concilia*, i, p. 218.

parchment so that he could make notes of the bishop's wishes and take home with him a copy of any decrees which were passed.[1]

The synod would normally be held in the cathedral of the diocese. Little is now left of the great Saxon cathedrals, most of which were pulled down to build Norman churches. But, from contemporary descriptions, many of them, such as the 'White Church' at Durham, consecrated in 999, must have been noble buildings. The plan normally adopted was that of the Carolingian churches in France, which was unlike that of the churches of later times in that it provided for an altar and transepts at the west end of the nave as well as at the east. If there were an entrance in the west wall the altar was normally placed in a gallery over the door. Towers, whether of wood or of stone, and generally in the form of a series of receding tiers of blind arcading, were very popular at this time, many churches having one at each end of the nave besides several smaller towers containing spiral staircases. Another feature of the Saxon church was its height in comparison with its width, a device which was probably due to the desire to place the unglazed windows well above the heads of the worshippers.[2]

The original cathedrals had been run by a body of secular priests under the immediate supervision of the bishop. From the eighth century onwards attempts were made to organize these corporations, and to persuade them to adopt a rule of life. The leading figure in this movement was Chrodegang of Metz (c. 755) whose *decretulum* became the normal pattern for all such churches. According to this rule the canons were placed under vows of celibacy and obedience and lived a common life in dormitory, refectory and cloister; but individual property was allowed and in time the canons abandoned the communal life and began to build their own private houses around the church. A rule similar to that of Chrodegang was introduced at Christ Church, Canterbury, by Archbishop Wulfred about 813 and several other cathedral churches were run on similar lines.[3] So also were the greater collegiate churches such as Southwell and Beverley. After the revival of Benedictine monachism in the tenth century, however, there was a tendency to change the constitution of some of the cathedrals from secular to monastic. In some places

---

[1] Edgar's laws, 960, in Wilkins, *Concilia*, i, p. 225.
[2] A. W. Clapham, *English Romanesque Architecture*, i, pp. 77-100.
[3] K. Edwards, *The English Secular Cathedrals in the Middle Ages* (1949), pp. 3-9.

4

the secular canons had lapsed from their original rule, had grown rich and worldly, and were living in their own houses with their wives and children. S. Dunstan, with his strict views on celibacy and his devotion to the monastic ideal, was horrified at this, and at several places, such as Winchester, Worcester and Canterbury, the secular corporations were replaced by monks.

The parish churches of the tenth century had mostly been built of wood and have, therefore, long since disappeared. One only has survived, at Greenstead in Essex, built of split oak logs.[1] Of the stone churches, however, many are still standing in whole or in part. A few are quite large buildings (such as Deerhurst in Gloucestershire) but most are small village churches of a simple design and without transepts. The style of architecture is rugged and strong, often using stones of enormous size, and the exterior of the churches was often ornamented with pilaster strips (as at Earls Barton in Northamptonshire), while the interior was often richly decorated.

By the tenth century the parish had become well established as the ecclesiastical unit. It remained still the property of the local lord, though in a few places, mainly in the towns and in the Danelaw, the people had acquired possession of their church.[2] Parish churches were not all of the same status, some being described as *principales*, some as *mediocres*, while a distinction was generally drawn between those which possessed a graveyard and those which did not.[3]

The parish priests, known in contemporary legislation as 'altarthegns', were mainly local men, simple in their tastes and with only a rudimentary education. In spite of the fulminations of reformers, few of them were pluralists or had acquired their benefices by simony. On the other hand, a good many of them were married, especially in the north. In the Laws of the Northumbrian priests (c. 950) the marriage of a priest was regarded as perfectly normal and legal. The reformers, however, soon began to make their influence felt, so that by 963 it was becoming common (at any rate in the south) for men to separate from their wives at ordination and to vow themselves to celibacy. But things moved slowly, for by 1009 it was necessary to entreat the clergy not to marry though 'some have two (wives) or more; and some, though they dismiss her whom they

[1] E. Tyrrell-Green, *Parish Church Architecture* (1924), p. 65.
[2] R. R. Darlington, 'Ecclesiastical Reform in the Late Old English Period', in *E.H.R.* 1936, p. 413.
[3] G. Baldwin-Brown, *The Arts in Early England* (1903), i, pp. 308-9.

formerly had, afterward take another, the former living, as it becomes no Christian man to do'.[1] It is clear, therefore, that the efforts of the reformers were not meeting with an unqualified success.

The clergy were instructed to teach their people to observe the Lord's day from Saturday afternoon to Monday morning. The laity were to be encouraged to attend church on the Saturday evening to hear evensong and nocturns, and to come again on the Sunday morning, not to one of the early Masses but to the High Mass, complaints being made of those who 'hear Mass early in the morning, and then presently, all the day after, serve their own belly, not God, by drunkenness and junketing'. The laity were to communicate regularly, at least every Sunday during Lent, and some people of special holiness, 'widows and minstermen', might communicate every day if they wished. Communion was given in both kinds, the lay people often drinking the wine not directly out of the chalice but through a small pipe made of silver or ivory.[2] Fasting before communion was enjoined, the canons declaring 'that no man take the housel after he hath broke his fast except it be on account of extreme sickness'.[3]

Attempts were made to enforce the recitation of the Hour Services, known as 'uht-song, prime-song, undern-song, midday-song, noon-song, evensong and night-song', and the clergy were encouraged to preach to their people and to teach them to say the Creed and the Lord's Prayer. They were also to instruct the children of their parishes, as the *Capitula* of Theodulf (994) declare: 'Mass-priests ought always to have a school of learners in their houses, and if any good man will commit his little ones to them to be taught, they ought gladly to accept them and to teach them at free-cost'.[4]

In addition to the sermons preached by the clergy there was, at this time, an abundance of homiletic literature in the vernacular for those who could read. Examples of this are the *Blickling Homilies*, written largely to prepare people for the expected end of the world in the year 1000, and the various writings of Aelfric. In addition to vernacular translations of the Bible and of the Fathers, Aelfric, who became novice-master at Cerne Abbey in 987, composed two series

[1] J. Johnson, *Laws and Canons of the Church of England*, i, pp. 377, 437, 483; Wilkins, *Concilia*, i, pp. 219, 233-4, 287.

[2] D. Rock, *The Church of Our Fathers*, ed. G. W. Hart and W. H. Frere (1905), i, p. 130.

[3] Johnson, *op. cit.* i, pp. 410, 419, 466, 477; Wilkins, *Concilia*, i, pp. 227, 245, 273, 280.

[4] Johnson, *op. cit.* i, pp. 392, 393, 461-2; Wilkins, *op. cit.* i, pp. 252; 270.

of *Homilies*, each intended to cover the Church's year, the second series being rather more elaborate and discursive than the. first. Aelfric's ambition was to introduce the more simple of his country-men to the religious thought of the west, especially as expressed in the writings of S. Augustine. He was not in himself an original thinker, but a great interpreter and, 'not only the greatest prose-writer, he was also the most distinguished English-writing theologian, in his own time, or for five centuries afterwards'.[1]

Yet in spite of much preaching and the production of homiletic literature heathenism died hard, if it can ever be said to have died at all. Ecclesiastical laws of this period forbid people to indulge in the 'worship of fountains, necromancy, auguries and enchantments, sooth-sayings, false worship and legerdemain', or to bow down to idols and heathen gods or to the sun or moon, or to resort to special stones and trees as holy places.[2] And if superstition was the beset-ting sin of the laity, worldliness seems to have been the bane of the clergy. Constant appeals are made to the clergy to dress as their office demands and not as laymen, and, above all, to avoid the sin of drunkenness.[3]

The general impression of church life which is conveyed by the surviving records of the age shortly before the Norman Conquest is one of vigour and progress. The bishops were clearly exercising some real control both over the monasteries and over the secular clergy, valiant efforts towards reform were being made, and a high standard both of worship and of Christian life was the ideal towards which the Church aspired. That there was much ignorance and superstition to combat, and that there were many parishes where b᾿ h clergy and people had been barbarized by war and neglect is undeniable, but the Church as a whole was aware of the abuses and anxious to promote reform.

ii. *The Later Danish Invasions*

The tenth century had been, on the whole, a period of peace and progress for the people of England. The supreme courage and

---

[1] *Cambridge History of English Literature*, i, p. 127.
[2] Johnson, *op. cit.* i, pp. 415, 513; Wilkins, *op. cit.* i, pp. 226, 306.
[3] Johnson, *op. cit.* i, pp. 402, 459; Wilkins, *op. cit.* i, p. 268.

wisdom of Alfred had saved the country from destruction and had given self-confidence and strength to the Church. This was followed by the gradual conversion of the Danes and by steady progress in the government of the country, the administration of justice and the reform of the Church. But towards the end of the tenth century, and for the next few years, a series of calamities took place which threatened to undo the good work which had been done.

In 978 Edward, the young King of Wessex, was assassinated, leaving the throne to the incompetent Ethelred, an event which the Vikings took as an opportunity for renewing their raids on the south coast. In 1011 Canterbury was sacked, its cathedral burnt and many of its citizens, including Alphege the archbishop, were taken captive. Alphege was kept a prisoner for some months, until on his refusing to burden the poor with the task of raising a ransom for him, he was clubbed or stoned to death (April 19, 1012) near Greenwich. For a moment it looked as if the Lord had deserted His people, and as if Church and State must inevitably relapse into barbarism and heathendom.

By 1016 the second Viking invasion had been so far successful that the Danish King, Cnut, had made himself master of England; but his victory was not, as might have appeared, a victory for paganism, for Cnut was a Christian. In the Winchester *Liber Vitae* is a drawing of Cnut, standing by the altar with his hand upon the cross while an angel places the crown upon his head. This picture demonstrates the attitude of his subjects, for Cnut soon made his mark in England not as tyrant and oppressor but as the protector of the Church.

From the beginning of his reign he worked in the closest alliance with the Church, conscious that in so doing, he had much to learn. In his own country of Denmark the Church was young and inexperienced: in England it was by now a venerable institution with a long history behind it. Cnut was content to listen to what the Church had to teach him about the duties of a Christian monarch, and relied much upon churchmen for advice. He passed many laws protecting the Church, gave many gifts to the monasteries, filled his court with royal clerks (thereby creating a new type of civil servant), went on pilgrimage to Rome, and generally behaved as a loyal and dutiful son of the Church. That his private life, and especially his matrimonial affairs, caused some anxiety to church leaders is undeniable, for there was a good deal of the barbarian in him and he could be very cruel; but, on the whole, his reign from 1016 to 1035 was a time of peace and prosperity for the land and, perhaps even more so, for the Church.

iii. *Edward the Confessor*

Cnut's death was followed by eight troubled years, after which the English monarchy was restored, and Edward, son of Ethelred the Unready, was crowned king in 1043. Edward had lived in Normandy since he was about ten years old and was now forty. A saintly man, who earned for himself the title of 'Confessor', he was ill-fitted to govern a turbulent country in which he had little interest. His sympathies and his friends were Norman. He scarcely spoke any English, a language which he despised. Unlike Cnut who, though a foreigner by birth, had a great admiration for the English, Edward was a native of this country but with considerable contempt for its people whom he regarded as more or less uncultivated barbarians. It would have been difficult to find anyone less suited to guide the affairs of a great country at so critical a time.

It soon became clear that the country was divided into two parties. At the court was Edward, the 'crowned monk',[1] surrounded by his Norman clerks and anxious to fill the highest offices in the Church with his friends from overseas, men such as Robert, Abbot of Jumièges, whom he made Bishop of London in 1044 and Archbishop of Canterbury in 1051. Edward also kept in close touch with Rome and was happy to welcome papal legates to this country to advise him on ecclesiastical affairs.

The other party was represented by the great earls like Godwin and Harold. These men bitterly resented the intrusion of foreigners into England, and did their utmost to acquire some of the high offices for their supporters. One of these, Stigand, was thrust into the primacy in 1052 when Robert, its lawful holder, was in exile. Stigand was not an attractive character. He continued to hold the see of Winchester and several abbeys in plurality with Canterbury, until he was eventually deposed as a schismatic and usurper in 1070. If Stigand was one of the worst of English prelates, Wulfstan was one of the best. Brought up as a monk at Worcester he devoted much

---

[1] C. Dawson, *The Making of Europe* (1932), p. 273.

of his time to preaching and was eventually elected Bishop of Worcester, with Edward's consent, in 1062. He was the only English bishop who won the confidence of the Conqueror.[1]

In spite of his personal holiness, Edward the Confessor allowed the Church to deteriorate during his reign. His appointments were foolish and arbitrary and he allowed favourites like Leofric to be abbot of as many as five monasteries at once.[2] Sees became filled with a poor type of bishop, wealthy and worldly in their tastes. The clergy as a whole were poor and ignorant, and little was done to improve them. The one positive monument to Edward's reign was the building of the abbey at Westminster, a magnificent church which was consecrated on the Innocents' Day 1065. The king was too ill to attend the ceremony and died six days later.

Harold was king for only a few months, for, on the death of Edward the Confessor, his kinsman, William, Duke of Normandy, to whom Edward had promised the throne, decided to invade England. William regarded his exploit almost as a crusade. He sought and received the blessing of the pope, Alexander II, and the support of Hildebrand, the influential Archdeacon of Rome. He came as a churchman with the express purpose of reforming the Church in England, and when he landed at Pevensey many of the church leaders were prepared to welcome him.

With the defeat and death of Harold at Hastings the Church in England entered upon a new stage in its history. For five hundred years it had gone its own way, very much cut off from the general flow of Church life in the rest of Europe. For the next five hundred years it was to be brought more and more under the influence of Rome and thus to lose some of its independence and distinctive character. That the Conquest brought many advantages to the Church in England no one would deny, but one cannot see the passing of the Saxon Church without regret. It was to some extent provincial, and there were times when it lost its high ideals; but it did a great work for the people of England, evangelized North Germany and Scandinavia, and produced some of the greatest men whom the Church delights to honour. When we recall the holiness of Cuthbert, the zeal of Wilfrid, the courage of Boniface and the learning of Bede, and realize that behind them lay a host of faithful souls, some of whom

---

[1] See the *Vita Wulfstani*, ed. R. R. Darlington (1928).
[2] Peterborough, Burton-on-Trent, Coventry, Croyland and Thorney.

have left no memorial, we cannot but salute the Church which produced them and which they loved and served.

NOTE ON BOOKS

GENERAL and church histories as before. See also G. O. Sayles, *Medieval Foundations of England* (1948), pp. 131-211 and R. R. Darlington, 'Ecclesiastical Reform in the late Old English Period', in *English Historical Review* (1936). For laws see either D. Wilkins, *Concilia Magnae Britanniae et Hiberniae*, vol. i (1737) or J. Johnson, *A Collection of the Laws and Canons of the Church of England*, vol. i in the *Library of Anglo-Catholic Theology* (1850). Daniel Rock's *The Church of our Fathers*, 4 vols. edited by G. W. Hart and W. H. Frere (1905) is a mine of liturgical information. See also W. Page, 'Some Remarks on the Churches of the Domesday Survey', in *Archaeologia*, vol. lxvi (1915).

THE MIDDLE AGES

CHAPTER VI

ENGLAND UNDER THE NORMANS
(1066–1109)

i. *The Effect of the Conquest on English Church Life*

THE chief effect of the Norman Conquest was to give new life and vigour to the English Church and to bring it more into line with the Church on the continent. For some years the English Church had been showing signs of weakness. The rash policy of the Confessor in inviting Norman favourites to England had divided the Church and left it weak. For fifty years there had been little leadership, and deterioration and decay had set in. The Church in England was sorely in need of reform.

It was as a reformer that William liked to regard himself. During his lifetime considerable reforms had been taking place in Europe, with most of which William was in sympathy. But there was one aspect of church policy which William was not prepared to support; he would not allow the pope to interfere with what he regarded as the king's lawful business. Since 1046 there had been a great increase in papal claims, and both Alexander II and Gregory VII liked to think that William would govern his realm with due deference to their wishes. They were much mistaken. William was old-fashioned; his idea of reform meant producing a better Church, not greater subservience to Rome. He consequently made it clear from the start that he regarded himself as the head of the Church in England. He nominated his bishops and abbots and invested them with ring and staff. He summoned Church Councils. He expected his churchmen, just as much as his laymen, to pay respect to his wishes, and he refused to allow any foreign interference with his sovereignty.

Meanwhile papal power was increasing, and when the reformer, Hildebrand, became pope as Gregory VII in 1073 he was both shocked and indignant at the barrier imposed by William. But the king stood his ground. Although he would allow his subjects to seek advice from Rome, he firmly resisted any attempt on the part of the pope to interfere, on his own initiative, in English affairs. Gregory pleaded in vain, warning William of the terrible consequences of disobedience. 'As I have to answer for you at the awful Judgment,' he wrote, 'in the interests of your own salvation should you, can you, avoid immediate obedience to me?'[1] William apparently felt that he could. He was not prepared to submit to what he regarded as new-fangled ideas;[2] and to safeguard his independence he issued a number of decrees saying that no baron or royal minister might be excommunicated without the king's consent, that no bishop might go abroad without his permission, and that no letter from the pope might be received by anyone in England until it had first been read to the king.

William's policy for the English Church was, therefore, clear. It was to be brought into the main stream of continental church life, but it was to remain under the leadership of the king. Meanwhile the English prelates were gradually replaced by Normans, men whom William already knew and trusted. At the time of the Conquest there were already several Norman bishops in England, protégés of Edward the Confessor. But the Archbishopric of Canterbury was held by the usurper Stigand, and a number of sees were held by English bishops. William quickly made arrangements for the deposition of all those who were likely to be troublesome. A Council was held at Winchester in 1070 at which Stigand was deposed, Leofwine of Lichfield resigned (being a married man with a considerable family), and two other bishops lost their sees. This broke the back of the English party, and, before long, only one of those who had held office before the Conquest remained—Wulfstan, the saintly Bishop of Worcester. The way was thus laid open for an influx of church leaders from Normandy. By far the greatest of these was Lanfranc, Abbot of Caen, whom William chose for the primacy.

But the Conquest brought to an end not only the line of English bishops but the whole Anglo-Saxon culture. 'Hardly ever before or since has a national culture been so easily, so rapidly, or so completely submerged as was the Anglo-Saxon in the last thirty years of the eleventh century.'[3] The English language went underground for three centuries; English art and architecture were replaced by continental styles; and no Englishman had the slightest hope of promotion

[1] Migne, *Patrologia Latina*, vol. cxlviii, col. 569.
[2] See his letter to Gregory in H. Bettenson, *Documents of the Christian Church* (1943), p. 217.
[3] A. W. Clapham, *English Romanesque Architecture*, ii, p. 1.

for many years to come.

The effect of this on the Church was quickly seen in new styles of architecture. The Normans were enthusiastic builders and lost no time in pulling down many of the Saxon churches and replacing them with new buildings of their own design. Each of the two great churches at Canterbury, and those of Winchester, Worcester, Gloucester, Norwich, Ely, St. Alban's and, above all, Durham bear witness to the zeal and genius of the Anglo-Norman masons. To later generations this early Norman work may seem over-austere (and it was soon replaced by a more florid and ornate style), but for strength, dignity and simplicity it has never been surpassed. In its massive, rugged strength it was, in some ways, typical of the new régime. Under the leadership of the Conqueror the Church in England increased greatly in strength. But even William would have been greatly restricted had he not had the constant support and advice of his archbishop, Lanfranc.

ii. *William and Lanfranc*

Lanfranc was born at Pavia about the year 1010. As a young man he was a student of law, but in 1036 he left Italy and made his way northwards into France where he settled for a time at Avranches. A few years later he was attacked by robbers in a wood, but managed to reach a neighbouring monastery, the abbey of Bec, now rising to fame under the rule of its abbot Herluin. Lanfranc settled down as a monk and added prestige to the monastery by his great skill as a teacher. In due course he became prior and in 1063 was transferred to be abbot of William's new foundation at Caen.

Lanfranc and William had, therefore, known each other for some years when the vacancy at Canterbury occurred and the king had to find a successor to Stigand. In choosing Lanfranc William brought over a loyal servant. Lanfranc, like his master, was a keen reformer, and, like his master, he saw reform from the traditional point of view. Having left Italy ten years before the 'cleansing of the papacy' and the rapid growth of papal intransigence, Lanfranc had no difficulty in accepting William's views on the relationship between Church and State. King and archbishop were, therefore, able to work happily together in pursuit of a policy which commanded the allegiance of them both.

The first problem to be tackled was that of the organization of the English Church. In 1070 William appointed to the archbishopric of York a Norman called Thomas of Bayeux. Lanfranc saw at once that steps must be taken to convince Thomas that, although he was an archbishop, yet he must regard his see as inferior to that of Canterbury. Thomas refused to accept any such ruling, and a dispute ensued which lasted for some time and was won by Lanfranc only with the use of some documents which were almost certainly forged, though Lanfranc himself may not have been aware of the fact. Lanfranc engaged the support of William in the argument by pointing out that an Archbishop of York who claimed independence might set up a rival kingdom in the north and even crown some foreign king to reign over it.[1]

Having achieved unity in the government of the Church Lanfranc turned to questions of reform which he hoped to carry out by a series of Church Councils such as had been held in the old days. A Council was therefore summoned to meet at Winchester in 1072, another at London in 1075 and one at Winchester in the following year. At these Councils considerable reforms were carried through. Regular synods were to be held in each diocese twice in each year; archdeacons were to be appointed; simony was to be prohibited; vagrant clerks and monks were to be rounded up. But on the subject of the celibacy of the clergy Lanfranc was prepared to go slowly. The papacy would, no doubt, have liked a complete prohibition of all clerical marriage, but the English Councils were not prepared to go as far as that. Canons of secular cathedrals and collegiate churches were, indeed, ordered to put away their wives, and in future no married man might be ordained; but all parish clergy who were married were allowed to keep their wives. Attempts were also made to protect the parish clergy against exploitation by unscrupulous Norman barons.[2]

Another move towards greater efficiency in the Church was the removal of sees from the smaller places to the principal town in each diocese. This had already occurred in Devon in 1050 when the see had been moved from Crediton to Exeter. Now and during the next few years a number of other transfers were made—Dorchester to Lincoln, Sherborne to Salisbury, Selsey to Chichester, Lichfield to

[1] A. J. Macdonald, Lanfranc (2nd ed. 1944), p. 78.
[2] For decrees of these Councils see Wilkins, Concilia, i, pp. 363-7.

Chester and later to Coventry, Elmham to Thetford and afterwards to Norwich. Under Norman government the towns were to rise in importance and it was a wise move to put the seat of ecclesiastical jurisdiction in the most conspicuous place in the diocese.

Meanwhile king and archbishop were making changes in the administration of justice by the separation of the courts Christian from the civil courts. Hitherto all causes, spiritual as well as lay, had been heard in the same courts, the bishop sitting side by side with the earl. From now onwards ecclesiastical law was to be administered by church courts presided over either by the bishop or by the archdeacon. The promoters of this scheme can hardly have foreseen the trouble which this would cause in later years.

Finally Lanfranc, who had long studied the ideals of the monastic life, was busy reforming the monasteries. He himself presided over his monks at Canterbury, for whom he wrote a set of Constitutions which were regarded as the standard for all Benedictine houses in England.[1]

In all this work Lanfranc and William worked happily together. William was a successful soldier and able administrator, but he was illiterate and therefore bound to depend upon some faithful colleague who could do the things which he could not do. Lanfranc was ideal for this post, and the co-operation of the king and his archbishop was one of the most successful partnerships in history. Both were interested in reform, and, fortunately, both agreed upon the methods which should be employed. The result was that by the time of William's death in 1087 the Church in England was much stronger and more efficient than it had been for many years.

Lanfranc was regarded as one of the great churchmen of his day. He was consulted by bishops in Scotland and Ireland and by both bishops and abbots in Normandy. He kept in close touch with Rome, though always jealous of his own rights and independence. He was a great builder, especially at Canterbury, Rochester and St. Alban's. He also built almshouses and did much to help the poor relatives of his monks. And, in addition to all this, he was no mean scholar, for he was able to hold his own in theological dispute with men like Berengar of Tours. At the critical moment of the Norman Conquest and of the changes which were bound to affect the Church, England was fortunate in having not only a king of the quality of William but also so outstanding an archbishop as Lanfranc.

[1] See *The Monastic Constitutions of Lanfranc*, ed. M. D. Knowles (1951).

iii. S. Anselm

The partnership, so valuable for both Church and State, of William and Lanfranc was brought to an end by the death of William in 1087. Lanfranc supported William Rufus out of deference to his father's dying wish, but he must have realized that there could never be any real intimacy between him and the new king. Lanfranc, however, did not have to serve him for long, for he himself died on May 28, 1089, being then about eighty years of age.

The young king was no doubt glad to be relieved of the presence of the old archbishop with whom he would soon have quarrelled, for William had no real love for the Church. Falling under the influence of bad companions like Rannulf Flambard, he regarded the Church mainly as a possible source of revenue, and soon entered upon the most shameless robbery of church goods. His chief method of spoliation was to appropriate the income of all bishoprics during a vacancy. As the king normally appointed the bishops vacancies were made to last as long as possible, to the great financial advantage of the crown. If an abbacy fell vacant the king confiscated the whole income of the monastery and gave the monks a mere pittance on which to live. The harm done to the Church by this evil practice was incalculable.

The see of Canterbury being one of the richest benefices in England, it was in the interest of the king to delay as long as possible before appointing a successor to Lanfranc. Four years passed by without anything being done, and the vacancy might have gone on even longer had not Rufus fallen dangerously ill in 1093, and thus been frightened into making some act of restitution for the wrongs which he had committed on the Church. The greatest need was for a leader, and Rufus reluctantly agreed to nominate a man for the primacy. There was only one churchman for whom he had any respect and that was Anselm, the Abbot of Bec, who was in England at the time. Anselm was most unwilling to accept the offer, but the popular demand was so great that he could not refuse. He was consecrated at Canterbury on December 4, 1093.

Anselm, like Lanfranc, was an Italian, a native of Aosta, born about 1034. Like his predecessor he also left his native land and travelled north to the abbey of Bec, attracted, no doubt, by the fame of

Lanfranc. When Lanfranc went to Caen in 1063 Anselm succeeded him as prior, and, on the death of Herluin in 1078, he was promoted as abbot. He had thus ruled the monastery for fifteen years when he moved to Canterbury.

Anselm's extreme reluctance to accept the primacy was due not only to modesty. He knew enough of William Rufus to realize that they could never work together in harmony. 'What good', he said, 'would come of yoking together an untameable bull and an old and feeble sheep?'[1] But even had Anselm had to do with as good a king as the Conqueror, there could never have been harmonious co-operation between them, for Anselm's views of kingship were very different from those of Lanfranc. Lanfranc had been a reformer, but a reformer of the old school who was quite prepared to allow a king considerable independence in his own kingdom. Anselm had lived in Italy for some years after the reforms of the papacy in 1046 and had come to accept papal authority in a way which Lanfranc had never done. Anselm, therefore, knew that he must work to curtail the power and independence of the king while increasing the influence of the pope, and it was for this that he fought his long battle, first against William Rufus and then against Henry I. In the early days he fought almost alone; but gradually he won over the bishops and abbots to his side, and by his death in 1109 he had broken the old independence of the kings of England and given the papacy a greater control over the affairs of the country than it had ever had before.

Anselm may have fought a lone fight in England, but in the Church as a whole he was but one of many who were engaged in the great struggle over the question of Investitures. The mere act of investing a prelate with ring and staff was not, in itself, a matter of much importance; what was of supreme importance was the status of the bishop, whether he was to regard himself as the king's nominee and servant or not. The difficulty was, of course, enormously exaggerated by the great temporal estates of the bishops. A bishop was not only a great spiritual leader, he was also a feudal tenant-in-chief with very considerable powers, and it was therefore essential to a king that he should have some control over the appointment of such magnates. The Church, on the other hand, with its concern for reform, was equally determined that the choice of bishops should be in its own hands and not in those of any lay power. It was true that bishops and

[1] R. W. Church, *St. Anselm* (1870), p. 221.

5

abbots were landowners on a very large scale, and, as such, must take their place in a feudalized society, but first and foremost they were there to guide and reform the Church. To ecclesiastical eyes, therefore, it was essential that bishops should owe allegiance primarily to the Church and its laws and not to any temporal power.

Such was the issue being so fiercely fought out in Europe when Anselm became Archbishop of Canterbury in 1093. He saw at once that there was bound to be trouble, and he prepared himself for a long and bitter struggle. It began immediately after his consecration when he applied to the king for permission to go to Rome to fetch his *pallium*, the long stole which popes granted to metropolitans as a mark of rank. William immediately raised objections. The battle had begun.

In the long struggle which followed, and which kept the archbishop out of England for six years at a time when his presence was most needed, behind the actual and often petty subjects of dispute lay the fundamental question: What was to be the relative position of king and pope? If a conflict of loyalties occur, which of the two has the greater claim?

Anselm had no doubt about the answer. The pope was the head of the Church on earth and must take precedence over every temporal ruler. But at first there were not many in England who were prepared to accept this point of view, and when the Council of Rockingham met in 1095 to try to reach some agreement between the king and the archbishop, various parties began to emerge. The king, following the example of his father, was determined to keep a tight hold on the Church and to claim his full rights of nomination and investiture. Over against him stood the archbishop, a child of the continental reform movement, equally determined that royal power over the Church must be curbed. In theory this was sound; in practice, a bad and unscrupulous king like Rufus made it essential. The bishops, looking back to the more peaceful days of the Conqueror and Lanfranc, distrusted Anselm and his papalism and voted against him, while the barons tended to support him in the hopes of using him as an ally in their struggle against the king.

The Council of Rockingham decided nothing; it led only to an uneasy truce which lasted for a couple of years. At the end of this time Anselm decided to force a decision. He again asked for permission to go to Rome. The king again refused. So the archbishop took the law into his own hands and went. He did not attempt to return until after the death of Rufus in 1100.

Henry I was a much better king than his brother, William; but he was equally determined to maintain his independence and his rights over the Church. There was, therefore, little hope of reconciliation, especially as Anselm, during his sojourn abroad, had taken part in two Councils in Italy which had flatly forbidden lay investiture, and had become even more intransigent than before. Anselm returned to England in 1100 and even managed to hold a Council at Westminster in 1102 at which some reforms were carried out. But the deadlock over the question of investitures remained, and in 1103 Anselm returned to the continent refusing to set foot in England again until Henry had given way. Three years later some sort of compromise was reached: the king gave way on the question of investitures and the archbishop made certain concessions in the matter of bishops doing homage to the king. Anselm then returned to England and resumed his functions as archbishop. But he did not live long after this, for he died on April 21, 1109.

Anselm had, throughout the struggle, regarded himself as bound to fight for the new canon law against the usurpation by native law of powers which must really belong to the Church. He had come to England knowing that he must fight that battle. Under William Rufus there was no doubt that Anselm was right. Rufus was a bad king who was letting the Church go to ruin. Only papal interference could save it, and Anselm fought hard to try to persuade his bishops that this was so. But the bishops let him down, perhaps because they were shrewd enough to see the dangers which lay behind this policy. Disappointed in his prelates Anselm was driven abroad, where he became more fanatical in his support of the papacy. He returned, under Henry I, more determined than ever not to give way; and, in the end, he won. He would never have returned unless he had been sure of victory. Anselm won; the freedom of the Church was safeguarded; but at a price—the price of growing papal control.

So much of Anselm's time was taken up with controversy and with affairs of state that he had little opportunity for exercising his great talents as a scholar of remarkable ability. While he was at Bec he produced two treatises which put him in the first rank among creative theologians—the *Monologion* and the *Proslogion*—in which he attempted to prove the existence of God from pure reason and by the argument from ontology. Later in life, during his years of tribulation and exile, he wrote his famous book *Cur Deus Homo?* in which he discussed the doctrine of the Incarnation and the Atonement. By nature a scholar and a monk, Anselm's sense of duty is nowhere more clearly shown than in his willingness to surrender the life which he loved and to plunge into public affairs which he must have found most uncongenial. For this, if for nothing else, Anselm has earned his place among the saints.

iv. *The Growth of Monasticism*

At the time of the Norman Conquest there were, in England, thirty-five monasteries and a few nunneries. They all followed the Benedictine rule, and were mostly well established and well endowed. In spite of Edward the Confessor's predilection for Normans these monasteries were mostly filled with English monks and proved one of the chief obstacles to William's occupation of the country. This might have led to harsh measures; but, on the whole, William treated the monasteries leniently. He had a great respect for the monastic life and was anxious to foster the religious houses in his kingdom. The arrival of Lanfranc in 1070 greatly strengthened the king's hand. From then onwards Norman abbots were imported in increasing numbers from the French abbeys of Jumièges, Fécamp, Caen and elsewhere. These abbots did not always find it easy to win the respect and confidence of the English monks, and there was often an uneasy period of adjustment; but in the end English monasticism was much strengthened by these importations.

With the coming of the Normans monachism went ahead rapidly. Many houses were rebuilt in the Norman style, the numbers of the monks increased, and a large crop of new monasteries appeared in England. In 1066 there were thirty-five houses but by 1100 this number had grown to fifty independent houses, twenty-nine dependent 'cells' and forty-five alien priories or dependencies of foreign monasteries. There was an increase also in the number of nunneries. Lanfranc also did much to reform the existing houses and to enforce a more strict observance of the Rule. For his own monks at Christ Church, Canterbury, he wrote his *Consuetudines*[1] which, like

[1] See above, p. 63.

the *Regularis Concordia* of Dunstan, set a standard for English Bene-dictine monachism. Meanwhile, with the moving of some of the sees to the more important towns a number of cathedrals gave up their secular government by dean and canons, and became monastic, under the rule of a prior and convent.[1] The years which followed the Con-quest were thus a time of considerable expansion and progress for the English Black Monks.

The first half-century of Norman rule also saw the introduction into England of a number of new orders of religious. Early in the tenth century a reform had taken place in France which had led to the formation of a new body, known as the Order of Cluny. Whereas each Benedictine house was an independent unit, the Cluniac monasteries were all more or less ruled from Cluny itself. Such supervision certainly made for greater discipline, though all Cluniac houses were exempt from episcopal jurisdiction. Within these monasteries great stress was laid upon worship, which gradu-ally came to occupy more and more of the day, to the virtual exclu-sion of all other forms of activity. The first Cluniac house in England was at Lewes in Sussex, founded by William de Warenne in 1077. By the end of the century three other houses had been founded— Wenlock (*c.* 1080) and Bermondsey and Castle Acre in 1089. Eventu-ally there were eleven abbeys of this order in England with a number of smaller dependencies.

About the year 1100 a new kind of religious life was introduced with the first houses of 'canons regular'. Groups of priests living to-gether under some kind of rule had existed from early times, but in the eleventh century attempts were made to bring these into a general organization with a vow of poverty, and a Rule was devised, based largely on the writings of S. Augustine. This gave them the name of 'Augustinian canons' and, as such, the order first appears in England in the reign of William Rufus.[2] Once introduced they spread rapidly and became one of the most popular orders in the country with over two hundred houses. Their monasteries, though smaller than the Benedictine houses, were built on the usual monastic pattern, and their daily life differed only slightly from that of the monks.

---

[1] During the Middle Ages the 'monastic cathedrals' in England were Canterbury, Rochester, Winchester, Worcester, Ely, Durham, Norwich, Carlisle, Coventry and Bath. All were Benedictine except Carlisle, which was Augustinian.

[2] J. C. Dickinson, *The Origins of the Austin Canons and their Introduction into England* (1950), pp. 98-108.

Similar to the Augustinian or Black Canons were the White Canons of the Premonstratensian Order. This order was founded by S. Norbert at Prémontré about 1120 and took its name from the place of its origin. It was introduced into England at Newhouse in Lincolnshire in 1143, and in time had thirty-one abbeys up and down the country. The rule of the order was much like that of the Augustinians, but bore some traces of Cistercian influence.[1]

The first part of the twelfth century also saw the creation of a small English order, the Gilbertines. If the Augustinians were called after a book, and the Premonstratensians after a place, this order took its name from its founder, Gilbert, rector of Sempringham, who wished to found an order for nuns based on the rule of the Cistercians. On the Cistercians refusing to take on the responsibility for this, S. Gilbert provided the nuns with a small body of canons and thus revived in England the old idea of a double monastery containing both men and women, though minute regulations were drawn up to keep the two elements apart. The order eventually extended to twenty-seven houses in England, but it never spread overseas.[2]

By far the greatest foundation of the early years of the twelfth century was the Cistercian order, an austere and simplified type of Benedictinism, which played a very important part in English medieval life. The order originated at Cîteaux near Dijon and owed much to an Englishman, S. Stephen Harding, who became Abbot of Cîteaux in 1109. Harding did much to set the order on its feet, but it was his pupil, S. Bernard of Clairvaux, who added lustre to it by his scholarship and by his sanctity. By cutting out all superfluities of food and dress, by choosing the most barren and desolate places for their houses, and by a strict simplicity both in the design and decoration of their churches, the Cistercians made a valiant effort to return to the early days of monasticism when S. Benedict had lived with his first companions at Monte Cassino. The experiment proved popular, postulants flocked to the Cistercian houses, and the order spread rapidly.

It was introduced into England at Waverley in Surrey in 1128, but the first house to achieve any real fame was Rievaulx in Yorkshire which was colonized by a group of monks from Clairvaux in 1132.

---

[1] H. M. Colvin, *The White Canons in England* (1951).
[2] For the history of the order see R. Graham, *St. Gilbert of Sempringham and the Gilbertines* (1901).

Hidden among the rolling hills of the Yorkshire moors Rievaulx soon became a famous monastery and has the distinction of having produced one of the most distinguished men of the twelfth century, Ailred of Rievaulx, the 'Bernard of the north', a peculiarly lovable character, typical of the best that monasticism could produce.[1]

The coming of the Cistercian monks to Rievaulx also had the effect of causing a crisis in the Benedictine abbey of S. Mary at York. This abbey had been founded in 1078 but had already departed a good deal from its first loyalty, and a small group of monks, under the leadership of Prior Richard, were seriously distressed at the drift which was taking place. They caused so great a disturbance by their demands for reform that the archbishop, Thurstan, had to be called in to restore peace among the brethren. The advent of the archbishop, however, only led to further trouble, the outcome of which was that the thirteen dissatisfied monks left the abbey and were taken for a time into the archbishop's household. All this occurred in the autumn of 1132; and three months later, in the depths of winter, the monks were taken to Ripon, given some land in the uninhabited valley of the Skell, and left to fend for themselves. All through that winter they suffered terrible privations. They built themselves some huts under a large elm-tree and fed themselves on anything edible which they could find. Thus they lived through the winter, but in the spring they got into touch with S. Bernard and adopted the Cistercian Rule. Thus was born the famous Cistercian abbey of Fountains, taking its name from the springs which watered the valley where it stood. For two years the life of the monks remained very austere and hard, but in 1135 they were joined by Hugh, Dean of York, and two canons whose coming brought money, land and books ; and it was not long before a handsome church and convent were built. From this time onwards the Cistercian order grew rapidly in England, and by 1200 had sixty-two abbeys.[2]

Among the minor orders which found their way into England in the twelfth century was the order of Carthusians, founded by S. Bruno at the Grande-Chartreuse in 1086. Unlike most of the other monastic orders the Carthusians were hermit-monks, who renounced the corporate life and lived each in his own cell, where he did his

[1] See F. M. Powicke, 'Ailred of Rievaulx' in *Ways of Medieval Life and Thought* (1950), pp. 7-26.
[2] For the early history of the Cistercians see M. D. Knowles, *The Monastic Order in England* (1940), pp. 208-66.

work, cooked his own food and said his prayers. The community met only for the night-office, Mass and vespers. For the rest of the day each monk lived the life of a solitary.[1] The first Carthusian house in England was founded about 1178 at Witham in Somerset, and this was followed by Hinton Charterhouse early in the thirteenth century. The order never made much progress in England, for the life was very hard and the standards remained very high.[2] It produced, however, one of the most saintly characters of the medieval English Church—S. Hugh of Avalon, who came over to found the charterhouse at Witham in 1178 and in 1186 was elected Bishop of Lincoln, where he lived for fourteen years, setting an example of what a really pastoral bishop might be. The 'Angel Choir' in Lincoln Cathedral was built in his honour.[3]

With the exception of the Carthusians each order had houses for women—the Black Nuns of the order of S. Benedict, the White Ladies of the Cistercians, a few Cluniacs, and the Augustinian and Premonstratensian canonesses. By the year 1200 there were about seventy-six houses which followed the Benedictine Rule, twenty-eight Cistercians, two Cluniacs, nine Augustinian and two Premonstratensian. In addition to these were the Gilbertine houses and three similar double monasteries which took their origin from Fontevrault.

Mention should also be made of the Military Orders, the Hospitallers and Templars. Each of these orders had started in the Holy Land to provide hospitality and protection for pilgrims to Jerusalem and the holy places. They had spread to England and founded a number of houses, or 'preceptories' as they were called. In addition were the numerous hospitals in all parts of the country. These were small religious houses where a few elderly and infirm people were accommodated and cared for by a small group of men or women living under religious vows.[4]

The vast number of monastic houses founded in or about the twelfth century shows that this type of life was highly valued. Wealthy landowners vied with one another in setting up monasteries where they and their families might be prayed for, and where a quiet

[1] The most complete remains of a Carthusian house in England are at Mount Grace in Yorkshire.
[2] For a history of the order in England see E. M. Thompson, *The Carthusian Order in England* (1930).
[3] The *Magna Vita S. Hugonis* was published in the Rolls Series in 1864. There is a modern life by R. M. Woolley (1927).
[4] R. M. Clay, *Medieval Hospitals of England* (1909).

and peaceful life could be provided in the midst of war and tumult. At this time there were few who doubted that the monastic life was the highest form of Christian endeavour to which a man could dedicate his life.

NOTE ON BOOKS

THE standard history for this period is in F. M. Stenton, *Anglo-Saxon England* (1943), chapter xviii, and A. L. Poole, *From Domesday Book to Magna Carta* (1951), being vols. ii and iii of the *Oxford History of England*. See also *Cambridge Medieval History*, vol. v. For church history W. R. W. Stephens, *The English Church from the Norman Conquest to the Accession of Edward I* (1901) is still the main work. Z. N. Brooke, *The English Church and the Papacy* (1931) is essential. Reference should also be made to A. J. Macdonald, *Lanfranc* (new ed. 1944) and to R. W. Church, *Saint Anselm* (1870). For monasticism see M. D. Knowles, *The Monastic Order in England* (1940) and M. D. Knowles and R. N. Hadcock, *Medieval Religious Houses: England and Wales* (1953). A. W. Clapham's *English Romanesque Architecture*, 2 vols. (1934) is of great interest.

CHAPTER VII

THE STRUGGLE FOR POWER
(1109–1216)

i. *The King and the Pope*

THE struggle in which Anselm had been involved, and which he had virtually won, was part of the great battle over the question of Investitures, behind which lay the ultimate question of authority. In the ordering of society two powers were struggling for precedence —Pope and Emperor, Church and State, Archbishop and King. This tension was to continue for many years, and indeed, in a sense, must always be present so long as men have a dual allegiance to the Church and to society. Anselm, on his accession to the primacy in 1093, had found a bad and tyrannical king whose power over the Church must be broken. He had lived on into the reign of a much greater king who really had the welfare of his subjects at heart. But Anselm had felt bound to continue the fight, and had won. The authority of the Church had been vindicated. The independence of the Conqueror, which had so baffled and angered the pope, could never again be revived.

For five years after the death of Anselm the primacy was vacant, but at last, in 1114, Ralph d'Escures was elected amid expressions of general satisfaction. This satisfaction was not, however, shared at Rome, where the pope complained that he had not been consulted, and declared that he was responsible for the appointment of fit persons to high ecclesiastical rank. The election being obviously valid, the papal objections were not upheld, and the new primate entered upon his office. But the pope decided that the time had come for a revival of the practice of keeping a legate to England to watch over his interests on the spot and, if necessary, to override the decisions of the English bishops. Abbot Anselm, a nephew of the late archbishop, was therefore sent off from Rome as legate, but Henry I refused to allow him to enter the country, perhaps because of his close kinship with his old enemy. The next legate, Peter of Cluny, was allowed to land, but the king saw to it that he was given no opportunity of doing anything.

Shortly after this a resurgence of the old dispute between the Archbishops of Canterbury and York, and the death of Ralph d'Escures in 1122, encouraged the pope to make yet another attempt to establish a footing in England. This time he sent as legate Cardinal John of Cremona who soon made his presence felt by asserting his precedence over all, assuming the rights which normally belonged to the Archbishop of Canterbury, and summoning a Council to meet at Westminster in 1125. The latter was much resented by the English people, Gervase of Canterbury writing of it as 'a thing hitherto unheard of that a clerk who was only of the rank of priest should occupy a throne above archbishops, bishops, abbots and all the nobility of the realm'.[1] The Council passed various reforms, but the cardinal, having himself been found guilty of a breach of one of his own decrees, was obliged to leave the country in haste, and, for a time, the Archbishop of Canterbury, William of Corbeil, was allowed to act as legate.

Henry I died in 1135 and for nearly twenty years the country was torn by fierce quarrels and at times by open hostilities. Stephen had such difficulty in maintaining his hold on the throne that he tried to bribe the Church by making all kinds of desperate promises far beyond anything that Anselm would have dared to ask. None of these promises was kept, and the gulf between the king and the Church grew steadily wider, reaching its widest point when Stephen arrested and imprisoned the Bishops of Salisbury and Lincoln. From 1139 onwards the primacy was held by Archbishop Theobald, 'the last archbishop to wield unquestioned influence as the first adviser of the crown, in virtue of his ecclesiastical position'.[2] Theobald surrounded himself with a group of very able young men, including Thomas Becket and John of Salisbury, and his household was the home of all that was best in English thought and learning. But the times were evil; Stephen was in process of plunging the country into civil war, and the eyes of many were looking overseas to Henry of Anjou as the man who could restore order and prosperity. In October 1154 Stephen died and Henry promptly entered into his inheritance.

---

[1] W. R. W. Stephens, *The English Church from the Norman Conquest to the Accession of Edward I* (1901), p. 141.
[2] F. M. Powicke, *Stephen Langton* (1928), p. 109.

ii. Henry II and Becket

Henry II was a wise and strong ruler who was determined to restore law and order after the chaos of Stephen's reign. He looked back to the days of his grandfather, Henry I, with admiration and esteem, and set himself to establish a strong government and a respect for authority. He had to some extent been influenced by the revival of legal studies on the continent, and he realized that the prime necessity for the country was a just legal system justly administered. There must be no respect of persons, no suspicion of 'one law for the rich and another for the poor', and no exemptions. The law must be equal for all and universally applied.

Between the king and the achievement of this ideal lay various obstacles, among them the privilege known as 'Benefit of Clergy'.[1] This had been introduced soon after the separation of the spiritual from the civil courts in the time of William I and meant that any clerk could claim the right to be tried by the ecclesiastical courts for any crime above the level of misdemeanours, with the one exception of high treason. Thus for such crimes as murder and manslaughter, theft, rape, pillage, assault and highway robbery a man had only to prove himself a clerk to have his case transferred to the ecclesiastical courts where he could often reckon on going unpunished, for the procedure in these tribunals had become little better than a farce.[2] The test of clerkship was the wearing of the tonsure, and there are cases on record of men bribing their gaolers to shave them in order to claim Benefit of Clergy.

To a wise and ambitious king like Henry II, determined to establish one law for all, this privilege was most objectionable. 'Criminous clerks' must stand their trial like other men and suffer the same penalties if found to be guilty. On this point the mind of the king was perfectly clear. The Church, however, saw it in quite a different light. The question was not one of justice but of authority. If the Church were a mere department of state then, no doubt, its officers would be obliged to submit to secular jurisdiction; but if the Church were, in fact, an authority separate from and superior to the state, then it

[1] On this, see the article in Ollard, Crosse and Bond, *Dictionary of English Church History* (1948), and L. C. Gabel, *Benefit of Clergy in England in the Later Middle Ages* (1929).
[2] See Pollock and Maitland, *History of English Law* (1895), i, p. 426.

had the right to try its own men according to its own laws. The quarrel, therefore, between Church and state in the reign of Henry II was part of the long and universal struggle which was being fought out all over Christendom. Hitherto it had been largely concerned with the question of appointment to high office; now it had become a matter which affected the life of the humblest clerk. Is he amenable to the law of the state or only to the law of the Church which he serves?

It was not long before Henry found himself bitterly opposed on this point by his archbishop, Thomas Becket. Becket, a Londoner of Norman stock, had, as a young man, entered the household of Archbishop Theobald where he had shown himself efficient and reliable, though ambitious and egotistic. His ability was rewarded by his being made Archdeacon of Canterbury, and it was as such that he became friendly with Henry II. Henry was immediately attracted to him, and, in 1154, appointed him to one of the highest positions in the land, that of Chancellor of England. For eight years king and chancellor saw much of each other, and a warm friendship was established. Becket, having a clear idea of what a chancellor should be, took infinite pains to make his court and household the most magnificent in the kingdom. He entertained on a lavish scale, he hunted and hawked, he surrounded himself with the richest and most influential men in the country. Even the king himself could scarcely rival the magnificence and opulence of his chancellor.

Then in 1161 the old Archbishop Theobald died, and the question of his successor arose. For about a year the king hesitated, and then announced to Becket that he wished him to succeed to the primacy. Becket at first treated the suggestion as a joke, and warned the king that he would regret it. But Henry insisted; and, in spite of considerable opposition from some of the monks at Canterbury, the election was made. Thomas was ordained priest on June 2, 1162 and consecrated archbishop on the following day.

Immediately his whole manner of life changed. He threw aside his old life and adopted the life of the ascetic, living in almost monastic seclusion at Canterbury. To some this has appeared as hypocrisy; but it was not so. Nor was it a sign of sudden conversion. The explanation is that he was one of those men who visualize the part which they are to play and then adapt their lives to the type which they have created in their own minds. As chancellor Becket had seen himself as

the magnificent courtier, glorious in his apparel, reckless in his hospitality. As archbishop he saw himself as the leading churchman in
England, fighting for God and the freedom of His Church against
tyranny and oppression; and he was able to adapt his life accordingly.[1]
Henry was baffled and infuriated. The man whom he had regarded
as his greatest friend and whom he hoped to make his staunchest ally
had, in a night, become utterly estranged from him, with every
appearance of turning into his bitterest enemy. The scene was thus
immediately set for a quarrel on the grand scale. As Henry himself
said: 'England is not a bush that can hold two such robins as the
archbishop and myself'.

It was not long before the conflict began. At first it was concerned
with minor questions, but soon the problem of the 'criminous clerks'
arose. Henry was determined that the clergy should be brought
within the framework of the law and demanded that clerks, having
been convicted in the ecclesiastical courts, should be degraded and
handed over to the secular courts for punishment. Becket regarded
this as a gross infringement of the liberties of the Church, declared
that degradation was itself a punishment and that Henry's plan ran
counter to the elements of justice by punishing a man twice for one
offence. He therefore insisted that only for a second offence could
the civil courts punish a man who had once been ordained.

A deadlock was therefore reached, and it was to deal with this and
other problems that Henry summoned first the Council of Westminster in 1163 and then the Council of Clarendon in 1164. At the
latter a set of Constitutions was drawn up in which an attempt was
made to codify the ancient law, especially in the matter of the relations between Church and State. The Constitutions tried to prohibit
appeals to Rome without the king's consent, and to prevent clergy
leaving the country. They also dealt with the question of criminous
clerks, declaring that a clerk once tried, convicted and degraded in
a bishop's court should then be punished as a layman and may no
longer claim the support of the Church. A long debate took place
on this proposal, which Becket regarded as a direct attack upon the
rights of the Church. He therefore opposed it with all his strength,
though with little support from the bishops. Borne down by threats,
pleas and persuasions Becket at last gave his consent; but immediately
afterwards he repented of his action and sought opportunity for

[1] On this see Z. N. Brooke, *The English Church and the Papacy* (1931), pp. 193-4.

showing his utter disapproval of what had been done. For a time he was miserable and ashamed, knowing that, in a moment of weakness, he had not lived up to the ideal which he had set himself. All that he needed now was an opportunity of publicly declaring his entire dissatisfaction with the king's policy. Almost any incident would serve for this purpose.

Becket did not have to wait long. A minor difficulty over the archbishop's estates in Sussex served as an opportunity for him to make his stand against what he regarded as tyranny and oppression. He was summoned to appear at the Council of Northampton in October 1164, and it was there, after some months of indecision, that he threw down his challenge to the king. The time had come for action. There must be no further 'halting between two opinions'. Men must decide which they were to serve—Church or king. Striding into the hall, bearing his primatial cross in his own hands, he defied the king, refused to hear the judgment pronounced upon him, threatened with excommunication any who dared to consent to his trial, and solemnly walked out through the crowd of infuriated courtiers, not one of whom dared to touch him. 'It was the first of the two occasions when, for a whole act's length, he stood in the centre of the stage of English history.' [1]

Becket fled overseas and, for six years, remained abroad, mostly at the Cistercian abbey of Pontigny where he immediately adopted the full rigours of the monastic life. During these years of exile he brooded over his wrongs and became more stubborn than ever. For a man who had always lived a life full of activity and adventure and who, for many years, had been always in the limelight, the forced inactivity, obscurity and sense of helplessness which assailed him were very bitter. He grew more hard, more determined, more ruthless. He saw himself now as the persecuted champion of the Faith, God's suffering servant, the sole survivor of those who had refused to bow the knee to Baal. The quarrel about 'criminous clerks' had now been largely forgotten. Becket's mind had moved away from a local dispute on a matter of justice; what troubled it now was the question of ultimate authority. He, at least, was determined that he should not render to Caesar the things that are God's.

After a time conferences began to take place, and messengers

<hr />

[1] M. D. Knowles, 'Archbishop Thomas Becket, a Character Study', in *The Historian and Character* (1963), p. 113.

passed between king and archbishop in the hope of reaching a settlement. It was not, however, until 1170 that some kind of truce was made and Becket felt free to return to England. He crossed to Sandwich on December 1 and had a triumphant progress to Canterbury, where he was warmly received by the crowds. But his mind was full of forebodings. All through life he had loved the centre of the stage. Always he had been driven on by 'a fierce desire to excel'. Was his ride into Canterbury—like the Master's ride into Jerusalem—to be the prelude to tragedy—and triumph?

The return of Becket greatly alarmed his enemies in England, especially the Archbishop of York and the Bishops of London and Salisbury, whose excommunication he had procured from Rome. These three prelates immediately went over to France to lay their grievances before the king who, sick and tired of the whole weary business, complained bitterly of the trouble which the archbishop had caused him.

Four knights—Reginald FitzUrse, Hugh de Morville, William de Tracy and Richard le Breton—heard this burst of anger and immediately laid a plot to murder Becket. They crossed the Channel and arrived at Canterbury about midday on December 29. They forced their way into the archbishop's chamber while he was at dinner, and a stormy altercation took place over the excommunication of the three bishops. Becket refused to retract, and the four knights went away with murder in their hearts. An hour or so later they returned fully armed. The monks barricaded the house and dragged the archbishop into the great church. This they also tried to defend, but Becket refused to allow the house of God to be turned into a fortress. The murderers now approached from the cloisters, pushed through the crowds into the church, and encountered Becket in a chapel in the north transept where he had placed himself by a pillar.

By this time all his companions had fled with the exception of Edward Grim, who stood by him to the last, though his arm was broken in attempting to defend his master. Within a few minutes all was over. Becket lay dead on the floor of the church, while his murderers marched unmolested through the terrified crowds who filled the cloisters on that dark winter afternoon.

The news of the murder spread rapidly and came as an immense shock to the whole of Christendom. Archbishops had been murdered before, but the butchering of an archbishop in his own cathedral by some of his own people was an event which rang through the world. Henry II was horrified, and immediately attempted to justify himself by swearing that he had not intended the archbishop's death, that he would be faithful to the pope, that he would allow appeals to Rome, renounce any attempt to introduce customs detrimental to the Church, and, if necessary, go on Crusade. Some years later he visited Canterbury where he publicly underwent the most rigorous penance at the tomb of the archbishop.

'Saint and Martyr rule from the tomb' says the Fourth Tempter in Eliot's *Murder in the Cathedral*, and Becket certainly won, by his death, the fight which he had come so near to losing in his life. In 1173 he was canonized, and his fame spread far and wide.[1] His shrine at Canterbury became one of the most famous objects of pilgrimage in Europe, and the roads of Kent were often thronged with parties who set out, like Chaucer and his friends, 'the holy blisful martir for to seke'. For over three hundred years the shrine of S. Thomas at Canterbury stood as a witness to the triumph of Church over State. It was no wonder, therefore, that in 1538 Henry VIII took steps to have it destroyed and the martyr's bones scattered.[2]

iii. *The Reigns of Richard I and John*

The four knights who had murdered the archbishop escaped overseas, and the king made no attempt to bring them to justice. But this would not have worried the dead man. He slept in peace, having won his battle. No one now dared to raise again the question of 'criminous clerks', and Benefit of Clergy remained on the statute-book until 1827. More important, Henry had acknowledged the legality of appeals to Rome which now increased greatly in number. Yet in spite of this reverse Henry II managed to carry through the main part of his policy, which was to encourage respect for the law and to build up a stable government. It was because of this that England was able to survive the neglect and mismanagement of Henry's two sons

---

[1] See T. Borenius, *St. Thomas Becket in Art* (1932).

[2] The literature about Becket is copious, beginning with the original sources in *Materials for the History of Becket*, 7 vols. in the Rolls Series. For modern lives see Richard Winston, *Thomas Becket* (1967) and M. D. Knowles, *Thomas Becket* (1970). See also M. D. Knowles, *The Episcopal Colleagues of Thomas Becket* (1951).

who followed him on the throne—Richard I (1189–99) and John (1199–1216).

Richard took only a passing interest in the affairs of his kingdom, for his life was so totally absorbed by the Crusades that, out of his whole reign of ten years, he spent only four or five months in England. Meanwhile the government of the country was carried on by his ministers, most of whom were bishops and many of them far more interested in the details of political organization than in the routine of pastoral duties. Hubert Walter, who was Archbishop of Canterbury from 1193 to 1205 held, in addition to the primacy, the offices of legate, chief justiciar, chancellor and vicegerent. But he was a good and conscientious man, a great civil servant anxious to make a success of his labours and to guide the country through an exceedingly difficult time. William Longchamp, Bishop of Ely (1189–97), who was also chancellor, was a less attractive character who made himself much disliked by his domineering and extravagant ways. Geoffrey Plantagenet, an illegitimate son of Henry II, had far less claim to ecclesiastical preferment; yet he became Bishop of Lincoln at the age of fourteen and Archbishop of York seven years later, though his interest in the affairs of the Church was of the very slightest and he spent most of his time abroad. One bishop alone stands out as a shining example of pastoral devotion, and that was S. Hugh of Lincoln.

The absence of the king, the intrigues of prelates and barons in England, and the constant financial drain on the country's resources in aid of foreign wars did much to undermine the good work which Henry II had done. Nor did the death of Richard in 1199 bring any relief, for he was succeeded by his brother John, under whom things went from bad to worse. John was a 'tough, rather stout, energetic little man' of amazing versatility. He has been described as 'cruel and ruthless, violent and passionate, greedy and self-indulgent, genial and repellent, arbitrary and judicious, clever and capable, original and inquisitive'.[1] His unreliability meant that he soon quarrelled with the leading men who had been trying to keep the ship afloat during the reign of King Richard. The one hope for the country was for the king to surround himself with a group of wise counsellors, but this John steadfastly declined to do.

[1] A. L. Poole, *From Domesday Book to Magna Carta* (1951), p. 425. Cf. Sir F. M. Powicke's description of him as 'very mean, very astute, very reckless and irresponsible, and also very thorough in all his ways' (*Stephen Langton* (1928), p. 101).

Hubert Walter died in 1205 and some of the monks of Canterbury rashly tried to rush through an election. The younger monks met within a few hours of the death of the old archbishop and elected their sub-prior, Reginald. This annoyed everybody, and the king promptly nominated one of his friends, John de Gray, Bishop of Norwich. Both sides now appealed to Rome for a decision, and Innocent III solved the problem by choosing a third party, Stephen Langton, who at the time was lecturing in theology at the *curia* and was a man well qualified for the position.

John was furious, declared that his rights had been ignored, and refused to allow Langton to set foot in England. So, like Anselm and Becket, Langton was obliged to live abroad for the next six years while the Church in England suffered from lack of any real leadership. John, however, scarcely realized that he was setting his strength and wit against one of the most courageous and prudent men who have ever occupied the chair of S. Peter. Innocent soon made it clear that he had no intention of allowing John any quarter, and, on the king's continuing to defy him, he struck hard and swiftly with the most powerful weapon in his armoury and, on March 23, 1208, placed England under an Interdict.

Immediately the churches were closed, Mass ceased to be said, the gathering together of the faithful to worship God was forbidden, and only the barest essentials of baptism and burial were allowed to continue. The country suffered considerably from this blow, a blow which fell most heavily upon the humble and the devout; but the king cared nothing for it and actually used it as a means of raising more money for his own use.[1] He began by seizing all ecclesiastical property, out of which he provided small allowances for clergy who remained in the country, while confiscating the entire profits of those who went overseas. Many bishops left the country, the clergy lost their civil rights and the laity the ministrations of the Church. In 1209 Innocent went a stage further and excommunicated the king.

After four years of this, Innocent found that he had still made little impression upon the king, and decided to give another turn to the screw. So in 1212 he threatened John with deposition and ruin. John might have ignored this had he not been aware that Philip of France was planning an invasion of England. As it was, his resistance was

[1] See C. R. Cheney, 'King John's Reaction to the Interdict on England', in *Transactions of the Royal Historical Society*, 1949, pp. 129-50.

broken; and in the following year, he surrendered his crown and his kingdom to the pope, receiving them back from the pope as his vassal and promising to pay him an indemnity of 1000 marks a year. The invasion was then called off, Stephen Langton returned, and John was absolved, though the Interdict went on until 1214.

When Stephen Langton came to take up his office as Archbishop of Canterbury he found the country seething with discontent and a strong anti-royal feeling which, to some extent, was also anti-papal; for John, having made his submission to the papal legate, had risen to high favour at Rome. From the moment of Langton's return attempts were made to circumscribe the power of the throne in order to prevent such a disastrous and disgraceful episode from happening again. The culmination of these efforts was Magna Carta which John was obliged to accept in 1215. The first clause of the Great Charter declares that 'the English Church shall be free' which means that it shall have freedom to elect its officers according to Canon Law. This may have been a blow to the royal prestige, but in fact it did little to promote the independence of the English Church since, in every disputed election, the papacy now had power to intervene.

In all this Stephen Langton fared very badly. Consecrated archbishop by the pope in 1207 he had not been able to enter upon his office for six years. By the time of his arrival in England John had become a papal vassal, and Langton, in co-operating with the barons for the restoration of law and order, was now suspended from office by the pope for not supporting the king! The archbishop thus again found himself in exile, and by the time of his return, after the death of John, the country had fallen so much into the hands of papal legates that he had little opportunity of influencing either Church or State. It was not until 1221 that he could begin to act as Archbishop of Canterbury, by which time he had held the office for fourteen years.

iv. *The Intellectual Revival*

One result of the Norman Conquest had been the impetus which it had given to learning in England. Both Lanfranc and Anselm had been scholars of international reputation as well as great teachers and champions of the faith, and they had tried to encourage the study of theology in England, though mainly in the monasteries. Meanwhile the secular cathedrals had been developing their organization, and the office of chancellor had been introduced with the express purpose of providing lectures for the clergy. William de Monte who taught at Lincoln about 1190 was probably the most learned and active of the early chancellors, though by this time the office seems to have been established at all the secular cathedrals with the possible exception of Exeter.[1]

In the monasteries the emphasis had moved from the study of theology to the writing of histories and chronicles. The father of English historians is Bede and various writers in later years attempted to continue his work. Shortly after the Norman Conquest men such as Florence of Worcester, Simeon of Durham and William of Malmesbury were busy recording the events of the past and of their own times. Probably the greatest of them was the Augustinian, William of Newburgh (1136–c.1201), whose *History of English Affairs* ranks high among all historical works. Outside the monasteries Henry, Archdeacon of Huntingdon, Ralph de Diceto (Dean of St. Paul's) and Roger of Hoveden (or Howden) all made most valuable contributions to the study of history. This active and prolific group of English historians in the twelfth century paved the way for the great school of St. Alban's in the following century which produced first Roger of Wendover and then Matthew Paris.[2] Mention should also be made of that fascinating character Giraldus Cambrensis, or Gerald of Wales, whose wild denunciations, amusing characterizations and bitter criticisms of contemporary society have delighted many generations of readers.[3]

Of the twelfth century theologians the most distinguished was John of Salisbury (c. 1120–80) who, having studied at Paris and Chartres, returned to England where he became a close friend and adviser of Becket. Driven from England in the latter part of his life he became eventually Bishop of Chartres. He was a humanist, well read in the literature of the past and with a comprehensive and acute mind. Living in the midst of the universal struggle between Church and

---

[1] K. Edwards, *The English Secular Cathedrals in the Middle Ages* (1949), pp. 178–87.
[2] C. Jenkins, *The Monastic Chronicler and the Early School of St. Albans* (1922); R. L. Poole, *Chronicles and Annals* (1926).
[3] See *Autobiography of Giraldus Cambrensis* (ed. and trans. H. E. Butler, 1937) and 'Gerald of Wales', by F. M. Powicke in *Christian Life in the Middle Ages* (1938). Innocent III kept a copy of the *Gemma Ecclesiastica* for bedside reading.

State he tried to form a picture of the ideal state in which there should be a perfect union of both spiritual and temporal power. This he described in a book called *Policraticus*, which had considerable influence on his own time and upon later thinkers.[1]

While the monks were busy with their chronicles and other minds were busy with philosophy, considerable progress was being made with education at the more elementary level. There were, in the twelfth century, six types of education for boys in their early years, of which the chief was the Cathedral School. If the cathedral were monastic the school would be outside the precincts and the boys would be taught by masters employed by the monks; if the cathedral were secular the school was under the general direction of the chancellor, though the actual teaching was given by a grammar-master. In addition to these there were, at the Cathedrals, Song Schools, kept quite separate from the Grammar Schools and under the supervision not of the chancellor but of the precentor. The boys in these schools provided the 'children of the choir' for the daily offices but received also a general education. Separate from the cathedrals we find, as the third type of school, the Grammar Schools attached to collegiate churches and to the larger parish churches. There was a considerable growth of such institutions in the twelfth century, so that, by 1200, most towns of any size had a school of this sort. Besides the larger Grammar Schools there appear to have been, fourthly, a certain number of small village schools, though the evidence for these is scanty and very little is known of their history. But the idea of a village school goes back to the eighth century, and no doubt there were some parish priests in the villages who were glad to gather a small group of boys together and help them over the early stages of their education.

The fifth type of education was that given to oblates in the monasteries. The *Rule of S. Benedict* presupposes that a certain number of small boys shall be brought up in each monastery and, in time, duly professed. The custom continued for many years and is frequently referred to in Lanfranc's *Constitutions*. But in the twelfth century it was beginning to die out. Boys offered by their parents at the age of seven did not generally make very satisfactory monks, and the system was allowed to disappear and was never revived. Finally, it was

---

[1] R. L. Poole, *Illustrations of the History of Medieval Thought and Learning* (2nd ed. 1920), pp. 176-97, 204-10; C. C. J. Webb, *John of Salisbury* (1932).

a common custom for sons of the nobility to be boarded out in the houses of bishops and abbots, where they learnt good manners and were given some education by the chaplains and clerks of the household.

For most boys the object of education was as a preparation for ordination. Vast numbers of men were in either major or minor orders at this time, and most of these must have been able to read and write Latin tolerably well. Some elementary arithmetic was probably added, for the keeping of accounts was generally entrusted to a 'clerk', and any candidate for ordination would also need to be more or less familiar with plain-chant. But on the whole the schools were for the teaching of Latin grammar, hence the name by which they were afterwards called.[1]

The importance of the schools attached to the cathedral and collegiate churches was very great, yet it was from neither of these that the earliest English universities took their origin. The idea of a university or *studium generale* developed out of the more advanced of the cathedral schools in France and Italy in the earlier part of the twelfth century. In one or two places, such as Bologna and Paris, the schools acquired great fame and attracted large numbers both of teachers and of pupils. Organization quickly followed, the masters forming themselves into gilds, with the bachelors taking the place of the apprentices, while the ceremonies of inception were closely modelled on those which obtained in gild ritual.

The first trace of a true university in England was at Oxford in 1167. No doubt there must have been schools in Oxford before that date, but little is known of them. In that year, however, Henry II, in the midst of his quarrel with Becket, summoned any English clerks studying at Paris to return to England. Many settled at Oxford and established the kind of schools with which they had been familiar at Paris. Immediately the numbers increased as the fame of the university spread throughout the country. When Giraldus Cambrensis visited it in about 1185 he found there masters in several faculties. A true *studium generale* had come into being.

As Oxford was founded by a migration from Paris, so Cambridge appears to have begun by a migration of students from Oxford. In 1209 three clerks at Oxford were hanged, probably unjustly, and the university, to show its disapproval, dispersed, some going to Reading,

[1] See A. F. Leach, *The Schools of Medieval England* (1915).

some to Paris and some to Cambridge. Once again there must have been good schools already at Cambridge to have attracted them there, but we know little of them. And as Oxford had reproduced the organization already established at Paris, so Cambridge followed the practice of Oxford.

The normal course which the medieval student pursued was based upon what were called the 'Seven Liberal Arts'. This began with the *Trivium* (grammar, rhetoric and dialectic) which was followed by the *Quadrivium* (arithmetic, astronomy, music and geometry), the whole course taking seven years to complete. Theology was a post-graduate course taken by only a few men and those mainly professional scholars. This is not to be wondered at when it is realized that the full course took about seventeen years and included a good deal of lecturing as well as disputations and examinations. The standard text-books were, first of all, the Bible, followed by the *Sentences* of Peter Lombard—a vast collection of authorities designed to supply an answer to any problem which might be posed. Canon Law, which was also studied after the Arts course, was largely based upon the *Decretum* of Gratian which had appeared about 1140.[1]

Education of the laity was practically non-existent, for many of those who went up to the universities were already in minor orders (some being already beneficed), and most boys attending grammar and other schools were destined for the ministry. With few exceptions the laity of the twelfth century were illiterate, but attempts were made to teach them by means of pictures whether in the form of wall-paintings or of historiated windows.

Wall-paintings in the churches go back to Saxon times; but, by the twelfth century, they were becoming more popular, and, by the latter part of the medieval period, every church in England was covered from floor to roof with pictures, some of which have survived until this day. These paintings, which represented scenes from the Bible, or from the lives of the saints, or some symbolic or eschatological subject, were put there not for decoration but to teach and to admonish.[2]

There is today very little coloured glass in England of the twelfth century, but such as there is shows that the art was well developed

[1] H. Rashdall, *Medieval Universities of Europe* (ed. Powicke and Emden, 1936), vol. iii; R. S. Rait, *Life in the Medieval University* (1912).

[2] For the paintings of this period see E. W. Tristram, *English Medieval Wall Painting, 12th Century* (1944); see also F. Kendon, *Mural Paintings in English Churches during the Middle Ages* (1923).

at that time. The size and shape of the windows largely affected the designs of the glaziers, which often took the form of a series of circular or otherwise geometrical medallions set in a background of conventional foliage. Occasionally this plan was amplified into a 'Stem of Jesse' window, of which a fragment may still be seen at York. Canterbury Cathedral had at one time a fine collection of late twelfth-century glass, but much of this was destroyed during the Commonwealth when the Puritan who had charge of the church boasted that he had 'rattled down proud Beckett's glassie bones'. The glass of the twelfth century was rich in colour, and the surviving windows give an impression of great strength and dignity.[1]

Meanwhile, for the literate, some magnificent books were being produced, often with highly decorated initial letters. The most superb examples of these were the Bibles, especially that which may be seen in the Cathedral Library at Winchester.[2] In the earlier part of the century the style shows a strong Byzantine influence. The clothes cling to the bodies of the wearers; the colours are rich and brilliant; the whole impression is one of solemnity and starkness. But as the century wore on, the stiffness began to disappear and to give place to a much more natural and graceful interpretation.

This was typical of the period. Throughout the twelfth century there was a steady movement away from the massive grandeur of the Romanesque towards the softer grace and delicacy of the Early English. This shows itself most clearly in building, where the introduction of the ribbed vault, flying buttress and pointed arch about 1150 opened the door to a whole new field of architectural expression. But the same movement is visible in other forms of art, especially in painting. The earlier style was hard and conventional, but gradually a lighter and more tender style begins to take its place. This may be seen by comparing, for example, the twelfth-century painting at Canterbury of S. Paul at Melita with the early thirteenth-century roundel of the Virgin and Child on the wall of the Bishop's chapel at Chichester.[3] The comparison is striking, and will serve to show that in spite of wars, rebellions, murders and interdicts a civilizing process was going steadily on in the twelfth century and preparing the way for the Golden Age which was to follow.

[1] See Philip Nelson, *Ancient Painted Glass in England* (1913).
[2] W. Oakeshott, *The Artists of the Winchester Bible* (1945).
[3] Both have been reproduced many times, *e.g.* as plates 6 and 23 of W. Oakeshott's *The Sequence of English Medieval Art* (1950).

NOTE ON BOOKS

GENERAL and other histories as on p. 73. See also H. W. C. Davis, *England under the Normans and Angevins* (1915) and the volume of essays edited by him under the title of *Medieval England* (1924). *Stubbs' Select Charters*, ed. Davis, is important for official documents. Reference should also made to F. M. Powicke, *Stephen Langton* (1928) and M. D. Knowles, *The Episcopal Colleagues of Archbishop Thomas Becket* (1951). See also F. W. Maitland, *Roman Canon Law in the Church of England* (1898), C. H. Haskins, *The Renaissance of the Twelfth Century* (1927) and H. Rashdall, *The Universities of Europe in the Middle Ages* (new ed. by F. M. Powicke and A. B. Emden, 3 vols. 1936).

CHAPTER VIII

THE THIRTEENTH CENTURY
(1216–1307)

i. *The Reign of Henry III*

WHEN Henry III succeeded to the throne of his father, King John, in 1216, he was a boy of only nine years of age. It was necessary, therefore, that a regent should be found; but the difficulties were great. The country was divided by civil war; a foreign prince was in control of much of the kingdom; the Archbishop of Canterbury was in Rome; most of the regalia had been lost; and for a moment it looked as if chaos must ensue. One man, however, stepped into the breach and began to organize the nation, and that was Cardinal Guala Biachieri, the papal legate. It was he who created the small council which virtually governed the country, and it was he who arranged that from henceforth Rome should have her say in all matters which concerned the governance of England. England, since John's capitulation, had been regarded as in a special way subject to the see of Rome, and the pope saw to it that he was well represented in the country and that his interests were well served. Guala, who was legate from 1211 to 1218, was succeeded by Pandulf (who died as Bishop of Norwich in 1226), Otto (1237–41), and Ottobuono (1265–68). Each of these men exercised a great influence on the history of England in the thirteenth century. Wise, conscientious and determined, they introduced an element of stability at a time when the danger of collapse was very great.

Yet their presence and their power were more and more resented as time went on. As Henry grew to manhood he naturally turned to the legates for advice, for it was easier to consult these foreigners than to get involved in the clash of family and political interests in England. But his action, though natural, was unpopular. Men felt that England was being governed from Rome, and as Roman demands for money became more insistent, resentment was fanned into active opposition.

For Rome in the thirteenth century was in process of a vast development in centralized, curial administration. Innocent III was convinced that the struggle for supremacy both over the temporal powers within Christendom, and against the menace of Islam from without, could only be carried on by increasing the central power of the papacy and by building up a strong monarchical authority which all men must respect. But this needed money—new money and in large quantities; and the pope was forced to examine every possible source of supply. The most obvious source was taxation, and many attempts were made to increase the amounts collected from this field; but an even more profitable source of income was found in the system of 'provisions'. The policy of centralization meant a vast increase in the number of officials. These officials had to be paid. What better way of providing for them than by presenting them to benefices from which they could draw a considerable income while, where necessary, paying a small stipend to the priest on the spot? From the time of John's submission in 1213 such 'provisions' became common in England. In so far as most of the benefices which the pope claimed for his clerks were canonries and prebends at cathedral and collegiate churches, the system did not in fact interfere very seriously with the religious life of the country. More serious was the provision of foreigners to English country livings, which they never visited and which were regarded simply as sources of revenue. And the system was certainly abused. Italian boys of ten or twelve years old were 'provided' to canonries and archdeaconries the very names of which they could never have pronounced, papal chaplains who never set foot out of Italy were encouraged to amass a plurality of English benefices, and even laymen were sometimes provided with ecclesiastical appointments for which they were totally unfitted.

It was no wonder that the system was resented by the English. To some it seemed a scandal that church property should be used in this way and that spiritual responsibility should be so completely subordinated to financial convenience. To many the system was obnoxious simply because it meant so much good English money going out of the country to support an establishment the very nature of which they were inclined to resent. On the side of the pope it could be argued that in every case of a 'provision' care was taken to see that the spiritual needs of the people were met, and that many English noblemen used the benefices in their gift in precisely the same way and for far less worthy objects. But such arguments did not easily reach those on the spot, and Matthew Paris's outcry against the 'wretched men without manners, full of cunning, proctors and "farmers" of the Romans, seizing whatsoever in the country is precious and serviceable and sending it away to their lords living delicately out of the patrimony of the Crucified'[1] would have found a good many supporters among his fellow-countrymen.

Popular resentment flared up in 1231 when a small secret society was formed under the leadership of a man called Robert Tweng who had estates in Yorkshire. Infuriated by what he regarded as papal aggression, he organized some rioting and burning down of property held by Italians. Little came of the movement, which was suppressed in the following year. But the country continued to feel resentment against the whole system of Provisions until the *Statute of Provisors* was passed in 1351 to put an end to the whole business.[2] Meanwhile responsible churchmen were sometimes goaded into anger on the receipt of letters from Rome telling them that they must confer some benefice upon a member of the papal court. The classic example of this was when Robert Grosseteste, Bishop of Lincoln, emphatically refused to present a nephew of the pope, Frederick de Lavagna, to a canonry at Lincoln in 1253. Grosseteste was a man of strong convictions and the most vigorous prelate of his time. On several occasions he had complained of papal interference. Now in the last year of his life he could stand it no longer. After stating his reasons at some length he concludes: 'With all filial respect and obedience I will not obey, I resist, I rebel'.[3]

Grosseteste's outburst was dictated not only by dislike of the whole system of Provisions but also by a growing sense of patriotism. Although no one doubted the unity of Christendom and the importance of the papacy, men were beginning to be more conscious of nationalist feeling, and therefore more and more resentful both of interference from outside and of the constant drain of English money into Roman pockets. This nationalist feeling grew steadily during the reign of Henry III, who allowed himself to be guided by his papal advisers. A party was formed, under the leadership of Simon de Montfort, which was determined to control the king and to see that

---

[1] M. Paris, *Chronica Majora* (ed. H. Luard, 1872–83), iii, pp. 389–90.
[2] See below, p. 116. Cf. also G. Barraclough, *Papal Provisions* (1935) and H. Mackenzie in *Anniversary Essays by Students of C. H. Haskins* (1929).
[3] *Epistolae R. Grosseteste* (ed. H. Luard, 1861), p. 436.

national interests took precedence over papal. Simon de Montfort was a close friend of Grosseteste, who did much to support the national cause and to advise its leader. In 1258 things had become so serious that Parliament set up a committee to keep a watch on the king. This was part of the Provisions of Oxford, but it was an uneasy arrangement and lasted only a few years. When it came to an end in 1264 civil war broke out. At the Battle of Lewes in that year the barons won a victory over the king, only to be beaten at Evesham in the following year, when Simon de Montfort was killed. But his cause triumphed, for Henry never recovered despotic power, and his son, Edward, was far too wise a man to attempt to revive it.

So far as the life of the Church was concerned, the reign of Henry III showed considerable advance and reform. The king himself was a devout and loyal churchman who did much to promote the building and decorating of churches, and himself rebuilt Westminster Abbey in the Gothic style which was now so popular.

It was a time also of great leaders in the Church. At least three bishops of this reign—the primate Edmund Rich, Richard of Chichester and Thomas Cantilupe of Hereford—were canonized, and Grosseteste probably would have been if he had not angered the pope by his outspokenness and disobedience.[1] There were others, too, of outstanding ability among the episcopate, though their effectiveness as a body was bound to be limited by the presence of royal favourites, most of whom added no lustre to the bench. Those who had the welfare of the Church at heart were fully conscious of the need for reform and determined to do what they could to achieve it. Many of the English bishops attended the Fourth Lateran Council at Rome in 1215 and returned to their dioceses full of zeal and energy. Synods were held and sets of statutes were published in almost every diocese. The earliest was probably that of William of Blois at Worcester in 1219 and was followed by the magnificent set of decrees put out by Richard le Poore at Salisbury. Others followed suit; especially Walter Cantilupe at Worcester in 1240 and Robert Grosseteste at Lincoln about the same time. How far these decrees were observed it is hard to say, for evidence is not always obtainable; but of the desire for reform, and of the efforts to achieve it, there can be no doubt.[2]

[1] See R. E. G. Cole, 'On the Canonization of Robert Grosseteste' in *Associated Architectural Societies' Reports* (1915–16).

[2] See *Councils and Synods* (ed. F. M. Powicke and C. R. Cheney) II, Pt. 1 (1964), pp. 52, 57, 265, 294.

Many of the statutes deal with the clergy. Pluralism and its attendant evil of absenteeism were sternly rebuked. Parishes were to be properly staffed by men sufficiently educated and adequately ordained. Efforts were made to improve the private life of the clergy, to make them dress in clerical attire, attend to their duties and spend less time in the taverns. The long-standing problem of the clergy who kept concubines was tackled, and attempts made to bring this to an end. Then there was the question of the services in the churches. Many decrees deal with the right and due celebration of the sacraments, with the provision of service-books and ornaments for the church, and with the importance of teaching and preaching. Finally, the bishops were not afraid to rebuke the laity for their low standards of morality, their ignorance, their slackness in church-attendance and the savage and lustful lives which many of them lived. As an attempt to reform the church the decrees of the thirteenth-century diocesan synods, together with those of provincial councils and of the legates Otto and Ottobuono, were of the greatest importance and are a witness of the life and vigour with which so many of its leaders were inspired.[1]

ii. *The Secular Clergy in the Thirteenth Century*

Of the cathedral churches of England during the Middle Ages eight were monastic and seven were secular.[2] In these latter there had now come to be a regular system of dignitaries, canons and priest-vicars. The dignitaries were normally four in number—the Dean, who was the head of the corporation; the Precentor, who was in charge of the music and the choir; the Chancellor, who was the theologian and responsible for all educational work; and the Treasurer, who looked after the cathedral treasures and property. The titles were not always uniform, but the system was the same everywhere. Next to the dignitaries came the canons or prebendaries, some of whom were resident but many were not. By now most of the canons, besides the dignitaries, were living in their own houses in the close, for the old idea of a corporate life had been abandoned. Each non-residentiary was supposed to have his own priest-vicar or vicar-choral

[1] See M. Gibbs and J. Lang, *The Bishops and Reform, 1215–72* (1934); R. Cheney, *English Synodalia of the Thirteenth Century* (1940) and J. R. H. Moorman, *Church Life in England in the Thirteenth Century* (1945), chaps. xvi and xvii.
[2] See above, p. 69.

who deputized for him during his absence. These *ministri inferiores* were now beginning to form separate corporations of their own. They lived a communal life in the 'vicars' close' and were becoming increasingly conscious of their rights and dignities.

The vast structures which these men served were not parochial, for most cathedral cities were well supplied with parish churches for the laity. Nor were they intended for large gatherings of diocesan clergy and laity. Rather were they designed to provide dignified and impressive settings in which a small group of priests might offer daily worship to God. The men who did this were mostly well endowed, and many were pluralists and absentees, but some were always in residence assisted by the priest-vicars.[1]

Similar to the cathedrals, but on a slightly smaller scale, were the collegiate churches such as Ripon, Beverley or Southwell. These were also provided for by a corporation consisting of a dean, provost or warden supported by his prebendaries and a number of vicars, sing-ing-men and boys. On some of these foundations the prebendary drew his income from a parish church associated with his prebendal stall, and an absentee was therefore obliged to provide himself with two vicars, a vicar-choral to deputize for him in the cathedral, and a parochial vicar to manage the affairs of the parish.

In early days the incumbent of a parish was always styled 'rector'. He was generally chosen by a lay patron, was instituted by the bishop, and enjoyed his benefice as a freehold. From the twelfth century on-wards, however, there began a system known as 'appropriations' whereby the patron, who regarded himself in a sense as the owner of the church, gave it away to some religious body, generally a monas-tery. There was at this time so great a desire to found or support the religious houses, that the system of appropriation became very popular, and about half the parish churches in England changed hands in this way. The donor lost nothing by it except the right of patron-age; but the monks benefited greatly, for they could generally arrange for a stipendiary priest to do the work at a low figure while they themselves kept what remained of the income of the living.

Occasionally a monastery would provide for the spiritual needs of an appropriated church by appointing one of its own inmates as parish priest. This was very rare among monks, but was more common among the canons regular (Augustinians and Premonstra-

[1] See K. Edwards, *The English Secular Cathedrals in the Middle Ages* (1949).

tensians) for the performance of parochial duties had often been regarded as a suitable occupation for a canon. But by far the most common arrangement was for the monks to employ a priest, as they employed chaplains for their own altars, and to make their own arrangements as to his stipend and obligations. This system, however, proved unsatisfactory. The tendency was to secure the services of the cheapest man available, with obvious disadvantages both to the parish and to the employee who had no security and often a totally inadequate wage.

It was to remedy this that a number of bishops in the thirteenth century instituted the system of 'vicarages'. Where a church had been appropriated efforts were made to draw up a contract with the chapter concerned to see that the man appointed had a definite stipend and security of tenure. Hundreds of these documents have been preserved in bishops' registers and elsewhere, and they show what great care was taken to safeguard the rights of the vicars. But still the monasteries stood to gain considerably. The standard stipend for a vicar was five marks a year (£3. 6s. 8d.), but most livings were worth at least three times that amount.

In churches which were not appropriated the incumbent continued as rector. Rectors in the thirteenth century were, roughly speaking, of two kinds. By far the majority were local men who held but one living and served it personally. Drawn from the families of small-holders and the upper ranks of the peasants, they were not as a rule highly educated, and they lived very much as their parishioners, tilling their own land, looking after their few cows and sheep, and joining with their neighbours in the day-to-day affairs of village life. Chaucer's 'pore persoun', it may be remembered, had as his brother a simple ploughman. A few rectors, however, belonged to quite a different class. These were the wealthy pluralists, mostly scions of illustrious families, who regarded their benefices simply as sources of income, and hired stipendiary priests to do the work. Some of these pluralists became immensely rich, for there was practically no limit to the number of livings which they managed to acquire. Bogo de Clare, a son of the Earl of Gloucester and Hertford, collected so many benefices that, at the time of his death in 1291 he had an income of some hundreds of thousands of pounds a year in

---

¹ See A. H. Thompson in *Associated Architectural Societies' Reports* (1916–17), pp. 53 ff.

7

modern money. Some of them never troubled to proceed to holy orders—indeed there was little necessity for them to do so, as they seldom, if ever, visited their parishes. Many were boys at school or at the university, who paid their fees out of the profits of their parishes. Most lived in luxury and ease and were satisfied so long as someone could be found to relieve them of their parochial duties. Bogo de Clare spent more in one year on preserved ginger than he paid to a priest to serve one of his many livings.

The value of livings varied enormously in the Middle Ages and for long after. Some were worth as little as three or four pounds a year. A few, like Bamburgh and Lindisfarne were worth several hundreds. The average gross income appears to have been about £10 a year.

This income was derived partly from the land and partly from the offerings of the people. Every parish church was supposed to have some land attached to it as 'glebe'. This might be just 'a toft and a croft' or it might include many acres. Whatever it was, the rector held it as a freehold, without servile duties, and normally farmed it himself with the assistance of his page. More valuable to the priest was his tithe, his right to one tenth of all produce of nature within his parish whether of the soil or of beasts. The most important was the 'garb tithe' or tithe on corn, but the rector was entitled also to a tithe on hay, vegetables and even fallen timber. He drew his tenth also on the produce of animals whether in the form of young or in such things as milk, eggs, butter, cheese, honey and wax. Where there were difficulties in collecting it—for example, in the case of foals, where perhaps but one was born in each year on any farm— tithe was normally commuted to a money payment. Where artisans and tradesmen were concerned, a tithe was taken on their profits or wages. So important to the Church was this source of revenue, and so anxious were the laity to avoid paying it, that the ecclesiastical lawyers never ceased to devise ways of ensuring that the tax was paid. No matter what a man's occupation was, no matter how he made his living nor how slender it was, the Church's net was made with so fine a mesh that not even the smallest could escape.

Apart from the land the rector drew a certain proportion of his income from what was known as 'altarage' or the offerings of the people—the 'accustomed oblations' at the festivals, the mass-pennies, the anniversaries and trentals, the 'confession-pennies' and various offerings in kind such as bread and wax, eggs at Easter, cheese at Whitsuntide and fowls at Christmas. When a man died, the parish priest was entitled to collect a 'mortuary' (normally the second best possession of the dead man) in lieu of unpaid tithes.

Not all this income belonged exclusively to the parish priest. By ancient law the income of a benefice was supposed to be divided into four parts between the priest, the bishop, the upkeep of the church, and the relief of the poor.[1] By the thirteenth century the bishop's portion had been assessed in each parish and was payable in the form of 'synodals and procurations'. It also remained the custom for the rector of the parish to be held responsible for the upkeep of the chancel while the laity were responsible for the nave of the parish church. The clergy were also expected to provide a certain amount of poor-relief, though visitation records often complain that this was not being done and that certain clergy 'do no good in the parish'. Yet that there were many loyal, conscientious and devout men among the parochial clergy is beyond doubt. Much is often made of Chaucer's famous description of the 'pore persoun' who is presented to us as a model of pastoral zeal and devotion. There may or may not have been many men like him, for we must beware of using fiction as evidence. More important are the records of visitations like that of Branscombe in Devon where, in 1301, the sidesmen declare that 'Thomas their vicar beareth himself well in all things and preacheth willingly, and visiteth the sick, and doth diligently all that pertaineth to his priestly office'.[2]

In addition to the incumbent, whether rector or vicar, each parish contained also a number of assistant clergy known as 'chaplains', 'stipendiaries', 'annual priests' or 'ministers'. Few of these ever received benefices of their own, but remained for the whole of their lives in a subordinate position and on a wage which was often very low. Calculations based on the ordination lists, visitation returns and other sources show that there were, in the thirteenth century, about 40,000 secular clergy in England besides about 17,000 monks, canons and friars.[3] This is more than the present number of clergy of all denominations in England, although the population is now nearly

---

[1] See above, p. 14.
[2] G. G. Coulton, *Social Life in Britain from the Conquest to the Reformation* (1918), p. 261.
[3] J. R. H. Moorman, *Church Life in England in the Thirteenth Century* (1945), pp. 52-5, 412.

twenty times as great as it was then. How they lived and how they managed to fill in their time it is difficult now to say; but if some of them lost the sense of their high calling, or wandered about the countryside in search of a better job, they can hardly be blamed.

Normally the incumbent and his staff lived together in the parsonage house attended by the 'prestes page'. A few houses were well built of stone, but the majority of them were little two-roomed huts made of wood and clay. Around the living-house were generally some farm-buildings, since most clergy farmed their own glebe; but the standard of living of many priests and their assistants must have differed very little from that of the peasants from whom they were sprung and who formed so large a part of their congregation.

iii. *Administration*

From the foundation of the diocese of Carlisle in 1133 to the reign of Henry VIII there were seventeen dioceses in England and four in Wales. These varied very much in size, Rochester and Worcester being quite small, while Lincoln covered eight counties from the Humber to the Thames, and York stretched from the west coast of Cumberland to Nottingham. Each diocese was divided into two or more archdeaconries and each archdeaconry into a number of rural deaneries. The machinery for administration was all there; its efficiency depended upon the men who worked it.

The thirteenth-century bishops were a very mixed body of men. Since about half of the cathedral chapters were monastic it is not surprising that on several occasions one of their own members or a monk from some other house was chosen as their bishop. Towards the end of the century friars were appointed; notably the two Archbishops of Canterbury—Robert Kilwardby the Dominican and John Pecham the Franciscan. Many bishops were scholars who had achieved distinction in the universities, but most of these proved themselves to be able administrators as well as distinguished scholars, especially Grosseteste, Richard le Poore and Richard of Chichester.

But the largest section of the bishops was drawn from the royal favourites. These were either men who had served the king loyally for many years or who had some other claim on his generosity, for though the election of bishops was technically in the hands of the cathedral chapters, the king was generally able to induce them, whether by persuasion or by threats, to accept his nominee. Such men did not, as a rule, make very good bishops. Their interests were political rather than ecclesiastical, and their natural place was in the king's court rather than on a bishop's throne. Many of them visited their dioceses only on rare occasions, leaving most of the work to their chancellors and to Irish bishops or bishops *in partibus* who were glad to supplement their meagre incomes by serving their richer brethren.

Once appointed, a bishop became a landowner on a large scale. The endowment of a medieval bishopric was the ownership of a number of manors, often as many as thirty or more. This was essential since the bishop was the head of a large household, or *familia*, of legal officers, chaplains, clerks, stewards, bailiffs, servants and pages. The feeding of this large household meant that the bishop, like any other magnate, had to be constantly on the move from manor to manor, for the difficulties and dangers of transport were so great that it was easier for the family to go to the food than for the food to be brought to the family. Bishops who were mainly occupied in the affairs of state were normally attached to the royal household and travelled from manor to manor with the king; but those who wished to serve their dioceses were also constantly moving from place to place, staying a few weeks in each and conducting their diocesan business as they went.

Often, on their peregrinations, they took the opportunity of visiting the parishes, interviewing the clergy, examining the books and ornaments of the churches and listening to the evidence of the laity. Monastic chapters who had not managed to acquire exemption from episcopal control were also liable to be visited, their affairs discussed and their sins rebuked. Confirmation could also be held on these journeys, though, on the whole, the medieval bishop seems to have been reluctant to confirm children, and often procured the services of some more impoverished bishop to relieve him of this burden. Ordinations were also held at the Ember seasons, when large numbers of young men were ordained to the 'first tonsure' or as acolyte, subdeacon, deacon or priest.

But by far the greatest part of a bishop's time and energy was spent in the hearing of disputes and in the administration of the law. 'The benignant idea of a father in God and a shepherd of souls, with the tenderness and patience which it implies, no doubt existed in theory.

But the prevailing aspect of a bishop's paternity was its severity, and in the attitude of the pastor to his flock the spirit of correction was more prominent than that of compassion.'[1] Clergy who failed in their duties were tried and punished by fine, suspension, deprivation or imprisonment. Laymen, of whatever distinction, who offended against the moral laws of the Church were liable to public floggings inflicted generally by the rural deans. Patrons who tried to go beyond their powers were excommunicated. In fact, the bishop and his legal advisers were a formidable body whose ill-will even the most powerful magnates had cause to fear.

Meanwhile the bishop was concerned also with the administration of his estates and with all the multifarious problems, both personal and material, which this occasioned. Much of this could, no doubt, be left to stewards and bailiffs, but the responsibility remained with the bishop, who was never free from the anxieties of the owner of much property. Thus as pastor and landowner, judge and magistrate, civil servant and member of parliament, a bishop's time was fully occupied. Yet the more scholarly of them found time also to read and write, and several collected what would then be regarded as considerable libraries, for Richard Gravesend at his death in 1303 left eighty volumes valued at £116.[2]

iv. *The Coming of the Friars*

The early years of the thirteenth century saw the inauguration of a great experiment in Christian discipleship. New forces, intellectual and social, were moving in the world, forces with which neither the parochial clergy nor the regulars were fitted to deal. The returning army of crusaders had brought back strange heresies from the East which found a fertile soil among the discontented peasants and the growing populations in the towns. But the Church could do little. The secular clergy were far too ignorant, and the monks too remote and exclusive. The situation demanded a new type of Christian minister who would be a 'regular' in the sense that he would be under discipline, and yet free to go among men wherever he could

[1] A. H. Thompson, *The English Clergy and their Organization in the Later Middle Ages* (1947), p. 40.
[2] Milman, 'A Catalogue of the Books of R. de Gravesend', in *Philobiblon Society Miscellanies*, vol. ii (1855-56).

find an opportunity of witnessing by word and by example to the faith that was in him.

It was this new type of 'religious' which was provided by the orders of mendicant friars, the greatest of which were the Dominicans and the Franciscans. The first of these, the Order of Preachers, owed its origin to the courage and zeal of S. Dominic, who collected together a band of men who were to be trained to preach the truth, to expose error and, as far as possible, to convince the gainsayer. Soon parties of trained preachers were moving about the roads of Europe in their black-and-white habits, preaching everywhere, arguing, disputing, wrestling with heresy and unbelief wherever it chose to rear its head.

Meanwhile a greater than Dominic, S. Francis of Assisi, was also trying a new experiment in Christian living. Beginning as a solitary who had heard the call of God to a life which meant nothing less than a literal imitation of Christ in poverty, humility and suffering, he had soon collected around him a band of disciples who wished to share in this life and witness for Christ. Unlike the Dominicans the Friars Minor, or Franciscans, were not, at first, a learned order; their witness was to be rather by example than by art of human word. So they too began to move along the roads of Europe or settle in the cities, sharing the hardships and squalors of the poor, proclaiming everywhere the gospel of love and service and humility.

The first friars to reach England were a party of thirteen Dominicans who came over from France in 1221. They were welcomed by Peter des Roches, Bishop of Winchester, who took them to Canterbury and introduced them to the Archbishop, Stephen Langton, who was so much impressed by their preaching ability that he took them under his protection. They did not, however, remain long at Canterbury, but pressed on first to London and then to Oxford where they hoped to settle among the members of the university. Three years later a party of nine Franciscans, of whom four were clerks and five laymen, landed at Dover and made their way, first to Canterbury and then to London and Oxford. Their progress, however, differed from that of the Preachers in that they left a few of the brethren in each of these three cities to form the nucleus of a community.

From these beginnings both orders spread rapidly. Many of the bishops welcomed them, hoping that they would help in the reforming movements which they had at heart. The pious King Henry took them under his protection and soon began to give them money and materials for building. The townspeople opened their arms to them and provided them with lodgings or money with which to build. Young men were rapidly drawn to a life which, whether as Preacher or Minor, offered so striking a challenge to the world. In the first twenty years the Dominicans were able to establish nineteen houses, mostly in the larger towns such as London, Oxford, Norwich, York and Bristol. By 1300 they had fifty-one such friaries. Meanwhile the Franciscans progressed even more rapidly, for in the first twenty years after their arrival they founded thirty-nine houses, and by 1300 had fifty-five. Meanwhile many other orders of friars had come into existence of which the most important were the Carmelites (or White Friars) and the Augustinians (or Friar Hermits). The former of these were introduced into England in 1241 and the latter in 1250. Altogether, in the first eighty years after the coming of the friars, 169 new religious houses had sprung into being, representing some ten new orders.

In the early days the friars mostly suffered great hardships. Unknown and unendowed, they depended for their very existence upon the good-will of the laity; and though this was often given, there were times when it was refused and great privation ensued. Often they were hungry and cold as they tramped barefoot through the snow or left the print of blood upon the ice-bound roads. Yet wherever they went their lives spoke of love and sacrifice and of the poverty which maketh many rich.

Most of the orders of friars made it their business to settle in the university towns. In the case of the Dominicans this was part of a policy of establishing a footing in the academic world so that their young friars might have an opportunity of acquiring the best education available. With the Franciscans it was dictated partly by the same reason and partly by the hope of attracting young students into the order. But the result was that both at Oxford and Cambridge the friars began, soon after their arrival, to play a very important part in the development of the young university. Their zeal for knowledge, their power of attracting good scholars, and their contacts with foreign schools, did much to help the growing universities, especially in the foundation of the faculties of theology. At Oxford the Dominicans soon established a school of theology which produced a number of celebrated scholars like Robert Bacon, Robert Kilwardby and John of Darlington. Meanwhile the Franciscans, having persuaded Robert Grosseteste, chancellor of the university, and the greatest scholar of his generation, to become their lecturer, rapidly built up a school whose fame eclipsed that of almost every other theological school in Europe, for Grosseteste was the first of a series of theologians—Roger Bacon, John Pecham, Thomas of York, William of Ockham, John Duns Scotus—whose names are among the most famous in the history of medieval philosophy.[1]

While the more learned friars were busy disputing in the schools of Oxford and Cambridge their brethren were busy preaching the Gospel in the towns and villages of England. At this time a sermon was a rare event in most parish churches, most secular clergy having neither the ability nor the inclination to preach. The friars, however, were trained preachers who quickly attracted large audiences. Racy, provocative, entertaining, informative, their sermons were packed with illustrations and stories taken from their own experiences or from the books of *exempla* which were compiled for their use. It was no wonder that they were popular. Contrasted with the formal and sometimes rather drab services which the parish churches offered on Sunday mornings, the pyrotechnics of the friars provided a welcome change. Religion became more homely, more personal, more vital. In the universities and in the country lanes, in city slum and on the village green, in the castles of the rich and the hovels of the poor, everywhere the friars made their influence felt, and the country was the richer and the happier for the new hope and strength which were grafted into its spiritual life.

But the high standard which marked the early days of the movement was not maintained. At first the friars had been content with simple accommodation—a cellar under a school at Canterbury, an empty house at Oxford, an old prison at Cambridge; but soon they wanted buildings of their own, modelled on those of the older religious houses with spacious churches in which they might preach to their congregations and bury their benefactors. Their desire to excel in the academic world meant the accumulation of libraries. Their only means of subsistence being begging, they organized the business on a large scale, appointing certain friars as 'limitors' to see how much they could collect within the 'limits' assigned to them, and even farming out the begging rights at a fixed rent. Rather less austere habits began to appear, such as the keeping of servants, better

[1] See D. E. Sharp, *Franciscan Philosophy at Oxford in the Thirteenth Century* (1930).

food, more comfortable houses. Then followed disputes and quarrels
between various houses, between the several orders, and between the
friars and the seculars.

The quarrel between the friars and the seculars was fought out in
two spheres—at the universities and in the parishes. At the universities the friars had quickly made their mark. Their schools of theology
were so good that the regent masters could not ignore them, yet the
friars, while claiming the privileges of full membership of the university, refused to submit to its authority and control. Here lay the
seeds of dissension, and it was not long before, first at Oxford and
then at Cambridge, trouble broke out. In each case the result was a
compromise which settled the immediate problem but did nothing
to remove the cause of it. The friars continued to act as a constant
irritant to the university authorities, yet were too powerful and too
valuable to be turned out.

In the parishes the dispute turned upon three issues—the friars'
right to preach, to hear confessions and to bury the dead in their
churches and cemeteries. The problem here was partly one of prestige and partly of finance. Naturally a parish priest with cure of souls
objected to the presence of wandering friars who drew people
away from his church, usurped the right to act as their spiritual
directors and finally to bury them. But the problem was also financial, for sermons, the advice given in confessions and the last obse-
quies of the dead could be easily used as means of raising money.
This the friars did not hesitate to do, with effects which were often
disastrous to the parish priest. The problem was troubling the
Church all over Europe and was settled in 1300 by the bull, *Super
Cathedram*, which brought into being a system of licences without
which friars might not preach nor hear confessions, and ordered a
proportion of all funeral offerings to be given to the parish priest.

From this time onwards the influence of the friars began to
dwindle. But in their great days they did much to regenerate the life
of the Church. They brought new life into the parishes and new hope
to the people, they stirred up the clergy to greater effort and efficiency, they captured the universities by their knowledge and sincerity, they set up a whole network of schools from which all could
benefit, and they provided a way of life, simple, austere and holy,
in which those who were prepared to forsake all for Christ's sake
could find their spiritual home.

v. *The Older Religious Orders*

The twelfth century had seen the 'golden age' of English monasticism when the monasteries were full, new houses sprang into being, and men of high character and ability were being attracted into this way of life. But by the year 1200 the great days were over. Benefactors were beginning now to devote their alms more to schools and universities, or to the new orders of friars, or to the foundation of chantries. Only two independent Benedictine houses were founded after 1200, a few Cistercian and rather more Augustinian.

Most religious houses of the thirteenth century contained five different groups of people. There were, first of all, the choir monks, all duly professed and mostly in holy orders. The numbers varied greatly. A few of the larger Benedictine and Cistercian houses had as many as sixty to eighty monks, but there were not many as large as this. The average number was about twenty-five to thirty. The houses of canons regular, Augustinians and Premonstratensians, were about half as big as the houses of monks, the larger establishments containing about thirty canons, the smaller about fifteen, while some had a mere handful of four or five. Nunneries varied very greatly in size, a few being very large; but nuns always tended to exceed the statutory number while monks tended to fall below it.

In addition to the professed monks most monasteries contained a number of novices, though never very many since, even in the larger houses, there was seldom more than one vacancy a year. Reference has already been made to the system of 'oblates' whereby small boys were placed in monasteries by their parents at a very early age, and so, in due course, became monks whether they wished it or not.[1] This system had been in practice in England at the end of the eleventh century, but from that time onwards it had gradually died out. Such men often made very discontented and unsatisfactory monks and much trouble was caused. Conscious of these dangers the new orders of Cistercians and Carthusians forbade the practice altogether, and by the thirteenth century the only boys found in monasteries were those living there as boarders under the supervision of the abbot.

Thirdly, there were, in most monasteries, a number of lay-brothers, or *conversi*, who had been brought in to do some of the rougher and

[1] See above, p. 86.

more menial work, took vows of a simple kind, and had their own quarters in the monastic buildings. Such lay-brothers had formed a very important part of the Cistercian movement and often outnumbered the choir-monks by as many as three to one.[1] But, in the thirteenth century, the weaknesses of the system had become apparent. Lay-brothers tended to become unruly and difficult, conscious of their subordinate station, and anxious to improve their lot. As a result, the monks allowed the practice to die out and replaced the lay-brothers with hired servants whom they found much more manageable.

The number of servants employed in the average monastery was very large, sometimes as many as two to each monk.[2] They did the manual work of the establishment both indoors and out. Many were employed in the kitchens and sculleries, in the laundry, the church, the gardens and the farms. Some lived within the monastery, some outside it.

Finally, in many monasteries a certain number of people could be found, both clerical and lay, who were living there as lodgers or 'corrodars'. Desperate for ready money, the heads of religious houses sometimes sold what were known as 'corrodies' or annuities, whereby a layman, upon payment of a sum of money, could obtain the right to board and lodging, for himself and his family, in the monastery in his old age. A similar arrangement was sometimes made by secular clergy who wished to provide for their retirement. The result was that, in many monasteries, rooms had to be set aside as 'flats' for retired gentry whose food was sent up to them from the monastic kitchens and their needs attended to by monastic servants.

This varied population, living within the surrounding wall of a monastery, made the place a hive of activity. The ordering of life for so large a community with so many interests required considerable organization, and the monks' daily programme tended to get very full. In the *Rule of S. Benedict* provision is made for the division of a monk's time into three periods devoted to prayer, study and manual work. The daily offering of prayer and praise continued to provide the framework into which the daily life of the monk was fitted. The Hour Services, beginning with the 'night service' at 1.30

---

[1] E.g. at Rievaulx in the twelfth century there were 140 monks and 500 lay brothers (F. M. Powicke, *Ailred of Rievaulx and his Biographer* (1922), p. 97 and n.).

[2] E.g. at Norwich 62 monks employed 146 servants (H. W. Saunders, *Introduction to the Rolls of Norwich Cathedral Priory* (1930), p. 163).

or 2 A.M. and continuing at intervals throughout the day until sunset, kept a regular rhythm for the life of the community. As so often in liturgical matters, the tendency was for services to be multiplied and lengthened, so that the daily programme occupied more and more of the monk's waking hours, though not all the monks attended every service.

Sacred study, the *divina lectio*, was the second feature of the monk's daily life, and time was set apart for it in the daily horarium. By the thirteenth century monastic libraries had increased and many communities had noble collections of books.[1]

But by this time, although a good deal of reading and writing went on in the cloisters, the monasteries had lost the initiative in scholarship, which had now passed to the universities and to the friars. To the scholarly monk there was opportunity for study, but the monasteries had ceased to be the great centres of learning which they had once been. As for manual work as a part of the monk's duties this had now almost entirely disappeared, having been handed over, first to lay-brethren, and then to servants.

The monastic time-table had thus changed considerably as time went by, but this is not to say that the monks were idle. On the contrary, they were very busy men, for much of their time had to be devoted to the management of their estates. These were often very extensive and sometimes scattered over many counties. The rich Benedictine abbey at Bury St. Edmunds owned no less than 170 manors, while the Cistercians of Fountains Abbey had land in 151 different parishes. The management of these estates, and the legal, social and personal problems to which they gave rise, formed a large part of a monk's daily life and often took him far from his cloister for considerable periods.

For some time there had been a tendency towards the division of monastic estates into separate and independent portions. This had begun with the separation of the lands of the abbot from those of the convent, a stratagem originally designed to safeguard the monks' property during a vacancy of the abbacy and to prevent it falling into the hands of the king. The greater abbots, therefore, lived much like bishops, maintaining large households and often visiting their manors. That delightful picture of medieval monastic life, *The Chronicle of*

---

[1] See, for example, the catalogues of the libraries at Canterbury in M. R. James, *Ancient Libraries of Canterbury and Dover* (1903).

Jocelyn of Brakelond,[1] reveals how little time even the most conscientious of abbots was able to spend with his monks. When at home, he lived very much apart from his brethren, eating in his own house and worshipping in his own chapel.

A similar division of property into separate departments was also taking place in the common funds of the monks. The monk in charge of each department was called an 'obedientiary' and within his own sphere he tended to be despotic. Whether prior, sacristan, cellarer, chamberlain, librarian, infirmarer, guest-master or whatever office he held, he had his own manors and rents, his own staff of clerks and assistants and his own office, and was, at any rate in the early days, often responsible to no one. As the numbers of monks diminished and 'obediences' were multiplied it meant that almost any monk of any ability would sooner or later take charge of one of these departments and devote much of his life to its management. Thus 'save in monasteries such as Winchester, Canterbury and St. Albans, where strong intellectual or artistic interests existed, business of this kind was the career which absorbed all the talent of the house'.[2]

This fissiparous tendency in the case of monastic property often led to much incompetence, extravagance and debt, and in the later Middle Ages most chapters were disturbed by financial anxiety. Attempts were, therefore, often made by visiting bishops to restore financial stability by demanding economy, proper audit of accounts and, in many cases, a central treasury in each monastery through which all money had to pass. In the latter part of the thirteenth century the monks themselves also tried to put their finances on a better footing by improving their methods of farming. By this time trade was expanding, many country towns had their own markets, and there was beginning to be a regular trade with the continent, especially in wool. The monks, therefore, began to take more and more of their land, which had previously been let out, into their own hands, and to improve it by draining, clearance, deforestation, manuring and ploughing. Led by such men as Henry of Eastry at Canterbury,[3] their fortunes began to improve. Meanwhile many monasteries, especially among the Cistercians, had discovered the great profit which could be made from what had been regarded as unpromising land, by the

[1] See *The Chronicle of Jocelyn of Brakelond*, edited and translated by H. E. Butler (1949). There is an earlier translation by L. C. Jane in the *Medieval Library* (1922).
[2] M. D.Knowles, *The Monastic Order in England* (1940), p. 438.
[3] On whom see R. A. L. Smith, *Canterbury Cathedral Priory* (1943).

breeding of sheep and the sale of wool. Many monks became greatly interested in agricultural pursuits, visiting the farms and granges and supervising the work. Chaucer's monk in the *Canterbury Tales,* 'an out-rydere that lovede venerye', was one of these.

The religious houses were thus, for the most part, very active even if the type of work had changed from what had been originally intended by the fathers of monasticism. Nor had the introduction of new interests been altogether a good influence on the internal affairs of the cloister. The records of visitations, of which many have survived from the thirteenth century,[1] give us some idea of the condition of the monasteries and show that many had lost some of their early idealism. The world had, in various ways, invaded the cloister. The simple standard of living, with which the earlier monks had been content, had given way to relaxations in the matter of food and clothing and in the keeping of silence. Many of the monks were often out of their cloisters, not always on the business of the chapter. Hunting, hawking and other field-sports were becoming more and more popular and interfered with the more spiritual and ascetic duties of the monks.

Laxity, in varying degrees, was very common, as visitation returns show. But the Church and the best of the monks were aware of this, and reform was in the air. The Lateran Council of 1215 had ordered the setting up of General Chapters to pass decrees applicable to all monasteries, especially those exempt from episcopal control. Reforming bishops did much in the houses to which they had right of entry, to see that the Rule was kept and that the finances of the monks were put upon a reasonable footing. Meanwhile the monks themselves were anxious for reform, especially in the intellectual sphere by the establishment of lectures in the cloister and by acquiring premises at the universities where their more promising members might become qualified to act as theological teachers to their brethren. The foundation of two colleges at Oxford—Gloucester College for the southern province in 1284 and Durham College for the north in 1289—and of a house for Gilbertine canons at Cambridge in 1290 shows how anxious the religious were not to be left out of the academic movement of the day.

Yet, in spite of such attempts at reform and advance, the fact

[1] See C. R. Cheney, *Episcopal Visitation of Monasteries in the Thirteenth Century* (1931).

remains that the older religious orders had departed a good way from their ideals. Morally the monks were probably above the average standard of either the secular clergy or the laity, but they were 'men of the world', absorbed in their business dealings, content to enjoy the solid security and comparative comfort which the monasteries provided. Meanwhile for those who desired austerity or solitude there were always the houses of the Carthusians and the scattered hermitages where a man could mortify the flesh to his soul's content.

vi. *The Reign of Edward I*

Edward I, though a loyal son of the Church, was not prepared to have his policy dictated to him by ecclesiastics whether in England or in Rome. He had seen the disastrous mistakes which his father had made, and was determined to profit by them. Known in later years as 'the English Justinian' his chief ambition was first to codify and define the laws of England, and then to see that they were justly and universally enforced. Probably more than any of his predecessors he felt the stirrings of that 'nationalist' spirit which was to prove so strong in later years. Certainly he was jealous of his rights, impatient of advice, and ambitious for success.

He was served during his reign by three Archbishops of Canterbury, with each of whom he found little in common. The first of them, Robert Kilwardby (1273-78) was a Dominican friar, a good scholar, Provincial Prior of his order, and the first mendicant to occupy the chair of S. Augustine. Kilwardby proved a conscientious archbishop, but he had no real interest in political matters, and, after five years, was appointed a cardinal and retired to Rome. His successor, John Pecham (1278-92), was also a friar, a Franciscan. Ascetic, holy, learned, cultivated, he was a man of many parts and brought distinction to his office. Like Kilwardby he had been 'provided' to the see of Canterbury by the pope, regardless of the wishes either of the king or of the monks of Christ Church. Pecham was an ardent reformer, tireless in visiting his province, holding a large number of councils, and doing his utmost to improve the standards of clerical life both in the parishes and in the religious houses. He worked hard for Edward I; but they had little in common and Edward was often infuriated by the rebukes of this courageous friar. The third archbishop,

Robert Winchelsey (1294–1313), also a distinguished scholar, was canonically elected by the monks of Canterbury with the king's consent, though in the end Edward found him the most intransigent and least tractable of the three. An uncompromising churchman, Winchelsey fought hard against what he regarded as unreasonable and illegal demands and suffered greatly for it, losing all his goods and being driven into exile.

Not only these three archbishops but many other churchmen were deeply concerned with the need for ecclesiastical reform. The king, however, had other reforms in mind, some of which had the effect of limiting the power and independence of the Church. Four acts were passed during this reign, each of which served, in some way, to strengthen the hands of the state. The *First Statute of Westminster* (1275) made it illegal for bishops to release criminals from their prisons unless they had very good reason for so doing. Four years later (1279) the *Statute of Mortmain*,[1] by prohibiting the assignment of landed property without consent of the feudal superior, struck a hard blow at the religious houses by making it impossible for them to accept any further benefactions without special licence from the king, though this was often granted.[2] Then, in 1285, was issued the writ, *Circumspecte agatis* (addressed to the judges and intended to act as law), which attempted to draw more clearly the dividing line between the civil and ecclesiastical courts.[3] Finally the *Statute of Carlisle* (1307) prevented any further money being sent overseas by the religious houses.

But if the clergy were being hit by legislation they were suffering even more from the burden of taxation. Possessed of incomes which could be easily assessed, they presented an easy prey to both Church and State. We have already seen how the growing demands of the *curia* had led to the system of 'provisions', but this was by no means the only way in which the pope tried to extract money from the English clergy. Time after time demands were made and collectors appointed to take their tenth or their fifteenth from the clergy, and new assessments were constantly made in the hopes of raising the sum which could lawfully be collected.[4]

[1] Gee and Hardy, *Documents* pp. 81–2.
[2] See K. L. Wood-Legh, *Studies in Church Life under Edward III* (1934), chap. iii.
[3] Gee and Hardy, *Documents*, pp. 83–5.
[4] See W. E. Lunt, *The Valuation of Norwich* (1926) and *Financial Relations of the Papacy with England to 1327* (1939).

8

Meanwhile the king was also desperately in need of money to support his wars in France, Wales and Scotland. Naturally he also turned to the clergy as a convenient source of revenue; but the canon lawyers raised the question as to whether the Church was really under any obligation to pay for purely civil expenses such as war or defence. While the matter was being argued in England the pope, Boniface VIII, issued a bull known as *Clericis laicos* (1296) forbidding any prelate or ecclesiastical body to pay taxes to the state without papal permission.[1] This put the clergy in a most difficult position, especially those who were prepared to shoulder their responsibilities as citizens and patriots. Winchelsey, however, supported the pope, and in January 1297 the English clergy were for a time outlawed by the king.

There was thus a considerable tension in the latter part of the thirteenth century. Under Edward's firm rule the nationalist spirit was growing, battling against old traditions and the ever more extravagant claims of the papacy. Between these two opposing forces, each striving for supremacy, lay the clergy both secular and regular, their loyalties divided and their minds confused.

[1] H. Bettenson, *Documents of the Christian Church* (1963), pp. 157–59.

NOTE ON BOOKS

FOR general history, see Sir M. Powicke, *The Thirteenth Century, 1216–1307*, being vol. iv of the *Oxford History of England* (1953). For church history see W. R. W. Stephens (as before) and W. W. Capes, *The English Church in the Fourteenth and Fifteenth Centuries* (1900). On church life of this period see J. R. H. Moorman, *Church Life in England in the Thirteenth Century* (1945), H. G. Richardson, 'The Parish Clergy of the Thirteenth and Fourteenth Centuries' in *Transactions of the Royal Historical Society* (1912), R. A. R. Hartridge, *A History of Vicarages in the Middle Ages* (1930) and G. R. Owst, *Preaching in Medieval England* (1926). F. S. Stevenson's *Robert Grosseteste* is an important work. For the regulars, see M. D. Knowles, *The Religious Orders in England*, vol. i (1948) and R. H. Snape, *English Monastic Finances in the Later Middle Ages* (1926). The literature on the friars is very extensive. Reference should be made to A. G. Little, *Studies in English Franciscan History* (1917) and A. R. Martin, *Franciscan Architecture in England* (1937), and to Bede Jarrett, *The English Dominicans* (1921) and W. A. Hinnebusch, *The Early English Friars Preachers* (1951).

CHAPTER IX

THE AGE OF WYCLIF
(1307-1400)

i. Troubled Times

THE fourteenth century was an unhappy time for the people of England. Weak government, pestilence, insurrection, lack of leaders and heavy taxation all contributed to a feeling of insecurity and anxiety. After the great achievements and brilliant personalities of the thirteenth century the earlier part of the following century seems dull and stagnant; and just at the moment when some kind of revival might have taken place, the great pestilence known as the Black Death struck the country, leaving it sore and bewildered; and the period ended in civil war.

When Edward II succeeded his father in 1307 the Church in England was weak and divided. Archbishop Winchelsey was in exile, and there were few bishops of outstanding merit. Abroad, the papacy had abandoned its ancient home at Rome and was about to settle at Avignon in the south of France where it was drawn more and more under the influence of the French, the natural enemies of England. It is therefore no wonder that anti-papal feeling grew more acute among the English during this period, and that steps were taken by the government to limit the powers of the papacy so far as this country was concerned.

In 1308 the pope demanded the suppression of one of the military orders, the Templars, which he accused of being disloyal to the Church. In England the order was by no means unpopular, and there was no natural support for this attack upon them; but the pope sent inquisitors to see that the work was done and gave orders for torture to be applied if confessions could not otherwise be extorted. To English people the whole business was distasteful, and it exacerbated such anti-papal sentiment as already existed. Added to this was the heavy taxation which the papacy continued to demand, so much of which went only to support political and military schemes which were directly opposed to the interests of the English people.

In the second half of the fourteenth century the government there-fore took up this question and passed a series of acts based on the assumption that the power of the papacy in England 'has increased, is increasing and ought to be diminished'. The first of these was a *Statute of Provisors* (1351) which declared invalid all papal 'provisions' to English benefices. It was followed in 1353 by the *First Statute of Praemunire* which attempted to stop appeals to Rome by declaring that any one who took to a foreign court any matter cognizable in the king's court should suffer the penalties of outlawry.[1] In 1365 a further act was passed extending to those who should attempt to obtain benefices or citations from Rome the heavy penalties attached to *Praemunire* and for a time the ancient practice of paying 'Peter's Pence' was suspended. In 1390 came the *Second Statute of Provisors*,[2] and in 1393 the *Second Statute of Praemunire*,[3] each of which was intended to make more definite what had been attempted in the previous acts.

These five acts of Parliament were the official expression of a grow-ing nationalist feeling which was uttered in more homely language by the Monk of Malmesbury when he cried: 'Lord Jesus! either take away the pope from our midst or lessen the power which he pre-sumes to have over our people'.[4] Such a *cri du coeur* would certainly have been applauded by many English people, for the chronicles and other literature of the time are full of similar laments. Nor was it the papacy alone which came in for criticism. Worldly and venal bishops; idle, absentee clergy; rich, sporting monks; hypocritical and grasping friars—all came under the lash of the satirists and of those who cham-pioned the cause of the downtrodden and oppressed. William Lang-land, in *Piers the Plowman*, attacked the clergy for the abuses which disgraced the Church and divided the nation. His personification of Sloth as a parson who had been more than thirty years in his parish yet could read not a line of his books though he was well able 'to fynde in a felde or in a fourlong an hare',[5] may well have been based upon personal experience of the men whom he had met. And if Langland was, on the whole, sympathetic towards the monks he was bitter in his criticisms of the friars, who professed poverty but man-

[1] Gee and Hardy, *Documents*, pp. 103-4.   [2] *Ibid.* pp. 112-21.   [3] *Ibid.* pp. 122-5.
[4] From the *Vita Edwardi II*, quoted by T. F. Tout in the *Political History of England*, (1905), iii, p. 257.
[5] *Piers the Plowman*, passus B, v. 424; ed. W. Skeat (1924), i, p. 168.

aged nevertheless to grow fat on 'sondry metes, mortrewes (hashed meat) and puddynges, wombe-clouts (tripe) and wylde braune, egges yfryed with grece'.[1]

Such criticisms are a sign of a *malaise* which affected the country in many ways and which was made worse by the tragedy of the Black Death and the social disturbances which followed it. The bubonic plague made its first appearance in England in 1348 and spread rapidly through the country. By May 1350 the epidemic had more or less died down, though spasmodic outbreaks occurred for some time. During the height of its power the mortality was certainly very high. Estimates of the number of deaths vary greatly, some historians thinking that as many as half of the population of England died during those years. The mortality was almost certainly heaviest among the clergy, both secular and monastic. The parish clergy, by the exercise of their normal duties, were inevitably brought into close contact with the dying and the dead; the friars were mostly living in the more congested districts of the towns where infection was likely to be most severe; and the monks lived in close and sometimes unhealthy quarters.

But the greatest problem left behind by the Black Death was not the replacement of those who had died, but social and economic unrest. Labour became scarce throughout the whole country, wages inevitably rose steeply, many serfs bought their freedom, and a new class of yeoman farmers arose—poor, but independent and ambitious. Faced by a number of problems, the government attempted to introduce legislation which would dispel the danger of insurrection, but their efforts were stupid and unimaginative. The *Statutes of Labourers* from 1349 onwards, and the Poll Tax, exacerbated feelings which were already strong, and led eventually to the rising known as the Great Revolt of 1381. With these feelings many of the clergy, especially the humbler parish priests, heartily agreed. Prices rose after the Black Death and the clergy were hard hit. Nor did the bishops show them much sympathy, for Archbishop Islip gave it as his opinion that no parish priest should receive more than £4 a year, though his own income was in the region of £1500. A further blow to the 'inferior clergy' was the decision of Convocation in 1380 that instead of a graduated tax according to income, all clergy should now pay at a flat rate of 6s. 8d. each, regardless of what their financial

[1] *Ibid.*, passus B, xiii, 63-4 (p. 390).

resources were. It was no wonder, then, that in 1381 the rebels were aided and abetted by a number of discontented clergy like John Ball, or by some who sympathized with what they regarded as the cause of justice and progress.

The Revolt was short-lived, but in the struggle for London the Archbishop of Canterbury, Simon Sudbury, who was also Chancellor of England and was regarded as largely responsible for the oppression which the government had shown, was savagely murdered by the mob on Tower Hill. A few monasteries were attacked —notably St. Albans and Bury St. Edmunds—by crowds which were always ready to score off their old enemies, and there was a wholesale destruction of charters and documents which were too easily regarded as weapons in the hands of the landlords. Otherwise the Church was not greatly affected by the rising.

But among those who had supported the rebels were some of the 'Poor Preachers' who, instigated and inspired by John Wyclif, were now wandering about the country intent upon a great spiritual and moral renaissance. By the end of the fourteenth century a new force had come into being, clothed in the shining garments of fanaticism, and destined to play its part in the history of the English Church in the next century and a half.

ii. *John Wyclif*

John Wyclif was born in the North Riding of Yorkshire at either Hipswell or Wycliffe about the year 1328. As a boy he went to Oxford, probably as a scholar of Balliol College which had special connections with the north. About the year 1358 he was appointed master of his college, but in 1361 he left Oxford upon being appointed rector of Fillingham in Lincolnshire. In the following year he was provided to the prebend of Aust at Westbury-on-Trym, so becoming a pluralist, though on a small scale. A few months later he became also an absentee, since he obtained leave of absence from his parish and returned to Oxford where he took lodgings in Queen's College and entered again into the rich and vigorous life of the schools. For two years, from 1365–67, he was Warden of Canterbury Hall, a hostel for monks from Christ Church, Canterbury. In 1368 Wyclif gave up his living at Fillingham in exchange for the benefice of Ludgershall in Buckinghamshire, probably because it was nearer to Oxford. He did not, however, take much interest in his parish, for in 1372 he entered the service of the Crown, and in 1374 was sent to Bruges as a Royal Commissioner, receiving the princely salary of 20s. a day, which was about what his vicar at Ludgershall received in three months. On returning from Bruges, Wyclif settled again at Oxford, where he was busy disputing in the schools and writing controversial pamphlets. These made so vigorous an attack on the Church that some kind of response was inevitable. In the summer of 1377 the pope issued five bulls condemning the opinions of Wyclif, who was formally imprisoned at Oxford. He appealed to Parliament, and a trial was staged at Lambeth in March 1378, only to end in fiasco. In 1381 he left Oxford on becoming rector of Lutterworth in Leicestershire which was his home for the next three years. Soon after he went there he was tried by a Council held at the Blackfriars in London. Wyclif did not attend the trial and was little affected by its decisions. He died at Lutterworth, as the result of a stroke, on December 31, 1384.

From this brief summary of his life it will be seen that Wyclif, although technically a parish priest, was in fact an Oxford don. Except for the last three years of his life he took very little interest in the parishes from which he drew his income, preferring to spend his time at Oxford in the more stimulating atmosphere of the schools. It is therefore a great mistake to compare him with John Wesley who had a burning zeal for the souls of men. Wyclif was far more interested in ideas and debates than he was in people.

Wyclif was a scholar and a critic. A man of strong feelings, his indignation was quickly aroused by what he regarded as abuses, and he was always ready to strike out, often with more courage than discretion. His keen mind and merciless tongue and pen made him a notable and formidable figure in Oxford for over thirty years.

When we examine his teaching we find that it was closely bound up with the idea of 'dominion'. Feudalism taught that each man held whatever position and authority he had from his immediate superior to whom he was responsible. Such position was his 'dominion' in which he had certain rights. The Church adopted a similar doctrine, and had for long been engaged in a struggle to make the secular and temporal dominion dependent upon the spiritual. In 1302 Boniface VIII had issued the bull *Unam Sanctam* in which he had accepted the theory of the 'two swords', the material and the spiritual, but had declared that both were in the power or dominion of the Church. This had been challenged by such thinkers as Marsiglio of Padua and the English Franciscan, William of Ockham, and the 'Babylonish Captivity' of the pope, coming so soon after *Unam Sanctam*, had made the papal claims look rather foolish. But the struggle continued.

Wyclif struck at the whole theory of dominion, whether temporal or spiritual, by declaring that all dominion is derived directly from God. Such doctrine, if pressed to its conclusions, would have cut right across the whole idea of authority in Church and State; and this was indeed what Wyclif proceeded to do. In his book *De Dominio Divino* he argued that, since each man is responsible to God alone, there can be no need for a hierarchy and no distinction between priest and layman. All are equal in the sight of God. Shortly afterwards he followed this up with his book *De Dominio Civili* in which he claimed that, since dominion or lordship was 'founded in grace', the un-worthiness of the holder deprived him of any right to exercise any authority or power. This applied to spiritual as well as temporal ownership. If the Church abused its trust then it lost any claim either to its property or to its power.

These two theories so dominated Wyclif's thought that he began to lash out on all sides with great vigour. The Church was rich and powerful; but it was also corrupt: therefore it automatically forfeited its right to hold any property. Such was the argument; but it de-pended upon the evidence of corruption in the Church, and it was this that Wyclif set himself to expose. Beginning with the papacy he had an easy target, for the popes had long been exiles in France, and from 1378 the Great Schism set up two rival popes. Wyclif began with severe criticism of the papacy—its power, its worldliness, its shameless greed, its prostitution of spiritual authority for material ends—but criticism soon degenerated into abuse and the pope be-came 'a poisonous weed', 'the head vicar of the fiend' and 'a simple idiot who might be a damned devil in hell'.

From attacks on the papacy Wyclif turned to criticize and con-demn the secular clergy. Believing that a priesthood was really un-necessary and that authority depended upon character, he had little difficulty in producing evidence of worldly bishops, rich pluralists and negligent priests. But he went further than this, for he was con-vinced that the power of the clergy rested upon false teaching about the sacraments, especially the Eucharist. The Real Presence of Christ Wyclif never denied, but the formal doctrine of Transubstantiation shocked him both on logical and practical grounds. He substituted first the theory of Consubstantiation, though he did not call it by this name, and then accused the secular priests of teaching a doctrine which was untrue in order to bolster up their own authority and power over the laity.

Towards the monks, or 'possessioners' as he called them, Wyclif showed bitter hostility. He objected to monastic life in theory since it tended to break up the unity of the Christian body, and in practice because the monks had deteriorated so much from their pristine asceticism and discipline. To Wyclif the wealthy and easy-going monks wallowed in 'the religion of fat cows'; he could detect no grain of usefulness in their lives and thought that all monasteries should be dissolved. The friars, on the other hand, he at first admired, even going so far as to say that the Franciscans were 'very dear to God'. But further acquaintance with the mendicants led him to change his views; and when the friars challenged his eucharistic teaching, Wyclif turned against them and became very scathing in his denunciations of their apostasy and degeneration. In his later years the wickedness of the friars became an obsession with him, and his writings abound in the most savage and bitter attacks upon them.

Wyclif was thus essentially a critic and satirist, lashing out at the abuses which were so obvious to him. But to counteract the evils of the day he made two positive contributions. Conscious of the ignorance of the laity, ground down by tyrannical priests, he conceived the idea of translating the Bible into English in order that the ordinary literate layman might himself study the Scriptures and form his own judgments. With the assistance of some of his followers, notably Nicholas of Hereford and John Purvey, the whole Bible was translated into English during the last few years of Wyclif's life, and copies soon began to circulate. This stupendous task, carried out in the teeth of considerable opposition and danger, represents Wyclif's greatest work for the Church. His other positive contribution was the assembling together of a body of disciples and enthusiasts who were prepared to go about the country, as the early friars had done, preaching the Gospel to all men wherever they might make themselves heard. These 'Poor Preachers' were mostly priests, some were scholars, many were simple and humble men. As they went out they took copies of the Scriptures in English with them and laid much stress on the Bible as the sole standard of faith and action. Their positive preaching of the Gospel was undoubtedly mixed with a good deal of vulgar criticism of monks, friars, bishops and rich clergy—for the Poor Preachers were disciples of Wyclif—and some of them stimulated social unrest by encouraging the demands of the disaffected labourers; but the fact remains that Wyclif was able to inspire a band of enthusiasts ready to face danger and hardship in the cause which they believed to be right.

And here, perhaps, lies the core of Wyclif's genius. In himself he is, to us, an unattractive character, for we know him almost solely from his own writings, which are full of bitterness and contempt, and from the attacks of his enemies. Yet behind all this there must have been a flame of real concern for the welfare of God's people. 'So much a scholar and so little a saint',[1] Wyclif was yet able to arouse men to such passionate zeal for righteousness that they willingly gave their bodies to be burnt for the faith that was in them. With all his faults Wyclif succeeded in lighting a candle which burnt steadily through many years of trial and which is by no means extinguished at the present day.[2]

iii. Popular Religion in the Fourteenth Century

By far the most conspicuous building in any medieval village was the parish church, which towered majestically over the squalid huts of the people, a perpetual reminder to them of things spiritual and eternal. Much building, restoring, altering and improving of churches was going on at this time, and we owe much to the care and liberality of those who looked after our parish churches in the Middle Ages. Inside the churches highly painted walls and historiated windows served as 'the poor man's Bible', teaching him Bible stories, legends of the saints or moral lessons.

On Sundays the Mass was by far the most important service,

---

[1] M. Deanesly, The Lollard Bible (1920), p. 226.
[2] H. B. Workman, John Wyclif, 2 vols. (1926) is the standard life. See also R. L. Poole, Wycliffe and Movements for Reform (1892), F. D. Matthew's Introduction to The English Works of Wyclif (Early English Text Society, 1880), W. W. Shirley's Introduction to Fasciculi Zizaniorum Mag. Johannis Wyclif (Rolls Series, 1858) and B. L. Manning, 'John Wyclif', in Camb. Med. Hist., vol. vii.

though Mattins and Evensong were also said. William Langland writes of a man's duty:

> Upon Sonedayes to cease. godes servyce to hear
> Bothe matyns and messe. and, after mete, in churches
> To hear their evesong, every man ouhte.[1]

Mass was probably said about nine o'clock in the morning and preceded by Mattins, which appears to have been poorly attended, for Robert Manning complains of people who prefer to stay in bed 'to lygge and swete and take the mery mornyng slepe'.[2] Mass, on the other hand, would normally be attended by most of the parishioners. As there were no seats in the church, people tended to wander about, talking and gossiping, except when the sanctus-bell rang and reminded them of their devotions. They communicated only about once a year, at Easter, and then in one kind only, since the chalice was generally withheld from all except the celebrant from about the middle of the thirteenth century onwards.

In the thirteenth century a sermon had been a rare event in any English parish church, though occasionally some instruction was given on the Creed, the Lord's Prayer or the Ten Commandments. But a revival of preaching took place with the coming of the friars, who laid so much emphasis upon the spoken word, and were themselves often such good preachers that many parochial clergy were forced to reconsider their duties and try their hand at a sermon. In the fourteenth century, preaching became more common, books being written to assist preachers in preparing their sermons, and pulpits appearing in a few churches from about 1340 onwards. But though there was some revival of preaching, most clergy were reluctant to add this burden to their labours, and reformers continued to complain of 'unpreaching prelates' until the days of Hugh Latimer.[3]

Every church was provided with a font in which infants were normally baptized on the day of their birth. The service was in two parts, the first taking place outside the door of the church, the second at the font. The service was long and elaborate and full of symbolism such as the exorcism of the evil spirit, the 'effeta' or unction with spittle,[4] the anointing with oil and the putting on of the white

---

[1] *Piers Plowman*, C, x, 227-9 (ed. Skeat, i, pp. 240-41).
[2] R. Manning, *Handlyng Synne*, ed. Furnival (1901), p. 143.
[3] See the two books by G. R. Owst, *Preaching in Medieval England* (1926) and *Literature and Pulpit in Medieval England* (1933).
[4] From 'Ephphatha' in Mark vii, 34.

chrisom cloth which the mother of the child returned when she came to be 'churched'. Confirmation was administered at a very early age, generally between the ages of one and three, though the neglect of this sacrament shown by some bishops must have meant that many people were confirmed only later in life, if at all.

Marriage, like baptism, began with a ceremony at the church door where, it may be remembered, the Wife of Bath had (most properly) married her five husbands. After the promises and vows the party moved into the church to the altar-step and the service ended with the nuptial Mass. Finally the priest visited the couple in bed and sprinkled them with holy water. But marriages among the rich were often little more than moves in the game of building up family fortunes, and moralists were loud in their denunciation of child marriages, of young girls given to 'olde febles', boys to widows, children of four or five years of age mated with grown men and women in order to further the plans of ambitious parents.

The sacrament of Penance was the normal preparation for the annual communion, and, where properly conducted, was made into a thoroughgoing spiritual examination in faith and morals. The Visitation of the Sick was often referred to in synodal statutes, and clergy were encouraged to perform this most important part of their ministry with the zeal of Chaucer's 'pore persoun' who, though 'wyd was his parisshe and houses fer a-sonder', never failed in his duty of visiting those in sickness or 'meschief'. Unction, though originally intended as a sacrament of healing, had by this time become little more than a preparation for death and was surrounded with a good deal of superstition. Burials of the dead were often stately and dignified affairs, especially in the case of rich people who left considerable sums of money to ensure that they were buried in style. Only the very rich were buried in coffins, the rest were wound in a 'cere-cloth' and so laid in earth.[1]

Although Chaucer clearly knew the Scriptures fairly well, Bible-reading among the laity was rare throughout the Middle Ages. There were two reasons for this; one was that most lay people were illiterate, the other that Bibles were extremely expensive books. Until the invention of printing, the writing of a Bible took so long

[1] See W. Maskell, *Monumenta Ritualia Ecclesiae Anglicanae*, 2nd ed., 3 vols. (1882); J. R. H. Moorman, *Church Life in England in the Thirteenth Century* (1945), chap. vii; H. S. Kingsford, *Illustrations of the Occasional Offices of the Church taken from Medieval Pictures* (Alcuin Club Collections, xxiv, 1921).

to complete that the price could not be anything but very high. Consequently, although scholars—whether lay or clerical, secular or regular—had access to Bibles in libraries and sometimes possessed their own, Bible-reading by the laity scarcely existed at all. The only lay people who are known to have owned copies of the Scriptures in the fourteenth century are a few great men and noble ladies.[1]

For the ordinary illiterate parishioner the walls and windows of the church, an occasional sermon and the presentation of religious drama, both liturgical and otherwise, had to provide such knowledge of the Bible narratives as he was ever likely to acquire. In a sense all worship in the early church was dramatic; but gradually, by means of processions and dialogue, the great facts commemorated-in the Church's year were brought more vividly before the people. The earliest liturgical drama was concerned with the Nativity (especially the coming of the shepherds to the stable) and with the Resurrection —in the famous *Quem quaeritis* ceremony at the Easter Sepulchre. These became very common, and by the middle of the thirteenth century had become a normal part of the life of most parishes. From that date onwards a change took place. The plays were now taken over more by the laity and performed in gild-halls or in the open air instead of in the churches. The language also changed from Latin to English and the plays became less liturgical and more didactic and popular. Under the name of 'miracle' plays, new themes were introduced such as the 'Harrowing of Hell' or a Passion Play. Early in the fourteenth century such vernacular plays, organized by the municipality or by some gild, were becoming popular at such places as Chester, York, Beverley, Coventry and Norwich. Often they were long pageants, each episode of which was acted by the members of a gild, and they dealt with the whole story of man's redemption from the Fall of Lucifer to the Day of Judgment. Still later came the 'moralities', which were allegorical dramas intended to drive home some lesson and brought in representative characters such as Everyman, Vices and Virtues, Perseverance, Curiosity, and so forth. Finally, in the fifteenth century, 'interludes' were introduced between the scenes of the drama, often of a lighter and more secular nature, to give comic relief.[2]

[1] M. Deanesly, *The Lollard Bible* (1920) and B. Smalley, *The Study of the Bible in the Middle Ages* (2nd ed. 1952).
[2] E. K. Chambers, *The Medieval Stage* (1903), vol. ii; K. Young, *The Drama of the Medieval Church*, 2 vols. (1933).

The climax of the miracle-play was the Doom or Judgment which every man must one day face. This final event was something which dominated the thoughts of all men and of which the Church was never tired of teaching. Grim and lurid pictures of the Last Judgment decorated the chancel arches of many churches, a perpetual reminder to the worshipper of what his ultimate fate must be. In the centre sat Christ the Judge with the Book of Life, while on one hand were the blessed being led away by angels into paradise and on the other hand were the damned being pushed by devils into the yawning mouth of hell. But man was not left to struggle alone to avoid this terrible fate. Three things served to help him—the mercy of God, the intercessions of the saints, and the prayers of the Church militant. For if the Judgment could never be forgotten neither could the Cross. In the centre of the church stood the Rood, the great crucifix flanked by the Virgin and S. John; and as the cross stood over a man in church, so the thought of the cross stood over him throughout his life. 'The medieval Christian', it has been said, 'was a man of one event. The Passion of Christ was his daily meditation. . . . Over the whole medieval world lay the broad shadow of the Cross.'[1] Redemption through the sacrifice of Christ was man's first hope. His second was the intercessions of the saints, especially of the Virgin Mary. To her the layman was taught to say his prayers in the *Ave Maria*; through her intercessions lay hope for even the most hardened sinner. Other saints, according to their degrees, could also help if their interest could be aroused; and hence the frequent pilgrimages, often at great cost, to distant shrines. Finally, each man depended much upon the prayers of the Church, especially for the 'trental' or series of thirty daily masses immediately following his death. It was to obtain the prayers of good men that monasteries were founded, schools endowed, chantries set up, private Masses said. The greater the number of prayers said the better a man's chances of coming safely through the awful Judgment.

It was in some such mood that the layman of the fourteenth century faced the issues of life and death, of heaven and hell. So long as he was a loyal son of the Church he had hope, for the angels were on his side; but as soon as a man cut himself adrift from the Church, or failed in his duty towards it, woe betide him! Few men would then have dared to question the dictum that 'outside the Church there is no salvation'.

[1] B. L. Manning, *The People's Faith in the Time of Wyclif* (1919), p. 25.

iv. *Mystics and Writers*

Largely under the influence of the Franciscans a number of mystical writings had appeared in England in the thirteenth century. These, like the paintings of the period, were marked by their tenderness and sensitivity. They showed a deep interest in the Cross and Passion, in the Holy Name and in the details of Christ's earthly life. Most of the writers were solitaries or writing for solitaries, and, since their works were addressed to educated but not academic readers, they wrote in English. The most famous work of this class which comes from the thirteenth century was *The Ancren Riwle*, sometimes attributed to Richard le Poore, Bishop successively of Chichester, Salisbury and Durham.[1]

The fourteenth century produced four mystical writers of great distinction. The first was Richard Rolle of Hampole in Yorkshire (*c.* 1300–49). A Yorkshireman by birth, Rolle went up to Oxford, where he was deeply influenced by the Franciscans. Instead of joining their order, however, he heard the call to an anchoritic life and returned to his native county where he became a hermit and missionary. Like S. Francis, Rolle was a born romantic and poet who developed an intense, personal devotion to poverty and humility. At first he suffered considerable persecution, 'with wordys of bakbyttingis', from his friends and relatives; but he persisted in the course to which he felt himself called, clad in a rough habit which he himself made out of material given to him by his sister. During the long solitary hours which he spent in his cell Richard Rolle tried to express in words the experiences which had come to him in his search for God. The experiences were of three kinds which he expressed by the words 'Heat', 'Sweetness' and 'Song'. The sense of fire, common to so many mystics, was intensely real to Rolle and was described in his book, *The Fire of Love*. 'I sat', he says, 'in a chapel, and whilst with sweetness of prayer or meditation muckle I was delighted, suddenly in me I felt a merry heat and unknown.' This sense of heat or fire was something almost physical, and gave place afterwards to that feeling which he describes as 'Sweetness', and finally to 'Song' which often expressed itself in delightful and tender lyrics or in analogies from

---

[1] See Ancrene Riwle, trans. by M. B. Salu (1955).

music. A moralist and an individualist, believing intensely in liberty of conscience and personal inspiration, Richard Rolle had considerable influence on Wyclif, as indeed on all religious thinkers of the later Middle Ages, especially in the north.[1]

About the time of Rolle's death in the year of the Black Death a work appeared, known as *The Cloud of Unknowing*. Its author's name and condition are not known, though attempts have been made by some to prove that he was a monk, by others that he was a parish priest. What is certain is that it was addressed to a solitary, a young man who had already embraced the eremitic life. The author, who had already translated the *Mystical Theology* of the writer known as Dionysius the Areopagite, was much more philosophical than Rolle. He is absorbed with the thought of the transcendence of God dwelling hid in the 'dark cloud of Unknowing' which can be pierced only by 'the sharp dart of longing love'. So deep is this mystery that it can never be wholly apprehended by the mind; in the end it is love and love alone which wins through to the vision of God.[2]

The third of the great English mystics of the fourteenth century was Walter Hilton (died 1396), an Austin canon of Thurgarton in Nottinghamshire. Hilton, who was a well-read theologian, addressed his most famous work, *The Scale of Perfection*, to an anchoress attached to some monastery. His other work, *An Epistle on Mixed Life*, was intended for men living in the world. Hilton, who was deeply influenced by Rolle, was much interested in ordinary people whom he wished to help in their spiritual progress and ascent. Christian perfection may be found in divine contemplation but it may also be achieved in the faithful performance of the ordinary duties of everyday life, the truth which Brother Lawrence was later to make so familiar and which Hilton expresses in the warning to people 'not to tend God's head and neglect his feet'. As might be expected, Hilton's work became very popular in England, many copies being made in the days before printing, and many printed editions appearing from 1494 onwards.[3]

The Lady Julian of Norwich (*c.* 1343–*c.* 1413) was an anchoress

[1] See H. E. Allen, *Writings ascribed to Richard Rolle* (New York, 1927); F. M. M. Comper, *The Life and Lyrics of Richard Rolle* (1928); *The Fire of Love and the Mending of Life*, ed. F. M. M. Comper (1914); *The Form of Perfect Living*, ed. G. Hodgson (1910).

[2] *The Cloud of Unknowing and other Treatises*, with a Commentary on *The Cloud* by Fr. A. Baker. Edited by Dom Justin McCann (1924).

[3] The most convenient edition is that published in the Orchard Books in 1953.

living in a cell built in the churchyard of S. Julian's at Norwich. At
the age of thirty she had a severe illness during which she fell into a
trance which lasted for five hours early one morning. During this
time she received a number of revelations or 'shewings' upon which
she afterwards meditated at great length. These *Revelations of Divine
Love* she recorded in two forms, the first written shortly after the
event took place, the second some twenty years later when the significance of the revelations had been more closely examined and considered in her mind. The outstanding feature of the Lady Julian's
mysticism is her all-conquering faith expressed in the message of
Christ that 'it behoved that there should be sin; but all shall be well,
and all shall be well, and all manner of things shall be well' (13th
Revelation). This is not mere optimism, but a clear faith in the cross
and passion of Christ and the ultimate triumph of love. 'In her
mingled homeliness and philosophic instinct, her passion for Nature,
her profound devotion to the Holy Name', says Evelyn Underhill
of the Lady Julian, 'she represents all the best elements of English
mysticism.'[1]

Meanwhile, in addition to the writings of the mystics properly so
called, a good deal of homiletic and devotional literature, mostly in
English, was being produced 'in symple speche for the luf of symple
men'. An educated laity was gradually emerging, hungry for books
of an edifying nature which would assist them in their spiritual pilgrimage. Perhaps the most famous writer of this kind of literature
was Robert Manning of Brunne (or Bourne in Lincolnshire) who
produced his *Handlynge Synne* in 1303. This work is a translation of
a French book called *Manuel des Pechiez*, though its author was an
Englishman called William of Wadington. *Handlynge Synne*, a long
poem of 12,630 lines, is a magnificent collection of exciting moral
tales designed to illustrate the teaching of the Church as expressed
in the Decalogue, the Seven Deadly Sins and the Seven Sacraments.
The stories, all of which are of a high moral character, are told not
only with great skill but with the purpose of arousing fear and con-
trition. The very titles—'The Story of the Adulterous Wife whose
Skeleton split in Two', 'The Sacrilegious Carollers made to dance
together for a Whole Year', or 'The Cambridgeshire Miser-parson
and how he stuft his Mouth with Gold'—will give some indication

---

[1] E. Underhill, *The Mystics of the Church* (n.d.), p. 127. See *The Revelations of Divine
Love recorded by Julian Norwich*, trans. J. Walsh (1961).

9

of the nature of this dramatic and didactic poem.[1] Another long poem, *Cursor Mundi*, written in the northern dialect, is a history of the world in which the Virgin Mary is the chief figure.[2]

Meditations on the Supper of the Lord,[3] perhaps also by Robert Manning, is based upon a work supposed to have been by S. Bonaventura. It begins with a long description of the Last Supper in which a great deal of apocryphal and imaginary detail has been added to the narratives provided in the Gospels. The same is true of the account of the Passion which follows. Here again the Virgin plays a prominent part, the last section giving a highly dramatized account of her sorrows.

Legends of the Holy Rood,[4] is a long story of the vicissitudes of the cross, beginning with the discovery by Seth of a miraculous tree in paradise and leading on to the finding of the cross by S. Helena. *The Eleven Pains of Hell*[5] gives us a vivid description of the place of the damned by one who claimed to have seen it in a vision. The descriptions of burning trees upon which are hung the souls of those who would not go to church, of vultures gnawing people's vitals, of venomous serpents, boiling lakes, frozen fens, heated ovens and vile dungeons were all intended to strike fear into the heart of the most hard-bitten and impenitent reader. Another famous work, the *Ayenbite of Inwyt* or *Remorse of Conscience* (1340)[6] by Dan Michel of Northgate in Kent, had much in common with *Handlynge Synne*, for not only was it a translation from a French book, but it was also a series of homilies upon certain documents, such as the Commandments and the Creed, treated allegorically and illustrated from legends and bestiaries.

This period also saw the publication of a number of books designed to assist both priests and people in the performance of their religious duties. John Mirc's *Instructions for Parish Priests*[7] was written about 1400 by a canon of Lilleshall in Shropshire. It is a translation into English poetry of a Latin work known as *Pupilla Oculi* and deals with the various duties of a parish priest, especially in the conduct of services and the care of the church and churchyard. So full is it of practical common sense that much of it could be put into the hands

[1] Edited by F. J. Furnival and published by the E.E.T.S. Original Series, Nos. 119, 123.   [2] E.E.T.S. Original Series, Nos. 57, 59, 62, 66, 68, 99.
[3] *Ibid.*, No. 60.   [4] *Ibid.*, No. 46.
[5] In *Old English Miscellany*, E.E.T.S. Original Series, No. 49.
[6] Published by the Roxburgh Club in 1855 and in E.E.T.S. Original Series, No. 23.
[7] E.E.T.S. Original Series, No. 31.

of the ordination candidate of the twentieth century as a useful hand-book of pastoralia. Meanwhile, for the laity, a book written in French about 1150 by a certain Dan Jeremy had been translated into English about 1300 under the title of the *Lay Folks' Mass Book*.[1] This describes, again in simple rhymed metre, the action of the Mass, giving instructions when to stand, kneel and sign with the cross; it provides suitable English prayers to be said by the worshipper while the Mass is in progress; and it gives paraphrases of the Creed and the Lord's Prayer for the edification and use of the layman. A similar production, the *Lay Folks' Catechism*,[2] was a translation of Archbishop Thoresby's *Instruction* of 1357. It complains of the ignorance of people through the neglect of teaching by 'prelates, parsons, vikers and prestes' and then gives paraphrases of the Lord's Prayer and Ten Commandments, the Fourteen Points of the Faith, the Sacraments, Vices and Virtues, and Works of Mercy.

Finally there was the production of 'Books of Hours' or *Prymers*[3] which became very popular in the later Middle Ages. The Prymer normally contained the 'Hours of Our Lady', the Seven Penitential Psalms and the Fifteen Gradual Psalms, a Litany, an Office for the Dead (called 'Matynes for dede men'), and a Commendation of all Christian Souls. Such books were intended for lay people to use at home, while such aids as the *Lay Folks' Mass Book* were meant to be used at church. A study of medieval wills shows that a good many lay people did in fact possess their own service books and books of devotion in the latter part of the Middle Ages.[4]

v. *Universities and Schools*

During the thirteenth and fourteenth centuries the Universities of Oxford and Cambridge made rapid progress both in numbers and in constitutional development. At Oxford the office of Chancellor appears by the year 1214 and at Cambridge by 1226. This meant that the regent masters had now formed themselves into a corporation under a duly appointed head, though in each university the bishop

---

[1] E.E.T.S. Original Series, No. 71.   [2] *Ibid.*, No. 118.
[3] H. Littlehales, *The Prymer*, 2 vols. (1891) and see E. Bishop, 'The Origin of the Prymer' in *Liturgica Historica* (1918).
[4] See the information collected by M. Deanesly in *The Lollard Bible* (1920), pp. 391-8.

of the diocese continued to exercise considerable power until Oxford obtained its freedom in 1395 and Cambridge in 1430.

Great impetus to the study of theology at the universities was given by the arrival of the friars, especially the Dominicans and Franciscans in the decade between 1220 and 1230. Each of these orders was now in a position to provide first-class teaching, and both at Oxford and Cambridge it was not long before the friars set up their own schools, which attracted large numbers of students. These schools were intended to form part of a plan for providing lecturers for each convent of mendicants in the country, but they soon began to play an important part in the development of the university. Almost immediately the question of the status of these schools forced itself upon the attention of the regent masters who were trying to direct the constitutional development of the growing university. The argument of the seculars was that if friars choose to come and set up schools in the midst of the universities they must submit to the discipline of the academic authorities. This the friars refused to do, with the result that great tension was created and much bad blood aroused. At first the universities accused the friars of claiming all the privileges of membership in the corporate body without submitting to its decrees; but in later years the quarrel took a more personal turn, when attempts were made to limit the number of friars who could graduate in any one year, or to prevent anyone under the age of eighteen from joining one of the mendicant orders. But the friars were in a strong position: they had papal support; they provided excellent teaching; and they had their own buildings which were often far better than those to which the university could lay claim.

One of the factors in breaking the power of the mendicants was the growth of colleges at the two universities. Until the latter part of the thirteenth century boys coming into residence were either obliged to find lodgings in the town or were herded together in hostels where there was little supervision. Discipline was so lax that it was no wonder if studious youths were attracted into the orders of mendicants where proper arrangements could be made for their studies. But from about 1250 onwards a new development took place with the foundation of a number of colleges where scholars could live and work in disciplined and quiet surroundings. University College at Oxford was founded in 1249, Balliol and Merton soon after 1260, and Peterhouse at Cambridge in 1284.

Early in the fourteenth century new colleges appeared rapidly at both universities, and though these were mainly quite small—catering for a master or warden and about eight or a dozen scholars—they showed that the question of providing the right atmosphere for study was being tackled, and in this way limited the appeal of the friars.

The basis of all study was the arts course followed, by those who so desired it, by a post-graduate course in theology, law, or medicine. Since the friars refused to let their members take a degree in arts it was in the faculty of theology that they made their largest contribution to thought and education. The course in theology included, besides attendance at lectures, some lecturing and participation in the 'disputations' which formed so important a part of medieval academic life. It was in these disputations that the great battles between rival schools of philosophy took place.

The history of medieval philosophy is the history of an attempt to reconcile Christian doctrine first with the teaching of Plato and then with that of Aristotle. In the earlier Middle Ages the works of Plato had been known and studied largely through the writings of the Neo-platonic school of Plotinus and S. Augustine. The works of Aristotle were then practically unknown except the *Logic*. But in the thirteenth century, partly as a result of the Crusades, a great deal of new material was introduced into Western Europe, including the remaining books of Aristotle and the works of Arab philosophers such as Averroës and Avicenna. The schoolmen, or Christian philosophers, were now faced with the task of finding some synthesis between Biblical theology and pagan philosophy. Such synthesis, however, could not always be found; and, where tension remained, the Christian thinker was driven to consider the respective claims of Reason and Authority. The sense of authority was so strong in the medieval Church that at first Reason had to submit to it; but this did not satisfy the more acute minds, who felt that truth must be one, and that there could not therefore be any real clash between the discoveries of pagan philosophers and the revealed truths of the Bible. Thus in the thirteenth century the great schoolmen, such as Alexander of Hales, Albertus Magnus and Thomas Aquinas, were all engaged on the attempt to produce a *Summa* which would resolve the apparent tension between the dogma of the Church and the teaching of 'the philosopher', Aristotle.

Of these three great men the first, Alexander of Hales was an

English Franciscan teaching at Paris. In England the schoolmen were doubtful of the value of such attempts to reach a synthesis, and were especially critical of Aquinas. It was a member of the Dominican order, Robert Kilwardby, who persuaded the University of Oxford to condemn a number of Thomist propositions, while the great Franciscan thinkers were his natural rivals and critics. John Pecham and Roger Bacon both challenged the conclusions of Aquinas, but the man who did most to give a new direction to philosophic thought was John Duns Scotus, a man of the most delicate and penetrating mind, who revived the Realist school of Anselm, profoundly influenced the teaching of theology at both Oxford and Cambridge, and was in later years looked upon as the typical 'Schoolman', splitting hairs over metaphysical trifles.[1] Scotus himself was challenged by another Franciscan, William of Ockham, the very personification of common sense, who applied his 'razor' to cut out all unnecessary argument and to get back to fundamentals.

In the fourteenth century the debate raged between the rival schools of Scotus and Ockham until John Wyclif appeared upon the scene and took the whole controversy into quite a new field. Hitherto both sides, though differing to the point of bloodshed over philosophic argument, were united in accepting the discipline of the Church. With the coming of Wyclif, himself essentially a schoolman, this hitherto unquestioned discipline was challenged, and the whole debate was taken from the realm of philosophy to that of authority. Thus, by the end of the fourteenth century, the old controversy between Realism and Nominalism had begun to take on less importance as the larger question of Heresy against Orthodoxy, of private judgment against dogma, of the individual conscience against the authority of the Church, took the field.

Throughout the whole of the medieval period, therefore, theological and philosophical controversy was strong in the universities, fanned by many winds, such as the rivalry of Franciscans with Dominicans, of friars with seculars, of north against south. It was, therefore, into a vigorous and lively atmosphere that the young student entered when he came into residence. It was customary at that time for scholars to begin their university studies at about the

---

[1] The Renaissance scholars were so exasperated by the intricacies of Duns' thought that they coined a word 'dunce' to mean a 'stupid man'. Duns Scotus, however, was the very opposite of stupid. See C. R. S. Harris, *Duns Scotus*, 2 vols. (1927).

age of fourteen, having previously learned enough at a grammar school to be able to profit from lectures and disputations held always in the Latin tongue. Most of these boys were already in minor orders, and some had already been instituted to livings. Their life was often very lax and undisciplined, and the boy ran many risks of having his head broken either upon his journeys to and from the university city or in some 'Town and Gown' riot while he was there. But for those who survived the dangers and endured the hardships of academic life the university offered a fine field for the exercise of wit and memory in the endless disputation and debate, both in public and in private, which absorbed the attention of the scholars and laid the foundations of modern thought.[1]

In order to keep up a supply of boys qualified to enter into the life of a university it was essential that there should be a large number of good grammar schools where the foundations of education might be laid. This demand was met mainly by the schools attached to the cathedral and collegiate churches, but also by a growing number of more independent schools which were founded by wealthy ecclesiastics, gilds or laymen. Of these the most illustrious and ambitious was the college founded at Winchester by the bishop, William of Wykeham, in 1382. This, which was part of a plan for a better educated clergy, was designed to take seventy poor boys who would proceed, in due course, from Winchester to the sister foundation of New College at Oxford and so complete their education. Other similar foundations followed to meet the growing demand for good schools, so that, by the close of the Middle Ages, England was well provided with free grammar schools where boys could prepare either for a university course or to enter that growing class of educated laymen who were now beginning to play so important a part in the life of the country.

[1] See H. Rashdall, *The Universities of Europe in the Middle Ages*, ed. Powicke and Emden, 3 vols. (1936); R. S. Rait, *Life in the Medieval University* (1912); H. C. Maxwell-Lyte, *History of the University of Oxford* (1886); J. Bass Mullinger, *The University of Cambridge from the Earliest Times to 1535* (1873); A. G. Little, *The Grey Friars in Oxford* (1892) and J. R. H. Moorman, *The Grey Friars in Cambridge* (1952).

NOTE ON BOOKS

FOR general history, see M. McKisack, *The Fourteenth Century, 1307-1399*, being vol. v of the *Oxford History of England* (1959). For church history

CHAPTER X

THE CLOSE OF THE MIDDLE AGES
(1400–1509)

i. *The Church in the Fifteenth Century*

In the retroquire of Winchester Cathedral stand, on either side of the grave of S. Swithin, two magnificent canopied tombs. These were erected in memory of two bishops who, between them, governed the see of Winchester for almost the whole of the fifteenth century— Henry Beaufort from 1404 to 1447 and William Waynflete from 1447 to 1486. Each, in his way, was typical of his period. Beaufort was an aristocrat, a son of John of Gaunt, and a man whose interests lay far more in the affairs of state than in the dull routine of diocesan administration. Bishop of Lincoln at the age of twenty-four and Chancellor of England at the age of twenty-nine, he was, throughout his life, immersed in the political life of his country. Waynflete, who was the son of a country squire of Lincolnshire, owed his preferment to his ability, for he was a successful schoolmaster, first at Winchester and then at the newly founded college at Eton. Although, by his ability and his position, he was drawn into politics and was for a time Lord Chancellor, his real interests were scholastic, and his greatest gift to posterity the foundation of Magdalen College, Oxford.

These two bishops, lying side by side in their cathedral, represent the two chief concerns of the leading churchmen during the fifteenth century—politics and education. For this century, with all its wars and divisions and destruction, was still a period of advance and of progress towards that more civilized and intellectual life which we associate with the Renaissance. Such progress as was made was mainly in the towns where trade was flourishing, fortunes were being made, gilds were being formed, and a new class of prosperous and educated citizens was coming into being.

Yet the century was one of almost continuous war. The revolution of 1399 which brought Henry IV to the throne came in the middle of the Hundred Years' War which had begun far back in 1337 and dragged on until 1453, when the English were finally driven out of France. Back came troops and adventurers to their native land without occupation and without settled homes. These were men who, whether as commanders of armies or as private soldiers, were trained for fighting and had little interest in the humdrum affairs of civilian life. It was, therefore, not altogether surprising that, two years after the return of the soldiers from France, civil war should break out in England, the so-called Wars of the Roses, which, though they caused much damage and loss of life, broke the power of the great barons and made possible the stern, strong government of the Tudors. When Richard III fell on Bosworth Field in 1485 and Henry Tudor ascended the throne, the chief need of the country was for security and order. This Henry set himself to achieve by what appeared to many as a dull and pedestrian policy, but it was a policy which, while paying due deference to the rights of the people, enormously strengthened the power of the throne. The result was that by the end of the century the country was far more united, far more self-conscious and far more alert than it had been for many centuries.

Into the complicated politics and rivalries of the time most of the leading churchmen were inevitably drawn, for many were members of the families most closely involved, or owed their preferment to the favour of the king or of some magnate. But, behind personal and family quarrels, lay a growing desire for national solidarity and unity. Men were beginning to dream dreams of a country where men would live together in freedom and unity, where trade and industry would flourish, and where religion and learning would advance together in the ways of wisdom and truth. A new day was breaking; new opportunities were arising; ideas and customs which men had long accepted as natural were now beginning to look a little tarnished and out of date. All this, with the rise of a new class of educated laymen, did much to arouse a sense of dissatisfaction with the existing state of affairs and a desire to sweep away all abuses and injustices in both Church and State.

For some two hundred years there had been, in England, a growing uneasiness at the development of papal policy. Apart from a few hot-heads, no one denied for a moment the necessity of the papacy, but papal pretensions and exactions, especially where they affected the political and economic life of the country, came to be more and more resented. The 'Babylonish Captivity' of the fourteenth century, which identified the papacy with the natural enemies of England, had been succeeded by a greater degradation when, for nearly forty years, the papacy was divided and two rival popes reigned, one in Avignon and the other in Rome. The Great Schism did much to intensify the existing distress and anxiety which many thoughtful men felt about the future of Western Christendom, and when one council after another was shipwrecked on the rocks of personal pride and political ambition men began to despair of any hope of reform.

The Great Schism ended with the election of Martin V in 1417, a strong and ambitious pope who was anxious to restore the power and wealth of the papacy and did his utmost to secure the repeal of the anti-papal legislation which had been passed by the English Parliament in the preceding century.[1] Recognizing Henry Beaufort as the most influential prelate in England, he made him a cardinal in order to win his support, and heaped insults and threats on the head of Archbishop Chichele, whose half-hearted attempts to persuade the House of Commons to repeal the statutes of *Provisors* and *Praemunire* met with no success. But though Martin's vigorous policy came to little, later popes continued to press their claims, and managed, at a time when the country was torn by civil war, to get some of their nominees appointed to English bishoprics, the *Statutes of Provisors* notwithstanding. Many of the bishops in the latter part of the fifteenth century and down to the breach with Rome were, in fact, appointed by the pope, and a number of them were Italians, especially at Worcester.

Meanwhile the Church in England had domestic problems of its own to face. John Wyclif had died in 1384 leaving behind him a number of highly controversial pamphlets and a body of disciples prepared to face danger and death in the propagation of their faith. These disciples, who came to be known as 'Lollards',[2] were a mixed group containing some discontented clergy as well as a number of educated laymen, but they were united in their desire for reform in the Church and in their belief in Wyclif as a prophet. Unfortunately their practical demands for reform were often mixed with a good deal of vulgar criticism of the clergy, both secular and regular; and

[1] See above, p. 116.
[2] The original meaning of the word was 'a wandering chanter', but it came to be associated with the Latin word *lolia*, tares; see H. B. Workman, *John Wyclif*, i, p. 327.

it was inevitable that action should be taken against them. A demand that they should be silenced led in 1401 to the savage statute *De heretico comburendo*,[1] which enacted that such as refused to abjure their heretical opinions should be tried by their bishop and, if found guilty, be handed over by him to the civil authorities to be publicly burnt.

The act was quickly applied. William Sawtre, a leading Lollard, was seized, tried, condemned and burnt to death on March 2, 1401—the first of a long line of martyrs, both clergy and laity, who suffered the supreme penalty rather than abandon their beliefs. At first the persecution did little to stop the spread of Lollard ideas, and in 1407 Archbishop Arundel, that 'hammer of the heretics', was obliged to summon a provincial council at Oxford to institute a censorship of books, while he himself carried out a most unpopular visitation of the University of Oxford four years later. Finally he turned against one of the most conspicuous of the Lollard party, Sir John Oldcastle, a soldier, scholar and friend of the king. Oldcastle was examined and convicted, but while awaiting execution he escaped from the Tower and was at large for four years before being recaptured and burnt in 1417.

The first quarter of the fifteenth century was, therefore, an uneasy time. Heresy, which had been common in many parts of Europe since the twelfth century, had not hitherto caused much trouble to the Church in England; but, for a short time, the disciples of Wyclif managed to make themselves very troublesome to the church authorities. By about 1430 the movement had been more or less silenced and suppressed, though it went on underground for some time, stirring up hostility to all church endowments, especially those of the monks, making and distributing copies of the Bible in the vernacular, and trying to persuade men of the wickedness of the friars and the falsity of the doctrine of transubstantiation.

ii. *Bishops and their Clergy*

When Edward Story, Bishop of Chichester, visited the parish of Selmeston in 1479 he found that the vicar, though a canon regular, was wearing the habit of a secular. He immediately ordered the man to be arrested and taken to Chichester, where he was locked up in the

[1] Gee and Hardy, *Documents*, pp. 133-7.

prison within the bishop's palace.[1] This trifling incident in the normal business of a medieval prelate will serve to remind us that, in the eyes of his clergy, a bishop was often far more a magistrate and administrator than a loving father-in-God. Nor is this to be wondered at when we consider who the bishops were and how they came to be appointed.

When a vacancy occurred, the king selected a man whom he thought would be useful to him and forwarded his name to the pope for ratification. If the pope did not agree, the see remained empty until some settlement had been reached. When the candidate had been finally selected, the cathedral chapter, who in theory were the electors, were ordered to choose the man proposed. Neither the chapter nor the archbishop had much influence on the election which, as often as not, was merely the result of a bargain between king and pope. Having been formally elected by his chapter the bishop-designate did homage to the king and was duly consecrated and enthroned.

His next task was to carry out a 'primary visitation' of his diocese to check up on his clergy and to satisfy himself that their 'letters of orders' were correct and that they were all legally entitled to their benefices and preferments. Having done this the bishop, as often as not, retired from his diocese and devoted himself to the affairs of state, paying only infrequent visits to his flock and leaving the administration of the diocese to his vicar-general and official-principal. To these officers was delegated the legal and formal work of the diocese, while the spiritual side was commonly farmed out to suffragan bishops, who frequently held Irish sees or bishoprics *in partibus* and were glad of a little extra money. The diocesan, therefore, played little part in the spiritual life of the parishes and was identified in the minds of his people with a set of legal officials who were much to be feared. 'The language of the episcopal chancery is pious and edifying; the preambles of its common forms are full of unction; but the objects for which the whole organization has been built up are legal and judicial.'[2]

The growth of the bishop's chancery and the concentration of power in the hands of his legal officers had largely undermined the authority of the lesser diocesan officials, the archdeacons and rural deans. In the past, these officers had held regular courts and wielded

---

[1] MS. Register of Edward Story, i, f. 21.
[2] A. H. Thompson, *The English Clergy and their Organization in the Later Middle Ages* (1947), pp. 70-71.

considerable power, but by now their authority had been largely usurped by the bishop's legal staff and their offices had become little more than sinecures.

The great cathedral chapters continued much as they had done in the past. Pluralism and absenteeism among dignitaries and prebendaries continued as before, but the work of the cathedral was carried on mainly by a small group of residentiaries and by the priest-vicars. These latter were in process of organization and had formed themselves into corporations modelled upon the chapter. They often lived together in a college with their own common hall and chapel. They elected one of their own number as warden or provost and appointed other members as chamberlain, bursar, pitancier and so forth. They drew up statutes which received official sanction and employed servants to look after them.[1] But, in spite of this, the number of priest-vicars was falling, largely owing to the introduction into the cathedrals of paid singing men or lay clerks whose services were necessary for the performance of the more complicated polyphonic music which was now coming into favour.

Out in the parishes the conditions remained much as before. Appropriations of benefices continued, though on a much smaller scale and more often to educational foundations rather than to the religious houses. One of the practices which caused some concern to the authorities was the exchange of livings between incumbents. This had become so common that brokers set themselves up to accommodate those who were anxious for an exchange, and the system of 'chop-churches' came under episcopal disfavour.[2]

The parochial clergy continued to cultivate their land as they had done for many centuries. They were still poorly educated, for the universities could provide for only a very small proportion of those who entered the ministry each year, and most of those who had received any higher education were destined for an academic or legal career. The ideal of an educated man and a graduate in each parish was of much later date. But though simple and poorly educated, the parochial clergy of England were by no means illiterate or immoral, and Thomas More could write of them that 'in learning and honest living' they were 'well able to match, number for number, the spirituality of any nation Christian'.[3]

---

[1] See F. Harrison, *Life in a Medieval College* (1952).
[2] Wilkins, *Concilia*, iii, pp. 215-17.   [3] *Dialogue*, Bk. iii, chap. 11.

A few parishes continued to be served by regulars—monks, canons, and even friars. The general decay of the religious orders had, in fact, meant an increase in the number of regulars who preferred the comparative liberty of the parish church to the restrictions of the cloister. Over twenty Franciscan friars received papal licence to hold benefices in England in the fifteenth century.

The later Middle Ages saw the growth in importance and power of the laity in parochial life. The office of churchwarden, originally known as *oeconomus*, came into being early in the twelfth century. In early days these officers had charge of certain small funds raised by rents from land and by the letting out of implements. The wardens, who might be either men or women, were elected by the parishioners, and held office normally for one year only. As time went by, their authority and responsibilities increased as money or land was left under their care for the upkeep of the church. They were expected to keep accounts of their stewardship and to provide not only for the laity's share in the repair of the fabric, but also in the provision of books, ornaments and all other things necessary for the performance of divine worship. The accounts which they kept provide one of the most interesting sources for our knowledge of parish life in the fifteenth and sixteenth centuries.[1]

But perhaps the most distinctive development in parochial life in the fourteenth and fifteenth centuries was the growth of chantries. Before this time those who wished for the prayers of the Church after their death normally obtained them by endowing or giving money to a monastery or other religious foundation. In exchange for such gifts the monks inscribed the names of the benefactors in their 'book of life' and saw that they were remembered in their prayers. As men's confidence in the monastic orders began to wane their benefactions were transferred to the foundation of chantries or endowment of priests to say daily Masses for the souls of the benefactors and their families. By the fifteenth century all the larger churches contained a number of such chantries, often signified by a separate altar or chantry-chapel, and there were probably few parish churches in England without some such foundation.

A chantry was a benefice to which a priest was duly instituted, and

[1] See J. C. Cox, *Churchwardens' Accounts* (1913) and such interesting transcripts as *Churchwardens' Accounts, 1349–1560*, ed. by Bishop Hobhouse (Somerset Record Society, 1890) and *Medieval Records of a London City Church* (*St. Mary-at-Hill*) *1420–1559*, ed. H. Littlehales in E.E.T.S. Original Series, No. 128 (1905).

it could sometimes be very profitable. The work was light—for it entailed only the saying of a daily Mass with the Office for the Dead —and the remuneration was often generous. The demand for such posts was therefore great, and Chaucer commends his 'pore persoun' for sticking to his job and not rushing off 'to London, un-to seynt Poules, to seken him a chaunterie for soules'. Many chantries, especially those which were poorly endowed, were served by stipendiary chaplains who managed to supplement their slender incomes by doing a little teaching or other odd jobs, though the chantry itself was intended to be sufficient to support a priest. But the fact that there was so little to do, and that the chantry-priest was not under the jurisdiction of the incumbent of the parish, led to endless quarrels and many abuses.

The chantry system also led to the formation of a number of new collegiate foundations. In some instances a parish church was turned into a collegiate church served by a number of clergy each of whom was in a sense, a chantry-priest. In other places a college of chantry-priests was attached to a parish church as a separate foundation independent of the parochial clergy, though using the same building. A third type of chantry was the extra-parochial foundation of a college of priests such as S. George's, Windsor. Many of these latter foundations had a definite educational purpose or, as at Eton, had a school attached to them, and those which had such a purpose to fulfil were by far the most valuable element in the chantry system.[1]

iii. *The Decay of the Religious Orders*

The urge to found religious houses, which had been so strong in the twelfth and early thirteenth centuries, had practically spent itself by the year 1300. After that date very few new houses came into being, the chief exceptions being the seven Carthusian monasteries where a kind of asceticism was practised which the older orders had never attempted to provide, and the house of Bridgettine nuns and brethren at Syon in Middlesex. At the same time, although the number of men and women in the religious houses was falling steadily, and had done since about 1200, most monasteries managed to keep themselves going right up to the dissolution. The most noticeable loss to monasticism was the closing down of all the alien priories,

[1] See K. L. Wood-Legh, *Perpetual Chantries in Britain* (1965).

or houses owing allegiance to some foreign abbey. These were all dissolved during the French wars and their revenues and endowments diverted to educational and other work. The military order of the Knights Templars was, for other reasons, closed down in 1312. Otherwise very few religious houses went out of existence, and those that did had clearly outlived their day. The nunnery of S. Radegund at Cambridge, for example, was dissolved by the Bishop of Ely in 1496, since the number of nuns had been reduced to two, of whom one was living elsewhere and the other was of doubtful reputation.

The numbers attracted to the monastic life had been falling for some time before the Black Death, in 1349, killed off so large a part of the population. Men were not now being drawn to the life of the cloister. For those who wanted opportunities of study the universities provided a much more stimulating environment. For the ascetic and contemplative the hermitage became the natural home. Meanwhile falling receipts and rising costs also tended to keep the numbers down, since chapters were anxious not to have to maintain more than their funds would allow.

Early monasticism had offered a way of life which was austere and communal. Over many years the high standards of austerity had been gradually relaxed, and by the fifteenth century no one could suppose that the monk or canon lived a more rigorous life than did those outside the cloister. The list of necessary articles which each novice at Ely was required to provide for himself—including bed-linen, five habits, various undergarments, furs, silver, etc.[1]—shows that the standard of living was not as simple as it had once been. In food and clothing and the amenities and comforts of life the average monk was probably a good deal better off than his brother in the world. Meanwhile the old communal life of the monastery, when monks lived together and had everything in common, was beginning to break down. Private property, which had been so sternly condemned by visiting prelates, was now becoming more common, and most monks had acquired some measure of privacy either through becoming obedientiaries with separate rooms, or by the provision of 'carells' or divisions of the cloister which monks could appropriate to their own use.

Episcopal visitations and injunctions, of which a good many have

[1] Cf. R. H. Snape, *English Monastic Finances in the Later Middle Ages* (1926), p. 160.

10

been preserved,[1] give us a picture of a way of life which has obviously departed a good deal from the intentions of its founders. There was probably not as much immorality as is sometimes supposed, but the general picture is one of a number of easy-going communities of men (and of women) who enjoyed their sport, entertained their friends, dressed well and ate well and looked after their own affairs with the care and attention of trained business men. Owning a very large proportion of the land of England, they played a very important part in the social and economic life of their age. Among the poor they were not unpopular, since the monasteries continued to give alms, mainly in the form of food left over from the monks' meals; but among the landowners, and with the civic authorities of the growing towns, there was a good deal of hostility towards what could not but appear as an effete institution which had outlived its day and was living upon its spiritual and moral capital.

The various orders of friars had come in for a great deal of criticism at the hands of men like Langland, Chaucer and Wyclif. The chief accusation against them was one of hypocrisy, for men felt that the friars claimed for themselves a spiritual ascendancy to which they were in no way entitled. Certainly, by the fifteenth century they had lost much of their early fervour and idealism. Gone now were the days when they walked barefoot through the snow to tend the sick and poor in the slums of the cities. But that they continued to hold the respect of the people as a whole, apart from the satirical poets and writers, is shown by the fact that 'letters of fraternity' were eagerly sought by the laity, that burials in friars' churches continued to be popular, and that legacies to the friars went on right up to the eve of the dissolution.

At Oxford and Cambridge the friars were becoming more and more absorbed into the academic life of the universities. As the universities grew in self-consciousness, as they acquired statutes and constitutions, as they erected their own buildings, and, above all, as the collegiate system developed, the presence of the friars became more and more of an anomaly, and they were obliged either to submit to university discipline or to leave altogether. In fact they became absorbed into the academic life of the place, though, wedded as many of them were to the old scholasticism, their methods and

---

[1] See especially *Visitations of Religious Houses in the Diocese of Lincoln*, edited by A. H. Thompson, Lincoln Record Society, vols. 7, 14 and 21.

opinions were coming to look more and more barren and withered and out of date. The old battles had been fought out. Men's thoughts were turning now to other things, and the more intelligent of the friars realized this and joined forces with their fellow-scholars. Meanwhile in the Franciscan Order a new movement towards a stricter observance of the rule had been taking place in Europe. The minority of rigorists had preserved an unbroken succession from the time of S. Francis' death, and, by the fifteenth century, had become organized as a separate branch of the order, known as the Observants. Although this was officially recognized as early as 1415, it did not make any appearance in England until about 1480, when three new friaries were founded and three others changed over to the stricter observance. At first these were under the province of Cologne, but they became a province of their own in 1499. The Observant Friars mark the last attempt at the reform of any religious order before the dissolution.[1]

iv. *Art and Architecture*

At the beginning of the fourteenth century the English architects and designers were exercising their imaginations to the full on the style of building known as the 'Decorated'. This, which had grown naturally out of the Early English, lent itself to many kinds of elaboration, especially in the tracery of the windows and by the reintroduction of figure sculpture. But about the middle of the fourteenth century, in the West of England, a variation of style occurred which spread eastwards and produced the typically English style of the later Middle Ages known as the 'Perpendicular'. From the time of the narrow lancets of the twelfth century there had been a constant demand for larger windows, partly in order to give more light in the churches and partly to provide opportunities for coloured glass. By the introduction at Gloucester, about 1340, of the horizontal transom in the tracery of the windows, it was discovered that the area of glass could be enormously increased, and the goal for which designers had been striving for two hundred years or more had been reached. The new style became so popular that in the fifteenth century many

[1] See A. G. Little, *Introduction of the Observant Friars into England*, from the *Proceedings of the British Academy*, vol. xi (1923).

English churches and cathedrals were practically rebuilt. Coinciding as it did with the prosperity of the merchant classes, this discovery led to a great deal of new building, and parish churches all over the country were provided with new naves or chancels or aisles, or with new and larger windows. Meanwhile, also, the Perpendicular style was itself improved upon and elaborated, especially in such auxiliary arts as the invention of lierne and fan vaulting. By the latter part of the fifteenth century the architects were able to produce buildings of extraordinary grace and delicacy, made more brilliant by large areas of coloured glass. The chapel of King's College, Cambridge, provides a perfect example of the best that the new style could produce.

The vast windows, with their rectangular divisions, greatly encouraged the art of the glazier, lending themselves either to large pictures occupying the whole of a window, or to a series of scenes from the Bible or from the lives of the saints. Meanwhile in all parts of the church the tendency was ever more and more towards greater richness and elaboration. Stone and wood screens with rich carving or painting, alabaster figures and altar-pieces, effigies in wood or stone or bronze, canopied tombs, heavily carved sedilia, niches, font-covers, stalls and bosses, all worked out on the most intricate and elaborate designs, contributed to a splendour of decoration far surpassing anything which the country had so far seen. And if the Perpendicular style was itself, in comparison with the Decorated, somewhat monotonous and uniform, this was amply compensated for by the variety and virtuosity of the detail.

In the making and illustrating of liturgical and devotional books the later Middle Ages saw a vast increase of production with a corresponding decline in inspiration. In the early fourteenth century the most popular book had been the Psalter, many noble copies of which were produced and illustrated with a charm and fertility of imagination which has been the delight of later generations. The Ormesby Psalter,[1] the Tickhill Psalter,[2] Queen Mary's Psalter,[3] and the Luttrell Psalter,[4] are all magnificent specimens of this type of art. The chief glory of such works are the marginal sketches of beasts and monsters,

[1] 1285–1300, now in the Bodleian. Reproduced by the Roxburgh Club in 1926.
[2] 1303–4, now in the New York Public Library. See D. D. Egbert, *The Tickhill Psalter and Related MSS.* (New York, 1940).
[3] Early fourteenth century, now in the British Museum. Reproduced in 1912 with introduction by Sir George Warner.
[4] C. 1340, now in the British Museum. See *The Luttrell Psalter* with Introduction by E. G. Millar (1932).

of stories from the Bible and from the lives of the saints, and, above all, of scenes from the everyday life of peasants and country folk pursuing their ordinary occupations. In all this art there is a child-likeness and simplicity which is wholly delightful. But from the middle of the fourteenth century onwards much of this charm was lost. The *Book of Hours* became the popular devotional manual of the laity and was in great demand among the rising class of prosperous and educated lay men and women. Though technically the standard of production remained high, inspiration seems to have flagged a little, and much of the simplicity of the earlier art was lost in a much more mature and commonplace style. Finally, with the invention of printing, the whole art of caligraphy and decoration gave place to typography and the woodcut.

In the realm of church music the Gregorian plain-chant had been originally introduced into England by S. Augustine in 597 and had been spread by James the Deacon and Theodore of Tarsus. In later years it had been encouraged by men like S. Dunstan, himself an accomplished musician and organ-builder, and the standard of singing probably stood fairly high at the time of the Norman Conquest. The effect of the Conquest was to introduce part-singing and to make the music of the Liturgy more elaborate. John of Salisbury thought that this 'defiled the service of religion' by its 'womanish affectations in the mincing of notes and sentences',[1] while the Cistercian, Ailred of Rievaulx, complained both of the singing in parts and of the organ accompaniments. 'To what purpose', he cried, 'is that terrible blowing of belloes, expressing rather the crakes of thunder than the sweetnesse of a voyce?'[2]

By the thirteenth century the cathedrals and larger parish churches were beginning to employ choirs of men and boys and thus encouraged the development of polyphonic music, which, as time went on, became more and more complicated as the choirs increased in efficiency and technique. At first the music had all been prescribed by the Liturgy, but new works began to appear to supply material for the choirs, and, by the first half of the fifteenth century, an English school of composition, both sacred and secular, had grown up, encouraged by Henry VI, himself an accomplished musician. John

---

[1] *Policraticus*, i, 6.
[2] *Speculum Charitatis*, ii, 23; from Prynne's translation quoted in W. H. Hadow, *English Music* (1931), p. 11.

Dunstable, who died in 1453, was the most distinguished member of this school and the greatest composer in Europe at that period. By the close of the Middle Ages there is no doubt that church music in England was of a high order and acknowledged as such in other parts of the world.

v. *The New Thought*

While the greater part of the academic world was engaged in the subtleties of Scholasticism and the endless war between Realists and Nominalists fought out in the disputations of the schools, a few individuals had, for some time, been interesting themselves in a different and more scientific approach to truth. In the early part of the thirteenth century Robert Grosseteste had turned his encyclopaedic mind to the problems of the text of the Bible and had taken what was then the unusual step of learning both Greek and Hebrew in order to discover the real meaning of the Scriptures and the origins of Christianity. His pupil at Oxford, the Franciscan, Roger Bacon (*c.* 1214–92) had gone even further. Not only did he study Greek, Hebrew and Arabic, but he also developed a new method of acquiring knowledge by means of experiment, boldly publicising his conclusions even where they conflicted with the accepted doctrines of the Church. Bacon maintained the right of every student to pursue his search for truth no matter where it led, so challenging the Church's doctrine of authority. He carried out a number of experiments in the use of lenses, discovered the principle of the telescope and microscope, learned something of anatomy and the use of drugs, compiled a large number of mathematical tables and produced a new and better formula for the making of gunpowder. Bacon was, in most ways, far in advance of his times, and, like other pioneers, was misunderstood and persecuted. But he laid the foundations of all later scientific research, and was the most interesting thinker of his generation.[1]

The risks incurred by those who took an independent line were so great that perhaps it is no wonder that most men were content to follow the safer and more orthodox paths. Yet the study of the literal meaning of the Bible continued to attract scholars (among them the Cambridge Franciscan, Henry of Costesy, early in the fourteenth

[1] See *Roger Bacon: Commemoration Essays*, ed. A. G. Little (1914).

century) and was continued intermittently until the days of Erasmus and Colet on the very eve of the Reformation.

If Roger Bacon may be said to have stood for Reason rather than Authority, then we may discern a disciple of his in Reginald Pecock (c. 1395–1461). Pecock began as an opponent of the Lollards, taking up the defence of the clergy against Wycliffite criticism in his book *The Repressor of Overmuch Blaming of the Clergy*. Later he was himself accused of heresy, had all his books publicly burned, and, though Bishop of Chichester, was for a time imprisoned in Thorney Abbey. The charge against him was his rationalist approach to theology: all knowledge, he said, was to be subjected to 'the doom of reason'. It was this which led him to doubt some of the articles of the Christian faith—such as the descent of Christ into hell; and the Church naturally took action against him.[1]

Among those whose anger was roused by Pecock's speculations was Thomas Gascoigne (1403–58) Chancellor of Oxford University, a man of simple tastes, retiring, donnish, and pessimistic. His most famous book, *Veritates Collectae*, was written in the form of a theological word-book and was filled with criticisms of the clergy, both secular and regular. Like Giraldus Cambrensis, three hundred years earlier, he revelled in stories of ignorant clergy, and poured scorn on those who tripped up in their Latin or made foolish statements such as that of the Archdeacon of Oxford who declared: 'I believe there are three gods in one person; I believe what God believes'.[2]

Meanwhile in Italy the so-called 'Classical Renaissance' had begun. As early as the fourteenth century Petrarch had sung the glories of ancient Rome, and it was not long before a discovery of the splendour of Greek literature was made. The movement, which took Italy by storm, was slow in reaching England; but, by the end of the fifteenth century there was a group of humanists at Oxford, including Grocyn and Linacre, while Erasmus at Cambridge was encouraging the study of Greek and inspiring younger men like Roger Ascham.

Humanism had begun outside the universities which were, at first, suspicious and hostile. But it soon forced an entry, and largely changed the direction of men's thoughts and the methods of study. For, by now, the old Scholasticism was more or less played out. The

---

[1] V. H. H. Green, *Bishop Reginald Pecock* (1945). The *Repressor* was published in the Rolls Series in 1860, edited by C. Babington.

[2] Extracts from this work were published by J. E. T. Rogers under the title of *Loci e Libro Veritatum* (1881).

questions which it raised had all been discussed so long that there was really nothing new to say. Men were tired of the subtleties of metaphysic and interested more in history and the sifting of evidence. The discovery that certain documents, such as the 'Donation of Constantine', were palpable forgeries had had a twofold effect, for it had whetted men's appetites for scientific research and had struck a hard blow at Authority. Scholars were beginning to see, what Roger Bacon had seen nearly three centuries before, that truth depended not on the weight of authority but on the evidence of indisputable facts which could be hammered out, not by the old method of the schools, but by the newer method of the law-courts.

About the year 1500 there were three men in England who stand out as leading Humanists. The eldest of them was John Colet (1466–1519), born in London and educated at Oxford. In 1505 he became Dean of St. Paul's, where he proved to be a great preacher, intolerant of every kind of weakness and insincerity, critical of contemporary abuses, and with a great love of truth. His lectures on the *Epistle to the Romans*, in which he abandoned the old allegorical and mystical approach to the Scriptures and set himself to discover what S. Paul was really trying to say and the historical conditions in which the letter was written, marked a new step forward in Biblical research and exegesis. Anxious to balance his criticisms of the present with some positive contribution towards reform, he devoted much of his wealth to the foundation of St. Paul's school for 153 poor boys. His own great love for children and desire to win them for Christ gave him a great interest in his foundation for which he drew up elaborate rules. Stern, self-disciplined, courageous, generous, Colet represents the best type of practical scholar and reformer.[1]

His contemporary, Desiderius Erasmus (1467–1536) was a very different kind of man. Born in Rotterdam, he was early affected by the Italian Humanists, and was one of the first to bring the new learning to his native country. He was not, at first, specially interested in Biblical studies, but after his visits to England and his friendship with Colet, he turned his mind to a careful study of the text of the Greek New Testament. He worked for a while at Oxford, then at London and finally at Cambridge where he found a number of scholars engaged on similar tasks. As a result of his studies he published, first, the *Novum Instrumentum*—a corrected Greek text with prefaces and

[1] See J. A. R. Marriott, *Life of John Colet* (1933).

annotations—and then the *Paraphrases* or commentaries which became one of the standard books of the Reformation and in 1547 was to be compulsorily acquired by 'every parson, vicar, curate, chantry priest and stipendiary' in England.[1] Unlike Colet, Erasmus was a timid man who never came out into the open. Full of scholarship and wit, he yet hated to declare himself openly or to take sides in controversy. But his studies on the text of the Bible influenced the work of scholars for many generations.[2]

The third of the famous triumvirate, Sir Thomas More (1478–1535) represents the Renaissance ideal of the 'full man', equally distinguished as scholar, statesman, churchman and host. Trained as a lawyer, he was also a competent theologian and a critic of both Church and State. He sympathized with the new learning, especially in its desire to bring all that was best in the ancient thought of mankind to the service of his own day, but was bitterly opposed to the new ideas which the continental reformers were beginning to propagate. Steeped in Canon Law and in Augustinian theology, he was fundamentally a medievalist who, in the end, gave his life in the cause of the unity of the Western Church.[3]

vi. *Church and Society about 1500*

What place did the Church hold in the general life of the country about the year 1500? This is just the sort of question which the historian finds so difficult to answer. Leading events and great personalities make a mark on history and can be discussed and studied and adjudged. But the everyday affairs of the ordinary man—the merchant, the craftsman, the peasant, the tradesman—leave little record behind them. And if it is difficult to say what the ordinary man was doing, it is even more difficult to say what he was thinking.

Throughout the Middle Ages the Church had occupied a very important place in society. The responsibility of Church-membership was not then, as it is today, a matter of choice which a man may accept or refuse without in any way jeopardizing his position in society. In the Middle Ages everyone belonged to the Church and

[1] J. R. Tanner, *Tudor Constitutional Documents* (1922), p. 101.
[2] See P. S. Allen, *The Age of Erasmus* (1914).
[3] See R. W. Chambers, *Thomas More* (1935).

recognized the right of the Church to control his life in this world and in the next. Everyone expected the Church to levy a tax on his income, and acknowledged its right to do so. Everyone accepted the fact that if he were guilty of a breach of one of the Church's laws he would suffer for it by fine or imprisonment or a public flogging. Everyone looked to the Church to provide education, leadership, poor-relief, sick nursing and any other social amenities which were obtainable. Everyone acknowledged the right of the Church to deprive him of spiritual comfort in this world and to give him his ticket either to endless bliss or to unspeakable torment in the life to come. The power of the Church weighed heavily on the ordinary man, and its demands upon him were often very great; but there were very few who were inclined to question the Church's authority or defy its power.

It was in the thirteenth century that the Church had reached the summit of its power. By 1500 that power was beginning to wane. The extravagant claims made by earlier popes such as Gregory VII and Boniface VIII could hardly have been made after the 'Babylonish Captivity' and the Great Schism. The Church was now in close partnership with the secular power, but few churchmen would have dared now to say that the secular power existed only to serve the Church. The average churchman would by this time probably have been content to say what the writer of the *Epistle to Diognetus* had said in the second century: that 'what the soul is in a body, this the Christians are in the world'. More and more was it coming to be recognized that the State had its own existence and its own rights and privileges; it was the duty of the Church to provide the spiritual and religious background to the lives of men.

The typical village of the later Middle Ages was a cluster of tiny cottages with the church brooding over them with its lofty walls, massive tower and often soaring spire. Every man, woman and child in the village was thus kept perpetually aware of the presence of the Church and of its power. The same was true of the towns, which were packed with churches which jostled each other in the narrow streets.[1] And each church had its staff of priests, deacons and clerks, each chantry chapel or altar its stipendiaries, each religious house or hospital its community of religious. No man could have walked

[1] The little town of Chichester in 1500 in addition to its cathedral, had at least a dozen parish churches, two friaries and two hospitals.

many yards in any English town without meeting someone in holy orders, whether secular or religious.

Moreover the Church kept in very close touch with the lives of the people. In addition to the regular services on week-days and Sundays it controlled all education and all poor-relief. It provided, by processions, plays and spectacles, the chief recreation of the people. It formed the background of markets and fairs. It watched over and to some extent organized the gilds of craftsmen and tradesmen. And the churches themselves were respected and often loved by the people, who, according to their ability, showered gifts of vestments, books, ornaments and plate upon them, as early inventories and churchwardens' accounts will show.

In addition to the parish churches there was a large number of monastic houses varying greatly in size from the great abbeys like Westminster and St. Albans to the tiny 'cells' and hospitals which contained only a handful of men or women. Most of the towns had three or four religious houses in them while the countryside was studded with abbeys and priories; and the monk, canon or friar was a familiar figure in society. Yet the religious houses were, by the end of the fifteenth century, living very much on the past. Most of them were crippled with heavy debts, while the number of monks had been steadily decreasing for some considerable time. Apart from occasional hospitality and small doles to the poor, the religious houses counted for little in the lives of men, and they had long ceased to contribute much to the life of the Church. To the ordinary man they were a relic of the past, magnificent in their rather shabby grandeur but out of touch with the new spirit which was abroad.

But if the regulars seemed remote and preoccupied, what of the secular clergy? How were they regarded by the men and women who worshipped day by day in their churches? The answer is that the ordinary parish priest—simple, frugal, industrious and neighbourly —was undoubtedly loved and respected by his parishioners. Many of the clergy were of peasant stock and understood and were understood by their people. On the other hand, there were some clergy who sprang from the richer classes and who made themselves unpopular by their avarice and irresponsibility. Thomas Wynter, the illegitimate son of Cardinal Wolsey, was a pluralist of the old style and a man who looked upon his benefices simply as sources of emolument. Such men have always made themselves both disliked and despised.

The bishops often fell under the same condemnation, partly because many of them had begun as pluralists and owed their appointment to royal favour, partly because they wielded so much power and were so closely concerned with legal and criminal proceedings. Even the best bishops, who were real spiritual leaders, found it very difficult to break through the barriers of suspicion and fear which separated them from their flocks. With the best will in the world, their intentions were as liable to be suspected as their attempts to win the love of their people were liable to be repulsed. The feeling of the ordinary man towards a bishop was not likely to be one either of love or respect but of fear and of awe.

Such a feeling, but in a more intense degree, was aroused by the papacy. Rome had long been unpopular in England partly because so much good English money was annually sent out of the country, partly because the pope continued to appoint Italian courtiers to English benefices, and partly because of the system of appeals to Rome which often delayed the execution of justice or resulted in a miscarriage. No one doubted the necessity of the papacy or the importance of a united Church. Few, if any, had as yet any conception of, or desire for, a 'national church'. But the papacy as a whole was disliked and to some extent distrusted, and many of those who would have been horrified at the thought of a breach with Rome would gladly have welcomed some reform of abuses.

In his own inner life the average Englishman of the later Middle Ages was undoubtedly deeply religious. There was, of course, a certain amount of superstition and false emphasis. Most people were illiterate and consequently credulous and uncritical. Moreover their credulity was sometimes exploited for purposes which were not always above suspicion. Relics and wonder-working shrines can be made very profitable, and such famous objects of pilgrimage as the Holy Rood of Boxley or the Blood of Hayles were undoubtedly used for financial gain. But apart from a certain amount of superstition the English as a whole were a religious nation and impressed foreign visitors as such. Moreover they were becoming more educated and more intelligent. The large number of grammar schools were turning out, year by year, not only a steady flow of men for the priesthood but also a stream of educated laymen who were beginning to take an interest in literature and theology and the arts. The fifteenth century, both before and after the invention of printing, witnessed a vast production of books of devotion in both Latin and English, which were bought by laymen and women, and presumably read by them.

This educated laity formed an important element among those who were conscious of abuses and keen for reform. Men were aware that big changes were taking place—social, economic, national and international—and were anxious to see a Church alive both to its responsibilities and opportunities. In its present condition the Church gave the impression of being conservative, secular and, in some ways, decadent. It was certainly greatly in need of reform. But those who, at the close of the fifteenth century, cared most about reform would have been among those most distressed at the course which the so-called 'Reformation' took in the following generation.

NOTE ON BOOKS

FOR general history, see E. F. Jacob, *The Fifteenth Century, 1399–1485*, being vol. vi of the *Oxford History of England* (1961). For the life of the Church see A. Hamilton Thompson, *The English Clergy and their Organization in the Later Middle Ages* (1947), Peter Heath, *The English Parish Clergy on the Eve of the Reformation* (1969), H. Maynard Smith, *Pre-Reformation England* (1938), J. Gairdner, *Lollardy and the Reformation in England*, 4 vols. (1908–11), J. A. F. Thomson, *The Later Lollards, 1414–1520* (1965) and M. D. Knowles, *The Religious Orders in England*, vol. ii (1955). See also *The Paston Letters, 1422–1509*, ed. J. Gairdner (various editions), H. S. Bennett, *The Pastons and their England* (1922) and F. Seebohm, *The Oxford Reformers* (1867).

PART III.

THE REFORMATION AND AFTER

CHAPTER XI

HENRY VIII
(1509–1547)

i. *Henry, Wolsey and the Succession*

WHEN the body of Henry VII was laid to rest in the magnificent chapel at Westminster Abbey which he himself had built, the crown devolved naturally and peacefully upon his seventeen-year old son, Henry, who, since the death of his brother Arthur in 1502, had been the heir apparent. The young prince certainly stepped into a rich heritage, for the cautious policy of his father had left him a kingdom far more united and self-confident than it had been for many a day. Moreover, the young Henry was fully qualified to make the most of his inheritance. Young, clever, handsome and debonair, he was already a great favourite with his people. He appeared to be the ideal of the Renaissance prince. The age delighted in learning; and the king was a gifted scholar who could discuss the theories of Thomas Aquinas with the most accomplished of his theologians. It delighted in sport; and the king was of such magnificent physique and athletic skill that few could beat him in any sport they cared to choose. It delighted in the arts; and the king was an accomplished poet and musician who could write both words and music of a lyric and then sing it to his own accompaniment on the virginals. It was also a religious age, but there was none so devout as the king, or so punctilious in the performance of his religious duties. It was over a brilliant court that Henry presided, but none was so brilliant as the king himself. The reign of Henry VII may have been sombre and austere, but when young Harry ascended the throne the lights went up, the music began to play and 'jest and youthful jollity' became the order of the day.

With such gifts and such an inheritance we should not be surprised to find that Henry was also a determined egoist. Into whatever sphere of life he entered he expected to have his own way. And he generally succeeded in getting it, though not, at first, by naked tyranny but by extreme astuteness and by the gift of persuading people that what he

11
161

was doing was for their own good. Henry had a conscience, and in a curious way he respected the conscientious scruples of his people; yet his own conscience was wonderfully elastic and could generally be found to support his own interests. His power of self-justification was superb. He sacked Wolsey and persuaded people that he was saving them from a public enemy; he robbed the monasteries under pretence of getting rid of a vicious institution; he broke off his marriage with Katharine of Aragon on the grounds that he had done wrong to God in having ever married her. And so on. In all his work Henry was constantly appealing to the interests of his subjects—their patriotism, their prosperity, their consciences, their desire for order and progress after the Wars of the Roses. And people were prepared to put up with a good deal in exchange for a strong government.

Henry soon found a useful colleague in one of his father's civil servants, Thomas Wolsey. Wolsey, who was a native of Ipswich and of quite humble origins, entertained ambitions as great as, if not greater than, those of his master. Henry found him a most valuable servant and loaded him with preferment. He became rapidly Dean of Lincoln, Lord Chancellor, Abbot of St. Alban's, Bishop of Bath and Wells, Winchester, Durham and Tournai, Archbishop of York and a Cardinal. In 1529 he narrowly missed election as pope. If the king was the perfect Renaissance prince, Wolsey was the Renaissance prelate—immensely rich, powerful, hospitable, all but indispensable in both Church and State. The king loved him because he was ready to do all the jobs that Henry most disliked doing, and he persuaded the pope to create him *legatus a latere* in order that he might override the whole bench of English bishops. Wolsey's powers were, thus, immeasurable, and he made his influence felt in all walks of life. The bishops feared him; the nobility despised him; but the king trusted him, and the poor rejoiced in his hospitality. He was also a great benefactor to the cause of education, suppressing a number of small monasteries in order to found Cardinal College (Christ Church) at Oxford and a Grammar School at Ipswich as a nursery for scholars. Wolsey was thus a great power in the early part of the new reign and one can scarcely think of the king without the cardinal or the cardinal without the king. But the immense power of Wolsey had two effects. In the first place it showed how easily control of the Church in a country could find its way into the hands of one man—a lesson which was not lost on

the acute mind of Henry VIII. It also did much to foster anti-papal-
ism and anti-clericalism—a fact which probably also passed not un-
noticed by the king.

Wolsey shone with so bright a light during the years of his
ascendancy that the other bishops were thrown into the shade. The
gentle Warham at Canterbury had the mortification of being obliged
to take his orders from York, and the other bishops were in the same
plight. Most held conservative ideas: some looked back with nos-
talgia to the less flamboyant days of Henry VII. Few counted for
anything much in the policy of the state.

Meanwhile, however, a group of younger men was growing up,
who were beginning to take an interest in the new ideas which were
coming across the North Sea from Germany. In 1517 Martin Luther
had challenged the authority of the Church and started a movement
which soon had large areas of Europe hopelessly divided. Both his
theological and his political ideas soon began to find a footing in
England, where they were eagerly greeted by the remnant of the old
Lollard tradition which had lingered on, mainly in the south and
east of the country and among those engaged in the wool trade.

Early in the 1520's Lutheran teaching was being discussed at Cambridge where a group of enthusiasts was accustomed to meet at the
White Horse Tavern. Among these were Robert Barnes, who was
an Austin friar, Thomas Bilney, John Frith and probably a group
of future bishops and archbishops, including Thomas Cranmer,
Matthew Parker, Hugh Latimer and Nicholas Ridley. Here of an
evening Luther's works were read and his doctrines of Justification
by Faith or of the wickedness of the sale of indulgences were discussed. Similar discussions were also held in other parts of the country.
But the movement was looked upon with suspicion by those in
authority. The king much disliked what he had heard of Luther and
replied to his attack on the Sacraments by a counter-attack which
earned for him the pope's gratitude and that title of 'Defender of
the Faith' which the English sovereign still bears. But in spite of
royal disfavour the reforming movement continued to grow; and,
as disfavour hardened into active opposition, the reformers became
more courageous and determined. The issue was not clear, for many
of the reformers were implicated in the political as well as the religious ideas of the time, and the king was inclined to regard all who
disagreed with him as potential traitors. It was inevitable, therefore,

that those who went contrary to the policy of the king should suffer, and a number of men went gallantly to their deaths in defence of what they believed—Bilney in 1531, Frith in 1533 and Barnes in 1540.

Meanwhile a problem was arising far more serious than the aberrations of a few heretics. By the year 1527 Henry had been married for eighteen years, but although Katharine had borne him at least three sons and two daughters all, except one of the daughters, had died in infancy. Katharine being now forty years old it was becoming obvious that the chances of a male heir were slight. England had never been successfully ruled by a woman, and the outlook was serious indeed. Katharine had previously been the wife of Henry's elder brother Arthur who had died in 1502, and Henry would not in the normal course of events have been allowed to marry his deceased brother's wife. But in this instance the influence of the parents was so strong that the pope, Julius II, had been persuaded to grant a special dispensation. Then disaster had succeeded disaster, and the king was not the only one who began to wonder whether the whole thing had not been a mistake. True, a dispensation had been granted; but had the pope any power to override the laws of God? As early as 1514 rumours of a 'divorce' were going round, but the queen was then under thirty and there was still hope. By 1527 hope was practically dead.

It was then that Henry fell in love with Anne Boleyn, a lady of the court who possessed not only considerable personal charm but a number of intriguing and ambitious relatives. Henry was certainly in love with her, and the solution of all his anxieties about the succession seemed at hand. All that was needed was a papal indult declaring the previous marriage null and void and Henry would have been at liberty to marry Anne.

In normal circumstances this could have been done. Nullity decrees for distinguished and powerful people were often granted by the papal court, and Henry had a strong case. By marrying within the prohibited degrees he had transgressed the laws of God and had been punished.[1] To go on living with Katharine was to live in sin. Therefore the sooner it came to an end the better. Henry therefore summoned Wolsey and ordered him to make arrangements for the annulment of his marriage. Immediate application was made to Rome, but

[1] Cf. Leviticus xx, 21. For a detailed study of the legal problems of the divorce see J. J. Scarisbrick, *Henry VIII* (1968), pp. 163–97.

two major difficulties presented themselves. The first was the special dispensation granted by Julius II, the other the fact that at the moment the pope, Clement VII, could not afford to offend the emperor, Charles V, in whose hands he was then virtually a prisoner. Now Katharine was Charles's aunt.

The pope therefore played for time. If he could keep the matter in suspense for a year or two his political fortunes might change or Henry might tire of Anne. But time was the one thing which Henry could not afford to waste, and the next two years saw the king getting more and more exasperated while the pope procrastinated even to the extent of ordering his legates, Wolsey and Campeggio, to go as slowly as possible. After two years of disputes, discussions and delays the problem was no nearer solution and Henry's patience was exhausted. Egged on by the Boleyn family and the anti-clerical nobility he decided to get rid of Wolsey whom he now regarded as a block to all progress. Wolsey, at the height of his power and insolence, was indicted under the statute of *Praemunire* for having taken orders from a foreign power. He was deprived of his chancellorship and in 1530 arrested on a charge of high treason, but he died while on his way south and so was saved from having to face any earthly tribunal.[1] His place in the king's counsel was taken by Thomas Cromwell.

ii. *The Breach with Rome*

By 1531 Henry was becoming desperate. It was now four years since he had applied for the dissolution of his marriage and nothing had been done. Was the King of England to be thwarted and the future security of the country threatened because of the political fortunes of an Italian prince? So long as Wolsey was about, the personal representative of the pope in England, little could be done. But now that Wolsey had gone, the first obstacle had been overcome. But what of the rest of the clergy? Henry soon dealt with them. In 1531 he accused them all of a breach of *Praemunire* for having accepted Wolsey as legate, and then allowed them to save themselves from punishment on two conditions—one, the payment of a sum of £100,000; the other, the acknowledgment of Henry as 'Protector

[1] For Wolsey see M. Creighton, *Cardinal Wolsey* (1888) and A. F. Pollard, *Wolsey* (new ed. 1965).

and Supreme Head of the English Church and clergy'. The first condition they accepted; but the second was quite another matter. There was on earth only one head of the Church and that was the pope. To accept Henry's proposal would mean a personal insult to the pope and a complete break with the past. But the alternative was ruin. In the end a compromise was reached by the clergy acknowledging Henry as 'Singular Protector, only and supreme Lord, and, as far as the law of Christ allows, even Supreme Head' of the Church in England. Henry might not have got exactly what he wanted, but he had done remarkably well. He had made the clergy admit responsibility for a crime which they had not committed, and he had persuaded them to accept the Crown as an essential part of the constitution of the English Church. He could now turn again to the troublesome question of the divorce.

It was at this stage that a new figure appeared on the scene. The king, while lodging at Waltham Abbey in 1529, had made the acquaintance of a Cambridge tutor called Thomas Cranmer, who had put forward the suggestion that, in the matter of the legality of Henry's marriage (and therefore of the possibility of an annulment) the opinion of the academic world should be sought. Henry was grateful to the young don for this suggestion, and made a note of his name for future reference. The universities in England and many of those on the Continent had been circulated, and the reports were now coming in. Most of them were favourable to the king, but the means whereby they were obtained will not always bear investigation. Henry's cause was growing stronger every day.

His next move was to test the temper of Parliament and to play on the latent anti-clericalism of many of its members. A *Supplication against the Ordinaries*, which was a list of grievances against the bishops, was drawn up largely by Thomas Cromwell, passed by the House of Commons and presented to the king early in 1532. Gardiner, Bishop of Winchester, replied on behalf of the bishops, but the king was not interested in the reply. What interested him was not whether the charges were true or not, but how far they could be used to weaken any possible opposition from the clergy.[1]

Having cowed the clergy and made himself reasonably sure of the support of Parliament, Henry could now go forward with his scheme

[1] The *Supplication* is in Gee and Hardy, *Documents*, pp. 145-53, and Gardiner's reply on pp. 154-76.

for cutting England off from Rome and making himself, in fact as well as in name, 'Supreme Head' of the Church in England. Between 1532 and 1534 seven bills were passed through Parliament, each carefully designed to cut one of the threads which bound England to Rome.

The first act was the *Conditional Restraint of Annates*.[1] Annates were the first year's income of a see and were payable to Rome. The act complained of English money going abroad and declared that this must stop except for a small token payment of five per cent. And to make things easier for the bishops concerned, the act also stated that in future all bishops should be consecrated in England by the archbishop. In the meanwhile the Convocations had acknowledged the Royal Supremacy by pledging themselves not to make any new canons without the king's permission.[2]

In August 1532 Archbishop Warham died and the problem of his successor arose. Henry wanted Thomas Cranmer and the pope agreed, though he could not wholly approve of him since he had been associating with heretics, had married the niece of one of them, and had done a good deal to support the king's demand for a divorce. But Henry was not seriously worried about that, and Cranmer was consecrated on March 30, 1533. Henry was now in a hurry. He had been living with Anne Boleyn at least since December 1532; he had been secretly married to her in January 1533; and their first child was due in September. If this was to be the long-expected heir it was essential that he should be legitimate. But still the divorce proceedings were delayed, and Henry was in the most unsatisfactory position of having two wives living at the same time.

It was now that the second act was passed through Parliament, the *Act in Restraint of Appeals*.[3] Hitherto in all ecclesiastical causes the final appeal had been to Rome. This had long been unpopular, and the transference of all such appeals to an English court was naturally acceptable to Parliament. But this act also asserts that 'this realm of England is an empire' (that is, an independent, sovereign state) and that the king is supreme head of both Church and State. In this preamble lies the fundamental principle of the English Reformation. And it gave Henry just the extra power which he needed. He could now go forward rapidly, for no one could appeal to Rome against

---

[1] Gee and Hardy, *Documents*, pp. 178-86.
[2] *Ibid.* pp. 176-8.   [3] *Ibid.* pp. 187-95.

him. On May 23 Cranmer brought the long divorce proceedings to an end by declaring Henry's marriage to Katharine of Aragon null and void. Five days later his marriage to Anne Boleyn was made public. On June 1 Anne was crowned as queen. On July 11 a decree for the excommunication of Henry was drawn up by the pope; and on September 7 Anne's first child was born, the Princess Elizabeth.

From this point onwards there was only a certain amount of clearing up to be done, but Parliament was kept busy in 1534 putting the seal of legality on the breach with Rome. First came the *Submission of the Clergy and Restraint of Appeals*[1] which more or less re-enacted what had already been done; then the *Ecclesiastical Appointments Act*[2] which provided a formula for the election of a bishop and refers to the pope as 'the Bishop of Rome, otherwise called the pope'. This was followed by the *Dispensations Act*[3] which transferred the power of granting dispensations and licences from the pope to the Archbishop of Canterbury[4] and also abolished the ancient payment of 'Peter's Pence'. The next act, known as the *Supreme Head Act,*[5] not only gave the king the title which he had always sought (and that without any saving clause about the 'Law of Christ'); it also gave him the power to define doctrine and to punish heresy. The final act, the *Succession Act*[6] gave parliamentary sanction to the divorce, and made it possible for the king to demand an oath from any subject in favour of the new régime. Refusal to take the oath was regarded as misprision of high treason. It was under this act that More and Fisher went to their deaths.

Thus in the course of three years Henry had carried through a major revolution. For almost a thousand years the Church in England had been directly under the jurisdiction of Rome. Now, by a stroke of the pen, that ancient allegiance had been severed and all the powers which the papacy had exerted had been transferred to the king or the Archbishop of Canterbury. In carrying through this revolution the Church in England had played little part. The initiative had lain throughout with the king, though Henry had been wise enough and strong enough at each stage to carry his Parliament with him. It is, therefore, no exaggeration to say that the English Reformation, at

[1] Gee and Hardy, *Documents*, pp. 195-200.
[2] *Ibid.* pp. 201-9.   [3] *Ibid.* pp. 209-32.
[4] This explains why the archbishop today has power of conferring degrees and of granting special marriage licences.
[5] *Ibid.* pp. 243-4.   [6] *Ibid.* pp. 232-43.

any rate in its earlier stages, was 'a parliamentary transaction', or an 'act of state'.[1]

iii. *Public Opinion*

Considering the issues involved and the popularity of Katharine of Aragon, the 'divorce' and all that accompanied it passed off extraordinarily quietly and there was surprisingly little opposition. This was primarily due to the fact that people as a whole were satisfied with Henry's policy and thankful for the peace and prosperity which he had brought them. It was, no doubt, due also to some apathy and fear; but, whatever the cause, the people of England as a whole accepted the breach with Rome with a complacency which may have surprised the king himself.

The number of those who ventured to protest was very small. Elizabeth Barton, the 'Nun of Kent', denounced the king and was executed. A few Franciscan Observants deliberately preached against the divorce and suffered for it. Dr. Reynolds of Syon Monastery and the Carthusians of London found themselves unable in conscience to recognize the king's supremacy and were either left to die in gaol or were deliberately put to death. A few parish priests suffered the same fate. Of the whole bench of bishops only one, John Fisher of Rochester, stood out. He also refused to take the oath acknowledging the king's supremacy, was accused of misprision of treason, tried, found guilty and beheaded (June 22, 1535). A few weeks later he was followed to the block by that great Christian gentleman, Sir Thomas More, who suffered for the same cause. All of which showed that opposition was hopeless. The king was determined to have his way and did not shrink from crushing the noblest and holiest of his subjects if they attempted to resist him. The country was beginning to learn what 'Royal Supremacy' meant.

But 'Royal Supremacy' did not mean that England was to adopt the ideas and doctrines of the continental reformers. So far little had beeen done in England towards reform of either doctrine or worship. The breach with Rome was mainly a constitutional change: the 'reformation' in England had not yet begun.

This may partly explain the lack of effective opposition to Henry's policy. There must have been a number of men of conservative views

[1] F. M. Powicke, *The Reformation in England* (1941), pp. 1, 34.

who deplored the breach with Rome but who decided not to resist unto death, so long as the catholic doctrine and worship of the Church was not interfered with. This might account for the complacency of men like Gardiner, Tunstall and Fox. On the other hand, there was in the Church a reforming party which regarded the breach with Rome as merely the first step towards a true reformation. Among its members were those who had been at Cambridge in the 1520's and who were now to play an increasingly important part in the affairs of the Church.

In his choice of Cranmer as his archbishop in 1533 Henry found a most accommodating colleague and servant. Cranmer, the scholar and Cambridge don, was a man who shrank from the responsibilities of high office, but having once accepted them he served his king with a loyalty which amounted almost to idolatry. But, unlike Henry, Cranmer was sympathetic towards foreign theology and in close touch with the Lutheran movement in Germany. Once he had accepted the royal supremacy he struck out manfully against the papacy, while at the same time his mind was full of schemes for liturgical reform of which the king would not have approved. However, Cranmer kept these to himself and Henry had no cause to complain of the devotion of his archbishop.

Of those who were most closely involved in schemes for further reform there is none who wins our admiration more than Hugh Latimer who became Bishop of Worcester in 1535, a good, honest, blunt English yeoman who was not afraid to denounce abuses whether in Church or in State. Nicholas Ridley, who was eventually to be his brother in death, was equally courageous; but his outlook was more negative and puritanical than that of Latimer and Cranmer and he delighted in destroying relics of past devotion. These and other bishops such as Shaxton and Rowland and Edward Lee now began issuing injunctions for their dioceses in which they encouraged the reading of the Bible in English, ordered their clergy to devote more attention to preaching and to the teaching of the Creed and the Lord's Prayer to their people, while at the same time denouncing false relics as 'stinking boots, mucky combs, ragged rochets, rotten girdles, pyld purses, great bullocks' horns, locks of hair, filthy rags, gobbets of wood', and so forth.[1]

[1] W. H. Frere and W. M. Kennedy, *Visitation Articles and Injunctions of the Period of the Reformation* (1910), ii, pp. 15-60.

There is no doubt that popular feeling as a whole was on Henry's side, and there was a good deal of anti-papal demonstration. Charles Wriothesley, the chronicler, tells of a mock battle on the Thames between two barges, one representing the pope and his cardinals, the other the king. After a good deal of splashing about, the papal barge was sunk amid cheers—a 'goodly pastime'.[1] About the same time a Mr Forde, who was an usher at Winchester College, conceived a dislike to the statues in the chapel and 'tyed a longe coorde to the images, lynkyng them all in one coorde, and, being in his chamber after midnight, he plucked the cordes ende, and at one pulle all the golden godes came downe with *heyho Rombelo*'.[2] Meanwhile some of the shrines to which pilgrims had been wont to resort were being desecrated, and ancient objects of veneration exposed, such as the Holy Rood of Boxley, a crucifix fitted with invisible strings which moved the eyes and lips, to the great wonder of simple folk. This was brought to London and, after a good protestant sermon on the evils of idolatry, was thrown to the crowd 'and then the rude people and boyes brake the said image in peeces'.[3] But by far the most spectacular event of this kind was the destruction of the shrine of Thomas Becket at Canterbury, which in its great days had been the chief object of pilgrimage in England and a source of considerable wealth to its owners. But Becket's martyrdom fitted ill with the *Supreme Head Act*, and Henry VIII was anxious to remove anything which might encourage false ideas about kings and their archbishops. So in 1538 the shrine was totally destroyed and Becket's bones scattered 'because yt is founde that he dyed lyke a traytor and rebell to his Prince'.[4] His name was also removed from all church kalendars and service-books.

The 1530's therefore saw a wave not only of anti-papal feeling but also of protestant fervour which led to the destruction of much that was ancient and beautiful. Meanwhile more positive protestant ideas were beginning to cross the North Sea and affect the people of England. Although Canon Law still forbade the marriage of priests, a number of clergy in England, including Cranmer himself, had taken wives after the manner of the Lutherans. There is also evidence that in some places Mass was said in English,[5] though this also was illegal.

[1] *A Chronicle of England*, by Charles Wriothesley (Camden Society, 1875), i, pp. 99–100.
[2] *Narratives of the Reformation*, ed. J. G. Nichols (Camden Society, 1860), p. 29.
[3] Wriothesley, *op. cit.* i, pp. 74–6.   [4] *Ibid.* pp. 89–90.   [5] Cf. *Ibid.* i, p. 83.

But the most important innovation was the publication of an English Bible. Bibles in the vernacular had been known since Wyclif's time, but their distribution had of necessity been secret. Early in the sixteenth century the demand for an English Bible grew as the ideas of the reformers got more footing in the country. Opposition, however, remained as rigid as ever, and it needed the courage and zeal of a man like William Tyndale to set the movement on its way. Tyndale was completely dedicated to the task of producing, printing and distributing copies of the scriptures in English, and faced much opposition, and in the end death, in order to fulfil his mission. After working in secret in England he was obliged to flee to Germany in 1524; but he continued his work there, smuggling leaves of his English Bible into England in bales of wool. Unfortunately Tyndale was not content with a straightforward translation of the text, but added glosses and notes of a strongly protestant flavour which naturally aroused the anger of the more conservative churchmen in England. Tyndale, however, was beyond their reach until he was betrayed by one of his fellow countrymen. He was imprisoned and eventually condemned as a heretic and executed in October 1536.

His last prayer on the scaffold was 'Lord, open the King of England's eyes', but in fact the King of England's eyes were more open than Tyndale supposed. Since 1529 Henry had also been taking considerable interest in the production of an English Bible. So also had Cranmer and Thomas Cromwell, though for very different reasons. The difficulty was that it seemed impossible to produce a plain translation without a mass of highly controversial footnotes and tendentious glosses. The chief translator in England was Miles Coverdale who had probably for a time worked with Tyndale. Coverdale was not a very profound scholar, but, like Cranmer, he had an ear for good prose, as his translation of the Psalter, now part of the Book of Common Prayer, shows. His English Bible was produced in 1535 and dedicated to the king. In the following year Henry issued an injunction for the provision of a Bible in Latin and English in every parish. Little, however, was done since no one could agree on a text. But in 1538 the Great Bible, based on the work of Tyndale and Coverdale, was produced and, in time, copies found their way into the churches, not for use during divine service, but as works of reference to which the people might resort. Tyndale's hopes and prayers were, therefore, answered more quickly than he might have expected. From 1538 onwards it was possible, without risk of punishment, to study the Scriptures in the English tongue. But how far this privilege was taken advantage of by the people it is impossible to say.[1]

iv. The Dissolution of the Monasteries

By the year 1535 Henry was desperately short of money. Extravagance at home and expensive wars abroad had played havoc with the treasure so carefully stored up in his father's 'wall of brass'. There was not much hope of raising more money from the usual sources, but the 'Supreme Head of the Church' was quick to realize that new sources now lay ready to be tapped. Scattered up and down the country lay nearly two thousand religious houses (of which about half were hospitals) of varying size and importance, but all endowed with estates which had been given to them by pious benefactors. The potential income from these estates was enormous. Did the monks and nuns really need so much money? Were they really important enough to justify so much wealth?

Most reasonable men would have been obliged to admit that the answers to these questions were not altogether clear. The monasteries had to some extent outlived their day and were sadly in need of reform.[2] A few had already been closed down and their incomes applied to educational purposes. Of those that were left many were now very small—a mere handful of men or women; the 'religious life' had greatly deteriorated; and the whole institution presented a spectacle of decaying grandeur which fitted in badly with the high hopes and renewed vigour of the age.

In 1534 the king had ordered a general survey to be made of all ecclesiastical revenues, the results being recorded in the *Valor Ecclesiasticus*.[3] This gave Henry some idea of the prize which might be his if he played his cards well. In the same year the *Supremacy Act* gave the king power to visit any ecclesiastical institution, and Henry took advantage of this in 1535 by ordering Thomas Cromwell to appoint

---

[1] There is a plentiful literature about the history of the English Bible. The following should be consulted: B. F. Westcott, *History of the English Bible* (1905); A. W. Pollard, *Records of the English Bible* (1911); J. R. Dore, *Old Bibles* (1888); J. F. Mozley, *William Tyndale* (1937); S. L. Greenslade, *The Work of William Tindale* (1938); and H. Maynard Smith, *Henry VIII and the Reformation* (1948), pp. 276-350.

[2] See above, pp. 144-7.

[3] Published by the Record Commission in six volumes in 1810-34.

commissioners to visit and report upon the smaller monasteries. The commissioners, under the leadership of Dr. Legh and Dr. Layton, were no doubt told what was expected of them, and in due course produced a large mass of 'evidence' of the kind which the king required.

The next step was to draft an Act of Parliament in such a way as to convince people that these monasteries were not only redundant but a scandal, and that the king would be doing an act of service to the community if he brought these houses of iniquity to an end. A bill was therefore drawn up which opens with the words: 'Forasmuch as manifest sin, vicious, carnal and abominable living is daily used and committed among the little and small abbeys, priories, and other religious houses', etc. If any member of Parliament wished for corroboration of this statement, the *dossiers* so cunningly prepared by Cromwell's agents were always available. The bill goes on to declare that all monastic houses with incomes of less than £200 a year shall cease to exist and their incomes and possessions be transferred to the king. The monks might 'receive their capacities' (*i.e.* take a benefice) or go to other monasteries.[1] The bill passed both Houses of Parliament (though not without some difficulty), and, as a result, 376 religious houses went out of existence and their inmates were scattered abroad.

Henry thereby gained a very considerable sum of money, but the action alarmed the country as a whole. Wriothesley says that there was great lamentation among the poor who had relied upon the monasteries for daily doles of food.[2] This may be true; but in other respects the dissolution did not greatly concern the ordinary man, who tended to regard the monks with an envious eye. What alarmed the country was not the fate of the monks but the arbitrary action of the State. People began to wonder if this was the beginning of a general seizure of church property. Few people cared much about the monasteries; but what about the parish churches? Was the king about to lay his hands on them and despoil them of their treasures?

Such feelings of alarm and resentment burst into flame in a rising in Lincolnshire in October 1536. This came to nothing, but was shortly followed by a more serious rebellion in Yorkshire under the leadership of Robert Aske. The malcontents, who were not altogether sure of their motives or of their objective, liked to think of

[1] Gee and Hardy, *Documents*, pp. 257-68.   [2] Wriothesley, *Chronicle*, i, p. 43.

themselves as Crusaders and called their rising the 'Pilgrimage of Grace'. But Henry was a match for them and soon broke up their forces and hanged their leaders. The only effect of this demonstration of northern conservatism was to make Henry more determined than ever to carry on with his work of spoliation.

In 1538 most of the friaries were closed down, not by act of Parliament but by a series of more or less forced surrenders. Their property was so meagre that the king benefited little from their dissolution, but the friars had the reputation of being papal agents, and Henry was therefore glad to get them out of the way once and for all.

In the following year the remaining monasteries fell by the same process. No act was passed to give the king power to dissolve them; all that the act of 1539 did was to record the surrender of the monasteries and to legalize the king's taking into his hands all their possessions.[1] This time there was no rising on behalf of the monks. A few abbots resisted, but most of these were terrorized into submission. Those who showed any stubbornness—like the Abbots of Reading, Glastonbury and Colchester—were hanged.

So, in the course of three years, was expunged from the face of England one of the greatest and most ancient of her institutions. It was monks who had evangelized England, whether from Rome or from Iona. It was monks who had kept scholarship alive in the Dark Ages, who had established the earliest schools, who had provided hospitality for the traveller and the pilgrim, who had fed the poor and nursed the sick. Now by the rapacity of a king and the subservience of Parliament the whole thing was brought to an end, the monastic lands were transferred to lay owners, and the monastic buildings sank into decay and ruin, a useful quarry for farmers who wanted good stone to build their barns and fences.

Of the inmates of the monasteries, most of those in Holy Orders did fairly well. Many were absorbed into the parochial system or the cathedrals and chantries. A few got educational or academic jobs; some were provided with state pensions. The nuns presented a more serious problem, though some of them found husbands. There was also the problem of the monastic servants. Many of these went on with their same jobs though under lay management, but some also went to join the ranks of the unemployed and the 'sturdy beggars' who caused so much trouble to the Tudor governments.

[1] Gee and Hardy, *Documents*, pp. 281-303.

The extent of the wealth which passed from the Church to the State was enormous, for very little was devoted to ecclesiastical or educational purposes. Six new dioceses were created at Westminster, Bristol, Chester, Gloucester, Oxford and Peterborough, in each case the monastic church becoming the cathedral church of the new bishop. Similarly all the old monastic cathedrals[1] now received new statutes and were run by secular chapters. In some cases the prior of a cathedral monastery was made dean under the new system. As far as the monastic estates were concerned many of these were bought by local landlords, some of whom were obliged to pay pensions to ex-monks out of the rents. The monks had for long been closely connected with the local gentry, and in some cases their lands had been entirely managed for them by lay agents, so that the change-over from monastic to lay ownership made little disturbance to the country-side as a whole. In fact, it has been said that 'the "spoliation" did not imply a cataclysm so much as an infinite series of adjustments'.[2] The monks softly and silently vanished from the English scene, leaving only a few mouldering ruins to show where they had been.

The peacefulness with which this revolution was effected can only mean that the 'religious' themselves had largely lost faith in their own system and that many people regarded monasticism as out-dated and redundant. If there had been much that was worth pre-serving in the monastic system or if the religious houses had been making any noticeable contribution to either Church or Society, some effort would have been made to save at least a few houses. But apart from the half-hearted Pilgrimage of Grace, no one took up the cause of the monks. Nor did the monks themselves show much spirit, for there is practically no evidence of any escaping abroad in order to be faithful to their vows under happier conditions. In the dissolution of the monasteries Henry had made a bid for wealth and power. He had been surprisingly successful. Vast wealth had flowed into his exchequer, but even more significant was the assurance that the State was now in supreme control and had almost unlimited powers of overriding the rights of other bodies, even those more ancient than itself.[3]

---

[1] See above, p. 69 n.

[2] F. M. Powicke, The Reformation in England (1941), p. 23.

[3] See Letters relating to the Dissolution of the Monasteries, ed. T. Wright (Camden Society, 1843), G. Baskerville, English Monks and the Suppression of the Monasteries (1937), and M. D. Knowles, The Religious Orders in England, iii (1959).

v. *The Last Years of Henry VIII*

The last years of Henry VIII were incalculable. Glutted with power and wealth, the bonny prince had degenerated into a surly old tyrant, determined at all costs to have his own way. No one knew what was going to happen next, for much depended upon the intrigues and plots and alliances in which the king was engaged. The only certain thing was that anyone who criticized the king or stood in his way would be instantly crushed.

The religious policy of the king was just as incalculable as his political intentions. There was in the country a strong progressive party composed of good men like Cranmer, who really cared about reform, and bad men such as Thomas Cromwell who was constantly trying to draw his master into a protestant alliance with the German princes. But Henry kept his own counsel. Outwardly he remained a staunch catholic and 'defender of the faith', but this did not deter him from entering into various intrigues with the protestants, while he entrusted the education of his son and heir to avowed reformers like Richard Cox.

Henry certainly expected, as Supreme Head, to dictate what a man should believe as well as what he should do. In 1536 he had assisted in the passing by Convocation of the Ten Articles which were issued by the king with a preface which he himself had composed. With these went out a set of Injunctions in which the clergy were ordered to preach for no less than thirteen successive Sundays, and regularly after that, against the pope and his 'usurped power and jurisdiction'.[1] The doctrinal and homiletic problems which this created among a clergy but ill-trained in the art of preaching must have been considerable, and it is no wonder that there was much confusion and perplexity. It was largely to meet this that in 1537 a book was issued called *The Institute of a Christian Man*, known more familiarly as the *Bishops' Book*. Drawn up mainly by Cranmer, it was an attempt to help parish priests to know what the teaching of the Church was and so to aid them in their ministry. But it had little success.

In 1539 Henry issued another fiat in the realm of doctrine. This was the *Six Articles Act*,[2] described as 'an act abolishing diversity of opinions'. This dealt with six of the most highly controversial subjects of the day and not only dictated to people what they should

---

[1] Gee and Hardy, *Documents*, pp. 269-74.   [2] *Ibid.* pp. 303-19.

believe but made doubt or heresy a felony. The six subjects were: the truth of the doctrine of Transubstantiation; the adequacy of Communion in one kind only; the necessity of clerical celibacy; the obligation upon the laity to observe vows of chastity (*e.g.* by ex-nuns and lay-brothers); the importance of Private Masses; and the necessity of sacramental confession. To the reformers this 'bloody whip with six strings' was a cruel disaster, striking at many of their most cherished beliefs. As a result of it Latimer and Shaxton resigned their sees, Cranmer's wife returned to Germany, and a number of the married clergy resigned their livings and took up secular employment. Any who criticized the act or showed any resistance were burnt.

Henry followed up the act with another book called *A Necessary Doctrine and Erudition for any Christian Man* which was meant to be a reply to the *Bishops' Book* and consequently came to be known as the *King's Book*.[1] This, which was published in 1543, was a triumph for the reactionaries and was, in some ways, a commentary on the previous act. From now onwards the reformers were effectively silenced, the few who refused to hold their tongues (like Anne Askew) being put to death. Meanwhile the king made one more attempt to despoil the Church. This was in 1545 when he was at war with both France and Scotland, and again short of money. He had done so well out of the monasteries that he decided now to attack the chantries and hospitals. A bill was therefore prepared and passed through Parliament for the dissolution of all these and the handing over of their endowments to the king. But no vesting date was agreed upon, and the matter was in fact left over to the next reign. There is also some evidence that Henry had plans for the dissolution of the two universities, but was prevented from putting this into execution by the good offices of his last queen, Catherine Parr.

Henry's reign, therefore, ended amid fear and doubt and distress. During the twenty years since the question of the 'divorce' had been raised many great changes had taken place. England had repudiated her allegiance to Rome, which had been unquestioned since the Synod of Whitby in 664. The monasteries, which since the time of S. Augustine had been so familiar an aspect of the English scene, were now deserted and mouldering. A new ecclesiastical figure had arisen,

[1] Published by the Church Historical Society, with introduction by T. A. Lacey, 1932.

the king as 'Supreme Head in earth of the Church of England' with powers so great as even to include the definition of dogma. Yet in spite of all these fundamental changes, the religious life of the country remained much as it had always been. The parish churches looked just as they had always looked; the services remained what they had always been; the clergy behaved as their predecessors had behaved for centuries. To the ordinary villager the great changes of Henry's reign meant little. Constitutionally the Church in England had been revolutionized, but the changes which affected the daily lives of the people were yet to come.

NOTE ON BOOKS

THE literature for this period is very extensive. See *Tudor England* a bibliography compiled by Mortimer Levine (1968) esp. pp. 67-88. The following is only a selection from the more important and accessible books. E. Cardwell, *Documentary Annals of the Reformed Church of England* (1839) and J. Strype, *Ecclesiastical Memorials*, 3 vols. (1820-40) provide some early sources, to which should be added J. R. Tanner, *Tudor Constitutional Documents* (1922). C. Wriothesley's *Chronicle of England during the Reigns of the Tudors*, ed. W. D. Hamilton, 2 vols. (1875-77) and *The Grey Friars Chronicle of London*, ed. J. G. Nichols (1852) give contemporary accounts of great interest. Of more modern works, R. W. Dixon, *A History of the Church of England from the Abolition of the Roman Jurisdiction*, 6 vols. (1878-1902), J. Gairdner, *A History of the English Church in the Sixteenth Century from Henry VIII to Mary* (1904) and A. F. Pollard's *Henry VIII* (1905) and *Thomas Cranmer* (1904) are all valuable. Of recent books the most important are F. M. Powicke, *The Reformation in England* (1941), H. Maynard Smith, *Henry VIII and the Reformation* (1948), J. J. Scarisbrick *Henry VIII* (1968), E. G. Rupp, *Studies in the Making of the English Protestant Tradition* (1947), T. M. Parker, *The English Reformation to 1558* (1950), A. G. Dickens, *The English Reformation* (1964) and J. D. Mackie, *The Earlier Tudors, 1485-1558* (1952) in the *Oxford History of England*. In order to understand the Roman Catholic point of view, G. Constant, *The Reformation in England* (1939), Philip Hughes, *The Reformation in England*, vol. i (1950) and C. Haigh, *Reformation and Resistance in Tudor Lancashire* (1975) should also be read.

CHAPTER XII

ACTION AND REACTION
(1547–1558)

i. *Edward VI and Somerset*

IN spite of the breach with Rome, Henry VIII has generally been regarded as a champion of orthodoxy, the author of a treatise against Luther, proud of his title of 'Defender of the Faith', promulgator of such documents as the *Six Articles* and the *King's Book*. Yet, like his daughter Elizabeth, Henry remains doctrinally an enigma, for at the very moment when his orthodoxy was being most strongly expressed he was arranging for his son and heir to be educated by protestant teachers and was planning a council of regency with a strongly protestant bias. In 1547 Henry died, leaving the crown to a small and delicate boy of nine years of age. Henry had paid a high price for this boy. He had quarrelled with the pope, dismissed his first wife and killed his second. Was the child worth it? Was the succession any more secure than it had been when Henry had but one daughter living? No one could answer these questions or know what the future would bring. One thing seems clear: that Henry wished his son to be identified with the reforming party.

Henry had given so much power over the Church to the State that everything now depended on the personnel of the Council which was to govern for the next seven years until Edward was deemed to be of age. The Duke of Norfolk, who might have been favourable to Henry's religious views, was in prison, and conservative bishops like Gardiner were passed by. The Council took over, and Edward Seymour, shortly to become Duke of Somerset, an uncle of the king and a convinced reformer, soon got power into his own hands. It immediately became clear that reforms for which many in the country had been hoping and working for many years would now be put in hand. On January 29, 1547, the body of the old king lay in its coffin, the boy king arrived in London, and the reformers prepared for action.

Religious opinion in the country was at the time divided. Few had any hopes or desires of a return to Rome, but there was much controversy over such matters as Justification by Faith, the meaning of the Mass (with subsidiary questions of clerical celibacy and communion in one kind), images and relics, the infallibility of the Bible, and so forth. Somerset held advanced opinions, in many of which he was ably supported by Cranmer whose mind was increasingly influenced by foreign protestant theology. These two regarded the king's minority as a good opportunity for introducing considerable religious changes, using the extensive powers which Henry VIII had usurped for the crown. In these reforms the Church played only a small part. Convocation was seldom consulted and the bishops were too much divided to offer any united front. Thus the Reformation in the reign of Edward VI continued to be primarily an 'act of state'. Conservative bishops like Gardiner and Bonner who showed any opposition were immediately imprisoned, while the policy of the government went inexorably forward, using the machinery of commissions, injunctions and statutes.

Within a few months of Edward's accession the first set of royal injunctions was published,[1] ordering the removal of such images or paintings in the churches as might lead to superstition, reducing the lights on the high altar before the Sacrament to two, forbidding the ringing of bells during Mass and demanding that a copy of the *Book of Homilies* and of the *Paraphrases of Erasmus* should be procured for each parish church. The intention behind these injunctions was to discourage superstition and promote sound learning, for the *Paraphrases* were in the nature of a commentary on the Gospels and the *Homilies* provided a series of twelve sermons on the Scriptures, Justification, Faith, Good Works, etc. by Cranmer, Bonner, Latimer and Becon.[2] At the same time two Acts of Parliament were passed, the first repealing the *Six Articles*, the other dealing with the Mass.[3] The latter shows that, in the first few months of Edward's reign, as soon as the tyranny of the old king had been removed, the more advanced protestants had attacked the Eucharist, making fun of it 'in their sermons, preaching, readings, lectures, . . . rhymes, songs, plays and jests'. The most sacred words of the institution of the rite: *Hoc est corpus meum*, had been corrupted

[1] Printed in W. H. Frere and W. M. Kennedy, *Visitation Articles and Injunctions of the Period of the Reformation*, ii, pp. 114-30, and E. Cardwell, *Documentary Annals of the Reformed Church of England* (1839), i, pp. 4-23.
[2] On the *Homilies* see W. E. Scudamore, *Notitia Eucharistica* (1872), pp. 288-95.
[3] Gee and Hardy, *Documents*, pp. 322-8.

into 'Hocus-pocus', a word which came to stand for any kind of superstitious nonsense. People found guilty of such irreverence were to be punished, for decency and propriety must be maintained. The act also ordered the administration of the sacrament to the people in both kinds, thus restoring to the laity a right which had gradually been taken from them during the later Middle Ages.

In the same year shortage of money in the exchequer led to further steps being taken to despoil the Church, this time by the dissolution of the chantries. Such a proposal had been made by Henry VIII, but it had never been carried through. Now a new bill was drawn up and passed through Parliament ordering the immediate suppression of all chantries.[1] The preamble talks of devoting the money to education; but this was never done, and a great opportunity was thereby lost. The act was not popular, for many of the chantries were supported by gilds as well as by private families; but the government needed the wealth and could always justify itself by the complaint that the whole chantry-system was hopelessly wedded to medieval theology about the efficacy of private Masses and prayers for the dead.

Not many months, therefore, went by before considerable changes were taking place. The more conservative among churchmen were swept away by the rising tide of reform, while the progressives, filled with iconoclastic zeal, steadily and systematically began the spoliation of the parish churches. The churchwardens' accounts of the period show that great destruction was taking place. At Ludlow the 'image of saynt George that stode in the chapelle' was sold for 18d. and 'the dragon that the image of Saynt George stode upon' for 7d.[2] At S. Michael's in Bedwardine, Worcester, the churchwardens had a vast sale of lamps, censers, candlesticks, crosses, a platter, a holy-water pot, organ-pipes, bells, the organ case and the cloths that covered the shrines.[3] At S. Michael's, Cornhill, a collection of medieval plate, was sold for £80.[4] And so on. In every parish church in the country treasures of the past were taken out and men gave a few

[1] Gee and Hardy, Documents, pp. 328-57; cf. J. R. Tanner, Tudor Constitutional Documents, pp. 103-7 for extracts.
[2] T. Wright, Churchwardens' Accounts of the Town of Ludlow (Camden Society, 1869), pp. 33-7.
[3] J. Amphlett, Churchwardens' Accounts of S. Michael's in Bedwardine, Worcester, 1539-1603 (Worcs. Hist. Soc., 1896), p. 22.
[4] A. J. Waterlow, Accounts of the Churchwardens of St. Michael, Cornhill (n.d.), pp. 69-70.

pence for works of art which the Victoria and Albert Museum would now give many thousands of pounds to recover.

With the zeal for clearing old objects out of churches and old ideas out of men's minds went an equal zeal for edification, especially through a revival of preaching. It is to these years that we owe the sermons of Hugh Latimer which, although in style essentially medieval, belong in thought and intention to the days of reform. Racy, full of anecdote, reminiscence and humour, rich in homely English words like 'ugsomeness', 'dodipoles' and 'belly-cheer', these sermons[1] are an indication of the vigour and courage and outspokenness which belonged to the New Age. Latimer has hard words to say about the pope—'that Italian bishop yonder, the devil's chaplain'[2]—and about the falseness of images and relics,[3] of the Roman doctrine of the Mass,[4] and about the unworthiness of monks and friars.[5] But he attacks, also, his contemporaries, especially bishops and others who neglect the ministry of the Word and become 'unpreaching prelates'. Bishops, he says, are so taken up with 'ruffling in their rents, dancing in their dominions . . . munching in their mangers and moiling in their gay manors and mansions' that they have no time for preaching, while the devil 'the most diligent prelate and preacher in all England' is busy poisoning the hearts of men.[6] Social evils are fiercely attacked, especially enclosures which meant that 'where as there have been a great many householders and inhabitants there is now but a shepherd and his dog';[7] also the decay of charity towards poor scholars,[8] child marriages[9] and the corruption of the judges.[10] Latimer was not afraid to hit out where he saw injustice or falsehood or wrong, and in the end it cost him his life. His manner has a grandeur and ruggedness all its own; but in his matter he was typical of a large number of reformers who were using the pulpit to press their views and stir up the people to greater zeal for reform.

Further pressure was put upon the English reformers by the arrival in 1548 of a number of distinguished protestant theologians from abroad. Peter Martyr Vermigli, an ex-Austin canon, who had fled from Italy to Switzerland, came to England in this year and was

---

[1] Printed by the Parker Society in two volumes, *The Sermons of Bishop Latimer* and *The Remains of Bishop Latimer* (1844–45).
[2] *Sermons*, p. 74; cf. pp. 27, 50, 119, 205–6.
[3] *Ibid.* pp. 23, 49–50, 342, 497–9.   [4] *Ibid.* pp. 167, 445.
[5] *Ibid.* pp. 188, 292, 391–2, 478.   [6] *Ibid.* pp. 67, 70.
[7] *Ibid.* p. 100.   [8] *Ibid.* pp. 65, 178–9, 291, 349.
[9] *Ibid.* pp. 95, 243–4.   [10] *Ibid.* p. 140.

immediately appointed Regius Professor of Divinity at Oxford. At the same time Francisco Dryander, a Spaniard now turned Lutheran, was appointed Reader in Greek at Cambridge where he was shortly afterwards joined by Martin Bucer, a German ex-Dominican, as Regius Professor. John à Lasco, a Pole, who had identified himself with the Reform movement in Germany, also came over in 1548 to pursue his work in England. This group of foreign theologians played an important part in the history of the Church in England during the next two or three years. They were scholars, and, as such, men after Cranmer's own heart. He and they talked the same language and were interested in the same problems, and their influence upon the archbishop was undoubtedly very great.

Cranmer, at the time, was busy with his liturgical schemes and his plans for the supersession of the Roman service books by an English Prayer Book. By 1549 such a book was ready, and was imposed upon the country as a schedule to an *Act of Uniformity* which demanded that whereas in the past there had been a number of different 'uses' in England, from now onwards all clergy must use the new book on pain of imprisonment.[1] It was accompanied by an act legalizing the marriage of priests,[2] an act of which a good many clergy took advantage.

The Prayer Book seems, on the whole, to have been fairly well received by the parochial clergy. It was not, after all, unexpected, and it bore enough resemblance to the old service-books to satisfy all but a few of the conservatives. The chief trouble came from the extreme south-west, where complaints against the book 'because it is but like a Christmas game' were fomented into a rebellion which for a short time caused considerable disturbance and some bloodshed.[3]

The latter part of 1549 was, in fact, an anxious time for the Government. Kett's rebellion in Norfolk in protest against the enclosures, and the Cornish rising in protest against the Prayer Book, had shown that the Council was not altogether popular; and the Earl of Warwick, who afterwards became Duke of Northumberland, took the opportunity of seizing power into his own hands. Somerset was taken by surprise and thrown into the Tower. A new régime now took control.

---

[1] Gee and Hardy, *Documents*, pp. 358-66. See below, pp. 189-90.
[2] *Ibid.* pp. 366-8.
[3] See *Troubles connected with the Prayer Book of 1549*, ed. N. Pocock (Camden Society, 1884).

ii. *The Pace Quickens*

Northumberland, an unscrupulous and crafty man, allied himself with the more advanced reformers and greatly quickened the rate of change. The cautious and conciliatory policy of Somerset and Cranmer now gave place to more radical changes. With many of these Cranmer was in agreement, for, under the influence of the foreign theologians upon whose advice he relied, his mind was moving towards a much more protestant position. But Northumberland found his chief supporters among such men as Nicholas Ridley and John Hooper.

The year 1550 opened with an *Act against Books and Images*,[1] which led to further iconoclasm in the parish churches. Again the churchwardens' accounts reveal the extent of the damage, for at Great St. Mary's in Cambridge there is a record in this year of a big sale of plate and vestments which denuded the church of many of its richest treasures.[2] Ridley now succeeded Bonner as Bishop of London and immediately issued injunctions to his clergy to remove all stone altars from their churches, while the priest is not to 'counterfeit popish mass in kissing the Lord's board, washing his fingers after the Gospel, shifting the book from one place to another, licking the chalice . . . showing the Sacrament openly before the distribution, ringing sacring bell or setting any light upon the altar';[3] and Ridley himself commanded the lights on the altar at S. Paul's to be put out before he would enter the choir.[4] Meanwhile John Hooper, 'the father of nonconformity', was causing considerable difficulties for, having been appointed Bishop of Gloucester, he had refused to wear a surplice and cope at his consecration, declaring that he would countenance no ceremonies but such as could be justified by the New Testament.[5]

All this fitted in well with the policy of Northumberland, who liked

---

[1] J. R. Tanner, *Tudor Constitutional Documents*, pp. 113-15.
[2] J. E. Foster, *Churchwardens' Accounts of St. Mary the Great, Cambridge, 1504-1635* (Camb. Antiq. Soc., 1905), pp. 118-19.
[3] Frere and Kennedy, *Visitation Articles and Injunctions*, ii, pp. 241-5.
[4] *Chronicle of the Grey Friars of London*, ed. J. G. Nichols (1852), p. 66. In the following year he had the altar at St. Paul's moved from its customary place and set 'beneth the steepps in the middes of the upper quire' with the ends east and west (C. Wriothesley, *A Chronicle of England*, ii, p. 47).
[5] J. Gairdner, *A History of the English Church in the Sixteenth Century*, p. 282.

to see such changes taking place. Meanwhile the more conservative bishops were gradually weeded out. Gardiner had been in the Tower for some time and was now deprived. Voysey was turned out of Exeter and replaced by Miles Coverdale. Heath of Worcester and Day of Chichester were both deprived, and Tunstall of Durham was committed to the Tower. Thus all possible opposition was removed and a body of 'yes-men' created in readiness for the more sweeping doctrinal and liturgical changes which came in with the *Second Act of Uniformity* and the Prayer Book of 1552.[1] The Act identifies the Church and the State and, possibly under the influence of the Germans, tries to tighten up discipline by demanding universal attendance at the church services 'upon pain of punishment by the censures of the Church'. No provision is made for minorities or for religious scruples. The Church is to be the State at prayer. Meanwhile the annexed Prayer Book had carried reform much further by abandoning many of the old customs and ceremonies of worship, and by altering words and phrases to bear a much more protestant interpretation.[2]

The new book came into use on November 1, 1552, this time with even less opposition than before. In accordance with the new rubric all copes and eucharistic vestments now became illegal and many were destroyed. In 1553 inventories of church ornaments and plate were made for each parish in England,[3] and much was seized by the Government. Not since the days of the Danish raids had the churches presented so sorry a spectacle as they did at this time.

Meanwhile in 1552 an attempt had been made to define the doctrine of the Church of England in a series of Articles. Cranmer had drawn up forty-five, but these were reduced to forty-two before receiving the royal assent in 1553. They were aimed partly against the medieval doctrines of the schoolmen and partly against the antinomian teaching of the extreme protestants, now beginning to be called 'Anabaptists'. The Articles were intended to give a doctrinal 'platform' to the English Church and to set it upon that *via media* which, in later years, it was proud to tread.[4] A somewhat similar attempt to define the legal status of the Church by a *Reformatio Legum Ecclesiasticarum*, or reform of Church Law,

---

[1] Gee and Hardy, *Documents*, pp. 369-72.   [2] See below, pp. 190-1.
[3] See *The Edwardian Inventories for Beds. Hunts. Bucks. Exeter* and *Oxford*, in *Alcuin Club Collections*, vi, vii, ix, xx and xxiii (1905-20).
[4] See E. J. Bicknell, *A Theological Introduction to the Thirty-nine Articles* (1925), pp. 12-17.

came to nothing, and further work on this was postponed to a later date.

But at this point all further reform was brought to an abrupt end, for, on July 6, 1553, the young King Edward, at the age of fifteen, died from a tubercular infection of the lungs.

iii. *Liturgical Innovations*

At the death of Henry VIII in 1547 the churches of England looked much as they had always looked, and the services which were conducted in them were the services which would have been found in any other church in Christendom, then or during the previous five hundred years. But though the king had set his face against liturgical reform, the need for such was very much in the minds of many of his subjects. The whole system of worship needed overhauling and simplifying. Ancient customs had been allowed to disappear and new rites and ceremonies had crept in. There were, therefore, many, in England and elsewhere, who had set their minds to liturgical reform.

In England the man who did most to reform the liturgy was Thomas Cranmer. As a scholar and historian he had studied the life of the early Christians and was anxious to raise the worship of the Church in England as far as possible to the standards of the Primitive Church. The first need was for greater simplicity. The old services had become so complicated, and the rules and rubrics so involved, that 'many times there was more business to find out what should be read, than to read it when it was found out'.[1] The second need was for more congregational worship. In the later Middle Ages the laity had been thrown more and more into the position of spectators of ceremonies performed on their behalf by the clergy. This led to the third need, which was for a liturgy in the language of the people. If the laity were to be encouraged to take an intelligent part in the offerings of the Church then it must be in their own language. The fourth need was for the restoration of primitive customs such as the administration of the Holy Communion to the laity in both kinds. Finally, there was need for greater edification through sermons and reading of the Scriptures. It was along these lines that Cranmer was

[1] Preface to 1549 Prayer Book, 'Concerning the Service of the Church'.

working during the reign of Henry VIII, though there was, at that moment, little hope of any reforms being introduced. Among the works which Cranmer studied was the reformed Breviary prepared in 1535 by the Spanish Franciscan, Cardinal Quignon, for the use of the parochial clergy, but banned by Rome,[1] and a collection of revised forms for the Eucharist and the occasional offices put out by Hermann von Wied, a reforming Archbishop of Cologne, in 1543. On these and other sources Cranmer was undoubtedly working during the latter part of the reign of Henry VIII, thus laying the historical and theological foundations for the English Prayer Book which he hoped eventually to produce.[2]

The only liturgical innovation of any consequence during Henry's reign was the publication in 1544 of the English Litany. In that year war was threatening with France and Scotland and the king invited Cranmer to draw up a Litany in English to be said in all the churches. The archbishop based his litany on the Sarum *Processionale*, itself founded on a Greek liturgy brought to England about 700,[3] but he reduced the invocations of saints, grouped the petitions together and added versicles and responses suitable for a time of war.

With the death of the old king the door was opened for the introduction of reforms which many had long wished to see. Perhaps the keenest demand was for a greater use of the English language in the worship of the Church, and, as early as Edward VI's first Parliament in 1547, when the opening Mass was celebrated considerable portions of it were said in English, while by May 1548 the choirs at S. Paul's and other churches had started to sing all the services in English 'both mattens, masse and even-songe'.[4] This same year saw also the publication of the *Order of Communion*[5] which provided for a service in English to be inserted into the Latin Mass after the consecration. The new order included two exhortations, an appeal to sinners to withdraw, an invitation, confession, absolution, with the Comfortable Words, the Prayer of Humble Access, a form for the administration

---

[1] See *Second Recension of the Quignon Breviary*, ed. J. Wickham Legg, Henry Bradshaw Society (1908–12), 2 vols.
[2] J. Wickham Legg, *Cranmer's Liturgical Projects* (Henry Bradshaw Society, 1915), based on British Museum MS. Royal 7 B. iv. Cf. F. A. Gasquet and E. Bishop, *Edward VI and the Book of Common Prayer* (1890).
[3] E. Bishop, *Liturgica Historica* (1918), pp. 137–64.
[4] C. Wriothesley, *Chronicle*, i, p. 187; ii, p. 2.
[5] Edited by H. A. Wilson and printed in facsimile by the Henry Bradshaw Society, 1908. Cf. also the Parker Society volume, *Liturgies of King Edward VI* (1844), pp. 1–8.

of the sacrament in both kinds and the Blessing. Thus the priest, after the recitation of the Canon, broke off to conduct this office in English and then returned to the words of the Missal for the Post-communion.

The *Order of Communion* was probably but little used, for within a few months was published the *First English Prayer Book* (followed a few months later by the Ordinal) which entirely superseded the medieval Latin rites and brought to completion the task upon which Cranmer had been working for so long. The title page of the new book—'The booke of the common prayer and administracion of the Sacraments, and other rites and ceremonies of the churche: after the use of the Churche of England'—shows that the authors were anxious that the book should be regarded as in the direct line of catholic worship, a reform rather than an innovation. Like the wise house-holder 'who bringeth out of his treasure things new and old' the compilers of this book had made it their ambition to preserve all that was best in the treasury of Christian devotion while at the same time purging it of all accretions which might either encourage superstition or detract the mind of the worshipper from the true meaning of worship. Thus 'The Supper of the Lord . . . commonly called the Mass' was closely modelled on the medieval Sarum rite with the Gloria at the beginning and a long canon including the Prayer of Oblation and the Lord's Prayer. The office of Baptism retained the ancient ceremonies of exorcism, chrisom and unction; the Order of Confirmation directed the Bishop, besides laying his hands on the candidates, to 'cross them in the forehead'; and the Burial Service included a commendation of the soul to God and prayers for the dead. Naturally there was a good deal here that many found objectionable. To the conservatives the book was an unnecessary disaster, breaking up the unity of Christian worship. On the other hand the more progressive party regarded the book as timid and compromising and demanded far more sweeping innovations. But Cranmer knew what he was about. His ideal, as expressed in the epilogue 'Of Ceremonies',[1] is a high and sensible one. He knew that it was hopeless to please everyone, therefore 'it was thought expedient, not so much to have respect how to please and satisfy either of these parties, as how to please God, and to profit them both'.

Yet there is some evidence that Cranmer was already planning to

[1] Originally an epilogue to the Prayer Book, now printed among the Prefaces.

make further concessions to the more determined reformers by the production of a second prayer-book on more protestant lines.[1] He was, at the time, much under the influence of the foreign theologians, who found the 1549 Book far too conservative, and urged the archbishop to replace it by something more to their taste. The result was that, within three years, a new book had been prepared which appeared in 1552 as the *Second English Prayer Book*. This book shows that a considerable doctrinal change had taken place since 1549. The doctrines concerning the church, the ministry, the sacraments and the 'last things' have all undergone some modification. No longer is the book put out as containing 'the rites and ceremonies of the Church' but as the worship of the Church of England alone. Ceremonies intended to emphasise the priestly functions of the clergy are omitted or modified, especially in the wearing of eucharistic vestments and in the hearing of confessions. The sacrament of Baptism is much simplified, and all prayers for the dead are omitted. But the greatest changes occur in the Eucharist where the emphasis is shifted from the idea of sacrifice and the Real Presence to that of commemoration and communion. This is nowhere more clearly shown than in the words of administration of the sacrament, for whereas in 1549 the priest gave the bread to the people with the words: 'The Body of our Lord Jesus Christ which was given for thee ...' in 1552 he is made to say: 'Take and eat this in remembrance that Christ died for thee ...' Many ancient ceremonies and customs—such as the sign of the cross in Confirmation, the mixed chalice, reservation for the sick, the handing of the chalice and paten to a priest at his ordination, and commemoration of the saints—are omitted altogether. The protestant party was now very much in control. Moreover at the last moment, on the very eve of publication, a further addition, without the consent of either Convocation or Parliament, was made by the Council in the form of the *Black Rubric* which appears to have been inspired by a sermon by John Knox in London opposing the habit of kneeling at the Communion. The *Black Rubric* refers to the order in the new Prayer-book for kneeling but adds: 'it is not meant thereby that any adoration is done or ought to be done, either unto the sacramental bread and wine there bodily received, or to any real and essential presence there being of Christ's natural flesh and blood'. This gave the death-blow to catholic belief in the Real Presence of Christ in the

[1] Cf. E. C. Ratcliff, *The booke of common prayer* (1949), p. 15.

Sacrament and marks the furthest point to which the Church of England ever went in protestant teaching.

When the old Latin service books were all swept away in 1549 to be replaced by the new English services, the question of church music became acute. Cranmer, however, was interested in the subject and encouraged an advanced reformer called John Merbecke, who had narrowly escaped death as a heretic in 1543, to write suitable music to accompany the English words. The result was the publication in 1550 of *The Booke of Common Praier Noted* [1] containing music for the Eucharist and the daily offices in an easy, flowing, unison style based on medieval plain-song but simplified almost to the point of austerity and following Cranmer's rule of 'not full of notes, but, as near as may be, for every syllable a note'.[2] Merbecke's style fitted in very well with the new movement towards church music of a much more congregational and less professional character. The new style was taken up by Christopher Tye (*c.* 1500–72) who began the fashion of writing quite simple four-part anthems, and by Thomas Tallis (*c.* 1505–85) who, though he wrote mostly to Latin words, composed settings for the responses which have become much loved and are still almost universally used.

iv. *Mary and the Reconciliation with Rome*

The death of Edward VI in his sixteenth year was a great blow to the reformers. What doctrinal policy the young king would have pursued had he lived will never be known. But at least he had been educated by members of the reforming party and surrounded by such during his minority. Now, at his early death, the crown naturally went to Henry's eldest daughter Mary, a half-Spaniard and a fanatical Roman Catholic. Northumberland made a bid to get Lady Jane Grey proclaimed as queen; but the plot failed and, in due course, Mary entered London as Queen of England, while the crowds wept with joy and threw their caps in the air. Such enthusiasm must have warmed a heart long accustomed to sorrow and bitterness. Mary was now thirty-seven, but for the last twenty years she had

---

[1] See *Merbecke's Book of Common Prayer Noted*, ed. J. E. Hunt (1939), and extracts in S. H. Nicholson, *Quires and Places where They Sing* (1932), pp. 260–73.

[2] Letter of Cranmer to Henry VIII in 1544, in *Cranmer's Remains and Letters* (Parker Society, 1846), p. 412.

been obliged to live in close retirement, an object of scorn to some
and of pity to others. At the sensitive age of sixteen her security had
suddenly been removed, she and her mother had been driven out of
their home and she herself publicly proclaimed as illegitimate. The
shock of all this to an adolescent girl must have been great. No wonder
that the portrait we have of her is of a tight-lipped, severe woman
who has passed through the fire of suffering and is now in the grip
of a firm determination.

For Mary's policy was soon made clear: it was to undo all that had
been done by her father and brother and restore the Church in England to communion with Rome. Within a few months of her accession the bishops of the old school, who had been turned out in
Edward's reign, were restored to their sees, while such of the reformers as did not seek sanctuary abroad were imprisoned, including
Cranmer, Latimer and Ridley.

Mary naturally dropped the obnoxious title of 'Supreme Head of
the Church of England', but she continued to act as such whatever
she might call herself. It was she, as sovereign, who intended to
decide what the religious policy of the country should be, and, like
her father, she succeeded in carrying Parliament with her. Thus,
within a few months, Parliament had repealed all the Edwardian
legislation, so taking things back to what they were in 1547.[1] Nothing, however, was said yet about Henry's acts, nor about reconciliation with Rome.

The next step was the publication of a set of injunctions early in
1554[2] which required all bishops to restore the old order, to remove
all married priests from their cures, to see that holy days were kept
and to deprive all clergy holding heretical opinions. All this the
bishops were glad to do. Under Gardiner's leadership a purge was
carried out, as a result of which probably about twenty per cent of
the clergy were removed. Then began the restoring of the churches.
Stone altars were rebuilt to replace the wooden tables; ornaments and
images which had been lying in builders' yards were cleaned up and
restored; vestments which had survived were mended and brought
again into use, and there was a great hunt for plate and ornaments
and books. At the city church of S. Mary-at-Hill the churchwardens' accounts for this year record the purchase of many Latin

---

[1] Gee and Hardy, *Documents*, pp. 377–80.
[2] Frere and Kennedy, *Visitation Articles and Injunctions*, ii, pp. 322–9.

books, the building of stone altars, the buying of altar-cloths, albs, and amices, the 'puttyng out of the scrypture in the roode lofte' and the making of a 'bisshopes myter'. Finally a bishop was brought to reconsecrate the altars, the accounts recording: 'for boate hyer for the chargis of halowyng the altars, ii^d . . . for the dynner of the suffrycan that daye he halowed the altars and other that did service with hym, xiii^s . . . payde in Claret wyne, sacke and sugar, iii^s xi^d'.[1] And what took place at this church must have been happening all over the country, and apparently without much difficulty. There were a few disturbances, and no doubt a good many people regarded the reaction with dismay and sorrow; but on the whole the policy of the queen seems to have met, if not with approval, at least with acquiescence. The people had had only four years of the English Prayer-books and of the denuded churches, and many were undoubtedly glad to get back to the old ways with which they were familiar. The *theology* of reform did not greatly interest the working man of the sixteenth century, any more than it interested his descendants during the Tractarian revival. What the average man wanted was the kind of service to which he was accustomed.

Had Mary contented herself with a conservative policy which would have carried the country back to what it had been in the time of her childhood she might well have succeeded, for in ecclesiastical affairs man is naturally a conservative animal. But on January 12, 1554, Mary took a false step which was to be her undoing. On that day there was signed at Westminster a marriage treaty between her and her kinsman, Prince Philip of Spain. As soon as this became known the country was thrown into great alarm and despondency.[2] No one wanted England to be dragged into the Mediterranean political arena and to become a tool in the hands of Spain. But the tight lips were firmly closed. Mary had announced her intentions and was not prepared to listen to further argument. The marriage took place on July 25 and, since Philip could not for long be king of a country out of communion with Rome, preparations were put in hand for a reconciliation to take place.

---

[1] *The Medieval Records of a London City Church* (*St. Mary at Hill*), ed. H. Littlehales (E.E.T.S. No. 128, 1905), pp. 395-403.

[2] A contemporary chronicler says that the marriage was 'very moche mysliked . . . Eche man was abashed, loking daylie for worse mattiers to growe shortly after'; *The Chronicle of Queen Jane and of Two Years of Queen Mary*, ed. J. G. Nichols (Camden Society, 1850), p. 35.

The chief problem which lay in the path of reconciliation was a financial one. The legislation of Henry VIII had despoiled the Church of much of its property which was now in lay hands. Would reconciliation necessarily involve the restoration of all such property to the Church? Squires and merchants might welcome a return to the old ways so far as the worship of the Church was concerned: it was another matter when their estates were threatened.

It was to settle such problems and prepare the way for a healing of the breach that the pope now despatched to England one of the most gifted of her sons, Reginald Pole. Pole had been a great favourite of Henry VIII up to the time of the divorce, but since 1532 he had been living abroad and did not really understand what was happening in England. He could never accept Henry's policy, and wrote a book on the unity of the Church which Henry regarded as a personal insult. Consequently when, in 1541, Pole was made a cardinal and legate, Henry took his revenge by executing his mother and brother as traitors. But now that Henry was dead and his daughter sat on the throne with the truly orthodox Philip by her side, Pole was able to return to England with full legatine authority.

Pole reached England on November 24, 1554. In the same month Parliament passed two acts each designed to pave the way for reconciliation with Rome. The first[1] revived the old laws against heresy and so made resistance to the ecclesiastical policy of the State far more difficult and costly. The second, an *Act of Repeal*,[2] annulled all ecclesiastical legislation since 1528, with one exception—the dissolution of the monasteries. A bargain was thus struck with the papacy. The English Parliament agreed to retrace all the steps which it had taken in the last thirty years, but only on condition that the property of its members and other laymen was not touched. The preamble to the act is unctuous in the extreme, describing the coming of Cardinal Pole 'to call us home again into the right way from whence we have all this long while wandered and strayed abroad'; but the act was, in fact, largely a financial transaction intended to guard vested interests. However, it satisfied the pope; and on November 30 the cardinal graciously absolved the realm from its long-continued schism, the king and queen humbly kneeling before him.

[1] Gee and Hardy, *Documents*, p. 384.   [2] *Ibid.* pp. 385-415.

v. *Persecution and Disaster*

The reconciliation with Rome was the signal for the persecution of those who had espoused the protestant cause. Many of the reforming bishops were in prison; some fled overseas to await better times. Stephen Gardiner, as the leading prelate in the country, inaugurated a series of trials in an attempt to bring all to be of one mind in the state. There was at first no sign of injustice or pressure. Every opportunity was given to those accused of heresy to recant and save themselves. But things had gone too far. Men like Cranmer and Latimer knew where they stood and could not conscientiously deny what they believed to be true, whatever the consequences might be. So, also, with lesser men. The reforming movement had too tight a grip on the minds of Englishmen to be lightly broken. So the fires of Smithfield were lighted and the long stream of victims was dragged out there to suffer for conscience sake. Those who gave their lives were of all sorts—priests and prelates, nobles and commoners, learned men and illiterate peasants—as the pages of Foxe's *Acts and Monuments* will show.

Since April 1554 Cranmer, Latimer and Ridley had all been prisoners at Oxford. In September 1555 Cranmer was cited before a tribunal set up by the pope and was formally accused of heresy. Particulars were taken and a long account of the proceedings was sent to the pope. Meanwhile Latimer and Ridley had faced the judges and been condemned. On October 16 they were led out to execution on a spot close to Balliol College. Ridley's brother-in-law tied bags of gunpowder round their necks in the hopes of shortening the torment, but it was some time before they died. In the midst of their agony Latimer was able to cry out: 'Be of good comfort, Master Ridley, and play the man; we shall this day light such a candle by God's grace in England as I trust shall never be put out'.[1] Latimer died soon after this, but Ridley continued for some time in great agony until the fire reached the gunpowder and death released him from his sufferings.

Cranmer, meanwhile, remained in prison, though on December 4 he was excommunicated and Pole was appointed as his successor. Great pains were taken to persuade Cranmer to recant. Even Mary

---

[1] Foxe, *Acts and Monuments* (1877), vii, p. 550.

did not really want to burn the Archbishop of Canterbury, while his conversion would have been a triumph for the party in power. And, indeed, Cranmer did very nearly submit, writing a number of statements in which he did in fact repudiate some of the doctrines which he had long held. In his final confession he admitted that he had done this out of fear and in hopes of saving his life, but the issue was more complex than that. Cranmer believed whole-heartedly in the duty of the subject to obey his sovereign. During the reigns of Henry VIII and Edward VI he had been able to give his support to the changes which were taking place, not only because loyalty to his king demanded that he should, but also because his own mind was moving in the same direction. Loyalty and conscience went hand in hand. But with the coming of Mary and the return to the old ways Cranmer found himself in a new position. Loyalty bade him support the queen, but conscience told him that she was wrong. It was a fearful dilemma since anything but complete and unhesitating loyalty meant torture and death. Cranmer was now sixty-five years of age and, in a sense, his life's work was done. Yet in the evening of his life he was forced to make one of the most terrible choices which a man can ever make. It was a choice between a comfortable old age and a ghastly and most painful death. For a moment the old man wavered, but his conscience was too strong for him. He could not say he believed something which he knew to be untrue. So he faced his martyrdom, plunging the hand that had signed his recantations into the flames, crying: 'This hand hath offended'. And, we are told, 'as soon as the fire got up he was very soon dead, never stirring or crying all the while'.[1]

Cranmer had accepted the primacy in 1533 against his will, for he was a theologian and scholar rather than a statesman or leader. During the stormy years of his primacy he had kept his scholarly mind open to new ideas and had moved forward as he believed the Truth led him on. At the end it was his loyalty to Truth which, though it cost him his life, saved him from a betrayal of the best that was in him.

On the day of Cranmer's death Reginald Pole said his first Mass, having been ordained priest on the previous day. The next day he was consecrated as Archbishop of Canterbury and the restoration of the Church went on apace. While the crowd of victims—some three

[1] J. Strype, *Memorials of Thomas Cranmer* (1812 ed.), i, p. 558.

hundred or so—made their sad way out to face the fires of Smith-field, Masses were being said and monasteries refounded, notably at Westminster Abbey, the Observant friars of Greenwich, the Briget-tine nuns of Syon and the Carthusians of Sheen. But the efforts of Mary and Pole and Gardiner were soon to be brought to an end.

The last two years of Mary's reign were a time of much distress and foreboding. The reconciliation with Rome of 1555 soon came near to disaster, not on religious grounds but political; for Pope Paul IV, who was elected in the same year, soon quarrelled with the King of Spain who, of course, was also King of England. Pole tried hard to serve two masters, the pope and the king, but found the task im-possible, and the country was dragged into war with France which ended in disaster and disgrace. In the eyes of the English people Mary and all that she stood for were condemned together. National feeling ran high. If a return to papal allegiance meant loss of national prestige and power as well as persecution for those who resisted, then people desired nothing better than to get rid of it. Mary's unhappy death on November 17, 1558, followed within a few hours by that of Arch-bishop Pole, seemed like a providential deliverance.

From every point of view Mary's reign was a failure. She had come to the throne with a sense of vocation and had tried to carry out the policy which she believed to be right in the eyes of God. But it had failed; and the reasons for its failure were these. In the first place it came too late. In doctrinal matters too many men had made up their minds where they stood, and they could not go back. If Mary had immediately succeeded her father in 1547 things would have been different, but the five years of Edward's reign had seen changes which could not be suddenly reversed. Then again, the Span-ish marriage, however good the intentions which lay behind it, had always been unpopular and had brought nothing but disaster and shame. Again, the extent and savagery of the persecutions sickened and disgusted a people quite accustomed to a certain amount of rough justice. And finally, the fact that some of the clergy had taken advan-tage of the Edwardine legislation and had married wives and begotten children created various social problems, and a good deal of antagon-ism was aroused when they were told that they must either give up their wives or their livings.

Mary's attempt, therefore, at a Counter-Reformation in England ended in disaster, and when the news of the death of the queen and

the cardinal was made public then 'the same day all London song
and sayd *Te Deum laudamus* in evere chyrche in London'.[1]

[1] *Diary of Henry Machyn*, ed. J. G. Nichols (1847), p. 178.

NOTE ON BOOKS

MANY of the books mentioned above on p. 179 apply also to this chapter.
In addition there is much of interest in W. H. Frere and W. M. Kennedy,
Visitation Articles and Injunctions of the Period of the Reformation, 3 vols. (1910).
Reference should also be had to J. Foxe, *Acts and Monuments*, ed. J. Pratt,
8 vols. (1877). See also C. H. Smyth, *Cranmer and the Reformation* (1926),
W. Schenk, *Reginald Pole* (1950), G. Garrett, *The Marian Exiles* (1938) and
N. Pocock, 'The Condition of Morals and Religious Belief in the Reign of
Edward VI' in *English Historical Review* (1895). For the history of the Prayer
Book see F. Procter and W. H. Frere, *A New History of the Book of Common
Prayer* (1901, etc.), F. A. Gasquet and E. Bishop, *Edward VI and the Book of
Common Prayer* (1890), E. C. Ratcliff, *The booke of common prayer of the
Churche of England* (1949), M. Ramsey and others, *The Book of Common
Prayer of the Church of England, 1549–1662* (1963) and F. E. Brightman,
'The History of the Book of Common Prayer down to 1662', in *Liturgy
and Worship*, ed. W. K. Lowther Clarke (1932).

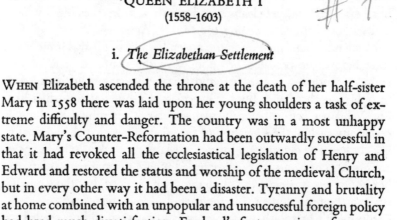

CHAPTER XIII

·QUEEN ELIZABETH I
(1558–1603)

i. *The Elizabethan Settlement*

WHEN Elizabeth ascended the throne at the death of her half-sister Mary in 1558 there was laid upon her young shoulders a task of extreme difficulty and danger. The country was in a most unhappy state. Mary's Counter-Reformation had been outwardly successful in that it had revoked all the ecclesiastical legislation of Henry and Edward and restored the status and worship of the medieval Church, but in every other way it had been a disaster. Tyranny and brutality at home combined with an unpopular and unsuccessful foreign policy had bred much dissatisfaction. England's first experience for many years of a woman on the throne had not given her much confidence in what John Knox called 'the monstrous regiment of women': and now here was another of them! Few people put much trust in this slim young woman of five-and-twenty, the daughter of Anne Boleyn; but all eyes were turned upon her as she took up the reins of government.

What would her policy be? Would she carry on as her sister had done? Was the breach with Rome and the Reformation in England which succeeded it just an insignificant incident which could now be forgotten; or would the new queen go back to the point where her brother had left off and carry on from there? The whole country was concerned in the answers to these questions, for much was at stake.

Ecclesiastically the country was divided into three groups. There were, first of all, those who had supported Mary in the return to Rome, and who were now in power. These included all the bishops, since any who had opposed Mary had either been burnt or had fled overseas. The parochial clergy who had not been turned out were all officially of the pro-Roman party. But a good many had been deprived, and it was among them that the nucleus of the protestant party was to be found. Many had gone abroad to await better times, but now made ready to return should the new régime show signs of a change of policy, while at home there were plenty who had lain low during Mary's reign but were now ready to come out into the open and join forces with any returning exiles. But between these two wings lay a middle party who wished to see neither servility to Rome nor subservience to Geneva but a Church of England truly catholic in all essentials and yet cleansed and reformed from the abuses which had gathered round it during the Middle Ages.

Much now depended upon the queen herself, but it was some little time before she revealed her policy. In the confused state of the country caution was essential, and Elizabeth was not to be hustled into showing her hand. But her selection of a moderate reformer like Sir William Cecil as her principal secretary, her refusal to allow a ceremony such as the Elevation of the Host in her chapel, and finally her choice of so definite a reformer as Matthew Parker to be the new Archbishop of Canterbury all revealed where her sympathies lay. As her policy became clear the moderate men rejoiced, but the Romanists and the protestants made them ready for battle.

Elizabeth's first Parliament met in January 1559 and proceeded to pass two acts of supreme importance—the *Act of Supremacy* and the *Act of Uniformity,* which together form what is known as the 'Elizabethan Settlement'. The *Act of Supremacy*[1] revived Henry's legislation against Rome and Edward's act to restore the administration of the Sacrament to the laity in both kinds. It abolished the jurisdiction in England of any 'foreign prince, person, prelate, state or potentate, spiritual or temporal', and imposed an oath upon all ecclesiastical and lay officials acknowledging Elizabeth not as 'supreme head' but as 'supreme governor' of both Church and State. This act, which passed with little opposition, undid much of Mary's legislation and reopened the breach with Rome, and there is some evidence that this was as far as Elizabeth intended to go for the time being. If no further action had been taken, Elizabeth's Parliament would in fact have restored the position as it was in 1547 except for the restoration of the chalice to the laity. But, under pressure from a protestant group in London, Parliament went on to pass the second bill, the *Act of Uniformity,*[2] which, playing upon the country's need for strength through

---

[1] Gee and Hardy, *Documents,* pp. 442-58; extracts in Tanner, *Tudor Constitutional Documents,* pp. 130-35.

[2] *Ibid.* pp. 458-67; cf. Tanner, *Tudor Constitutional Documents,* pp. 135-9.

unity, reintroduced, with severe penalties for disobedience, what was practically the Prayer Book of 1552. A few slight alterations were made: the objectionable 'Black Rubric' was omitted, the words of administration of the Sacrament from the 1549 book were joined together with those from 1552, and a restoration of the eucharistic vestments was carried out by the insertion of the so-called 'Ornaments Rubric' which stated that 'Such Ornaments of the Church, and of the Ministers thereof at all times of their Ministration, shall be retained, and be in use, as were in this Church of England, by the authority of Parliament, in the second year of the reign of King Edward the Sixth'.[1]

The choice of the 1552 Prayer Book rather than that of 1549 as the standard of worship showed that Parliament, in spite of the opposition of the spiritual peers, was under considerable protestant pressure, whatever may have been the personal wishes of the queen. The *Act of Uniformity* was shortly followed by a set of Royal Injunctions,[2] drawn up by Cecil and modelled upon the Edwardine Injunctions of 1547,[3] but adding new clauses dealing with clerical dress, encouraging kneeling during prayers and bowing at the name of Jesus, and enforcing more regular preaching and catechizing. The Injunctions also forbade any priest or deacon to marry until the lady of his choice had been interviewed and approved by the bishop and two Justices of the Peace.

These Injunctions and the oath which formed part of the *Act of Supremacy* were closely connected with a royal visitation of the country which took place in the summer of 1559. So many changes had taken place during the last twenty years that there was much confusion in the minds of both clergy and people and probably a good deal of disobedience to the new laws. The commissioners set themselves to see that uniformity was enforced.

The first problem was that of the bishops. Cardinal Pole had died within a few hours of the death of Mary and several other sees were vacant, but such bishops as remained were all of Mary's choosing and therefore inevitably hostile to the new policy. When the oath was administered to them, Bonner and eleven others refused to take it and were deprived. Five, including Tunstall of Durham, hesitated but,

[1] This is clearly intended to refer to the Prayer Book of 1549, though in fact the 'second year of the reign of King Edward the Sixth' had expired *before* the 1549 Prayer Book was authorized.
[2] Gee and Hardy, *Documents*, pp. 417-42.   [3] See above, p. 181.

with one exception, these all followed their colleagues into exile. Only one bishop—Kitchin of Llandaff—took the oath and threw in his lot with the new régime.

The parochial clergy gave very little trouble. Whatever hopes Elizabeth and Cecil may have entertained were amply fulfilled. What might have been a real crisis passed off remarkably quietly, probably not more than about two hundred of the clergy raising any difficulties, while the rest quietly accepted the new order and got on with their work. The laity, perhaps because they had less to lose, showed more independence. Most of them accepted the Elizabethan Settlement without demur, but a number stood out against it, especially in the north and north-west, where little pockets of recusants continued for many years to embarrass the government. Some also conformed outwardly by taking the oath and attending the necessary services in their parish churches while they remained Romanists at heart and received the sacraments from the hands of obscure priests. Meanwhile with the 'new reform' went a wave of popular iconoclasm. Altars, roods, images, ornaments, books and vestments which had been reintroduced into the churches during the reign of Mary were now disposed of, many of them being carried out into the streets and publicly burned. Henry Machyn, the diarist, described how he saw 'a-gaynst Yrmonger [lane] and a-gaynst sant Thomas of Acurs ij gret [bonfires] of rodes and of Mares and Johns and odur emages, ther thay wher bornyd with gret wondur'.[1]

Thus the Elizabethan Settlement was carried through with remarkably little opposition, though there were many difficulties ahead through the pressure from Romanists and Genevans. But the revolution had deprived the country of practically the whole of its episcopate and Elizabeth was faced with the very considerable task of finding enough outstanding men of her own way of thinking to fill the bench. For Canterbury her choice fell upon Matthew Parker. Parker had been at Cambridge in the days of Lutheran infiltration, and had been a friend of Ridley, Bilney, Barnes, Latimer and most of the reformers. He had certainly learnt much from them, but his scholarly mind and deep learning had prevented him from joining the ranks of the more extreme men. As Master of Corpus Christi College and

---

[1] *Diary of Henry Machyn* (ed. J. G. Nichols, 1847), p. 207; cf. pp. 208, 209. See also the account of similar bonfires in C. Wriothesley, *Chronicle*, ii, p. 146.

Dean of Lincoln he had held positions of some importance at Mary's accession, but, though he went into hiding, he remained in the country among his books and papers while others of his contemporaries were sitting at the feet of Calvin at Geneva. With the accession of Elizabeth his qualities were recognized, and, in spite of his extreme reluctance to be drawn into public affairs, he was elected archbishop on August 1, 1559, and consecrated at Lambeth on December 17 by Barlow, formerly of Bath and Wells, Coverdale, Scory of Chichester, and Hodgkin, suffragan bishop of Bedford, all of whom had survived from earlier days. Thus the apostolic succession was preserved and, by the new primate, other bishops were consecrated and the vacant sees filled. The first corner was successfully turned; Elizabeth had a bench of bishops and a clergy and laity all outwardly conforming to the policy which she wished to pursue. It was only later that cracks began to appear in the edifice.

ii. *Church and Papist*

Elizabeth had, at first, no wish to be hard on those who refused to accept the new régime. She realized, far more clearly than her sister had ever done, that men with tender consciences cannot be dragooned into a type of religion which does not command their allegiance. She was, therefore, prepared to wink at a certain amount of recusancy so long as it did not spread too far and so long as those who declined to conform were in other ways loyal subjects. But, as the reign progressed, relations between the government and the recusants steadily deteriorated, and that mainly as a result of pressure from outside England, which more and more forced the Roman Catholics into the position of subjects of a foreign and hostile power. The circumstances which brought this about were the attitude of the papacy towards Elizabeth, the Jesuit mission, Spanish interference and the intrigues of Mary Queen of Scots. As these, in their various ways, threatened the security of the throne and the physical safety of the queen, so government action became more and more severe against such as appeared to be implicated in them.

After the visitation of 1559 almost all the Marian bishops found themselves deprived of their sees, and most of them were in prison.

There is no evidence that they were ill-treated unless they were found to be intriguing with the Spanish ambassador, in which case sterner measures were taken against them. But as possible centres of plots and rebellions the government felt obliged to keep them under restraint. The visitation also led to the dissolution of such monasteries and religious houses as had been refounded in Mary's reign. Among these were Westminster Abbey, two houses of friars in London and the nuns at Syon; but so closely were these allied to the reactionary policy of Mary that it was thought dangerous to allow them to survive, and monasticism was brought to a complete end in the Church of England until its revival many years later.

Meanwhile the events taking place in England were being closely followed at Rome. At first the pope, Pius IV, appears to have entertained some hope of converting Elizabeth, and sent envoys to London with this purpose. But they failed. He also attempted to enlist the support of Philip of Spain, who, as ex-king of England, was looked upon as the natural protector of the papists in this country. But Philip had no wish to interfere in English domestic affairs, having plenty of troubles of his own to occupy his mind. But with the accession of Pius V in 1566 the papal policy took a more lively turn. The Council of Trent had now concluded its sittings and published its decrees. The Church of Rome was in a militant mood and determined that its will should be enforced. Pius therefore began to lay his plans for the humiliation of that proud young woman who sat upon the throne of England.

In 1568 the pope found a useful collaborator in Mary Queen of Scots, who, in this year, fled into England and did her best to rally the Romanists, especially in the north of the country. To many people her claim to the English throne was a good deal better than that of Elizabeth. Elizabeth was the daughter of Anne Boleyn whose marriage with Henry VIII had never been acknowledged by the Church of Rome, while Mary was directly descended from Henry VII through his daughter Margaret who had married James IV of Scotland. Not only did many people conscientiously regard Mary as the rightful Queen of England, but she herself had made it the ambition of her life to make herself accepted as such. Her arrival in England was, therefore, fraught with the greatest possible danger to the throne. Within a few months her presence had given new hope to the English recusants, and in November 1569 the Earls of Westmorland and

Northumberland raised a rebellion the purpose of which was to get rid of Elizabeth and restore the 'true and catholic religion'. The rebels entered Durham Cathedral where a Roman Mass was said and the English Prayer Book trodden under foot. But, in spite of some help from Rome, the Northern Rebellion was quickly suppressed and with great severity.

News of the rising and of its initial success did, however, reach Rome, where it was interpreted as a sign of general hostility to Elizabeth. The pope decided that the time had come for action. In February a formal 'trial' of Elizabeth was staged at Rome, witnesses being found among recusant exiles who had fled from England. As might have been expected, Elizabeth was found guilty, excommunicated and deposed, and all her subjects were dispensed from their oath of allegiance to her. The verdict was then embodied in a bull, *Regnans in excelsis*,[1] a copy of which was smuggled to England and nailed to the door of the Bishop of London's palace by a man called John Felton.

To the recusants in England the bull was a disaster of the first magnitude. Hitherto they had been able to live quietly as useful citizens, paying a small tax for the privilege of not having to worship in the parish churches. Now with the publication of this bull they were suddenly and without warning forced into the position of having to choose between obedience to the State and to the pope. If they chose to obey the pope they became, inevitably, traitors, for the bull had declared: 'we do command and charge all and every the noblemen, subjects and people and others aforesaid that they presume not to obey her or her orders mandates and laws' on penalty of excommunication. Each recusant in England was therefore faced with the choice between excommunication and death. No more terrible choice could be demanded of a man.

The papal bull of 1570 marks the final separation of England from Rome. Rome had now spoken in language which left no hope of future reconciliation. Meanwhile the English government replied to the papal bull by an act which tightened up the laws against recusancy, made it high treason to publish the bull in England, and declared that anyone caught introducing into England 'any crosses, pictures,

[1] The most important passages from the bull are printed in G. W. Prothero, *Statutes and Constitutional Documents, 1559–1625*, pp. 195–6, and a translation in Tanner, *Tudor Constitutional Documents*, pp. 143–6.

beads or suchlike vain and superstitious things from the Bishop or
See of Rome' should be declared guilty of *praemunire*.[1]

A deadlock was therefore reached and the pope began to look
around for means of implementing his threats. At first he hoped to
persuade the catholic princes of Europe to launch a crusade or *empresa*
against England; but the princes, knowing something of English sea-
power, failed to take up the challenge. But if military measures failed,
there remained another form of attack, by the work of missionaries.
In 1568 an English recusant, William Allen, had founded at Douai a
college to train men to serve as missionaries in England, and it was
not long before other colleges were established at Rome and elsewhere. A severe training was imposed upon the students, who were
to be fully prepared for martyrdom. They were to avoid all political
controversy and concentrate simply on the conversion of the English
people by every possible means. Many young Englishmen volun-
teered for this work, and by 1580 there were more than a hundred
priests at work in England as part of this mission. But their work was
constantly made more difficult by attempts from Rome to drag them
into political sabotage by fomenting disaffection or even encouraging
assassination of the queen on the grounds that 'whosoever sends her
out of the world with the pious intention of doing God service not
only does not sin but gains merit'.[2]

Many of those who took part in the mission to England were
members of the Society of Jesus, among them Edmund Campion and
Robert Parsons. Campion was a noble-hearted and fearless missionary who quickly made himself beloved and respected by the English
people, but Parsons was something of an adventurer and a lover of
intrigue. Campion's stay in England was short. After only a few
months of missionary work he was captured, tortured and executed
(December 1, 1581). But still the work went on. Other missionaries
arrived, were hunted down and, if caught, put to death. Meanwhile the government continued to tighten up the laws against
recusants and to make their position more dangerous and difficult.
An act passed in 1581[3] increased the fines for absence from church and
declared that anyone joining the Church of Rome should be regarded
as a traitor. In 1583, after the Throckmorton plot which threatened

---

[1] Tanner, *Tudor Constitutional Documents*, pp. 146-50.
[2] Letter of papal secretary to the nuncio at Madrid quoted in Meyer, *England and the Catholic Church under Queen Elizabeth* (1916), p. 271.
[3] Tanner, *Tudor Constitutional Documents*, pp. 152-4.

the life of the queen, further legislation was passed ordering all Jesuit
and seminary priests to leave the country.[1] Three years later the
government reluctantly decided that there could be no security so
long as Mary Queen of Scots was alive, stirring up trouble and
fomenting disobedience, and on February 8, 1587, she was executed.
Her death did more than anything else to break the back of the
Roman party, for many peaceful and law-abiding citizens conscientiously regarded her as the rightful Queen of England and felt
bound to support her claims. But with her death the Romanist
party became more and more identified with Spanish and papal
politics.

It was now some years since the pope had tried to launch a
military crusade against England, and at last he was getting some support for his scheme. Plans for an Armada were begun in 1585, and
much money was collected, but the powers concerned were completely misled about the state of opinion in England and were quite
unaware of the wave of patriotism which was sweeping across the
country. Nor did they fully appreciate the sea-power of their enemies;
and when the Armada sailed up the Channel in 1588, the English
admirals burnt or scattered the fleet and left the survivors to find their
own way back to Spain if they could. This rapid and complete rout
of the great force which had been assembled to conquer England and
restore the power of the papacy marked the end of any real danger
of foreign intervention in English ecclesiastical affairs, and left the
Roman Catholics in England to look after themselves.

Naturally the danger from the Armada led to further measures
against Roman Catholics in England. Recusants were now ordered
to return to their place of origin and were not allowed to move more
than five miles from their homes.[2] Many were suspected of subversive
propaganda and were imprisoned, though generally under quite
humane conditions.[3] Those who defied the laws and were prepared
to sacrifice themselves to papal claims were put to death, some 250
in all.[4]

[1] Ibid. 154-9; Gee and Hardy, Documents, pp. 485-92.
[2] Gee and Hardy, Documents, pp. 498-508; Tanner, Tudor Constitutional Documents,
pp. 159-63.
[3] See W. H. Frere, The English Church in the Reigns of Elizabeth and James I, pp.
268-9.
[4] J. B. Black, The Reign of Elizabeth (1936), p. 151. The total number of recusants
has been reckoned at about 120,000 (ibid. p. 374 n.).

iii. *Church and Puritan*

The danger to the Church from the Puritans was very different from that offered by the Roman Catholics. While the latter desired to *overthrow* the Church of England and restore the papal jurisdiction, the former wished to *transform* the Church according to their own ideas of what a Church should be. There was, therefore, nothing political about their activities. Though many of them were in touch with Geneva they were not commissioned by any foreign power, nor did they show any hostility to the queen herself. They could not therefore be tried for treason or imprisoned; on the contrary, there was nothing to stop them from holding positions of great power and responsibility within the Church which they wished to transform. To them the Elizabethan Settlement was wholly unsatisfactory, having set up a Church which they regarded as tainted with Romanism and untrue to Scripture. The motive power behind them was the influence of Geneva, many of them having become disciples of Calvin during their exile from England in Mary's reign. It was the full Calvinist system which they wished to reproduce in England as Knox was introducing it into Scotland. This would mean the abolition of episcopacy and the substitution of presbyteral government by assemblies and church-sessions, worship more in accordance with that of protestant communities elsewhere, an increase in the powers of the laity, and the prohibition of all vestments, ornaments and ceremonies which belonged to the past.

It was indeed to these that Puritan opposition was first directed. The Prayer Book of 1559 smelt of popery. It was 'an imperfect book, culled and picked out of the popish dunghill'.[1] It allowed such improper ceremonies as the use of the sign of the cross in Baptism, the imposition of hands in Confirmation and the ring in Marriage. It preserved the veneration of the saints through its Calendar and tolerated such customs as bowing at the Name of Jesus and kneeling at the Communion. Moreover, with the Prayer Book went certain discreditable adjuncts of worship especially the use of organs and other musical instruments and antiphonal singing—'the singing, ringing and trowling of psalms from one side of the choir to the other'. But

---

[1] 'An Admonition to Parliament' (1572), quoted in W. H. Frere, *The English Church in the Reigns of Elizabeth and James I*, p. 179.

the greatest dislike of all was to the vestments in which the priest clothed himself. The Ornaments Rubric in the Prayer Book of 1559 had allowed for the wearing of alb and chasuble or cope at the Eucharist and the surplice for the choir offices. The Puritans greatly disapproved of this, and many of the clergy whose sympathies lay with this party found themselves prevented by their consciences from appearing in church in even so innocent a garment as a surplice, while Edmund Grindal was doubtful whether he could accept a bishopric because it would necessitate the wearing of robes.

In the early years of the reign Puritan agitation was mainly confined to such comparatively minor matters, but as the years went by, the dispute moved into a wider sphere in which the critics of the Church began to attack not the externals of worship but the doctrines of the Church and the ministry which lay behind them. That the Church of England should preserve episcopal government had never for a moment been doubted by the framers of the Elizabethan Settlement, but to the Puritans it was anathema; and they set themselves to work for the abolition of episcopacy and the establishment of a presbyterian type of church government with a form of worship which gave complete liberty to the minister.

The Puritans found a vigorous leader in Thomas Cartwright, a scholar of Cambridge who had studied the New Testament and was determined to work for a Church which should be truly scriptural. Nothing, either in the worship or in the constitution of the Church, which could not be justified by the Scriptures was to be tolerated. A manifesto called *An Admonition to Parliament* (1572)[1] and Cartwright's translation in 1574 of Walter Travers' *Disciplina Ecclesiastica*[2] provided a platform for Puritan controversy and attack.

About the same time those of the clergy and laity who had Puritan sympathies were beginning to take matters into their own hands. The Prayer Book was enforced by law and must therefore be used; but this need not prevent other forms of worship being held at other times. Episcopacy was the only legal form of church government; but this need not prevent groups of clergy forming themselves into voluntary societies and placing themselves under a Calvinist form of discipline. It was found, in fact, that it was possible for a clergyman

---

[1] Printed in W. H. Frere and C. E. Douglas, *Puritan Manifestoes* (Church Hist. Soc., vol. lxxii), pp. 1-40.
[2] For Cartwright see A. F. Scott Pearson, *Thomas Cartwright and Elizabethan Puritanism* (1925).

14

to conform to the ordinances of the Church and yet conduct his ministry on what were practically Calvinist lines.

The first development was that of the 'prophesyings' which began at Northampton in 1571. These were meetings of clergy and laity on week-day mornings for the purpose of Biblical study, discussion and prayer. These seemed harmless enough so long as they did not replace the statutory worship of the Church. They could be, and often were, very edifying, especially if conducted by scholars and with a real desire for knowledge. But as they spread throughout the country the danger was to make them a substitute for Morning and Evening Prayer, or to comply with the statutes by saying Mattins quietly at an early hour and hold a 'prophesying' at the chief gathering together of worshippers on a Sunday morning. Some of the bishops approved of the 'prophesyings' and tried to encourage and control them, but the queen was bitterly opposed to them, thinking them disloyal and subversive. She tried her best, by a circular letter to all the bishops in 1577,[1] to have them forbidden, but many of the bishops, including Grindal, approved of them and refused to co-operate.

The second development was of the 'classis' system. Many Puritan clergy, disliking and disapproving of episcopacy, began to ignore the bishops as far as possible and put themselves under the discipline of a 'classis' or local committee of presbyters who came to wield considerable power. Candidates for the ministry, for example, were selected by these committees and privately 'ordained' according to the form of which they approved, being sent afterwards to the bishops for episcopal ordination in accordance with the laws of the land. The 'classes' also exercised great influence over the worship in the churches, criticized sermons and saw to it that extempore prayer only was used.

By these two developments the strength of the Church and the authority of the bishops was slowly undermined. Clergy were paying lip-service to the Establishment, and living upon its resources, while at the same time they were substituting for the Prayer Book their own type of worship, and were taking their orders not from their fathers-in-God but from local committees. A very serious and dangerous situation was thus developing, and one with which it was extremely difficult for the government to deal. There was no outward dis-

[1] Tanner, *Tudor Constitutional Documents*, pp. 184-5.

obedience, no political disloyalty, little breach of the law. From time to time, indeed, Puritan hostility flared up as in the 'Martin Marprelate' tracts which attempted to destroy episcopacy by ridicule and abuse, but these things were comparatively easy to deal with.

While the main bulk of the Puritans were content to work quietly for the overthrow of the Establishment, there were a few ardent and intolerant souls who could not brook delay and soon found membership in the Church of England more than they could bear. Most of these were either deprived of their benefices or resigned them voluntarily and began to throw in their lot with the Anabaptists, many of whom were refugees from Holland, fanatical protestants and antinomians.[1] Their preaching of civil disobedience led to stern measures being taken against them, and a few were burnt.

Among those who became 'Separatists' from the Church of England was Robert Browne, who, about 1580, formed an independent congregation of non-conformists at Norwich, while a similar movement was started by Henry Barrow in London.[2] But in the eyes of the government such experiments were regarded as fraught with danger, and in 1593 an *Act against Seditious Sectaries* was passed, imposing severe punishments of imprisonment, banishment and even death for such as refuse to go to church or who attend conventicles.[3] With such open defiance of the law the government was able to deal; but the quiet, elusive work of the main body of the Puritans went on unchecked.

There is no doubt that, to a large number of people the Puritan way of life held out great attractions. In a period of considerable confusion, Calvinism provided a clear-cut and authoritative system both of thought and of government which gave a sense of security. To many people the attitude of the government seemed deplorably vague and ambiguous. It seemed to be 'halting between two opinions', unable which to accept and what policy to follow. After a generation of rapid changes, people felt lost and insecure. This was supposed to be a period of reform, and yet so little real reform took place, many of the abuses such as pluralism and absenteeism, extremes of wealth and poverty among the clergy,

---

[1] For the Anabaptists, see C. Burrage, *The Early English Dissenters, 1550–1641*, 2 vols. (1912).

[2] For Browne and Barrow, see R. W. Dale, *History of English Congregationalism* (1907), and Tanner, *Tudor Constitutional Documents*, pp. 186–90.

[3] Tanner, *op. cit.* pp. 197–200.

ignorance and superstition continuing virtually unrecognized.

iv. *The* Via Media

'Ye shall pray', began the Bidding Prayer sent out with Elizabeth's Injunctions in 1559, 'for Christ's Holy Catholic Church, that is for the whole congregation of Christian people dispersed throughout the whole world, and especially for the Church of England and Ireland.'[1] In the eyes of those who were shaping the destiny of the Church in England there was no sense of separation from the rest of the catholic church. The Church in England was, as the title-page to the first Prayer Book had implied, a part of the catholic church, even though it had repudiated papal jurisdiction. It was catholic, but it was also reformed. Its roots ran back to the primitive church, but certain customs and ideas which had clung to it during the Middle Ages had now been cut away. The fundamental doctrines and constitution of the Church remained the same, but a number of genuine reforms had been carried out, such as the vernacular liturgy, the administration of the Sacrament in both kinds and permission for the clergy to marry. The chief constitutional change lay in the position of the sovereign as 'Supreme Governor'. This title had not been used before, though many sovereigns had acted as such without claiming the title. Strong monarchs such as William the Conqueror had appointed their bishops and controlled the affairs of the Church in their day with almost as much liberty as the Tudors.

The Elizabethan Settlement, therefore, though it reversed the policy of Mary, did not introduce much that was new. The question, however, which agitated the minds of the people was: How long will this last? On one side were the conservatives who hoped for a reconciliation with Rome: on the other the progressives who wanted to remould the Church according to the presbyterian pattern. Much depended upon the queen and her wishes. Like her father she could be reticent about her religious opinions. In her own chapel she liked to worship before an altar furnished with crucifix and candles and with a priest wearing the traditional vestments. But that was a private affair. In public her policy was to keep the Church in England free from foreign influence, whether from Rome or Geneva, and to allow it to develop on its own lines in accordance with the growing patriotism and national pride of which the queen herself so soon became the symbol. Elizabeth distrusted the papists because of their

[1] Gee and Hardy *Documents*, p. 440.

allegiance to Rome, and the protestants because of their allegiance to Geneva. People who took their orders from some continental power were not whole-heartedly English. And that was what Elizabeth wanted—an *English* church designed to meet the spiritual needs of the English people.

Elizabeth was, on the whole, successful in her choice of servants to promote her policy, especially men like Sir William Cecil and Sir Nicholas Bacon. She was successful also with two out of the three Archbishops of Canterbury who held office during her reign. Matthew Parker (1559–75) was a good scholar, a good administrator and a man of courage and vision. He was not afraid to stand up to the queen if he thought her policy mistaken, as, for example, over the question of clerical celibacy which Elizabeth preferred to a married clergy. Parker had a clear idea of what he wanted the Church of England to be, clearer probably than that of the queen. He wished it to be based upon true scholarship, drawing upon the best traditions of the primitive church, faithful to scripture, vital, honest, dignified. Himself a merciful man he did his best to avoid bloodshed or hardship even for those who were his worst enemies. It is to him, perhaps more than to anyone else, that we owe the type of churchmanship which we associate with 'Anglicanism'.[1]

His successor, Edmund Grindal (1576–83), who had been Bishop of London and Archbishop of York, was a much less successful leader of the Church. In his days a noticeable deterioration set in, and, in spite of Grindal's efforts, bishops and clergy showed signs of a growing materialism and worldliness which gave some excuse to the Puritan demands for the abolition of episcopacy altogether. Grindal himself was honest enough, but he was weak. His sympathies lay really with the Puritans rather than with the churchmen, and his support of the 'prophesyings' aroused the royal disapproval and led to his sequestration and to his spending the greater part of his primacy in retirement and disgrace.

John Whitgift, who succeeded Grindal in 1583, held office for twenty-one years and lived to crown James I in 1604. Whitgift, who had been Master of Trinity College, Cambridge, and Bishop of Worcester, was, in much of his doctrine, a Calvinist, but a staunch supporter of episcopacy. A strong man, like Parker, he had a clear

[1] J. Strype, *Life and Acts of Matthew Parker* (1711, etc.); and see 'The Importance of the Parker MSS.', by E. C. Hoskyns in *Cambridge Sermons* (1938), pp. 203–17.

vision of what he was working for and was fearless in carrying out his policy. Using the Court of High Commission he insisted that law and order should be preserved and the Prayer Book obeyed. The Puritans naturally thought him harsh and bigoted, but Whitgift regarded those who refused to conform to the established Church as potential traitors; and, in this, he had the support of the queen.[1]

Thus the official policy of both Church and State was that of the *Via Media*; and, though there was not a great deal of ecclesiastical legislation after 1559, many bishops, by means of injunctions and diocesan decrees, tried to carry out the same policy in their own dioceses.[2] The most notable document of this kind was the *Advertisements* drawn up by Archbishop Parker in 1566.[3] These were intended to be issued as royal injunctions; but the queen refused to commit herself and Parker was obliged to issue them in his own name. These demand the 'often and devout' reception of the Holy Communion, encourage preaching, demand the use of the surplice in parish churches and copes in cathedrals, and enforce the custom of kneeling at the Communion.

Meanwhile the Church had been considering its doctrinal position. In 1563 Convocation set itself to revise the 42 Articles of 1553 and reduced them to 39. When these were submitted to the queen she altered one or two of them and struck one out altogether as being offensive to the Roman Catholics. There were thus, for a few years 38 Articles until No. 29 was restored in 1571. These Articles have played an important part in the history of the Church, and are still regarded as one of the historic formularies to which every ordinand and new incumbent is required to affirm his loyalty. They are, in fact, a statement of the Church of England's attitude towards the doctrinal disputes which were convulsing Europe at the time, including such doctrines as Predestination and Transubstantiation.[4]

An attempt was also made to reform the Canon Law of the Church. Since Henry's reign the state of ecclesiastical law in England had been chaotic, as no one knew how much of the medieval system still applied. Various attempts to codify the Canon Law had been made but had come to nothing. Finally, in 1571, a set of 'certain canons'

[1] V. J. K. Brook, *Whitgift and the English Church* (1957). V. J. K. Brook, *A Life of Archbishop Parker* (1962).
[2] See Frere and Kennedy, *Visitation Articles and Injunctions*, vol. iii, and Kennedy, *Elizabethan Episcopal Administration*, 3 vols. (1924).
[3] Gee and Hardy, *Documents*, pp. 467-75.
[4] E. J. Bicknell, *A Theological Introduction to the Thirty-nine Articles*, (1925), pp. 17-21.

was passed dealing with bishops, deans, archdeacons and other cathedral dignitaries, parish clergy, preachers, schoolmasters, patronage and excommunication.[1] Such parts of the old *Corpus Juris Canonici* and of provincial statutes which were not abrogated by law were still regarded as binding, and to these were added the various acts of Henry VIII and Edward VI. But the Canons of 1571, like Parker's *Advertisements*, did not command the approval of the queen, who refused to sign them. Finally, in 1597, a small collection of twelve canons was made which the queen confirmed.[2]

The doctrinal and other controversies of this period produced a fairly large crop of literature, some of which was cheap and abusive, but some sober and scholarly. Among the apologists on the side of the Church were John Jewel, Bishop of Salisbury, and his pupil Richard Hooker. Jewel preached at Paul's Cross in November 1559 a famous sermon or challenge in support of the Elizabethan settlement. In this he appealed both to Scripture and to the practice of the primitive Church and challenged all comers to dispute his conclusions that the *Ecclesia Anglicana* was fully catholic. The sermon was followed up by a much larger work, the *Apologia Ecclesiae Anglicanae*, which appeared in Latin in 1562 and in an English translation by Lady Bacon in 1564.[3] This is a vigorous condemnation of Rome and defence of the Church of England and, as such, gave rise to much controversy.

Jewel made it his business to educate a number of boys, among whom was Richard Hooker who grew up to be Master of the Temple. By the time Hooker entered the field of controversy the danger from Rome was very much less than it had been in Jewel's day, while the Puritans had grown greatly in influence and prestige. Hooker set himself to provide Anglicanism with a philosophical and logical basis which he did in his book *Of the Laws of Ecclesiastical Polity*. This was planned on a large scale in eight books of which the first four, published in 1594, deal with law in general and with Church Law in particular. Hooker refutes the puritan argument that Scripture is the only test of what is correct, and defends the Church's right to make her own laws so long as they are not contrary to Scripture. All this served as a background to Book V, which is nearly twice as long as Books I–IV put together. It is described as 'Of our

[1] Printed in full in E. Cardwell, *Synodalia*, i, pp. 111–31, and extracts in Prothero, *Statutes and Constitutional Documents*, pp. 200–202, and in translation in Gee and Hardy, *Documents*, pp. 476–7.

[2] E. Cardwell, *Synodalia*, i, pp. 147–63. On this question see the Historical Introduction to *The Canon Law of the Church of England*, being the Report of the Archbishops' Commission (1947).

[3] Both published in *The Works of John Jewel*, third portion (Parker Society, 1848).

Lawes that concerne the publicke religious duties of the Church; and the manner of bestowing that power of order, which inableth men in sundry degrees and callings to execute the same'. It deals with the building and dedication of churches, preaching, prayers, psalms and canticles, the administration of the sacraments and occasional offices and of the learning that should be in ministers. It claimed that the Church of England had in no way separated from the catholic Church: 'in the Church we were and we are so still'. Thus Hooker's book is a defence of the Church of England against Puritanism, as Jewel's had been a defence against Rome, and it was written with much dignity, learning and restraint. But his book was not only a defence, it was an *irenicon*, designed to bring peace after much strife. Hooker was not a controversialist: he was too wise and too learned for that. He tried to see things rationally, and hoped by his work to draw together all men of good-will. But, above all, he was a man of deep religious conviction who tried to see every doctrinal problem in the light of eternity. Thus, after dealing at length with the eucharistic controversy over which so much ill-feeling had been stirred up, he can say: 'What these elements are in themselves it skilleth not, it is enough that to me which take them they are the body and blood of Christ, his promise in witness hereof sufficeth, his word he knoweth which way to accomplish, why should any cogitation possess the mind of a faithful communicant but this, "O my God thou art true, O my Soul thou art happy!"'[1]

v. *Church Life in the Elizabethan Age*

The Elizabethan Settlement was based upon two acts of which one was an Act of Uniformity; but the picture which we get of the Elizabethan Church is one not of uniformity, but of diversity. At one extreme were the old Marian clergy who paid lip-service to the Act of Uniformity but preferred the old ways and sometimes said a Latin Mass quietly from their old books. At the other extreme were the Puritans who disliked, and disapproved of, the Prayer Book and episcopacy, and introduced customs and rites which the Act of Uniformity would certainly not have allowed. Between these two were men of all shades of opinion, and what went on in the parish churches depended upon the opinions and tastes of the clergy and, to a lesser extent, of the laity. Even loyalty to the Prayer Book allowed for a

[1] *The Works of Mr. Richard Hooker*, ed. Keble, Church and Paget (1888), ii, p. 362.

good deal of variety then, as now; for additions could be made and rubrics could be 'interpreted' in all kinds of ways without causing undue anxiety to the average conscience. The queen kept demanding uniformity but to no purpose, for the utmost diversity prevailed. Grindal in 1565 described the condition of his diocese of London as follows: 'Some say the service and prayers in the chancel, others in the body of the church; some say the same in a seat made in the church, some in the pulpit with their faces to the people; some keep precisely to the order of the book, others intermeddle psalms in metre; some say in a surplice, others without a surplice; the Table standeth in the body of the church in some places, in others it standeth in the chancel; in some places the Table standeth altarwise, distant from the wall a yard, in some others in the middle of the chancel, north and south; in some places the Table is joined, in others it standeth upon trestles; in some places the Table hath a carpet, in others it hath not; administration of the Communion is done by some with surplice and cap, some with surplice alone, others with none; some with chalice, some with a communion cup, others with a common cup; some with unleavened bread, some with leavened; some receive kneeling, others standing, others sitting; some baptise in a font, others in a basin; some sign with the sign of the cross, others sign not; some with a square cap, some with a round cap, some with a button cap, some with a hat'.[1]

Apart from lawlessness and disobedience, church life was, in many ways, at a low ebb in the early part of the reign, but there was a steady improvement as time went on. Churches were restored and refurnished, worship was more reverently said, and the clergy showed increasing signs of responsibility and conscientiousness. The Elizabethan bishops, being all nominees of the queen, were all more or less in sympathy with the policy of the government. No recusant could hold office, and the keener Puritans refused to do so since they disapproved of episcopacy altogether.

At the beginning of the reign there was a considerable shortage of clergy, owing to the unsettled times of the previous twenty years, and the deprivations and executions. Many benefices stood vacant when Elizabeth came to the throne and for some time after. Meanwhile pluralism continued as before, with its attendant evils of non-residence and the entrusting of parishes to the care of ill-paid and ill-educated stipendiary priests. Benefices were also conferred on boys

[1] Quoted from Lansdowne MSS. 8, f. 16 in Gee, *The Elizabethan Prayer Book* (1902), pp. 164-5.

still at school or at the university. Clerical marriage, in spite of the disapproval of the queen, continued to increase, so that perhaps half the clergy of England were married, though Elizabeth refused to allow wives of the clergy to live in colleges and cathedral closes. The morals of the clergy seem to have been at a rather low ebb at the beginning of the reign but improved as time went on. Their standard of education was also raised. At first many were but poorly educated, but the bishops did their best to see that the clergy took some steps to improve their learning, and organized regular examinations. Clergy were ordered to provide themselves with Bibles, Paraphrases and notebooks, and there is evidence that this order was generally obeyed. They were commanded also to dress soberly and not in 'great barrel-breeches and flaunting ruffs'—possibly a necessary injunction as the social status of the clergy rose. Meanwhile, to supplement the clergy, the order of 'reader' was revived, though it did not last very long.[1]

The destruction of the chantries by Edward VI had led to the closing of many small schools and, for a time, elementary education suffered a serious repulse. But the Elizabethan age was deeply interested in education and saw to it that, at any rate for the sons of squires and merchants, educational facilities should be provided. The old grammar schools continued, and a number of new schools were founded, including Rugby, Harrow and Merchant Taylors. The education provided by these schools was still mainly confined to Latin; but, under the influence of men like Roger Ascham, author of *The Scholemaster*, the curriculum was widened by greater interest being taken in music and in physical exercise. At the universities the Elizabethan age saw a growth of the collegiate system. The medieval colleges had provided only for a handful of scholars while the main bulk of students lived in lodgings and hostels. Now these were done away with and all undergraduates were required to be members of a college. This meant the building of several new colleges, and led to greater discipline, which was sadly needed.

The parish churches had been roughly treated during the middle years of the century when many of their treasures had been destroyed. This continued into the early years of Elizabeth's reign when many ornaments and precious things which had been reintroduced under Mary's Counter-Reformation were thrown out again. But some

---

[1] See 'Injunctions to Readers' in Frere and Kennedy, *Visitation Articles and Injunctions*, iii, pp. 67-8.

churches managed to keep at any rate a few of their treasures—a set
of vestments, some old medieval service-books, a few silver candlesticks, and so on.[1] In place of the old stone altars were now movable
wooden tables which normally stood altar-wise at the east end but
were moved down into the body of the church during the Communion. The Lord's Prayer and Ten Commandments were now
inscribed on the wall of each parish church in place of old medieval
wall-paintings; pulpits were built in increasing numbers, and old
chantry-chapels were often converted into family pews for the
gentry.

Normally, the priest conducted Morning and Evening Prayer from
a seat in the nave, and the clergy were ordered to say the offices
audibly and not to 'mumble nor tumble all things without devotion'. They were encouraged to preach if licensed to do so; otherwise to read one of the Homilies, a second collection of which
appeared in 1562. The same year saw the publication of the whole
of the Psalter in metre for use in the churches. As far back as 1549
Thomas Sternhold had produced nineteen metrical psalms, to which
John Hopkins and others had made additions until the collection was
complete. The poetry was, with few exceptions, of poor quality; but
these new hymns appealed to a largely illiterate populace, especially
when good tunes were provided by Tallis and others. Meanwhile at
the cathedrals and collegiate churches, where good choirs were available, a school of English church music was developing which became a part of that great outburst of beauty in literature and music
which marked the latter part of Elizabeth's reign. The names of
William Byrd, Orlando Gibbons, Thomas Weelkes and Thomas
Morley are the most illustrious of a large company of most gifted
composers who did much to enrich the worship of the Church of
England.[2]

The Eucharist was celebrated generally about once a month at the
end of Morning Prayer, but there was much variety about the
manner of its celebration and about the ornaments of the altar and
of the ministers. The congregation came up from the nave into the
chancel at the Offertory or at the Invitation and gathered round the
altar, sitting in the choir stalls or standing beside the table. There
was no system of 'going up' to receive the Sacrament which was

[1] See, e.g., the inventory made at S. Michael's, Worcester, in 1561 in J. Amphlett,
Churchwardens' Accounts of S. Michael's, Worcester (1896), pp. 46-7.
[2] E. H. Fellowes, *English Cathedral Music* (1941), pp. 53-82.

normally carried round to the people as they stood, sat or knelt. It was in the appearance of the churches and in the character of the worship conducted in them that the Reformation had left its deepest mark on the Church. In spite of the strong opposition to Puritanism there had been a steady movement from the objective and sacramental worship of the medieval church to the more subjective worship which we associate with Protestantism. The reading of the Bible and the preaching of the sermon now took pride of place which had previously been held by the sacrifice of the Mass. However, in many parts of the country old customs lingered on—bells were rung and prayers said for the souls of the departed, faithful souls went quietly to old shrines and holy places or kept up old customs which their fathers had honoured. Authority could not approve of this, and the curate of Rufforth in 1581 was censured in that he 'did not onelye permit and suffer a Rishbearing within the churche' but did himself 'daunce skip leape and hoighe gallantlye'.[1] But it was impossible to stamp it out. Meanwhile, under Puritan influence, there was a great increase in the study of the Bible, in the observance of Sunday and in that sense of personal responsibility and integrity which is perhaps the greatest gift of Protestantism to the world.

[1] J. S. Purvis, *Tudor Parish Documents of the Diocese of York* (1948), p. 168.

NOTE ON BOOKS

FOR the reign of Queen Elizabeth I see J. B. Black, *The Reign of Elizabeth* (1936) in the *Oxford History of England*, and J. E. Neale, *Queen Elizabeth* (1934) and *Elizabeth I and her Parliaments, 1955–1581* (1953). See also A. L. Rowse, *The England of Elizabeth* (1950). For church history, W. H. Frere, *The English Church in the Reigns of Elizabeth and James I* (1904) is the standard work, to which should be added H. N. Birt, *The Elizabethan Religious Settlement* (1907), H. Gee, *The Elizabethan Clergy and the Settlement of Religion, 1558–64* (1898) and *The Elizabethan Prayer Book and Ornaments* (1902), A. O. Meyer, *England and the Catholic Church under Queen Elizabeth* (1916) and J. V. P. Thompson, *Supreme Governor: a study of Elizabethan Ecclesiastical Policy and Circumstance* (n.d.). W. P. M. Kennedy has collected some most interesting material in *Elizabethan Episcopal Administration*, 3 vols. (1924). For the Puritans see A. F. Scott Pearson, *Thomas Cartwright and Elizabethan Puritanism* (1925), and P. Collinson, *The Elizabethan Puritan Movement* (1967). *John Gerard, the Autobiography of an Elizabethan*, tr. P. Caraman (1951) is a contemporary account of the adventures of a Jesuit priest in England.

CHAPTER XIV

THE EARLY STUARTS
(1603–1649)

i. James I

JAMES VI of Scotland, having been crowned at Stirling in 1567 when he was only a few months old, had never known what it was to be anything but a king, even though it were of a small and impoverished country. But when, on the death of Queen Elizabeth in 1603, he was invited to unite the crowns of England and of Scotland he imagined that he would now be able to live in royal splendour, and entertained the loftiest ideas of what royal supremacy might be made to mean. His great-great-uncle, Henry VIII, had made his power felt by force of character and prowess; his cousin, Elizabeth, by tact and sagacity. James intended to base his claim to supremacy on theological grounds, the Divine Right of Kings.

When he made his journey south from Scotland in the summer of 1603 he found England much divided in its ecclesiastical allegiance. There was, first of all, a small but dangerous Roman Catholic party. Since the defeat of the Armada the recusants had been forced to lie very low, though pressure was constantly exerted upon them by priests and agitators. It is true that only 8500 declared their allegiance to Rome in the survey made in 1603, but there were probably a good many more who did not choose openly to commit themselves.[1]

On the other hand, the Puritan party was active, self-confident and aggressive. On the ecclesiastical side it represented those who wished to advance from the restrained conservatism of the Elizabethan Settlement to much greater liberty both in worship and in church government. It disliked both the Prayer Book and episcopacy because each put a curb on the liberty of the individual. On the political side Puritanism was in close alliance with the rising class of the squires who believed that the time was coming when the despotic power of

---

[1] See G. Davies, *The Early Stuarts* (1937), pp. 203-4.

the king should be broken and sovereignty be given to the people as represented in Parliament, especially in the House of Commons. This combination of religious and political fervour gave great strength to the Puritan party and made it a most formidable power in the land.

Meanwhile the Church was steadily consolidating its position under the leadership of men like Richard Bancroft, Richard Hooker and Lancelot Andrewes. Scholarly, devout, dignified, conservative, the Anglican Church stood for the ideals which appealed most to the new king. Though a son of Mary Queen of Scots, James had little sympathy with the papal party, whose loyalty he always suspected. He had seen enough of Scottish Presbyterianism to know that Puritanism would do him no good. He therefore entered into a close alliance with the established Church in which he found plenty of people to support both the theories and the policies which lay nearest to his heart. In the eyes of the king, monarchy and episcopacy stood together. The king ruled by Divine Right, and it was the duty of the Church to support him as he would support the Church. 'No Bishop, no King', cried James at the Hampton Court Conference; but, as the country was one day to learn, the saying had also its corollary: 'No King, no Bishop'.

James was, from the first, suspicious of the Roman Catholics; but he had no desire to persecute them. He would have liked to be tolerant, and genuinely hoped that a reconciliation with Rome might be possible, referring, in his first speech before Parliament, to the Church of Rome as 'our mother church'. This declaration of amity encouraged the recusants, and priests poured into the country hoping for a mass movement towards Rome. But any such hopes were rudely shattered by the Gunpowder Plot of 1605. On the eve of the opening of Parliament it was discovered that a group of fanatics had made preparations to blow up King, Lords and Commons in one enormous explosion. The chief conspirators were caught and executed, and any hopes which the king may have entertained of coming to terms with the papists were destroyed. The only possible result of such a discovery was a tightening up of the laws against recusants, who were now required not only to go to the Anglican churches but to receive the Sacrament.

An oath of allegiance[1] was now imposed with the hope of distin-

---

[1] J. R. Tanner, *Constitutional Documents of the Reign of James I* (1930), pp. 94-104.

guishing between those who were loyal to the state and those who were not. But the oath included a repudiation of papal claims and as such was unacceptable to many otherwise peaceable citizens. It was bitterly denounced by the pope and Cardinal Bellarmine who did their utmost to stir up English recusants against it. James himself entered into the controversy with a theological defence of the oath which was published first in English and then in Latin. Bishop Andrewes supported him with the weight of his learning and devotion, and John Donne, who had been brought up as a Roman Catholic but was now in process of transferring his allegiance to the Anglican Church, joined in with his book *Pseudo-martyr* which poured considerable scorn on some of the recusants who liked to pose as the victims of persecution.

The controversy dragged on for many years, but popular dislike of popery became more violent and bitter. The king might long for toleration, and the bishops might plead for charity, but to the people as a whole recusancy was but another name for treason, and Rome and Spain were the natural enemies of England. It therefore came as a great shock when James proposed to marry his son Charles to the Infanta Maria of Spain, and began promising concessions to the Roman Catholics in England. To the great joy of the people the negotiations broke down, but Charles's subsequent marriage to the French princess, Henrietta Maria, revived many of the fears which his previous suit had engendered and helped to stir up popular distrust not only of Rome but of James and the court as well.

The Puritans had hoped for great things from James, coming, as he did, from a Presbyterian country. On his way south from Scotland he was presented with the 'Millenary Petition',[1] said to have been subscribed by a thousand clergy of Puritan sympathies who were anxious to gain his support for their views. They raised a number of objections to the Prayer Book, demanding the abolition of such things as the sign of the cross in Baptism, the wearing of the surplice, the custom of bowing at the name of Jesus, and the reading of the Apocrypha in church. They also pleaded for more and better preaching. James listened to their demands, but referred the whole matter to a conference which was held at Hampton Court in 1604. This was presided over by the king himself who took an active part

---

[1] Gee and Hardy, *Documents*, pp. 508-11; G. W. Prothero, *Select Statutes and other Constitutional Documents, 1559-1625*, pp. 413-16.

in the debates. There were also present members of the Privy Council, nine bishops and five deans, Reynolds, Dean of Lincoln, being the spokesman for the Puritan party. The conference, which lasted for three days, made it perfectly clear that James was on the side of the Establishment and expected all others to conform, crying out that if they failed to do so 'I will harry them out of the land, or else do worse'. The positive results of the conference were a few minor additions to the Prayer Book, including the last part of the Catechism, and the plan for a new translation of the Bible which appeared in 1611 and is commonly known as the 'Authorized Version'.[1]

The Puritans were much disappointed with the Conference, from which they had hoped so much; but they continued to press their claims and to teach their own special doctrines. Among the latter was a strict Sabbatarianism which sought to prohibit all kinds of sport and merry-making on Sundays. In those places where Puritan influence was strong such prohibitions could be enforced, for in 1611 the Wardens of the Taylors' Company at Salisbury were sent to prison for patronizing morris-dancers on a Sunday. The king replied to this teaching by publishing, in 1618, the *Declaration of Sports*[2] which commended as suitable pastimes for Sundays such things as morris-dancing, the maypole and rush-bearing, to the great indignation of Puritans who could not but feel that the king was tolerating sin.

Indeed the distress and disapproval of many of the protestant party grew to such a pitch that they found the atmosphere of their native land intolerable and fled overseas to the Calvinistic consolations afforded by the Church in Holland. A group which settled at Leyden in 1609 afterwards decided to emigrate to the New World and in 1620 returned to England, made up a party of about a hundred souls, and sailed away in the 'Mayflower' from Plymouth on September 6 of that year. They landed at Plymouth Rock in Massachusetts on November 11, where they drew up a covenant to form a political and religious society under the strictest possible discipline and in conformity with the principles for which they stood.

Meanwhile, in England, James had to cope with the leaders of the Anglican Church, especially those of High Church proclivities.

---

[1] The best account of the conference is in T. Fuller, *The Church History of Britain* (1837 ed.), iii, pp. 172-93.

[2] Gee and Hardy, *Documents*, pp. 528-32. The Declaration was reissued by Charles I in 1633.

This party within the Church had now earned for itself the popular name of 'Arminian' from a Dutch theologian who had revolted against Calvinism in his own country.[1] The party, which drew its inspiration from men like Hooker and Andrewes, stood for a doctrine of the Church of England as both catholic and reformed. They were themselves mostly scholarly and devout men, conscious of the weaknesses which had revealed themselves in the medieval Church, and anxious to build up in England a Church which should approach to the purity and devotion of the first centuries of the Christian era. They studied the Greek fathers rather than the medieval schoolmen, took an interest in the early history of the liturgy, desired to improve the appearance of the churches and the standards of worship, worked for higher educational and moral standards among the parochial clergy, and generally sought to make the Church to which they belonged a model of what a Christian Church should be and an example to the world.

The first half of the seventeenth century certainly produced a fine crop of churchmen,[2] but this does not mean that the general standard throughout the Church was very high. Richard Bancroft, who was Archbishop of Canterbury from 1604 to 1610, was an able administrator who did much to enforce Church law and to improve the lot of the inferior clergy; but he was succeeded by George Abbot (1610–1633), a dim character who failed to win the confidence of the clergy, alienated both Puritans and High Churchmen, and was of little help to the Church during those most critical years in its history. In the parishes there was much variety—noble priests like George Herbert, ruffians like the men described in Richard Baxter's *Autobiography*, and all sorts and conditions of men in between. But if the general standard was not very high, attempts were being made to raise it by the more progressive and earnest churchmen.

The methods which they adopted were not only godly admonition and persuasion, but also the machinery of the law and the courts. In 1604 a set of 141 Canons had been promulgated with the purpose of providing a basis for disciplinary action by the bishops.[3] These Canons, which included a certain amount of medieval law, some of the statutes and injunctions of Edward VI and Elizabeth and some

[1] See A. W. Harrison, *Arminianism* (1926).
[2] See below, pp. 233-7.
[3] The Canons of 1604 have been often printed. The most convenient edition is that edited by H. A. Wilson (Oxford, 1923).

15

new material, were intended to assist in the enforcement of uniformity along the lines of the dominant church party. As such, they were much disliked by the Puritans who disapproved not only of the laws themselves but of the additional power which they put in the hands of the bishops. Meanwhile the Court of High Commission which, in Elizabeth's reign had developed from an inquisitorial court for the examination of heretics into a law court for the trial of all ecclesiastical causes, was brought more and more into action to deal with ceremonial and ritual irregularities, clerical misdemeanour, recusancy, sectarianism, immorality and divorce.[1] A powerful and dangerous weapon in the hands of the bishops, the High Commission was, naturally, very unpopular among the Puritans.

ii. Charles I and Divine Right

Charles inherited from his father a profound belief in the Divine Right of Kings, but, unlike his father, he was prepared to put his beliefs into practice and govern his kingdom according to this theory. James had held that 'Kings are not only God's lieutenants here below and sit upon God's thrones, but even by God Himself are called gods', and Charles, soon after his accession, declared 'I owe the account of my actions to God alone'. Charles, therefore, regarded himself as above the law. He could make laws and unmake them without consulting his people. He could make a solemn promise one day and break it the next if it suited him to do so. A king could do no wrong.

In adopting this attitude Charles was completely out of sympathy with the more progressive of his subjects. The seventeenth century was the age of revolt against authority and absolutism. It was the age when Parliament was beginning to be aware that it had duties beyond those of supplying financial aid and moral support for royal despotism. It was the age when men were beginning to revolt against sacerdotalism and ecclesiastical censure. All this Charles may have known; but if he knew it he ignored it. He entirely disapproved of the suggestion that his subjects should have any voice in the policy of the country. It was he, the king, who should decide what was to be done both in

[1] See article, 'High Commission', by R. G. Usher in Ollard, Crosse and Bond, *A Dictionary of English Church History* (3rd ed. 1948), and *The Rise and Fall of the High Commission*, by the same author (1913).

Church and State. Ministers of the Crown and bishops existed in order to see that the king's wishes were carried out.

In face of such doctrines it is not surprising that all Charles's early Parliaments were failures; and when they started interfering in religious issues, clamouring for action against the king's ecclesiastical advisers and passing a resolution that 'whosoever shall bring in innovation of religion, or by favour or countenance seek to extend or introduce popery or Arminianism or other opinion disagreeing from the true and orthodox Church, shall be reputed a capital enemy to this kingdom and commonwealth',[1] Charles decided to dissolve Parliament and govern by Royal Prerogative.

That was in 1629, and for the next eleven years there was no meeting of Parliament. Charles hoped by this means to stifle opposition and to govern according to the theories upon which his life was based. Secular affairs were left in the hands of the Earl of Strafford, while ecclesiastical matters were largely entrusted to the firm and capable hands of the Bishop of London, William Laud, who succeeded Abbot as primate in 1633. Whether or not such government could be rightly described as 'tyranny', it was certainly a time of strict discipline. There was no outlet for criticism or opposition. Country squires who objected to what they regarded as unwarrantable taxation were brought up before Charles's judges and heavily punished. Puritans who opposed the High Church measures of Laud were pilloried by order of the Court of High Commission or had their ears cut off. Everywhere men's hearts began to fail them for fear; but Charles was adamant. 'The king can do no wrong.'

The first sign of armed opposition to the royal despotism came from Scotland. Here the Reformation had gone much further than in England. In 1560 the General Assembly of the Kirk had broken with Rome, passing a decree that 'the bischope of Rome have na jurisdictioun nor authoritie in this Realme' and in 1567 the Kirk was established by Parliament. Yet it remained partly episcopal until, under the influence of Andrew Melville, about 1580, there was a swing towards Presbyterianism. The few bishops who survived had an uneasy time, and their relations with the General Assembly were not easy to define. James I, with his great love for episcopacy, did his utmost to support the bishops both before 1603 and after, he and they together fighting a losing battle for Anglicanism against

[1] Gee and Hardy, *Documents*, p. 527 n.

the power of the Kirk. Charles's ambition was to destroy the Kirk altogether and bring Scotland into line with England. To this end Laud and John Maxwell, afterwards Bishop of Ross, began, in 1629, the preparation of a Prayer Book for Scotland. After some interruptions the book was published in 1637 and, as a liturgy, had much to recommend it. But it was in some ways more 'catholic' than the English Prayer Book and, as such, was anathema to the Scots. The method of introducing the book into Scotland was badly mismanaged and led to a noisy scene in St. Giles's in Edinburgh and cries of 'The Mass is entered amongst us!' Scottish nationalism and Scottish presbyterianism were both fanned by this incident which led to the formation of the Covenant which laid on men an oath to resist all acts which might endanger the protestant Kirk. Practically all Scotland signed the Covenant, the General Assembly voted for the abolition of episcopacy as well as of the Prayer Book, and in 1639 war between England and Scotland broke out.

Even Charles could hardly hope to fight a war without the help of Parliament, and in 1640 the Houses were summoned, though they sat for only a few days. Meanwhile Convocation had also been called together, and, contrary to custom, was allowed to sit after the hasty dissolution of Parliament. Convocation took the opportunity of passing seventeen canons[1] designed to tighten the bonds between the Church and the king and to push forward the schemes of Laud and his party. The first canon declares that 'the most high and sacred order of Kings is of divine right, being the ordinance of God Himself, founded in the prime laws of nature and clearly established by express texts of both the Old and New Testaments'. A further canon, No. 6, sought to impose upon the clergy, schoolmasters and others an oath, known as the 'Etcetera Oath' which contained the words: 'Nor will I ever give my consent to alter the government of this Church by archbishops, bishops, deans and archdeacons, etc. as it stands now established'.[2] This oath caused great offence since the vague word 'etc.' might open the door to all kinds of innovations in Church government to which the swearer of the oath would have committed himself. Finally the canons demand the restoration of the altar to its ancient place in the churches.

The 'Short Parliament' had shown that Charles was still in a

---

[1] Printed in E. Cardwell, *Synodalia*, i, pp. 380-415.
[2] Gee and Hardy, *Documents*, p. 536.

despotic mood; but the continued disasters in the Scottish war led to a reassembly of Parliament a few months later (August 1640). This time the members were in a much more belligerent frame of mind. The country was faced with disaster, and action must be taken. One of the first acts of the new Parliament was to impeach Strafford, who was committed to the Tower and, in due course, executed. Then on December 11 Parliament received the *Root and Branch Petition*, a document said to have been subscribed by 15,000 Londoners and demanding the abolition, 'root and branch', of all government by archbishops, bishops, deans and archdeacons on the grounds that such government led only to the increase of Romish superstition and ceremonial.[1] A week later Laud was also impeached and committed to custody.

The following year, 1641, saw a steady drift towards civil war. Feeling ran high, as the war of pamphlets shows, and in December Parliament presented Charles with the *Grand Remonstrance*,[2] a long statement of grievances against the king and his party. Clauses 181-204 deal with religion and include a demand for the reduction of the power of the bishops, for the holding of a synod to which foreign protestants should be invited, and for steps to be taken to remove 'idolatrous and Popish ceremonies introduced into the Church by the command of the Bishops'. Charles, infuriated by this, and encouraged by the queen, outraged the privileges of Parliament by entering the House of Commons and attempting to arrest five members.

The *coup* failed, and Charles left London in January 1642 for Yorkshire. Everyone knew now that it meant war; and in August the king set up his standard at Nottingham. The question of the Divine Right of Kings was to be submitted to the ordeal of battle.

iii. *William Laud*

In the carrying out of his ecclesiastical policy Charles had been greatly helped by William Laud. Laud was born at Reading in 1573, and proceeded to St. John's College, Oxford, of which he became a fellow in 1593 and President in 1611. In 1616 he was appointed Dean

---

[1] *Ibid.* pp. 537-45.
[2] S. R. Gardiner, *Constitutional Documents of the Puritan Revolution* (1906), pp. 202-32.

of Gloucester, in 1621 Bishop of St. David's, in 1628 Bishop of London and Chancellor of Oxford, and in 1633 Archbishop of Canterbury.

Laud was, throughout his career, a bitter opponent of Calvinism and Puritanism. He desired to see the Church of England 'catholic and reformed' in the spirit of Jewel and Hooker but with more outward expression in ceremonial and ritual. He was consequently much disliked by the Puritans, who branded him as an 'Arminian' and accused him of wishing to undo the work of the reformers and effect a reconciliation with Rome. But Laud was no Romanizer. His first public performance was his controversy with Fisher the Jesuit in 1622 in which he strongly upheld the Anglican position and ought to have established his loyalty to the Church of which he was a member. But feelings were running high, and the fact that Laud was a favourite with Charles made him suspect in the eyes of the protestant party.

During the years of despotic government (1629-40) Laud worked in the closest contact with the king. The policy of 'Thorough' so rigidly enforced by Strafford in secular affairs was equally strictly imposed by Laud on the Church. Faced with the danger of separation and division, Laud hoped to preserve the unity of the Church by strict uniformity and by the rigid enforcement of the law. He found much slackness and disorder in the churches. Many were falling into decay; dirt and desecration were common; clergy neglected their duties or indulged their fancies in the conduct of worship. All this Laud was determined to stop. He demanded that such improprieties as cock-fighting in the churches should be prohibited. He gave orders that altars and fonts should be placed in their right places and kept clean and tidy. He demanded that residentiary canons should perform their duties and not, as at Chichester, employ 'riff-raff, shifters, Nonconformists, curates, young boys and Puritans'[1] to do their work for them. Above all, he demanded obedience to the bishops and to the Prayer Book, and he used his powers in the courts of law to see that such obedience was enforced. It was here that pamphleteers such as Prynne, Burton and Bastwick were tried for writing scurrilous attacks upon the bishops and were sentenced to have their ears cut off. For Laud was ruthless in his determination to see that authority was obeyed. He had a passion for reform, for putting other people right,

[1] See Bishop Montague's letter to Laud quoted in W. H. Hutton, *William Laud*, pp. 80-81.

for discovering breaches of order or discipline and demanding that the transgressors should be punished. He had the misfortune to think that he was born to set the world right. In no circumstances could he ever suffer a fool gladly. No allowance was made for carelessness or weakness; no attempt was made to meet people half-way; no plea of ignorance or misunderstanding was ever listened to. Laud never shrank from what he believed to be his duty whatever the consequences; and he was quite reckless of what other men thought of him.

This passion for reform shows itself nowhere more clearly than in his relations with the University of Oxford. In 1628 he was appointed its Chancellor and throughout his life he showed great affection for it. But he could not leave it alone. 'So soon as I was admitted to the chancellorship', he wrote in his notes, 'I thought it my duty to reform the University'.[1] His letters show how he proceeded to carry out this reformation. Hearing that one of the proctors, who had made himself unpopular, had been hissed by a group of noisy undergraduates he ordered the ringleaders to be sent down. When he discovered, later, that the Vice-Chancellor had merely had them thrashed he wrote angrily to say that 'if you do not banish them from the University I shall try how far my power will stretch'.[2] And when, in the following year, he heard that some elderly dons had left their seats during the reading of public letters and had gathered round the rostrum he ordered them to be committed to prison.[3] And it was the same with all ranks of Church and State. No one was safe for a moment. Churchmen and Puritans, Oxford dons and Scottish lairds, tradesmen and craftsman all came under the lash.

Laud was so closely identified with Charles's despotism, and he himself so autocratic, that he soon became very unpopular. On several occasions his life was in danger, and he was often publicly insulted, as when London street-urchins were heard crying: 'Give little *laud* to the devil!' When the House of Commons finally met, Sir Edward Deering expressed the general feeling of the Puritans when he said: 'I had rather serve a Pope as farre as *Tyber* than to have him come to me so neare as the *Thames*; a *Pope* at *Rome* will doe me lesse hurt than a *Patriarch* may doe at *Lambeth*'.[4] The tyranny of the king was bad enough, but a king had some excuse for trying to

---

[1] Laud, *Works*, v, p. 13.   [2] *Ibid.* p. 196.   [3] *Ibid.* p. 232.
[4] *Foure Speeches made by S* Edward Deering in the High Court of Parliament* (1641), p. 8.

exert his authority. There was no excuse for those who supported him in his tyranny, and Laud was one of the chief of those who did.

During the eleven years of government by royal prerogative Laud had a free hand to pursue his own policy and to force upon the Church and upon the country as a whole the type of religion which he advocated. But when the Long Parliament was finally summoned in 1640 it met in an angry mood and regarded Laud, no less than Strafford, as its natural enemy. Mr. Harbottle Grimston was expressing the feeling of a large section of the House when, in 1644, he declared: 'We are now fallen upon the great Man the Archbishop of Canterbury. Look upon him as he is in Highness, and he is the Sty of all Pestilential filth . . . the great and Common Enemy of all Goodness and Good men.'[1] From 1640 Laud was kept in custody for four years, but was then brought to trial. The charges against him were that he had attempted to alter the true protestant religion into popery, and that he had tried to subvert the laws of the kingdom. Against each of these charges Laud had an adequate defence. But the powers which were then in control were not prepared to let principle stand in the way of policy. In their eyes the removal of Laud was necessary for the public good, and if that could not be done through the ordinary legal channels then some extraordinary method, such as a bill of attainder, must be found. Such a bill was introduced into the House of Commons on November 1, 1644. It passed quickly; was accepted by the Lords on January 4; and within a week Laud was dead.

Laud fell chiefly because of the policy for which he stood. He had allied himself with despotism, and when that despotism was broken he was broken too. But he fell also because he was totally unable to make himself understood or appreciated by the world. Clarendon, who was one of his supporters, said of him that 'he could not bear contradiction in debate . . . with that patience and temper that was necessary; of which they who wished him not well took many advantages, and would therefore contradict him that he might be transported with some indecent passion, which upon a short recollection he was always sorry for, and would readily and heartily make acknowledgment'.[2] Laud had an ungovernable temper, but he had also a real desire to do justice. In trying Prynne, Burton and Bastwick in 1637 he refused to pass judgment upon them although they had

---

[1] Rushworth, *Historical Collections* (1659–1701), iv, p. 122.
[2] Quoted in Hook, *Lives of the Archbishops of Canterbury* (1860–84), xi, p. 300.

behaved so badly to him. 'For my part', he said, 'as I pity their rage, so I heartily pray God to forgive their malice'; and 'because the business hath some reflection upon myself I shall forbear to censure them, and leave them to God's mercy and the King's justice.'[1] Moreover, he was a man of vision and of great moral courage. In the turbulent times in which he lived, when the forces with which he was least in sympathy were daily increasing in power and influence, Laud had a clear vision of a national Church such as he believed had been the dream of the reformers. It was for the well-being of such a Church that Laud gave his life. His methods are open to criticism, and his manner was often unfortunate, but his vision remained always clear, and his courage never failed.[2]

iv. *The Caroline Divines*

Behind the political and constitutional issues which were dividing the country good work was quietly being done by a group of writers and thinkers who set themselves to proclaim to the world what they believed Anglicanism to be. The movement owes its origin to the work of Jewel and Hooker who, by their wit and learning, had defended the Church, the one against Roman, the other against Puritan, criticism. Their successors in the seventeenth century did much, by their lives as well as by their works, to give quality and strength to the Church of England and earned for the English clergy the title of *stupor mundi*, 'the wonder of the world'.

Among the most distinguished of these, apart from Laud, was a group of Cambridge scholars including such famous names as Lancelot Andrewes, Richard Montague, John Cosin, Thomas Fuller, Jeremy Taylor, George Herbert and Nicholas Ferrar. They worked not as a team, for in fact they saw little of each other; but each in his own way—by personal sanctity, by scholarship, by poetry, by the dedicated life—made his own contribution to the life of the Church and gave it that sense of self-confidence and inner strength which

[1] *A Speech delivered in the Starr Chamber . . . at the Censure of John Bastwick, Henry Burton and William Prinn* (1637), pp. 10, 77.
[2] See the *Works of William Laud*, 7 vols. (1847–60). The best life of Laud is that written by his chaplain, Peter Heylyn, and entitled *Cyprianus Anglicus* (1671). There are many modern lives of Laud of which the following may be read: W. H. Hutton, *William Laud* (1895), A. S. Duncan-Jones, *Archbishop Laud* (1927), H. R. Trevor-Roper, *William Laud* (1940), and E. C. E. Bourne, *The Anglicanism of William Laud* (1947).

enabled it to rise again after the disasters of the Civil War and Commonwealth.

The point of view which this group maintained may be summed up in the dying words of Thomas Ken who had inherited the great tradition laid down by the Caroline Divines. 'I die', he said, 'in the Holy, Catholic and Apostolick Faith, professed by the whole Church before the disunion of East and West. More particularly I dye in the *Communion of the Church of England* as it stands distinguished from all Papall and Puritan Innovations, and as it adheres to the doctrine of the Cross.'[1] These words indicate the basis of the work of the Caroline Divines. Theirs was an attempt to get back to the early Church before the accretions of the Middle Ages which the reformers had been so anxious to get rid of. The Anglicans stood between two great religious systems. On the one side was Rome, active and aggressive under the impetus of the Counter-Reformation, trying to rebuild a Christendom shattered by the cataclysms of the sixteenth century. But to the Anglicans there could be no return to Rome since the faith which she taught was, in their eyes, impure—corrupted by the 'innovations' which were no part of the 'Holy Catholic and Apostolick Faith' as taught by the Primitive Church. As Laud said, they could not return to Rome 'until she is other than she is'. On the other side were the Calvinists and Lutherans, who had separated from catholic tradition and had magnified certain doctrines out of all proportion. The Anglicans were equally clear that they could not fall into line with them since they had abandoned things which the Early Church thought essential. The Caroline Divines, therefore aimed at a *Via Media* between two extremes; but the *Via Media* which they sought was not a compromise, a 'lowest common denominator'; it was a real attempt to recover the simplicity and purity of primitive Christianity.

This point of view was unacceptable to the Puritans in England. Less well informed than the Anglicans, they could not understand what these scholarly men were trying to do. Because the High Churchmen stood out for episcopacy as essential to catholic order they accused them of wanting to restore the papacy; and because they fought for beauty and order in worship, for loyalty to the Prayer Book, for the offering of a liturgy worthy of a great Church, the Puritans thought they wanted to bring back the Roman Mass. The

[1] F. A. Clarke, *Life of Thomas Ken* (1896), p. 223.

Caroline Divines, therefore, found themselves out of sympathy with the Puritan party which was rising to power, and many of them suffered during the troubled years. But by their sound scholarship, their courage, the purity and sanctity of their lives, they saved the Church of England from destruction and laid the foundations upon which later generations could build.

The father of the movement was Lancelot Andrewes (1555–1626), a fellow of Pembroke College, Dean of Westminster, and then Bishop first of Chichester, then of Ely and finally of Winchester. Andrewes was a great scholar, administrator and preacher, but he will always be chiefly remembered for his prayers, the *Preces Privatae* which he wrote in Latin and Greek and which reveal his holiness of life.[1]

George Herbert (1593–1633) was the poet of the movement. Of aristocratic family, he proceeded to Cambridge where he became a fellow of Trinity in 1614. After some years he married and took the small, country living of Bemerton in Wiltshire where he died after a short ministry of only three years. His exquisite poems on the Church, called *The Temple*, and his prose work, *A Priest to the Temple*, which describes his ideal of the country parson, together make up a rich legacy from one who died at the age of forty.[2]

John Cosin (1594–1672) was Dean of Peterborough at the outbreak of the Civil War. He lived to become Bishop of Durham at the Restoration and was one of those who helped to re-establish the Church. A scholar and historian, he was also a liturgical expert who had some influence upon the Prayer Book of 1662, his own copy of which, with annotations in his own hand, is still preserved at Durham.[3]

Jeremy Taylor (1613–67) was, like Cosin, a scholar of Caius College, but afterwards became a fellow of All Souls, Oxford. His scholarship attracted attention and he became chaplain to the king and rector of Uppingham. His friendship with Charles led to his arrest in 1645; but he was released and retired to Golden Grove in Wales as chaplain to Lord Carbery. It was there that he wrote his most famous books, *Holy Living* and *Holy Dying*, practical handbooks for the use of the laity, and a treatise on moral theology called

[1] His *Works* were published in the 'Library of Anglo-Catholic Theology' and the Prayers have often been published. See also *Lancelot Andrewes*, by R. L. Ottley (1894), and *Lancelot Andrewes*, by Florence Higham (1951).
[2] See *The Works of George Herbert*, edited by F. G. Hutchinson (1941).
[3] His *Works* were published in the 'Library of Anglo-Catholic Theology', 5 vols., and his *Letters* by the Surtees Society.

Ductor Dubitantium. Towards the end of the Commonwealth he went to Ireland where he became Bishop of Down and Connor in 1661.[1]

Nicholas Ferrar (1593–1637) was brought up as a business man serving the Virginia Company, but his mind was attracted by the thought of reintroducing some kind of 'religious' life, not of the old monastic kind, but using the family as the basis. Accordingly in 1626 he and his household, consisting of his mother, his brother and sister-in-law with their three children and his sister with her husband and sixteen children, together with a number of servants, left London and settled in the manor house at Little Gidding in Huntingdonshire. Here they restored the church and devoted themselves to a life of religious seclusion and devotion. The chief purpose of their life was a regular round of prayer which, says Isaak Walton 'was done as constantly as the sun runs his circle every day about the world'. The family rose at 4 A.M. and the first office was said at 6. From then until 9 P.M. offices were said at frequent intervals, and much of the night was spent by one or more of the community in the 'Night Watch' when the whole Psalter was said kneeling. In addition to the offices, which formed the framework of the day's activity, much time was devoted to the making of Gospel Harmonies,[2] to study and discussion (the so-called 'Little Academy'), to educating the children of the household and those of the district, and to good works among the sick and poor. This regular routine was kept up from 1626 to 1637 when Nicholas died. In 1641 Puritan antipathy to the whole experiment found expression in a book called *The Arminian Nunnery,* and when the Civil War broke out the peace of the community was in great danger. It survived until 1646 when Little Gidding was sacked, many of its treasures were burnt and the family fled. The experiment, therefore, had but a short life, but in those twenty years something quite new in the pattern of the 'religious life' had been invented. It was a life of devotion, of simplicity, of austerity and of discipline; but whereas all previous experiments in the religious life had been inimical to the family, Nicholas Ferrar had set himself to preserve the family ideal in a monastic setting. How far he succeeded, and how far the ideal would have spread in happier circumstances, it is impossible

[1] *Works,* edited by R. Heber in 15 vols. (1839) and by C. P. Eden, 10 vols., in 'Library of Anglo-Catholic Theology'. See also C. J. Stranks, *The Life and Writings of Jeremy Taylor* (1952).
[2] Fifteen of these Harmonies or 'Concordances' are known to have been made, a number of which still survive in the British Museum and elsewhere.

to say. But, while it lasted, Little Gidding stood for something unique in the history of Christian thought and life.[1]

v. The Fall of the Monarchy

The Civil War began in August 1642 when Charles raised his standard at Nottingham. How far it was a religious and how far a political or class struggle is hard to say. Roughly speaking, on one side were ranged the king and Anglicanism (represented by episcopacy and the Prayer Book), but also autocracy and despotism; whereas on the other side stood Parliament and Puritanism (whether Presbyterian or Independent). Each side, of course, contained a good many adventurers who were just out for what they could get; but it had also its idealists, men fighting for a creed, for the deepest convictions of their hearts. On the king's side were men who sincerely believed that they were fighting to defend what was the will of God —civil government by the king, church government by the bishops. For all of this they had no difficulty in finding Biblical sanction. They believed in the monarchy and they believed in the Church. To them the parliamentary party stood for anarchy, antinomianism, protestant insurrection against the declared will of God. On the other hand, the Puritans were no less inspired by religious convictions and equally convinced that they had the Bible on their side. At the back of their minds lay fear of Rome and the belief that the bishops were trying to undo the work of the reformers. They stood for the protestant faith, for the individual conscience, for private judgment against royal authority, sacerdotalism and prelacy. But they were also fighting for civil liberty, for the right of the people not only to worship in their own way but also to decide the policy of their country. The fact that, on each side, religion and politics were in alliance meant that fierce passions were aroused and bitter divisions created.

As the scene of war moved about the country there was much destruction, especially of churches and church property. This was inevitable. The Parliament troops were fighting against the Church, and therefore churches and their ornaments were natural objects of

---

[1] A. L. Maycock, *Nicholas Ferrar* (1938); *Nicholas Ferrar, his Household and his Friends*, ed. T. T. Carter (1892); *The Ferrar Papers* (1938). A Society called 'Friends of Little Gidding' was formed some years ago.

destruction. Many noble works of art had been burnt or broken by the iconoclasts of the Reformation; of those that survived many were destroyed by the Puritans. Stained-glass windows were broken, church ornaments and fittings were burnt, books were torn up, vestments cut to pieces. The scars may be seen in many parish churches and cathedrals today. And the tragedy was that most of this destruction was not just the tragic and inevitable consequence of war, but was deliberately done by men who believed that they were doing what was right.

As soon as the war began, Parliament made plans for enlisting the support of the Scots. Having first abolished episcopacy, a meeting of Puritan leaders was held in London, known as the Westminster Assembly, which proceeded to draw up a religious agreement which might serve as a basis for an alliance with presbyterian Scotland. Scotland had declared its faith in the Covenant of 1638, and it was an amended form of this document which was discussed by the Westminster Assembly in 1643. The result was the publication of the *Solemn League and Covenant*[1] which was imposed upon all Englishmen over the age of eighteen. This declares that they have entered into 'a mutual and solemn league and covenant' for 'the extirpation of popery, prelacy (that is Church government by archbishops, bishops, their chancellors and commissaries, deans, deans and chapters, archdeacons, and all other ecclesiastical officers depending on that hierarchy), superstition, heresy, schism, profaneness, and whatsoever shall be found to be contrary to sound doctrine and the power of godliness'. It also declares their intention 'to preserve the rights and privileges of the Parliaments and the liberties of the kingdoms' though without any wish 'to diminish his majesty's just power and greatness'.

When this became law in February 1644 it meant the end of the Church of England wherever Parliament could make its will obeyed. Many of the clergy were Puritan at heart, and these signed the Covenant gladly and continued in their benefices as Presbyterian ministers rather than as priests of the Church. All those, however, who could not conscientiously subscribe to the Covenant were ejected from their livings, local committees being formed to examine, on matters of politics, religion and morals, any waverers. Of the ten thousand or so of beneficed clergy, between two and three thousand lost their

[1] Gee and Hardy, *Documents*, pp. 569-74.

livings. A few went abroad into exile as their predecessors had done a century earlier, some were committed to prison, some got posts as tutors or chaplains to such as could afford to support them. Parliament allowed a pension up to one-fifth of the benefice to be set aside for the wife and family of the evicted incumbent, but this was not often paid and great hardship was caused.[1]

The fall of episcopacy led also to the fall of the Book of Common Prayer, which in 1644 was declared illegal and was replaced by the *Directory of Public Worship*. This declared that 'the Leiturgie used in the Church of *England* (notwithstanding all the pains and Religious intentions of the Compilers of it) hath proved an offence, not only to many of the Godly at home, but also to the Reformed Churches abroad'. The book then proceeds to set out careful instructions for public prayer and preaching, for the administration of the sacraments of Baptism and the Lord's Supper, for the Solemnization of Marriage, Visitation of the Sick and Burial of the Dead. These instructions are in the form of rubrics and biddings, but no form of prayer is given, not even the Lord's Prayer.[2]

The *Directory* was soon followed by the setting up of a Presbyterian form of government for the Church in England with 'classes' and provincial and national assemblies. Meanwhile negotiations with the Scots were proceeding and there seemed a chance that the war, which was in danger of reaching a stalemate, might be brought to a conclusion in favour of Parliament. But Presbyterianism, whether as a theology or as a method of government, was proving no more popular in England than episcopacy. Many who had willingly taken up arms against the despotism of the king and the bishops were now finding a new form of tyranny in Calvinistic Presbyterianism. As Milton said: 'New Presbyter is but old Priest writ large'; there was no more liberty under the one than under the other.

Those, then, who really cared for liberty found themselves drifting away from Presbyterianism and supporting the rising men who called themselves 'Independents'. The most distinguished of these was Oliver Cromwell, whose victory over the Royalist troops at Marston Moor in July 1644 was the first decisive battle of the war

[1] See John Walker, *An Attempt towards recovering an Account of the Numbers and Sufferings of the Clergy of the Church of England . . . in the late Times of the Grand Rebellion* (1714), and A. G. Matthews, *Walker Revised* (1948).

[2] On the Directory see Procter and Frere, *A New History of the Book of Common Prayer* (3rd imp. 1907), pp. 158-62.

and gave great prestige to the Independent party. The religious enthusiasm of these men inspired the country far more than the sober erastianism of the Presbyterians. Men who believed that they were fighting for liberty and toleration for their own beliefs found in Independency a much better cause than they would ever find in Presbyterianism. The latter part of the year 1644, therefore, saw a decline in the strength of Parliament but a great increase in the power of the New Model Army which, by the victory of Naseby in 1645 and the fall of Oxford, brought the Civil War to an end.

The end of hostilities was followed by a period of endless intrigues between the king, Parliament, the army and the Scots. Parliament still believed in Presbyterianism and was utterly intolerant of everything else. It soon alienated those whose loyalty it might have won—the Church by its hostility, the army by its intolerance and meanness. Charles, if he had shown more wisdom and reliability, might have played off his rivals the one against the other, and so have done something towards the establishment of peace; but his irresponsibility exasperated all parties. Meanwhile the army was becoming more and more aggressive and impatient.

After two years of negotiations, during which little progress was made, Charles, in 1647, made a last bid for Scottish support by agreeing to establish Presbyterianism in England for three years, and fled to the Isle of Wight. This so aggravated the Independents that war broke out again immediately. This time the king had considerable parliamentary support; but the army, under Cromwell's leadership, was too strong for him. Cromwell was being driven more and more to the conclusion that there could be no peace so long as the king was alive. He became possessed with hatred of 'Charles Stuart, that man of blood', and is said once to have cried: 'We will cut off his head with the crown upon it'. From this point things moved rapidly. The House of Commons was 'purged' of any likely opponents, Charles was brought to London, a special court of commissioners was appointed to try him and, in due course, sentence of death was passed. On January 30, 1649, the king was beheaded on a scaffold outside the banqueting-house in Whitehall.

When the bleeding head was held up, the cry of horror from the crowd drowned the derisive shouts of the soldiers. During the trial and at the hour of death Charles had behaved with a quiet courage and dignity which had won many to his side, even among those who had been ready to take up arms against him seven years before. Royal despotism was a bad thing, but military despotism was worse. English people dislike the sight of blood; and the execution of a king sent a thrill of horror and detestation through the country which has never been forgotten. It has been described as 'a crime against England even more than against Charles'.[1] But not only did it outrage the deepest feelings of the country, it also alienated many who might have been Cromwell's supporters, and thus made a restoration of monarchy and Church inevitable in due course. The regicides little realized that in cutting off Charles's head they were cutting their own throats.

From 1662 to 1859 the execution of King Charles was commemorated in the calendar of the Prayer Book and special services were held each year on January 30. Charles thus came as near to canonization as it is possible to be in the Church of England. He stood as a symbol of the patient sufferer who lays down his life for his creed and for his Church. He was certainly a good man and devout. He had great courage and firm convictions. In his own way he was convinced that he was doing what was right. His father had taught him that the Divine Right of Kings was part of the will of God, and he had upheld this doctrine even unto death. Such devotion to duty, such readiness to die rather than surrender his belief, is worthy of honour. But his faith in Divine Right made him exasperating to others, especially his enemies. His duplicity and irresponsibility, to which, in his own mind, he was perfectly entitled, to others appeared as sheer dishonesty. To Cromwell there could be no peace for England so long as Charles Stuart was there to disturb it; hence the desperate remedy of a royal execution. So Charles died; but with his death the fate of Puritanism was sealed and the Church's future ensured.

[1] G. M. Trevelyan, *An Autobiography and Other Essays* (1949), p. 166.

NOTE ON BOOKS

FOR general history see G. Davies, *The Early Stuarts, 1603-1660* (1937) in the *Oxford History of England* and Basil Willey, *The Seventeenth Century Background* (1934). The most important documents will be found in G. W. Prothero, *Select Statutes and other Constitutional Documents illustrative of the reigns of Elizabeth and James I* (1894) and S. R. Gardiner, *The Constitutional Documents of the Puritan Revolution* (1906). For church history W. H. Frere, *The English Church in the Reigns of Elizabeth and James I* (1904) and W. H. Hutton, *The English Church from the Accession of Charles I to the Death of Anne* (1903) are the most important works, to which should be added Thomas Fuller, *The Church History of Britain*, vol. iii, P. E. More and E. L. Cross, *Anglicanism* (1935), a collection of extracts from Anglican writers with notes, and C. Hill, *Economic Problems of the Church from Archbishop Whitgift to the Long Parliament* (1956). See also G. W. O. Addleshaw, *The High Church Tradition* (1941), H. Hensley Henson, *Studies in English Religion in the Seventeenth Century* (1903), Horton Davies, *The Worship of the English Puritans* (1948), and H. R. McAdoo, *The Spirit of Anglicanism* (1965).

CHAPTER XV

COMMONWEALTH, RESTORATION AND REVOLUTION
(1649–1702)

i. *Commonwealth and Protectorate*

THE execution of Charles I marked the triumph of the Puritans, and they were proud of it. The 'man of blood' had been removed to where the wicked cease from troubling, and the road lay open to the new and glorious age. Firm government, just laws, and, above all, pure religion were to be established for all generations. The Kingdom of God was at hand.

So thought the more enthusiastic of the Puritans. But the country as a whole was depressed and uneasy. 'Who', cried David when God had delivered Saul into his hands, 'can stretch forth his hand against the Lord's anointed and be guiltless?' The New Age of the Cromwellians looked very fine; but what if it were built on blood? The soldiers may have cheered when Charles's head rolled from the block, but upon the country as a whole there settled a sense of horror, of guilt, of shame; and the consciences of many were uneasy. Consequently the little book called *Eikon Basilike: the Pourtraicture of His Sacred Majestie in his Solitudes and Sufferings*, which appeared almost simultaneously with his death, was eagerly bought and read.[1] To the horror of the Puritans, Charles the villain rapidly became Charles the hero and martyr; and Milton's reply to this in *Eikonoklastes* did nothing to stem the flood of popular feeling.

Meanwhile the religious life of the country was in a state of great confusion. Since the abolition of episcopacy there had been no proper organization or control. Most of the incumbents were Presbyterians, but a number were Anglicans at heart who conformed under protest, and a few were Independents. All that the government could do was to issue an order in 1650 to say that everyone must attend some place of worship or a place where religious exercises were held;

---

[1] It is thought to have been compiled by John Gauden largely from the king's own writings. It rapidly went through forty-seven editions and was translated into Latin.

but that meant very little. Then in 1653 was issued the *Instrument of Government*[1] which was intended to give some measure of toleration. According to this, people were not to be compelled to any 'public profession' of their faith, binding them to any particular church, but were to be free to go where they liked and to worship in the way which suited them best. 'Such as profess faith in God by Jesus Christ', it declared, 'though differing in judgment from the doctrine, worship or discipline publicly held forth, shall not be restrained from, but shall be protected in, the profession of the faith and exercise of their religion.' But there was a proviso which showed that the day of general toleration was still far off, for the act continued: 'provided this liberty be not extended to popery or prelacy'.

Cromwell was anxious to be broad-minded and tolerant. He did not expect uniformity. 'I meddle not with any man's conscience', he said.[2] But there were limits beyond which he was not prepared to go, and any measure of toleration stopped short of papists and Anglicans. Probably the reasons were political rather than doctrinal. The Roman Catholics had always been regarded as a source of danger. They were now in close touch with Charles's widow in France and there was no knowing what they might be up to. But there was no real persecution; papists were allowed to attend the embassy chapels in London, and, on the whole enjoyed more liberty under Cromwell than they had done since the days of Mary. This, however, did not apply to Ireland, where persecution of the priests was bitter and intense.

The Anglican Church represented the cause against which Cromwell had fought, and he knew that it was still his greatest enemy. All over England and beyond the seas were men longing and praying for the overthrow of the Commonwealth and the return of the monarchy. Unsympathetic with, and even hostile to, the new régime, these men had placed themselves outside the pale of the great protestant state and could neither expect, nor even ask for, toleration. They were the 'fifth column' which remained when Charles's armies had been beaten in the field, the 'running sore' in the body politic which sapped its strength and undermined its security.

Not that the whole Anglican Church was by any means united in

[1] S. R. Gardiner, *Constitutional Documents of the Puritan Revolution*, pp. 405-17, and extracts in Gee and Hardy, *Documents*, pp. 576-7. It was followed by the setting up of the Commission of Triers (1654) to fill vacant benefices. (See Gee and Hardy, *Documents*, pp. 577-82.)   [2] *Letter 110.*

its opposition to the puritan state. Far from it. The Church was deeply divided between the sixty per cent or so of those who conformed to the new régime, and the much smaller group of uncompromising Laudians who had retired into hiding or exile, with an intermediary group of disaffected conformists who accepted the new way under protest, grumbled a great deal about the restrictions and limitations on their freedom, said some of the Prayer Book offices in private, and continued to hold their benefices. To the High Church party, who were suffering so much for their convictions, the members of this middle group appeared as time-servers or worse. Were they honest? What about their ordination vows, and their oaths? Repeated attempts were made to get the bishops to stir these men into more active opposition; but no lead came, for the bishops themselves were just as much divided as were their clergy.

The initiative therefore passed more and more to the small group of Laudian clergy who were determined at all costs to keep the Church true and undefiled until this tyranny be overpast. Some remained to do what they could in England, many went abroad with the court or into exile on their own. But wherever they were they kept in close touch with each other and worked according to a carefully planned policy which would one day lead to a restoration of the king and the re-establishment of the Church of England.

The task which they set themselves was threefold: to see that the ministry was maintained, that the right influences were brought to bear on Charles II, and that the clergy and laity in England were prepared to play their part when the moment arrived. The problem of the maintenance of the ministry depended largely upon how long the interregnum was to continue. As far as priests and deacons were concerned, there is evidence that a certain number were secretly ordained by bishops in England in order that the supply might be kept up.[1] The consecration of bishops presented a more complex problem since the initiative lay with the king who, being in exile, was scarcely in a position to make any nominations. Various suggestions for overcoming this difficulty were made,[2] but none was found to be workable, and the problem was solved by the Restoration taking place before the situation had become desperate.

[1] See article, 'Ordinations under the Commonwealth', in *Theology*, June 1942.
[2] *E.g.* that the king should appoint Irish bishops or bishops suffragan who could eventually be translated to English sees.

Great efforts were made to ensure that the king remained faithful to the Church of England. Several of the more energetic members of the Laudian party made it their business to be at his court so that he might be prevented from going over either to Presbyterianism or to Roman Catholicism. The dangers were very great. In 1650 Charles went to Scotland where, in the hopes of enlisting Scottish support he accepted the Covenant; but he soon fell out with the Scots and returned a more convinced Anglican than before. Meanwhile his mother, Henrietta Maria, was doing her utmost to persuade him to allow himself to be received into the Church of Rome, but Charles was learning more and more to accept the advice of Edward Hyde, an Anglican much under the influence of the Laudian party.

Meanwhile in England efforts were made to ensure that the Anglican point of view was kept before the minds of those whose opinions would count most in the affairs of state if and when a restoration was carried through. It was to this end that a number of Laudian clergy got themselves appointed as chaplains and tutors in the houses of the nobles and squires where there were boys and young men whose ideas might be influenced.[1] At the same time, being forbidden to preach, they exerted themselves in writing books and pamphlets, which all helped to keep before men's minds the true nature of the Church.

In all these ways the Laudian party was working according to a well-planned policy. Their eyes were on the future when the monarchy should be restored, and they were determined that when this took place there should be a complete restoration of the Church of England as the one and only Church in the country. But until that restoration took place church life in England was at a very low ebb. Devout laity were deprived of the sacraments of the Church and obliged to attend Presbyterian forms of worship. The observance of Christmas Day was forbidden, and John Evelyn ran some risk of being assaulted or imprisoned when he attended a celebration of the Eucharist in Exeter Chapel on Christmas Day 1657.[2] Though many couples managed to get some kind of religious service, only civil marriage was officially allowed. Many churches lost their treasures

---

[1] Cromwell realized this and in 1655 issued a proclamation to try to stop it (Gee and Hardy, *Documents*, pp. 582-3).

[2] J. Evelyn, *Diary* (Bohn's ed.) i. p. 341. In 1652, 1653 and 1654 he could find no service on Christmas Day, but he found a sermon in 1655 and the sacrament administered in 1656 (pp. 297, 300, 322, 327, 335).

—books, ornaments and vestments. The dark shadow of Calvinism lay over the land, affecting not only the worship of the people but their everyday lives, for the government did its utmost to enforce the legislation of the Pentateuch and destroyed many of the simple amusements of the poor.

During the Commonwealth and Protectorate there was also a great increase in the number of independent sects, most of whom were despised by the Presbyterians who were staunchly erastian. The sectaries were united in their dislike of all forms of organized religion, in their love of 'enthusiasm' and in their conviction that they and they alone were the true Church. Otherwise they were entirely independent and exclusive.

The chief of these were the Congregationalists, who were descended from the Brownists[1] and were the true Independents. They regarded the congregation as the unit of church life and vested much power in the laity. The movement had grown during the Civil War and was strong in the army, in London, in East Anglia and in the towns of the south-west.[2]

The Baptists had broken away from the Brownists early in the seventeenth century when John Smyth had left England for Holland, where he baptized himself according to what he regarded as the true rite, and formed the first English Baptist church. A party came to England in 1612 and a number of local churches sprang up. These came to be called General Baptists to distinguish them from the much stricter Calvinists who constituted the Particular Baptists from 1633 onwards. After the Restoration the Baptists were much persecuted, John Bunyan spending twelve years in Bedford Gaol (1660–72).[3]

The seventeenth century also witnessed a growth of mysticism and of the belief in direct spiritual guidance. Those who were drawn to this way of life had no interest in a visible Church at all. Each individual made his own direct approach to God, depending from day to day and from hour to hour upon the inspiration of the Holy Spirit. Gradually small groups of such people got together, calling themselves the 'Family of Love' or 'Seekers'. These would probably have remained detached and largely unknown to one another had not George Fox rallied them by his vitality, courage and inspiration.

[1] See above, p. 211.
[2] R. W. Dale, *History of English Congregationalism* (1907).
[3] A. C. Underwood, *A History of the English Baptists* (1947).

Fox was a man of little learning and of no worldly wisdom, but of immense courage and unbounded zeal. A prophet who believed himself to be directly inspired, he devoted his life and all his powers to travelling about the country preaching what he regarded as the pure Gospel. His frank criticisms of the Church and clergy led to much hostility and persecution, and he was often in gaol. But he remained quite undaunted and continued his work as the Spirit directed him. His followers were at first called 'Children of Light' or 'Friends in the Truth', but the name which they finally acquired was that of 'Quakers', though at first it had been used as a term of abuse.[1]

In addition to these were large numbers of minor sects. There were the Fifth-Monarchy Men who were millenarians awaiting the return of Christ; there were Sabbatarians who, in their worship, observed the Jewish Sabbath rather than the Christian Sunday; there were the Adamites who wished to return to the conditions of man's innocency, and worshipped in the nude; there were Ranters, Muggletonians, Socinians, Philadelphians, Sweet Singers of Israel and many others.[2] In addition there were those sects which concentrated more on political and social activities than on the things of the spirit. Among these were the Levellers who believed in the destruction of class-distinctions, and the Diggers who thought that religion meant ploughing up other people's land and giving it to the poor. With the Church of England disestablished and silenced, and with Presbyterianism growing more and more unpopular, the soil was certainly favourable to the multiplication of sects which sprang up on all sides, and some of which have continued to this day.

ii. *The Restoration*

Oliver Cromwell died in 1658. His son Richard, who succeeded him as Protector, was a failure and resigned in 1660. At this point it became clear to most people that the wisest course would be to restore the monarchy; and the army, under the leadership of General Monck, got rid of the old Rump Parliament and arranged for the election of a new Parliament which invited the king to return.

[1] See George Fox's *Journal*, ed. N. Penney, 2 vols. (1911); W. C. Braithwaite, *Beginnings of Quakerism* (new ed. 1955) and *Second Period of Quakerism* (1919); T. Hodgkin, *George Fox* (1896) and R. Knox, *Enthusiasm* (1950), chap. viii.
[2] See C. E. Whiting, *Studies in English Puritanism* (1931), chap. vi.

Charles II arrived in England and reached London, amid universal acclamation, on May 29.

Before quitting Holland Charles published the *Declaration of Breda* in which he declared a general pardon to all except a few regicides, and declared his intention of allowing some measure of religious toleration. 'Because the passion and uncharitableness of the times', he said, 'have produced several opinions in religion, by which men are engaged in parties and animosities against each other ... we do declare a liberty to tender consciences and that no man shall be disquieted or called in question for differences of opinion in matters of religion which do not disturb the peace of the kingdom.'[1] From this declaration Presbyterians and sectaries took some comfort, believing that the tenderness of their consciences would be respected. Subsequent events, however, proved that their optimism was premature.

The religious situation when Charles arrived was exceedingly delicate. The Presbyterians were in power in the Convention Parliament which met Charles on his return, but the question of the restoration of episcopacy and the Prayer Book was bound to arise before long. Some of the Puritans were in favour of a compromise, a form of 'moderate episcopacy' on the lines of Archbishop Ussher's *Reduction of Episcopacy unto the Form of Synodical Government*, which had been published in 1641.[2] But they underestimated the zeal and determination of their opponents. The Laudian party had spent the last fifteen years preparing for this moment, and they were not in a mood for compromise. With the assistance of Edward Hyde, now Lord Clarendon, they intended to see to the restoration of the Church of England as they had known it in the days of Laud and Andrewes as the one and only legal and established Church of the land.

Thanks to the careful work which had been done, the king was on their side. The Book of Common Prayer was used in the king's chapel, and staunch Anglicans were appointed to cathedral dignities where, in due course, they proceeded to the election of sound churchmen to fill the vacant sees. The court, acting on the principle of 'No bishop, no king', assumed that the restoration of the monarchy

---

[1] S. R. Gardiner, *Constitutional Documents of the Puritan Revolution*, pp. 465-7.
[2] See R. Baxter, *Reliquiae Baxterianae* (1696), pp. 238-40; and *Theology*, January 1947.

inevitably involved the re-establishment of the Church of England. The Puritans' only hope now lay with Parliament; but here again the Laudians had done their work well. By holding tutorships and chaplaincies they had indoctrinated many of the young squires with true church ideas; and, when the Cavalier Parliament met, the majority were ardent churchmen. From that point onwards it was merely a question of tidying up. The new bishops set about their task with the vigour and earnestness of men who have long been kept waiting, and within a few months nearly 700 Puritan clergy had been ejected from their livings.[1]

Episcopacy had been restored without a struggle, but the Puritans were determined to oppose the reintroduction of the Book of Common Prayer with the various obnoxious customs which went with it such as the wearing of the surplice, kneeling at the Holy Communion, bowing at the name of Jesus, making the sign of the cross in Baptism and so forth. Various deputations of Puritan divines waited upon Charles, but he took little notice of them. All that he would promise was a conference between them and the Anglican clergy to settle their differences.

The Conference met at the Savoy Hospital on April 15, 1661. It was attended by twelve bishops and twelve Puritan divines (including Edward Reynolds, Bishop of Norwich, Edmund Calamy and Richard Baxter). Each side had also nine coadjutors. Sheldon, Bishop of London, who presided, assumed that the restoration of episcopacy inevitably implied the restoration of the Church's prayer-book, and left it to the Puritans to state their objections. This they did at considerable length, Baxter producing a list of *gravamina* which covers many pages of print.[2] Among them was the abolition of the surplice, the cross in Baptism and the habit of kneeling at the Communion, a demand for extemporary prayer and the running of collects and the Litany into one long prayer, the alteration of the word 'priest' into 'minister', 'Sunday' into 'Lord's Day', and so on. The zeal and energy of the Puritans was unbounded; but it went too far. The bishops were bored by Baxter's pedantry and his interminable speeches on matters which were really of very little significance. Had the objectors concentrated on one or two points of real doctrinal importance they might have made some impression on their

---

[1] A. G. Matthews, *Calamy Revised* (1934), p. xiii.
[2] See *Reliquiae Baxterianae* (1696), pp. 308-16.

opponents, but their absorption in details of little moment was their undoing. The bishops 'took up a strong and unyielding position behind primitive custom and catholic usage'[1] and refused to budge. After years of poverty and exile, when many of them had had no chance of using any kind of prayer book at all, they were determined now to have the kind of liturgy which they wanted. And they were in a strong enough position to carry the day.

While the Savoy Conference was sitting Convocation met, but nothing was done then about the Prayer Book. This was left to the winter session, by which time a revision of the book had been made by a liturgical committee and was now presented and approved. In the Preface reference was made to those who had tried to prevent its restoration, 'men of factious, peevish and perverse spirits' who have always 'a greater regard to their own private fancies and interests than to that duty they owe to the public'. The compilers, therefore, rejected all such proposals as appeared to them to be 'either of dangerous consequence (as secretly striking at some established doctrine, or laudable practice of the Church of *England*, or indeed of the whole Catholick Church of Christ) or else of no consequence at all, but utterly frivolous and vain'. Altogether about 600 alterations were made, but mostly on matters of detail. The main additions were the provision of a form of 'Baptism for those of Riper Years' to meet the needs of those who had grown up unchristened during the Commonwealth or for the use of converts 'in our plantations', the commemoration of the dead in the Prayer for the Church and the rubrics governing the manual acts in the Prayer of Consecration, a number of additional prayers, collects and thanksgivings, and the restoration of the so-called 'Black Rubric' but with the phrase 'no real or essential presence' changed to 'no corporal presence' of Christ in the Sacrament.

The new Prayer Book, like its predecessors, was introduced as part of an *Act of Uniformity*[2] which ordered the use of this book from S. Bartholomew's day, 1662, under penalty of deprivation. The act also required all clergy and schoolmasters to make a declaration that they believe it to be unlawful to take arms against the king, that they will use the Prayer Book of 1662 and none other, and that the Solemn

---

[1] Procter and Frere, *A New History of the Book of Common Prayer*, p. 189.
[2] Gee and Hardy, *Documents*, pp. 600-619; C. Grant Robertson, *Select Statutes, Cases and Documents*, pp. 37-53.

League and Covenant was an unlawful oath. Finally the act demanded the deprivation of all those who had not by this time received episcopal ordination.

Thus at Bartholomewtide the Church of England was fully and exclusively restored, and those who were not prepared to accept its liturgy and its discipline had to go. On the whole, it seems to have been well received, though there were some misgivings. 'I hear most of the Presbyters took their leaves today', wrote Pepys on August 17, 1662, 'and the City is much dissatisfied with it. I pray God keep peace among us, and make the Bishops careful of bringing in good men in their room, or else all will fly a-pieces.' Many of the Presbyterian clergy were ordained in order to retain their benefices, but nearly a thousand were ejected and either went abroad or found some other occupation in England.[1] About the same time the bishops were readmitted to the House of Lords.

Once in the saddle the new government, under powerful church influence, proceeded to take action against all its opponents. At all costs a repetition of the disasters of the last twenty years must be avoided. An England weak and divided would be a prey to all her enemies. Above all, religious disputes and bickerings must be controlled. Church and State were to be one, and such as refused to conform to the discipline of the Church could not expect the privileges of citizenship. A clear line, therefore, was to be drawn between conformists and nonconformists, and the latter must be penalized and controlled. Thus there came about a series of Acts of Parliament known collectively as the 'Clarendon Code'.

The Clarendon Code included the following. There was, first of all, the *Corporation Act* of 1661 which required all those holding civic office not only to renounce the Solemn League and Covenant, and to swear not to take arms against the king, but also to be communicants of the Church of England. In the following year the *Act of Uniformity* was passed and, in 1664, the *Conventicle Act* which made it illegal for anyone over the age of sixteen to attend any 'assembly, conventicle, or meeting, under colour or pretence of any exercise of religion, in other manner than according to the liturgy and practice of the Church of England'.[2] Two years later, in 1666, the *Five Mile Act* forbade any

---

[1] See A. G. Matthews, *Calamy Revised* (1934), for the history of those ejected.

[2] Gee and Hardy, *Documents*, pp. 623-32; C. Grant Robertson, *Select Statutes*, pp. 70-74. The act expired in 1667 and was re-enacted in 1670.

nonconformist minister to live or visit within five miles of any place in which he had previously worked.[1]

Such was the Clarendon Code which did so much to divide England permanently into conformists and nonconformists. From now onwards a clear line was drawn between those who accepted the teaching and discipline of the established Church and those who were determined to preserve their independence. The division cut right across society and affected politics and social relations almost as much as religion. The aristocracy and gentry with all their dependents, and the poor as a whole, were with the Church; it was among the artisans and tradesmen that dissent flourished.

A few years later, in 1673, the *Test Act* was passed, requiring all those holding any civil or military office to receive the Holy Communion according to the rites of the Church of England, to denounce the doctrine of Transubstantiation, and to take the oaths of supremacy and allegiance.[2] This, of course, was aimed at the Roman Catholics who were now becoming a danger to the peace of the realm. James, Duke of York and heir to the throne, was a recognized convert to Rome, and even the king himself was suspect. The Popish Plot in 1678 threw the country into much confusion and alarm, which was enhanced by the publication, in 1682, of the terms of the secret Treaty of Dover in which Charles had pledged himself to restore the Roman Catholic religion, if necessary with the help of French armed forces. The Anglicans may have felt that there was a world of difference between themselves and the protestant nonconformists, but they were united with them in their hatred of Rome. The situation, therefore, looked serious enough when Charles died in the arms of Rome on February 6, 1685, and was succeeded by his brother James who made no secret of the fact that he was a papist.

iii. *Life and Thought after the Restoration*

The world of Charles II was a very different one from that of his father. New ideas were in the air, new standards, new knowledge, new ways of thought. Men were dissatisfied with the old scholastic methods and dogmas which had served the Church so long, and were

---

[1] Gee and Hardy, *Documents*, pp. 620-23.
[2] *Ibid.* pp. 632-40; C. Grant Robertson, *Select Statutes*, pp. 80-84.

beginning to enquire into the nature of the universe in which they found themselves, its material structure and its purpose. But though there was a revolt from the old assumptions there was as yet no breach between science and religion. Indeed the alliance between the two was close. Robert Boyle and Isaac Newton were both convinced Christians, and the Royal Society which was incorporated by Royal Charter in 1662 was warmly supported by orthodox churchmen as well as by more detached enquirers. There were, of course, a few scholars who really belonged to an earlier generation but who had lived through the changes and disturbances of their times, bringing an air of old-world scholarship into the new age. Such were Jeremy Taylor who lived until 1667, John Cosin and Herbert Thorndike who both lived until 1672, John Pearson, known especially for his *Exposition of the Creed*, who lived until 1686, and Thomas Ken who survived right into the eighteenth century and died in 1711. These were the last survivors of the old school of Caroline Divines, interested mainly in patristics and the Early Church, and searching always for precedents for the kind of church life and worship which they loved. But the great days of the movement for which they had fought and suffered were past.

By the time of Charles II interest was concentrating not on the question of authority, nor of precedent, but of reason. Science, philosophy, theology—all were to be judged at the bar of Reason; and knowledge or opinions which were not founded upon a sound rational basis had little chance of being accepted. The most interesting group of Christian thinkers in the early stages of this movement was a handful of scholars known as the 'Cambridge Platonists'. With few exceptions they were all members of Emmanuel College, the leading Puritan community in the university, and the most distinguished of them were these: Benjamin Whichcote (1609–83), Ralph Cudworth (1617–88), John Smith (1618–52), Henry More (1614–87) and Nathaniel Culverwel (d. 1651). Their roots lay in Puritanism, but they brought to it a new meaning and a new quality. Like the Christian philosophers of Alexandria in the third century they set themselves to find a harmony between philosophy and religion; and living in times of bitter religious strife, they hoped to bring a new spirit into the Church. Polemic and controversy had so divided men into hostile camps that the true work of the Church had been seriously impeded. These things ought not to be. God is one; Truth is one; in the world of the Spirit harmony must take the place of strife. Their appeal, then, was to Reason, 'the very voice of God' as Whichcote termed it; and by Reason they meant the philosophical approach to truth but sanctified by God. Their favourite text was the phrase in Proverbs: 'The spirit of man is the candle of the Lord', for they believed that Truth is revealed to man by Reason, man's mind illuminated by God. 'They reject no article of the Faith, but they shift the emphasis of exhortation, affirming values where orthodoxy affirmed facts.'[1] To their minds the religious controversies which they had known had been cold and barren. Instead of purifying men's lives they had embittered them. But if a man is to apprehend truth his life must be pure and holy. So they themselves devoted much time to prayer and meditation and became, if not mystics, at least mystically minded. Not all of them lived to see the Restoration, and those who did lay outside the main stream of religious life and thought. But though they may not have had any great influence on their own generation their work and their holiness influenced those who came after them and is held in high honour today.[2]

The name originally applied to the Cambridge Platonists was 'Latitude-men', or 'Latitudinarians'; but this was later transferred to the school of liberal, rationalistic men who succeeded them in the latter part of the seventeenth century, men like Joseph Glanville (1636–80), Simon Patrick (1626–1707) who became Bishop of Ely, Edward Stillingfleet (1635–99), Bishop of Worcester, and two Archbishops of Canterbury, John Tillotson (1630–94) and Thomas Tenison (1636–1715). Many of these were Cambridge men who had sat at the feet of scholars like Whichcote and More, but they lacked the humility and reverence of their masters and were more self-confident and assured. They were, on the whole, broad-minded men, tired of controversy and the intensity of religious feeling in which they had grown up and anxious for a quiet life in the pursuit of goodness and righteousness. They believed intensely in Reason and had the utmost dislike and contempt for the various forms of ecstatic individualism which were then beginning to be known as 'Enthusiasm'. Their suavity and complacency made some men accuse them of trying to

---

[1] B. Willey, *The Seventeenth Century Background* (1934), p. 138.
[2] See F. J. Powicke, *The Cambridge Platonists* (1926) and selections from their writings in *The Cambridge Platonists*, ed. E. T. Campagnac (1901). Also W. R. Inge, *The Platonic Tradition in English Religious Thought* (1926), G. P. H. Pawson, *The Cambridge Platonists* (1930), and H. R. McAdoo, *The Spirit of Anglicanism* (1965), pp. 81–155.

make the best of both worlds, and their apotheosis of common sense appeared to their enemies to savour of 'Socinianism' and unbelief. But they were perfectly sincere, devoted much of their energy to the performance of good works, set a high standard of decency and morality in an age of loose-living, and pleaded for a spirit of charity and toleration among their fellow-Christians. If they lacked something of the intensity and spiritual grandeur of the Caroline Divines, and something of the depth and learning of the Cambridge Platonists, the best of the Latitudinarians represented a type of religion which was reasonable, sincere and within the range of ordinary men It may not have been heroic, but at least it was conscientious.

Meanwhile Reason was finding its leading prophet in the philosopher, John Locke. Locke's *Essay Concerning Human Understanding*, published in 1690, was the most important philosophical contribution which England made for many years. And it was deeply religious. Locke had not much faith in intuition; he believed that truth was to be discovered by reason and by effort; but he was convinced that philosophy led inevitably to faith. 'We more certainly know that there is a God', he said, 'than that there is anything else without us.' This point of view did much to establish the placid assurance of the eighteenth century. Newton in physics and Locke in metaphysics had both shown the orderliness of nature and of God. Locke went more deeply into the religious question in *The Reasonableness of Christianity as delivered in the Scriptures* (1695). His approach to the Bible was scholarly and profound. He had no use for the old method of arguing from individual verses. 'We must look into the drift of the discourse,' he wrote, 'observe the coherence and connection of the parts, and see how it is consistent with itself, and other parts of Scripture, if we will conceive it right. We must not cull out, as best suits our system, here and there a period or a verse; as if they were all distinct and independent aphorisms.'[1] Locke's study of the Scriptures led him to believe that the Christian faith was a much simpler thing than people had imagined. Centuries of theological argument and discussion had overlaid the essential faith with a heavy coating of unessentials. But though the true faith was simple it was no less profound and obligatory; and it must issue in morality, in the good life. Locke's Christian faith therefore rested upon three essentials—Reason, Simplicity

---

[1] *The Reasonableness of Christianity* (1695), p. 292; quoted in G. R. Cragg, *From Puritanism to the Age of Reason* (1950), pp. 131-2.

and Morality; and it is easy to understand how well this fitted in with the spirit of the age in which he lived.[1]

The scientific approach to knowledge was thus affecting many things besides physics and chemistry. It was being applied to the Bible, not only by Locke but by French scholars like Richard Simon, whose *Critical History of the Old Testament*, a forerunner of the higher criticism of the nineteenth century, appeared in an English translation in 1682. The scientific method was also being applied to history and archaeology; libraries and muniment-rooms were being searched and manuscripts read and copied. Some of the labour involved was no doubt inspired by the search for precedents to support some political or ecclesiastical opinion; but much of it also was done for the sheer love of learning. Dugdale's *Monasticon*, Rymer's *Foedera*, Wilkins' *Concilia*, Hearne's editions of medieval chronicles, Anthony Wood's researches into the history of Oxford and Burnet's *History of the Reformation* are only a small part of the vast output of learned works, many of which remain to this day as standard works of reference.[2]

Gilbert Burnet was Bishop of Salisbury. On the eve of his consecration in 1690, after a whole week of silent preparation, he wrote as follows: 'I will preach in season both in public and from house to house; I will not spare myself . . . I will give myself wholly to this great work. I will go round and be frequent in inspecting my clergy . . . I will be careful not to lay hands suddenly on any . . . I will shew all kindness not only to such as may differ from me but even to gainsayers: for I will love all men. I will live with my brethren of the clergy in all brotherly love and humility . . . I will set myself to do the work of a bishop in my diocese without ever designing to remove to aspire higher.'[3] Such was the ideal which he set and which, to a large extent, he achieved. Not all the bishops of the late seventeenth century were so conspicuous for pastoral duty as Burnet, but on the whole they were a conscientious body of men. In early days, Sancroft at Canterbury, Compton at London, Morley at Winchester, and Cosin at Durham, and later Ken at Bath and Wells, Gunning at Chichester and Ely, Stillingfleet at Worcester and Nicolson at Carlisle, were all, in their ways, distinguished men who made a determined effort to maintain a high standard of pastoral work in their dioceses.

---

[1] On Locke see A. S. Pringle-Pattison, *Preface to Locke's Essay Concerning Human Understanding* (1924).   [2] See D. C. Douglas, *English Scholars* (1939).
[3] H. C. Foxcroft, *A Supplement to Burnet's History* (1902), p. 538.

The need for wise and firm leadership was great. Considerable chaos and confusion had been left behind after the interregnum; ancient traditions of the Church had been interrupted and were often difficult to restore. Many of the clergy were ill-educated, ill-trained and ill-paid. Burdened often with large families, they lived among the poor and depressed and were often despised by the more cultured and wealthy of their parishioners. In the houses of the rich the chaplain ranked as little more than a servant and was obliged to retire from table in the middle of dinner 'picking his teeth, and sighing with his hat under his arm whilst the knight and my lady eat up the tarts and chickens!'[1] Many clergy had had very little education and entered upon their ministry without any real preparation. It was to meet this need that Burnet established at Salisbury ten young men to be trained for the ministry at his own expense under the direction of the precentor of the cathedral. The bishop himself took a close interest in the work and himself spent much time with the students.

In the parishes worship had sunk pretty low by 1660. Many children and young people had never heard the Prayer Book services. Worship to them meant metrical psalms and extemporary prayer. Even the Lord's Prayer had been regarded by some Puritans as a popish invention and therefore abandoned.[2] Many churches also were in a shocking state of dilapidation, especially in the north.

Gradually improvements were made. On Sundays, Morning and Evening Prayer were sung, with the Eucharist celebrated quarterly or monthly and, in a few town parishes, weekly. A number of churches restored the daily offices (Mattins at 6 A.M.: Evensong at 6 P.M.) and at least one church had a daily Eucharist in 1694.[3] The festivals of the Church's Year, which had been forgotten during the Commonwealth, were restored, and many old customs, such as bowing to the altar, came back into use. Churches were cleaned, restored and refurnished. Elaborate woodwork was often introduced in the form of pews, galleries and pulpits, the last often built in the 'three-decker' style. In some churches 'admonitory texts adorned the walls' where, in the Middle Ages, had been wall-paintings.

Many organs had been destroyed by the Puritans, who regarded

---

[1] J. Eachard, *The Grounds and Occasions of the Contempt of the Clergy* (1670) in E. Arber, *An English Garner*, vii, p. 258.
[2] G. W. O. Addleshaw, *The High Church Tradition* (1941), p. 21.
[3] *I.e.* S. Giles, Cripplegate (J. Wickham Legg, *English Church Life from the Restoration to the Tractarian Movement* (1914), p. 28).

them as inimical to true worship; but after the Restoration the organ was reintroduced into the larger churches, many splendid instruments being made by the great organ-builders such as Bernhard Schmidt ('Father Smith') and Renatus Harris. At the same time impetus was given to more elaborate singing in four parts, as in Playford's *Whole Book of Psalms* which appeared in 1671. Verse-anthems, in the form of a suite of movements for solo and chorus with *ritornelli* for organ or orchestra, were published, as well as many anthems in the more familiar style. Choirs also came back into fashion with the re-establishment of the Children of the Chapel Royal. This was largely due to the drive and energy of that remarkable man, Captain Henry Cooke, whom Pepys called a 'vain coxcomb',[1] who enlisted boys from all over England by royal warrant whether they wished it or not. Many of his boys became distinguished musicians, including Pelham Humfrey, John Blow and Henry Purcell. Meanwhile the old doggerel verses of the metrical psalms of Sternhold and Hopkins were replaced by a much better version by Nahum Tate and Nicholas Brady in 1696. George Wither's *Hymns and Songs of the Church* (1623) and some of the hymns by Thomas Ken were now sung to tunes by Orlando Gibbons and others.[2]

Sermons were as popular in the church of the Restoration as they had been in the days of the Presbyterians. George Herbert had recommended the country parson to preach for about an hour, and Isaac Barrow once preached a sermon before the Lord Mayor of London which lasted for three hours and a half. Lack of education and training, however, often made for very bad preaching, Eachard complaining of the 'high tossing and swaggering preaching' of clergy trying to show off their learning,[3] while Pepys often found the sermons soporific. But towards the end of the century a new style came in, the greatest exponents of which were men like John Tillotson and Robert South. These great seventeenth-century preachers rejected the old Puritan homiletic tradition which had become stiff and formal, overloaded with trite expressions and pedantry, and the matter analysed into countless divisions and subdivisions. In its place they put a new style, direct, clear, forcible, sometimes witty. Their matter may not have been immensely profound, but it was full of sound

[1] *Diary*, February 13, 1667.
[2] See C. H. Phillips, *The Singing Church* (1945), Part iii, and E. H. Fellowes, *English Cathedral Music* (1941).
[3] In E. Arber, *An English Garner*, vii, p. 268.

ethic and high moral tone. Though the note of prophecy is absent, the appeal to common sense is clearly sounded. The following passage from a sermon by Tillotson is typical of the age. 'The Virtues of his Life', he said, 'are pure, without any Mixture of Infirmity and Imperfection. He had Humility without Meanness of Spirit; Innocency without Weakness; Wisdom without Cunning; and Constancy and Resolution in that which was good, without Stiffness of Conceit, and Peremptoriness of Humour. In a word, his Virtues were shining without Vanity, Heroical without any thing of Transport, and very extraordinary without being in the least extravagant.'[1] When men could write and speak like that of the Incarnate Son of God it was a sign that the Age of Enlightenment was near.

The old medieval churches were not well adapted to pulpit oratory, but, where possible, aids to hearing, in the form of new pulpits, sounding boards and galleries, were now introduced. When, after the disastrous fire of London in 1666 new churches were erected they were built in a style very different from the series of separate rooms which formed the normal Gothic church. The new 'auditory' churches were designed for preaching, and therefore consisted almost entirely of one large room (the nave) with quite small chancel and sanctuary.[2] Plans had already been made for work on S. Paul's Cathedral when it was burnt down and an entirely new church was erected by Sir Christopher Wren and paid for by a tax on all coal entering the city of London.

Attendance at church seems to have been quite good, for, although the court was dissolute and there was much loose living in high society, there was also a good number of very devout lay people. John Evelyn the diarist, Isaak Walton the writer and fisherman, and Margaret Godolphin who preserved her integrity and nobility of character while living at the court of Charles II, were all deeply religious and were typical of a fairly large class. For such people there was a steady output of religious literature. Jeremy Taylor's *Holy Living* and *Holy Dying* were intended as religious handbooks for lay people. So was the anonymous work called *The Whole Duty of Man*, a statement of church doctrine and Christian ethics which ranked next to the Bible and Prayer Book in church circles. From the Puritan

---

[1] J. Tillotson, *Two Hundred Sermons*, ii, p. 241; quoted in C. H. Smyth, *The Art of Preaching* (1940), pp. 156-7.
[2] See G. W. O. Addleshaw and F. Etchells, *The Architectural Setting of Anglican Worship* (1948).

side came Richard Baxter's *The Saints' Everlasting Rest* and John Bunyan's *Pilgrim's Progress*, the greatest religious allegory in the English language. There were also many volumes of sermons.

Such an output of literature presupposes an intelligent reading public. The universities had suffered less than most religious institutions during the interregnum and were now turning out some good scholars. There was a fairly common feeling, shared by Locke and Burnet among others, that the universities might enlarge their curricula and give some more useful teaching; but even on the old system they managed to give men some degree of culture. Meanwhile the nonconformists, since they were debarred from the universities, set up academies of their own at Newington Green, Islington, Taunton, Warrington, and other places for the training of future ministers. Grammar schools flourished and many new foundations were made. Nor were the children of the poor forgotten, for a number of Charity Schools were opened about this time mainly as a bulwark against the spread of what appeared the two greatest evils of the day—popery and poverty.[1]

iv. *James II and the Revolution*

James succeeded quietly to the throne on the death of his brother Charles in 1685. He made no secret of the fact that he was a Roman Catholic, and the Coronation service had, therefore, to be curtailed since the king declined to receive the communion according to the rites of the Church of England. A Coronation is usually a joyful event, but on this occasion there was much misgiving, and John Evelyn, who enjoyed public occasions, confessed that he 'was not ambitious of seeing this ceremony'.[2] The last professing papist to sit on the throne of England had been Mary Tudor of unhappy memory. What did James propose to do? That there would be concessions to the Roman Catholics no one doubted, but what of the religion of the country as a whole? Would James do what Mary had done and lead the country back to Rome?

In his opening speeches James assured his subjects that he fully intended to protect the established Church, and there is evidence that he had hopes of an alliance between the Church of England and the

[1] See M. G. Jones, *The Charity School Movement* (1938).
[2] *Diary*, April 23, 1685.

Romanists against the republican nonconformists. But fear of Rome was too strong for that. If there was to be any kind of *entente* it was much more likely to be between the Church and the nonconformists against their common enemy, Rome. So the air was full of rumours and fears, and William Sancroft, who had succeeded Sheldon as Archbishop of Canterbury in 1678, knew that he would have a difficult task in steering the Church through the stormy seas which lay ahead.

The next few months saw a number of changes and disturbances. It began with the failure of Monmouth's protestant rising in the west, followed by Judge Jeffreys' 'bloody assize'. Then came the beginning of concessions to the Roman Catholics, the forbidding of bonfires on November 5, and an effort on the part of the king to get members of his religion into positions of influence and power in the army, navy and civil service by means of dispensations from the restrictions of the Test Act.[1] Further alarm was caused by the setting up in 1686 of a new Court of High Commission to try ecclesiastical cases. Jeffreys, as Lord Chancellor, presided over it, but Archbishop Sancroft refused to sit on it. The reasons which he gave were those of failing health, but it was generally believed that he was suspicious of the whole business. Next came James's attempt to introduce Roman Catholics into important positions at Oxford and Cambridge, procuring the appointment of Obadiah Walker as Master of University College and putting a number of Roman Catholics into Magdalen. New convents were also founded in London by Jesuits, Franciscans and Dominicans.

As a result of this campaign there were certainly many converts, especially among those in high position or in hopes of high position. Pressure was put on waverers to win them over, and clergy who preached against Rome were punished. Meanwhile fantastic rumours filled the air. 'All the land quakes for fear!' wrote Abraham de la Pryme in 1687; 'the jesuits and papists here bear all down before them, and many have been heard to say that they expect to wash their hands in heretick's blood before next Christmas.'[2]

James, however, liked to pose as the champion of toleration. In 1687, and again in the following year, he issued Declarations of Indulgence[3] in which, largely for the sake of trade and encouraging immi-

[1] See the case of Godden *v.* Hales in C. Grant Robertson, *Select Statutes*, pp. 384-8.
[2] *Diary of Abraham de la Pryme* (Surtees Society, 1870), p. 13.
[3] Gee and Hardy, *Documents*, pp. 641-4; C. Grant Robertson, *Select Statutes*, pp. 388-91.

grants, he declared his protection for the established Church but at the same time suspended all penal laws against nonconformists, Roman Catholic and otherwise. This struck such a blow at the legislation of the previous reign that Sancroft and six other bishops, including Thomas Ken, petitioned the king to withdraw it, and, upon his declining to do so, refused to read it. As a result of this refusal the seven bishops were committed to the Tower and duly brought to trial.[1] After an all-night sitting the jury brought in a verdict of 'Not guilty' which was received with great acclamation, the bishops coming from the court through 'a lane of people from the King's Bench to the waterside, on their knees, as the Bishops passed and repassed, to beg their blessing. Bonfires were made that night, and bells rung, which was taken very ill at Court.'[2] It was one of the few occasions on which bishops have been treated as popular heroes.

A few days before the trial of the bishops the queen had borne a son. This was a further incentive to the malcontents in the country to bring the Stuart dynasty to an end. Overtures to the protestant William of Orange and his wife Mary, daughter of James by his first wife, Anne Hyde, were made, and in July 1688 a formal invitation to them was secretly delivered. Feeling was now running high. Wild stories were circulated of papists armed with long knives and laying in supplies of 'great coppers full of oyl, and others of pitch, and tar, and lead, all which was to boyl hereticks in'.[3] Priests were hustled and assaulted in the streets of London, churches were demolished, and, as Evelyn said, 'the whole nation was disaffected and in apprehensions'.[4]

Meanwhile William was collecting his forces to invade England. Favoured by what men came to call the 'protestant wind' he sailed down the Channel and landed at Torbay on November 5. On December 18 James fled from English soil, dropping the Great Seal into the Thames in the course of his flight, and on the same day William entered London.

v. *William and Mary*

The flight of James created a number of problems both in Church and State. James had not abdicated: he had fled, and William had

---

[1] C. Grant Robertson, *Select Statutes*, pp. 392-406.
[2] J. Evelyn, *Diary*, June 29, 1688.
[3] *Diary of Abraham de la Pryme*, p. 16.   [4] *Diary*, August 23, 1688.

taken his place as king *de facto* if not yet *de jure*. But what of the future? Could James be deposed and the crown given to another? or should a regency be appointed? or was James to be regarded as the only lawful sovereign? There was much difference of opinion on these questions. Many felt that once a king had been crowned he ruled by 'divine right' which could never be taken from him. Those who held this view believed also in the doctrine of 'passive non-resistance' which laid upon the subject the duty of loyalty and obedience to the lawful king wherever he might be. Others, less doctrinaire, realized that so long as James continued as king in name there could be no security for the country. Parliament, therefore, acted quickly. It decided that James must go; declared the throne vacant; and then offered it to William and Mary jointly. It was, constitutionally, the only workable arrangement.

But many churchmen were uneasy. Divine Right and Passive Obedience had been important doctrines in the creed of the Laudian or High Church party; and, by Divine Right, James was still king and in a position to demand Passive Obedience from his subjects. It is true that, being a Roman Catholic, he was out of sympathy with the Church of England; but so was William, being a Dutch Calvinist. The Church was, therefore, much divided in its loyalty. Most of the clergy decided to accept the revolution. The spirit of tolerance, or at least of weariness, was growing. Men were tired of religious strife and longed for peace. After all, Mary was a good Anglican and William a protestant; surely that was good enough? Others accepted the new régime only with mental reservations as the best thing for the country and in hope of preventing further disturbances.

A small group, however, realized at once that they must resist; and, when called upon to take the oath of allegiance to William and Mary, they declined to do so. Among these Non-jurors were about four hundred clergy and six bishops including William Sancroft, Archbishop of Canterbury, Thomas Ken, Bishop of Bath and Wells and Thomas White, Bishop of Peterborough. These were men who, having fought all their lives for the doctrines of Divine Right and Passive Obedience, preferred to suffer rather than to abandon what they believed to be part of the divine will. To us, with our notions of a constitutional monarchy, the views of the Non-jurors may seem strange and unreasonable; but they were not so to them. It was all part of the problem of authority. Where should the seat of authority lie? To the Romanists, authority meant the pope; to the independents and protestants, it meant the people; to the Anglicans it meant the king. Against this authority no one had a right to rebel.

The offering of the crown to William and Mary, which entailed the virtual deprivation of James of his kingship, was an outrage to the teaching of these men. Conscience demanded that they should make their stand for what they believed, whatever the cost might be —to themselves and even to the Church. Attempts to hold them by altering the wording of the oath were of no avail. So on August 1, 1689, those who still refused to take the oath were suspended, and six months later they were deprived.

The men who made this stand were acting from the highest motives. They were prepared to lose all for the sake of what they thought to be right. Having made their stand, most of them desired only to sink into obscurity, from the archbishop himself down to the humblest curate. But matters were not so easy as that. These were men who held office in the Church, office to which they had been duly and canonically instituted. This they steadfastly refused to re-sign and had, therefore, to be deprived. But on what authority? Who had power to deprive a bishop of his see unless he were found guilty of some serious crime? And who had power to appoint another to take his place? Realizing these difficulties the government allowed the benefices to remain vacant for some time; but this could not go on indefinitely. Difficulties were then encountered in finding men will-ing to take high offices in the Church when their former occupants were still alive and claiming to be the rightful occupants. When, eventually, the places were filled, a schism inevitably occurred. But who were the schismatics? The Church as a whole naturally regarded as schismatic those who had abandoned her, but the Non-jurors con-sistently disclaimed all responsibility for the schism which, they said, had been caused when their opponents had instituted men to bene-fices which were not vacant. A breach was therefore created which time alone could heal.[1]

The conscientious stand which the Non-jurors made in 1689-90 showed that there were a few left in the Church who thought that

[1] On the Non-jurors see T. Lathbury, *A History of the Nonjurors* (1845); J. H. Overton, *The Non-Jurors* (1902); L. M. Hawkins, *Allegiance in Church and State* (1928); J. W. C. Wand, *The High Church Schism* (1951).

deprivation was better than compromise. Meanwhile, in the Church and country as a whole, further steps towards toleration were being taken. The hopes of an understanding between the establishment and the nonconformists which had arisen at the time of the Restoration had been quickly dispersed by the vigorous legislation of the Clarendon Code. The restored Anglicans were in no mood to give anything away. They believed that disunity in religion meant weakness in the body politic, and were unable to imagine that there could be more than one expression of religion in a united nation. But though the Church as a whole was intolerant, confusing dissent with dissension, there were a few writers who urged conciliation and tolerance. Edward Stillingfleet's *Irenicum a weapon-salve for the Churches wounds*, written in 1659, would allow freedom of thought but not of action and was a curious mixture of toleration and intolerance. The cause was further promoted, from the Anglican side, by Herbert Croft, Bishop of Hereford, in *The Naked Truth; or, The True State of the Primitive Church* (1675), from the point of view of the Quakers by William Penn in *The Great Case of Liberty of Conscience* (1671), and from the philosophical angle by Locke in his *Letters concerning Toleration* (1689-92).

By the time of the Revolution, therefore, toleration was very much in the air. Thoughtful men were beginning to realize that nonconformity had come to stay and that it was no good adopting an attitude of persecution and repression. One of the first deeds, therefore, of the new Parliament was to pass an act, generally known as the *Toleration Act*[1] which, although it removed none of the civil disabilities of nonconformists and refused to accept the free churches on anything like equal terms with the Church of England, allowed most of them to have their own places of worship so long as they met with doors unlocked and notified the bishop or his representative of their existence. These concessions did not apply to Roman Catholics, nor to Unitarians. There were, therefore, limits beyond which toleration was not yet prepared to go; but, within its limitations, this act must be regarded as the greatest measure of toleration so far achieved and the beginning of a new era in the treatment of religious minorities.

The last years of the seventeenth century also saw a considerable advance in the active life of the Church. As has been said: 'The re-

[1] Gee and Hardy, *Documents*, pp. 654-64; C. Grant Robertson, *Select Statutes*, pp. 123-8.

ligious life of England in the reigns of William III and Anne was better than its ecclesiastical history'.[1] Among the signs of this advance was the formation, from about 1678 onwards of Religious Societies composed of godly young laymen whose 'blooming piety' was an object of admiration to their seniors. These 'clubs', as they came to be called, met mostly in London and chose a priest as their director. They assembled regularly for prayer and discussion, pledged themselves to a monthly or weekly Communion, and interested themselves in philanthropic undertakings. John Wesley's father, Samuel Wesley, was one of their warmest supporters. Interest was also now beginning to be taken in the work of the Church overseas. Much colonization had been going on in North America and elsewhere, and that remarkable man, Dr. Thomas Bray (1656–1730), had begun his scheme of providing religious literature for the benefit of those cut off from libraries at home. It was out of this scheme that there emerged the Society for Promoting Christian Knowledge, founded in 1698 by Bray and a small group of religious laymen, for the purpose of 'promoting Religion and Learning in any part of His Majesty's Plantations abroad, and to provide Catechetical Libraries and free Schools in the parishes at home'.[2] Three years later Dr. Bray enlisted the support of Archbishop Tenison and several of the bishops for the creation of a new society to be called the Society for the Propagation of the Gospel in Foreign Parts, which was officially incorporated by royal charter in 1701. The objects of this society, as outlined by the Dean of Lincoln in 1702, were 'to settle the State of Religion as well as may be among our *own People* there (*i.e.* in the Plantations, Colonies and Factories) . . . and then to proceed in the best Methods towards the *Conversion* of the *Natives*'.[3]

There was also growing up a humanitarian concern for the poor in England which showed itself in an interest in prison reform and in the foundation of hospitals. Societies for the Reformation of Manners also grew up in an attempt to raise the standards of morals and decency. The method employed was chiefly that of the law-courts, and thousands were prosecuted for blasphemy, profanation of the Lord's day and other offences. But though some complained

---

[1] G. N. Clark, *The Later Stuarts* (1934), p. 151.
[2] J. McLeod Campbell, *Christian History in the Making* (1946), p. 35; cf. W. O. B. Allen and E. McClure, *Two Hundred Years: The History of S.P.C.K.* (1898).
[3] *Two Hundred Years of the S.P.G., 1701–1900*, p. 7; H. P. Thompson, *Into All Lands* (1951), pp. 20–21.

CHAPTER XVI

THE EARLY EIGHTEENTH CENTURY
(1702–1738)

i. *The High Church Revival*

WILLIAM III was a Dutchman whose chief ambition was to curb the rising power of France. He was also a Calvinist and therefore naturally out of sympathy with High Church Anglicanism which he could not understand and which he knew had only grudgingly accepted him at all. Most of the High Churchmen were Tories, a few were Jacobites, and none had much faith in a constitutional monarchy. William had found the English sharply divided on religious issues, but had hoped to unite them in the protestant cause. Like many foreigners, he found Anglicanism an enigma, neither wholly catholic nor wholly protestant, and was baffled by people whose point of view he was unable to comprehend. However, attempts were made to unite the country, religiously as well as politically, in order to build up a strong force against the French. In 1689 a bill was drawn up to modify Church order in such a way as to accommodate the Presbyterians, and plans were discussed for altering the Prayer Book so that it would be less obnoxious to puritans by changing the word 'priest' to 'minister', striking out certain saints' days from the Kalendar, revising many of the collects, and even trying to find a way round the barriers erected by the surplice and the sign of the cross in baptism.[1]

All these plans, however, failed; and when William was succeeded by Anne in 1702 the country was just as much divided as it had been thirteen years before. The people had passed through many years of strife and longed for peace. But it was not to come yet. 'The legacy of the seventeenth century was not peace but a sword',[2] and the early years of the eighteenth century were marked by fierce religious disputes which finally left the country exhausted and the Church too torpid to cope with the problem suddenly created by the activities of

---

[1] For details see Procter and Frere, *A New History of the Book of Common Prayer*, pp. 209-21.   [2] N. Sykes, *Edmund Gibson* (1926), p. 2.

the early Evangelicals. The religious differences were, moreover, closely connected with political allegiances, producing that intransigence which results from a mingling of man's deepest loyalties—religion and politics. 'The framework of the rival political parties', it has been said, 'was formed on a confessional basis, and dislike of the smell of one's neighbour's religion seemed the prevailing passion in man as a political animal.'[1]

When Anne ascended the throne in 1702 she found the High Church party active, aggressive and confident. She herself was in many ways ill-fitted for the heavy burdens which fell upon her. A chronic invalid, mourning the loss of all her fifteen children, reserved and rather dull, the queen presented a pathetic figure. But she was a good woman, kind-hearted and devout; and her sympathies were with the High Churchmen. Anne did not talk much about Divine Right and Passive Obedience; she knew that since the Revolution kings and queens were answerable to Parliament and not to God alone; but she had high ideas of the dignity of a queen and was glad to restore old-world customs such as the 'touching' of sick children supposed to be suffering from the King's Evil and therefore curable by the touch of the royal hand. She was also deeply concerned for the welfare of her clergy, especially those who were in want. The old medieval dues of 'First Fruits and Tenths', which the pope had always collected from the English clergy, had been annexed to the crown by Henry VIII and converted into a fixed tax which amounted to some £16,000 a year. Anne, moved by two of the bishops, Burnet and Sharp, gave all this money in 1704 to form a fund known as Queen Anne's Bounty from which the stipends of the poorer clergy might be augmented.

In 1702 the Tories were in power and in close alliance with the High Church party. Looking back over the past reign it was clear that the legislation introduced forty years ago in favour of the Church had been to some extent neglected or ignored. The chief problem was that presented by the 'occasional conformists'. In order to overcome the severe deprivations imposed upon dissenters by the Clarendon Code a certain number of men, who were not members of the established Church, had adopted the habit of occasionally making their communion at the parish churches in order to qualify as conformists. Some did it because they liked it, others because failure

[1] G. M. Trevelyan, *England under Queen Anne; Blenheim* (1930), pp. 283-4.

to do so cut them off from hopes of promotion or of office. But the Tories and High Churchmen did not approve of the custom. It was strictly illegal and seemed slightly dishonest. It meant that important and lucrative offices sometimes went to men who were not really entitled to them, or to men who were not pulling their weight as churchmen. Perhaps the most bitter opponent was that vigorous pamphleteer and bigot, Dr. Sacheverell, who denounced those 'insidious persons who creep to our altars' not with reverence and humility but only in order to get power with which to destroy the Church. The mild nonconformist, Daniel Defoe, wrote a pamphlet called *The Shortest Way with the Dissenters*, which was so obviously a skit on the Tory and High Church views that he was pilloried for it in London. Feeling ran high, and a bill to prevent nonconformists from circumventing the law by occasional conformity was introduced into the Commons in 1702, only to be thrown out, after great debate, by the Lords.

Another plank in the policy of the Tories was to get the Convocations of the Church restored to their lawful place. At the Restoration the Convocations of Canterbury and York had met again after the interregnum, but in 1664 a private agreement was made between Archbishop Sheldon and Lord Clarendon that in future the clergy should no longer tax themselves but should be liable to pay the ordinary taxes of the state. On the strength of this, Convocation had lapsed for some years. But the High Churchmen were not at all happy about it, and in 1697 Francis Atterbury published a vigorous appeal for the revival of these assemblies in his *Letter to a Convocation Man*. His appeal, in spite of opposition from William Wake and others, was successful; and in 1700 the Convocations met. At once it became apparent that, in the confused state of religious opinion, these meetings were going to do more harm than good. They immediately became centres of storm and controversy, the Canterbury Convocation being little more than a cockpit in which a group of discontented clergy sparred with the House of Bishops. Hand in hand with the religious controversies went political divisions, and, by 1717, the atmosphere had become so charged with friction and discontent that the Convocations were prorogued for several years. They met again in 1741 but only formally, and then virtually closed down for more than a century.

The silencing of the Convocations, during so important an epoch in the life of the Church, was a great disaster. It meant that the Church had no place where its members could meet to exchange opinions and air grievances. It meant that there was no opportunity for the Church to formulate a common policy on such burning questions as Methodism and the expansion of the Church overseas. It meant also that the clergy were deprived of their natural forum where men could be trained in the arts of debate. The quarrelsomeness of the clergy in the early years of the eighteenth century did much ill to the Church and to the cause of religion in England.

While Convocation was burning with dissension, further fuel was being added to the flames by Dr. Sacheverell who continued his attacks on Whigs, dissenters and Latitudinarians in the strongest language. But the political tide was beginning to turn; the Whigs came into power; and on November 5, 1709, Sacheverell, after a peculiarly virulent sermon, was arrested and impeached. In due course he was tried before the House of Lords in Westminster Hall amid scenes of the utmost excitement. The crowd was mainly on the side of Sacheverell, and a number of dissenting chapels in London were burnt down. In the end the verdict went against the accused, but the sentence was light—a prohibition against his preaching for three years. Sacheverell was immediately treated as a popular hero and was fêted as he journeyed across England after his trial.

It was largely as a result of the trial that the Whigs fell from power in 1710, bringing the Tories back with greater determination than ever. They immediately took up again the question of the occasional conformists and in 1711 passed the *Occasional Conformity Act*[1] which decreed that anyone holding any office, civil or military, who 'shall at any time . . . resort to or be present at any Conventicle, Assembly or Meeting . . . for the exercise of Religion in other Manner than according to the Liturgy and Practice of the Church of England . . . shall forfeit Forty Pounds' and be disabled from holding any further office. The penalty was so heavy that few could afford to take the risk of detection, especially as the execution of the act depended upon the employment of spies and informers. Three years later the *Schism Act*,[2] forbidding nonconformists to have their own schools, was passed with the view of keeping them out of the professions.

The year of the *Occasional Conformity Act* saw the death of the saintly Thomas Ken, the last of the bishops who had refused to take

[1] C. G. Robertson, *Select Statutes*, pp. 187-90.   [2] *Ibid.* pp. 190-94.

the oath of allegiance to William and Mary and had thus created the problem of the Non-jurors. Various attempts to win back the Non-jurors to the Church had failed, and the schism had been perpetuated first by the consecration of two new bishops, George Hickes and Thomas Wagstaffe, in 1694, and, after Ken's death, by the consecration of three more—Jeremy Collier the historian, Samuel Hawes and the devout Nathaniel Spinks—in 1713. This put all hope of a reconciliation out of the question, and the Non-juring church dragged out a somewhat miserable existence until well into the eighteenth century. Cut off from the main blood-stream of the Church, it tended to split up, especially over matters of worship and ceremonial, and after the rebellion of 1745 it fell into great disfavour, since it was largely Jacobite in politics and romanizing in religion.[1] Yet it captured the imagination and loyalty, at any rate for a time, of some great and good men, among whom were Robert Nelson, the friend of all good works, and William Law the mystic.

ii. *Conflicts in Theology*

While High Church Tory and Low Church Whig were fighting for precedence and privilege, a blow was being struck at the very foundations of the Christian faith by the rise of Deism. Deism is generally thought to have had its origin in the works of Lord Herbert of Cherbury (1583–1648) who aroused the interest of men in a 'religion of nature' unencumbered by creeds, formularies, and priesthood. The idea, fitting in so well with the growth of scientific thought and the love of Reason, was taken up by a number of thinkers later in the seventeenth century. John Locke's *Reasonableness of Christianity*, though intended as a strong plea for the Christian faith, laid much emphasis upon the simplicity of Christianity and thus encouraged those who were getting tired of dogmatic disputes and longed for a purer and simpler faith. This book appeared in 1695, and in the following year John Toland published his *Christianity not Mysterious*, with which the Deistic controversy began in earnest. Toland's idea was to take from Christianity all that was mysterious and supernatural and reduce it to what was natural and reasonable.

---

[1] *E.g.* in 1694 the question of the consecration of new bishops had been submitted to James II and by him to the pope for his advice.

18

It was followed some years later by Matthew Tindal's *Christianity as old as the Creation* (1730), sometimes known as the 'Deist's Bible'. Tindal laid great emphasis on the harmony of nature and the moral law. All truth is to be found in natural religion based upon reason. There could therefore be no fresh revelation of the divine will and therefore no need of an Incarnation. There was nothing new in Christianity, or, if there were, it was untrue.

Deism, therefore, though it assumed the Christian mask, was pantheistic and unitarian. It ignored the revelation of God in Christ and was content with a religion based upon the study of nature interpreted by reason. Making no great demands upon people, and couched in the phraseology of the day, it is easy to understand why Deism enjoyed considerable popularity in the early part of the eighteenth century.

One of the first to take up the cudgels against the Deists was the Non-juror, Charles Leslie, whose *Short and Easie Method with the Deists* was published in 1698. It was followed in 1713 by Richard Bentley's *Remarks on a Late Discourse of Freethinking*, and then the battle began in earnest. Books poured from the presses on both sides. Anyone who had any pretensions to theological ability thought it his duty to publish either a defence of Deism or an attack upon it. Of those who did most to refute and discredit the Deists three names stand out pre-eminently.

The most notable was Joseph Butler (1692–1752). The son of a prosperous linen-draper, Butler was brought up as a Presbyterian and was educated at dissenting academies. But as a young man he decided to join the Church of England and went to Oxford. He was ordained in 1718 and started preaching at the Rolls Chapel in London where his famous *Fifteen Sermons* were delivered. Some years later he went north to the diocese of Durham where he became Rector of Houghton-le-Skerne and then of Stanhope. In 1738 he was made Bishop of Bristol and in 1750 translated to Durham. It was while he was a country parson in County Durham that Butler wrote his most famous work, the *Analogy of Religion, Natural and Revealed, to the Constitution and Course of Nature* (1736). This, which is one of the most important and influential books in Christian literature, was written with great modesty and simplicity in an age of self-assuredness and subtlety. Butler accepts all that reason has to say about God but then goes on to the necessity of revelation. At a time when many believed that the Christian faith had been proved fictitious, Butler set forth again the fundamentals of Christian hope and pleaded for greater application to the Christian way of life.[1]

Among Butler's contemporaries was George Berkeley (1685–1753), an Irishman educated at Trinity College, Dublin, who became Dean of Dromore in 1722, of Derry in 1724 and Bishop of Cloyne in 1734. Berkeley was a man of a restless and benevolent nature who travelled over much of the world looking for ways of doing good. He took the greatest interest in missionary endeavour and was full of ideas and projects for the improvement of the world. But it is chiefly as a philosopher that Bishop Berkeley is remembered today, a Platonist opposed to the stern logic of Aristotelianism. His moral earnestness and deep spiritual feeling present a welcome contrast to the hard common sense of so many of his contemporaries. Berkeley's *Alciphron, or the Minute Philosopher*, written in America and published in 1732, was a philosophical argument in favour of the Christian faith in the form of an argument between Deists and Christians.[2]

The third of the great champions of Christianity was William Law (1686–1761). Law became a fellow of Emmanuel College, at Cambridge, but lost his fellowship in 1715 when he refused to take the oath abjuring the Stuart claims to the throne, and so joined the ranks of the Non-jurors though continuing in communion with the Church of England. His book, *The Case for Reason* (1731), was a reply to Tindal's *Christianity as old as the Creation*. In this work Law accepts Reason as a noble faculty in no way to be despised. But it is not enough; it has its limitations; and it is here that faith comes in to carry the believer onward to the fullness of truth and reality.[3]

While the Church was fighting the battle against Deism, two further skirmishes were taking place, one on the doctrine of the Trinity, the other on the doctrine of the Church. The Trinitarian controversy began with the works of Samuel Clarke (1675–1729) who was educated at Caius College, Cambridge, and afterwards became Rector of S. James, Piccadilly and Chaplain-in-ordinary to the King. In 1712 Clarke published his *Scripture Doctrine of the Trinity* in which

---

[1] See *The Works of Bishop Butler*, ed. W. E. Gladstone, 3 vols. (1896).
[2] See J. M. Hone and M. M. Rossi, *Bishop Berkeley; His Life, Writings and Philosophy* (1931) and J. Wild, *George Berkeley: a Study of his Life and Philosophy* (1936).
[3] The works of Law were published in 1893 in nine volumes, entitled *The Works of the Reverend William Law*. See also J. H. Overton, *William Law, Non-juror and Mystic* (1881).

he denied the orthodox teaching of the Creeds and brought upon himself charges of Arianism. He was answered, among others, by Daniel Waterland (1683–1740) in *A Vindication of Christ's Divinity* (1719) and a series of works which came almost yearly from his pen. The other dispute was on the doctrine of the Church. The more liberal thinkers were exasperated by the 'churchiness' and sacerdotalism of the High Church party and began discussing the question as to whether there is any necessity for a visible Church at all. The chief writer on this subject was Benjamin Hoadly, a prominent ecclesiastical careerist who was successively Bishop of Bangor, Hereford, Salisbury and Winchester. Hoadly was a friend and disciple of Samuel Clarke whose works he collected and published. The doctrine of the Church had been brought to the forefront by the Non-jurors, notably by Charles Leslie in his *Case of the Regale and of the Pontificate, stated in a Conference concerning the Independency of the Church upon any Power on Earth in the exercise of her purely Spiritual Power and Authority* (1700). This lengthy title explains the nature of the book, which was a defence of High Church doctrine and 'marks the culminating point of English sacerdotalism'.[1] Hoadly replied to this in 1717 with his *Preservation against the Principles and Practices of the Non-Jurors both in Church and State*, a solid defence of the Erastianism which was so marked a feature of the Broad Church. In Hoadly's view all that mattered was sincerity, and he followed up his book with a powerful sermon in the Chapel Royal on the nature of the kingdom or Church of Christ. Hoadly saw no need for a visible Church at all. He had no conception of sacramental religion, nor of the Church as the Body of Christ and continuation of the Incarnation. The Church was no more than 'the blessed company of all faithful people' and therefore had no need for creeds, orders or discipline. So shocking was this to High Church principles that it led to a dispute in Convocation so stormy as to result in the closing of the Convocations for many years.

Among a host of replies to Bishop Hoadly the most conspicuous was that of William Law in his *Three Letters to the Bishop of Bangor*. Law based his argument on the highest grounds—that the Christian Church is an essential part of the divine economy—whereas the bishop, he said, 'has left us neither priests, sacraments nor Church'. Other replies were more mundane: the visible Church was a part of

[1] J. M. Creed and J. S. Boys Smith, *Religious Thought in the Eighteenth Century* (1934), p. 244. The *Regale* was reprinted by the Tractarians in 1838.

the establishment, necessary to the keeping of law, order and decency in the State. Among the more utilitarian adversaries of Hoadly was William Warburton (1698–1779), an attorney who was ordained in 1723 and eventually became Bishop of Gloucester. Warburton was a man of very strong feelings, with the greatest possible dislike of papists and free-thinkers, enthusiasm and mysticism. He was completely and whole-heartedly attached to the Establishment whereby the Church surrendered its independence and authority in exchange for state patronage and protection. Doctrinal differences were to him immaterial, and he thought that whatever body contained a majority of the nation had the right to be regarded as the national Church.

Finally, behind all the dust and fury of battle lay the quiet thought and work of mystics like William Law. Law published, in 1726, his book on *Christian Perfection*, a treatise on practical Christianity based upon the imitation of Christ; and followed it up two years later with *A Serious Call to a Devout and Holy Life*. 'If we are to *follow* Christ', he said, 'it must be in our common way of spending every day. . . . If our common life is not a common course of *humility, self-denial, renunciation* of the world, *poverty* of spirit, and *heavenly* affection, we do not live the lives of Christians.'[1] He then goes on to illustrate, by a series of imaginary characters, the vices and virtues of men, and makes his great appeal to men to take their Christian profession seriously. This famous work soon began to have a profound influence on the religious life of England and was loved by such men as Samuel Johnson and John and Charles Wesley. It showed that under the noise of strife in the Church there was a quiet strain of piety and devotion which prepared the nation for the religious revival which was to come.

iii. *Church and State*

From 1705 onwards the Whig tide had been rising, and, by 1714, they had achieved power which they held until 1760. As soon as they were firmly in the saddle they began to undo some of the High Church legislation of the previous ministry. In the crisis of the rebellion of 1715 the nonconformists had played their part manfully in defending their country and deserved a reward. It came with the

[1] *The Works of the Reverend William Law* (1893) iv, pp. 11-12.

repeal in 1718 of the *Occasional Conformity* and the *Schism Acts*. The Whigs would like to have gone further and repeal parts of the Clarendon Code, but the Church was too strong for them. All they could do was to pass an *Act for Quieting and Establishing Corporations* which, under this clumsy title, allowed nonconformists to hold civil appointments if, after doing so for six months, their right to do so had not been challenged. Apart from this, the provisions of the Clarendon Code still stood, though, in fact, the law was not often put into operation. Toleration was in the air if not on the statute-book. But toleration had its limits. Roman Catholics, especially after the risings of 1715 and 1745, were still under considerable disabilities, being commonly regarded as traitors; and Quakers, who refused to pay tithes or to bear arms, were regarded as anti-social and dangerous.

The Whig government was warmly supported by the bishops, most of whom, as the years went by, owed their preferment to the fact that they had done good service to the party in power. A few still continued to hold political or diplomatic posts. All of them were closely connected with Parliament, forming a considerable section of the House of Lords and regarding attendance there for a large part of the year as of obligation. This meant that each bishop spent seven or eight months of the year in London, devoting only a few months in the summer to the care of his flock. A few failed to give even that much time to their dioceses, for Bishop Hoadly, though Bishop of Bangor for six years and Bishop of Hereford for the next two, practically never set foot in either diocese.

The expense of maintaining an establishment in the capital as well as a palace in the cathedral city laid a heavy financial burden on the bishops. The endowments of most of the sees were large, but they were seldom large enough to meet the needs of men who ranked among the highest in the land and expected to live on equal terms with the wealthy. Consequently many of the bishops were pluralists, supplementing their official stipends by holding deaneries, prebends or rectories *in commendam* and paying a small sum to an assistant curate to do the work for them. With the poorer sees such an ex-pedient was regarded as essential, but no rising prelate expected to be left in a poor see for long. Just as a clergyman regarded a succes-sion of canonries and dignities as stepping-stones to the bench, so, as bishop, he expected promotion to follow as more important sees fell vacant. Often a man started off with one of the poorer Welsh sees and gradually worked his way up to York, Winchester or Durham. The interests of the dioceses and the needs of the people do not seem ever to have been considered, nor would any bishop have been criticized for staying only a few months in a diocese if the chance of preferment to a more lucrative see came his way. But, of course, all preferment depended upon the good-will of the party in power. So long as a bishop devoted himself heart and soul to the promotion of the Whig interest he had some chance of bettering himself. If he failed to do so he would undoubtedly be passed over when the next shuffle took place.

Clergy who were ambitious, as indeed most of them were, knew how to play their cards and obtain preferment. He who had the good fortune to be born a member of one of the noble families began well ahead of his less privileged rivals. Against the man who had no such good luck the dice were heavily loaded; but by skill and fortune he might get into the graces of some aristocratic family, perhaps as a successful tutor or chaplain, and so win their support. The next thing was to preach the right kind of sermons, publish the right kind of pamphlets and do good work for your party in parish and county, and the rest followed in due course.

Bishops were naturally in a position to give peculiar assistance to the Government, even to the extent of military support, for Bishop Nicolson of Carlisle and Archbishop Herring of York both raised forces to crush the rebels in 1715 and 1745 respectively. But the chief assistance which the bishops gave was in more domestic affairs, especially at election times. Many a prelate could use his position in the county to influence the votes of the laity, while the hope of preferment or threat of censure was often enough to sway the minds of the clergy at a time when there was no secret ballot.

Yet in spite of the system being so bad, so open to corruption and sycophancy, there were a number of good and conscientious bishops who made a real contribution to the life of the Church. Gilbert Burnet at Salisbury from 1689–1715 was a highly conscientious man who genuinely cared for his clergy and was a father-in-God to his people.[1] John Sharp, Archbishop of York, 1691–1714, was a Yorkshireman of humble origin who worked his way up by his great gifts as scholar, administrator and preacher, and went back to serve the people of his native county for many years. Sharp was a close

[1] See T. E. S. Clarke and H. C. Foxcroft, *Life of Gilbert Burnet* (1907).

friend of Queen Anne, who greatly valued his advice, and he was naturally much engaged in political affairs. But he found time to say his prayers and to administer his vast diocese with skill and devotion, looking after his clergy and helping them to fight their battle against sin and ignorance in the villages of the dales.[1]

William Wake, Bishop of Lincoln, 1705–16, and Archbishop of Canterbury from then until 1737, was the son of a Dorset squire. Early in his career he was appointed chaplain to Lord Preston, the British ambassador in Paris, and began then to take a keen interest in the Gallican Church. He returned to England and quickly won promotion, first to the deanery of Exeter and then to a bishopric. Wake was a man of wide vision who worked hard for the reunion of Christendom and kept in close touch with Roman Catholics and Protestants in many countries.[2] In later years he retired much from public affairs to a life which he described as 'almost monastic', saying prayers four times a day with his family and household.[3]

Edmund Gibson, who succeeded Wake at Lincoln and was Bishop of London from 1723 to 1748, came from a modest Westmorland home but quickly made a name for himself as an antiquary and canonist. In 1713 he published his *Codex Juris Ecclesiastici Anglicani* which still ranks as an important authority on English canon law. His legal knowledge and native shrewdness made him useful in the councils of state, and he played an important part in the introduction of the Hanoverians. A man of strong opinions, he made a stand against some of the abuses in the Church of his day, expressed his disapproval alike of dissenters and Latitudinarians, urged the revival of the ecclesiastical courts, and ruled the complicated diocese of London with courage and vigour.[4]

Gibson was at the centre of affairs in London, but away in the lonely Isle of Man was another great bishop and administrator, Thomas Wilson, a Cheshire man, who was appointed in 1697 to the bishopric of Man, the poorest and most isolated of all sees. Though the endowment was so slender, Wilson refused to supplement it by holding other benefices and even managed to give nearly half of his income away in charity. During the fifty-seven years that he was Bishop of Man, from 1698 to 1755, he scarcely ever left the island,

[1] See A. Tindal Hart, *The Life and Times of John Sharp, Archbishop of York* (1949).
[2] See below, pp. 283–4.
[3] See N. Sykes, *William Wake, Archbishop of Canterbury*, 2 vols. (1957).
[4] See N. Sykes, *Edmund Gibson, Bishop of London* (1926).

refusing all offers of more lucrative sees on the mainland and devoting himself to the care of his clergy, the preparation of his ordinands, the promotion of education, and the evangelization of his people. He learnt the Manx language and translated Christian literature for the benefit of the humbler folk; he ran a college for students in his own house and taught there daily; he worked as a physician among the sick; he travelled all over the island, and ruled his people with severity, but a severity chastened by love.[1]

As the eighteenth century advanced, the number of outstanding men in the Church grew less. A quiet complacency seems to have brooded over the land after the storms and strains of the preceding years. The machine was kept in motion, but there was little inspiration or challenge to men of imagination and zeal. Enthusiasm was their chief bugbear, and even though we remember that by Enthusiasm they meant what would now be called Fanaticism, it is significant of the age. The learned and pious prelate, Joseph Butler, once said to John Wesley: 'Sir, the pretending to extraordinary revelation and gifts of the Holy Ghost is a horrid thing, a very horrid thing'.[2] Most of his fellow bishops would have concurred in this judgment. Peace and propriety were the qualities which the eighteenth-century Church most desired, and such as threatened to disturb the one or outrage the other were deeply suspect.

iv. *The Church of England and her Neighbours*

At the time of the Restoration there were many who hoped for a reconciliation between the Anglican Church and Presbyterianism; but the determination and vigour of the returning exiles quickly made this impossible. The Savoy Conference followed by the legislation known as the Clarendon Code, made a gulf between the Church and all other Christian communities which could not easily be healed. The tentative proposals of men like Tillotson, who genuinely desired greater comprehension, met with little response, and the country divided itself into two great camps: those who were within the established Church and those who were outside it. By the middle of the eighteenth century, although the direction of the Church was largely

---

[1] C. Cruttwell, *Life of Thomas Wilson* (1781) and *Life*, by J. Keble in *Works of T. Wilson* (Library of Anglo-Catholic Theology, 1863). See also *The Diaries of Thomas Wilson*, ed. C. L. S. Linnell (1964).

[2] J. H. Overton, *John Wesley* (1891), p. 100.

in the hands of Broad Churchmen they were no more disposed to compromise with nonconformity than their High Church predecessors. The Hanoverian bishops had made themselves so snug and secure that they had no intention of sharing their good things with others. If the dissenters wished for the privileges of the establishment, well, they knew what to do. The doors of the Church were open, but there could be no compromise.

Continental protestants were, however, regarded in a very different light. Even the High Churchmen in England were fully conscious of their own essential protestantism, and looked upon members of the reformed Churches of Europe as their fellows. Fear of Rome was so strong that all who had cast off the Roman yoke in the sixteenth century felt themselves drawn together in alliance against a common enemy, however much they might differ in other ways. Moreover in the protestant world the Church of England was looked up to as 'the chief and most flourishing of all the protestant Churches'.[1] It was therefore customary for members of the continental Churches, whether Lutheran or Calvinist, to communicate at Anglican altars in England and for English Churchmen to worship with Calvinists in France and Holland or with Lutherans in Germany. Even a High Churchman like Dean Granville of Durham had no scruples about communicating with French protestants, and Bishop Ken warmly welcomed the Huguenots to England when Louis XIV drove them out of their native land.

In the eighteenth century attempts were made to get into closer touch with protestants abroad. John Sharp, a High Churchman, took a great interest in the affairs of the Lutherans and Calvinists in Prussia and was called in to help with a plan, promoted by the Moravian, Ernst Jablonski, for a reunion of these two bodies on the basis of episcopacy and the English Prayer Book translated into German. Archbishop Wake felt the divisions among protestants so deeply that he declared that he would welcome a closer union amongst all the reformed bodies 'at almost any price'.

Meanwhile, nearer home, there was a sister Church in Scotland, the Episcopalians, for whom the Church in England clearly had some responsibility. The Episcopalian Church had been restored in Scot-

[1] *Omnium Protestantium Ecclesiarum praecipua et florentissima*; see letter from *Unitas Fratrum* to Archbishop Wake quoted in N. Sykes, *The Church of England & Non-episcopal Churches in the Sixteenth and Seventeenth Centuries* ('Theology' Occasional Papers, Series, No. 11, 1948).

land at the return of the monarchy in 1660; but it had never been popular, and many of its bishops were of a poor type. At the Revolution in 1689 many of the Episcopalian clergy were deprived and 'rabbled' by the crowds, who knew that the 'Piskies' were largely Jacobite in sympathy; and in the following year the Scottish Parliament passed an Act to make Presbyterianism the national religion of Scotland. Apart from the north and east, where Episcopalianism was strongly entrenched, most of the clergy were thrown into great want, and appealed to their brethren in England to help them. Archbishop Sharp and others raised money and did all that they could to bring succour to the afflicted, and feeling about the hardships of these men was so strong that in 1712 Parliament was obliged to recognize the Episcopalian minority and to pass an Act of Toleration to protect them.

The Church of Rome has always presented a problem so great as to be in quite a different class from every other question of reunion. The unhappy experiences of Mary's reign, the plots against Elizabeth I and James I, and the desertion of James II had all helped to build up a monstrous fear of Rome which centuries have not been able wholly to dissipate. Even so, in the early part of the eighteenth century an attempt was made to open negotiations with the more liberal section of the Roman communion in France known as the Gallican Church. Wake had made contacts with French priests when he was in Paris, and in 1717 a correspondence between him and Dr. Du Pin of the Sorbonne was opened with some support from the Archbishop of Paris. Wake was immensely interested in this approach, but quite determined not to compromise the Anglican Church or to allow it to be thought of as in any way inferior to the Church of Rome. For two years a considerable correspondence took place and some agreement was reached; but in 1719 the negotiations came to an end through the death of Du Pin and the complete submission of the Archbishop of Paris to pressure from Rome.[1]

Finally there was the great Orthodox Church of the East. During the seventeenth century a college for Greek students had been founded at Oxford, but it had never flourished. From time to time small groups of students had come, but their conduct had not been satisfactory and none had stayed very long. In 1701 the Archbishop of

[1] See J. H. Lupton, *Archbishop Wake and the Project of Union between the Gallican and Anglican Churches* (1896).

Philippopolis came to England, followed a few years later by an Armenian patriarch. Compliments were exchanged between them and the English hierarchy, but no proposals for reunion were made. Then, in 1716, the Non-juring bishops made overtures to the Church in Russia with the hope of finding some means of drawing closer together; but, being separated from the Church, they spoke without authority, and in 1725 Wake had to intervene to explain this to the Russians, even though it meant the end of negotiations.

All this shows that the Church in England, smug and self-satisfied though in some ways it was, was fully aware of the divisions of Christendom and anxious to heal the breaches. That it failed was due not to lack of a desire for unity so much as to the depth of the divisions. The day of Christian unity was not yet.[1]

v. *Church and Society*

As each bishop was obliged to spend more than half the year in London, the administration of the dioceses had to be largely left to archdeacons and others, except for the four or five months during the summer when the bishops left London and made their way to their own sees to take up the multifarious business of their dioceses where they had left off eight months previously. This meant, for any conscientious bishop, a busy round of visitations, confirmations, ordinations and entertainments.

Distances were so great, roads so dangerous, means of travel so slow, and English weather so treacherous that, with the best will in the world, a bishop could hardly see much of his clergy or even know who they were. Moreover the difference in class between a prelate and a poor parish priest was so great that they could have had little in common. As has been said of the inferior clergy of the period: 'These humble and ill-paid pastors and their wealthy fathers-in-God rarely saw one another, and even when they did, the social distance between them was so great that little human intercourse was possible'.[2]

Confirmations in the eighteenth century were done on a large

[1] See J. H. Overton, *Life in the English Church, 1660–1714* (1885), chap. ix; J. Wickham Legg, *English Church Life from the Restoration to the Tractarian Movement* (1914), chap. xiv; N. Sykes, *The Church of England and Non-episcopal Churches in the Sixteenth and Seventeenth Centuries* (1948). Much useful material will be found in *A History of the Ecumenical Movement, 1517–1948*, ed. R. Rouse and S. C. Neil (1967), pp. 123–66.
[2] B. Williams, *The Whig Supremacy* (1939), pp. 78–9.

scale. As work which nowadays fills most of the year had to be crowded into four months, and as there were no suffragan bishops to relieve the strain upon the diocesan, it was customary to collect together vast crowds of children when the day for the Confirmation arrived. Wake, when Bishop of Lincoln, confirmed as many as 1200 at one sitting at Grantham in 1709, and numbers between 500 and 1000 were quite common.[1] Such services were inevitably very lengthy, lasting sometimes from nine in the morning till seven at night with only short pauses for refreshment; it is therefore not surprising that a few bishops tried to lessen the fatigue by merely giving a general blessing without any laying on of hands at all. Often the length of the service and lack of control led to scenes of wild disorder and confusion, and occasionally the number of candidates was increased by people presenting themselves for confirmation more than once, as did some old ladies at Bury St. Edmunds who were confirmed every time that the bishop came to the town on the grounds that you cannot have too much of a good thing.[2]

Ordinations were also held in the dioceses during the summer months if the bishop were there. If he were not, the candidate would be obliged to acquire Letters Dimissory and present himself to some other bishop. Men desiring to be ordained during the winter months would normally be obliged to make the journey to London in search of their bishop. Finally, the bishop's residence in his diocese was regarded as an opportunity for a round of social calls upon his more influential laymen, and the exercise of hospitality on a large scale in his own palace. Some bishops even kept open house for their clergy, but it is doubtful whether many of the inferior clergy would have had the courage to avail themselves of this condescension.

As far as the parochial clergy were concerned, everyone agreed that there were far too many of them. Little reform of church life had taken place since the Middle Ages, and there still remained a small class of wealthy clergy side by side with a large mob of ill-trained, ill-paid priests who were hard put to it to make a living for themselves and their sometimes very large families. Pluralism, non-residence, nepotism, sinecures all flourished, with disastrous results for the spiritual life of the Church.

[1] See the figures in N. Sykes, *Church and State in England in the XVIIIth Century* (1934), Appendix A, pp. 429-36.
[2] *Ibid.* p. 134 and see S. L. Ollard in *Confirmation* (S.P.C.K. 1926), vol. i, chap. iii.

Pluralism had been forbidden by an act of Henry VIII's reign, but so many exceptions had been introduced that the act made practically no difference. Those who were in a position to claim the patronage of the crown or of the nobility did very well for themselves. They generally managed to collect a number of parishes, prebends and dignities which enabled them to live on terms of equality with the rich. Some of these men, if a good 'family living' became vacant before its time, obtained a dispensation to be ordained under the canonical age, were ordained deacon and priest on the same day, and immediately instituted to the living which they then held for life. From that point onwards further benefices could be added and a very substantial income assured.

With pluralism went, inevitably, non-residence; and it has been estimated that well over half the incumbents of English parishes in the eighteenth century were absentees.[1] This meant the employment of a number of poor curates to do the work in the parishes. Many of these were very poorly paid since in an overstocked market the jobs tended to go to the lowest bidders. £30 to £40 a year was considered handsome and many had to manage on much less than that, even as little as £5.[2] As at the same time many benefices were valued at over £500, and several of the bishops received over £5000 as official income apart from 'commendams' and sinecures, the variations in clerical income were very great. But if curates were ill-paid, many beneficed clergy were very little better off. At the time of the foundation of Queen Anne's Bounty it was estimated that there were 5597 benefices in England worth less than £50 a year, so that Goldsmith's parson who was 'passing rich with forty pounds a year' had many with him in the same boat. Such glaring inequalities, though accepted as part of the changes and chances of an unjust world, bred a good deal of bad blood and jealousy. 'There the old rascal goes', cries the curate in *Roderick Random* after encountering his vicar in the inn, 'and the d—l go with him. You see how the world wags, gentlemen. By Gad, this rogue of a vicar does not deserve to live; and yet he has two livings worth 400*l per annum*, while poor I am fain to do all his drudgery, and ride twenty miles every Sunday to preach; for what? why, truly, for 20*l* a year.'[3] With such underpayment and insecurity

[1] N. Sykes, *op. cit.* p. 217.
[2] The average wage for agricultural labourers early in the eighteenth century was 7s. 6d. a week, or about £20 a year; see B. Williams, *The Whig Supremacy*, p. 120.
[3] T. Smollett, *Roderick Random*, chap. ix.

it is no wonder that some of the clergy were reduced to a life of vagrancy.

The eighteenth-century clergy were, as a class, unpopular. The rich were despised as ambitious hypocrites and the poor as ignorant peasants. Moreover the controversies of the past had left the clergy with a reputation of being quarrelsome and intolerant. But things improved as the years went by. Many of the clergy in their parishes, though neglected by their bishops and fighting a hard battle against poverty, did their best, according to their lights, to carry out their duties faithfully. They visited the sick, relieved the poor, taught the children, conducted the Sunday services, preached the Gospel and wrestled with the devil in his attempts to capture the souls of their parishioners.

In country churches the ideal aimed at was Morning and Evening Prayer each Sunday with a sermon at one of them; but the fact that many priests had more than one church to serve made it impossible for even so modest an ideal to be maintained. Many churches therefore had but one Sunday service, either in the morning or in the afternoon. The Eucharist was normally celebrated quarterly at Christmas, Easter, Whitsuntide and Michaelmas. Some parishes had rather more than this; some had less. Town churches naturally did better, a few having weekly Communions and daily prayers. The infrequency of the Communions meant that often very large numbers attended. Devout laymen, like Dr. Johnson, treated the Sacrament Sunday with the greatest respect and made long and careful preparation for it.

In the offices of Morning and Evening Prayer the metrical psalms still largely held the field, though they were being gradually supplemented by hymns from the pens of such writers as Richard Baxter and Isaac Watts, 'the creator of the modern English hymn'.[1] Psalms were sung extremely slowly, and, as many of the congregation were illiterate, it was customary for the clerk to read out each line separately to be afterwards sung by the congregation. While this reading was going on, interludes were often played on the organ or some other instrument. Organs were common in town churches, but in the country the music was generally provided by a small band of instrumentalists, or 'musickers', who gathered with a group of singers in the west gallery of the church and accompanied the singing on a medley of instruments composed mainly of strings and wood-wind

[1] W. H. Frere, in *Hymns Ancient and Modern, Historical Edition* (1909), p. lxxxiii.

with an occasional horn or serpent or a few drums and harps. The quality of the music may not have been very high, but the intentions were good and the zeal of the players often unbounded.[1]

The sermon continued to occupy an important part in the service and was still, by modern standards, unconscionably long. Its length was supposed to be limited by the hour-glass which the preacher had beside him on the pulpit, but many a preacher was known, when the sands were running out, to turn the glass over and so give himself another hour for his discourse. If generalizations about the preaching are permissible, it might be said that the emphasis in the teaching tended to be more upon morality than theology; but that was in accordance with the sympathies of the age.

Church life in the parishes was formal, pedestrian and prosaic, but it was not dead. The Church still played an important part in the lives of the people, and the parson had his acknowledged place in the community. But there was little fire in the preaching, and little imagination in the conduct of services. The same was true of the cathedrals, where a higher standard might have been expected. But so many canons were absentees that the administration fell into the hands of a small group of residentiaries, some of whom were good scholars and all of whom took their place in polite society, entertaining the gentry in their pleasant Georgian houses in the close. The interiors of the cathedral churches were mostly very plain, for little interest was then taken in ecclesiastical furnishings. A few chapters tried to make their churches elegant and genteel, as Defoe found at Salisbury where he complained that the choir looked more like a theatre than a venerable church, being decked out with blue, white and gold paint.

Canons took life easily, as they thought they were entitled to do. There were not many services to attend, and sermons could generally be farmed out to priest-vicars or local clergy for a guinea or so. Meanwhile, with the help of minor canons and paid singing-men and boys, the worship continued. The music of the age was formal and Handelian and seldom rose to great heights, though the inauguration of the Three Choirs Festival in the western dioceses of Worcester, Gloucester and Hereford in 1724 was a sign of life and activity.

The Church was not dead, but it slumbered after the 'fitful fever' which had racked it for close on two centuries. But its sleep was not to be for long. By 1738 John Wesley had already begun to sound his

[1] See K. H. MacDermott, *The Old Church Gallery Minstrels* (1948).

trumpet-call. In both Church and State vast changes were about to take place which have altered the whole face of England. A new age was about to be born.

NOTE ON BOOKS

THE most important book for this period is N. Sykes, *Church and State in England in the XVIIIth Century* (1934), to which should be added his *Edmund Gibson* (1926) and *William Wake, Archbishop of Canterbury* (1957). C. J. Abbey and J. H. Overton, *The English Church in the 18th Century*, 2 vols. (1878), C. J. Abbey, *The English Church and its Bishops, 1700–1800*, 2 vols. (1887) and J. H. Overton and F. Relton, *The English Church from the Accession of George I to the end of the Eighteenth Century* (1906), George Every, *The High Church Party, 1688–1718* (1956) and G. V. Bennett, *White Kennett, 1660–1728, Bishop of Peterborough* (1957) and *The Tory Crisis in Church and State, 1688–1730* (1975) are all valuable. J. M. Creed and J. S. Boys Smith, *Religious Thought in the Eighteenth Century* (1934) contains extracts from some of the most important writers with explanatory notes. B. Willey, *The Eighteenth Century Background* (1940) is also important. W. K. Lowther Clarke has collected a number of essays in a volume called *Eighteenth Century Piety* (1944), and there is much liturgical matter in J. Wickham Legg, *English Church Life from the Restoration to the Tractarian Movement* (1914) and in W. J. Grisbrooke, *Anglican Liturgies of the 17th and 18th Centuries* (1958). For general history see B. Williams, *The Whig Supremacy* (1939) in the *Oxford History of England*.

PART IV

THE INDUSTRIAL AGE

CHAPTER XVII

THE AGE OF WESLEY
(1738–1791)

i. *The New Age*

THE latter half of the eighteenth century marks one of the great turning-points of history. Up to this time, although minor changes were bound to take place, man's life still went on very much as it had done for centuries. The only sources of power were the human body, domestic animals and a little wind and water. Consequently life was slow; and, because it was slow, it was constant and unchanging. A journey from London to York took as long as it had taken in the days of Paulinus, and the sailor crossing the Atlantic was as much dependent upon the direction of the wind as had been the early Vikings. London had a population a little short of a million souls, but outside the capital the largest towns—Norwich and Bristol —were not much bigger than the chief country towns of today. The country was, therefore, predominantly rural, and man's chief concern was the raising of food. There were no great industrial areas, where vast numbers of people were crowded together in acres of back-to-back houses around the mines, mills and foundries. The industrial areas of eighteenth-century England were places like Norfolk and Somerset where wool was spun and woven, places which are now among the most rural in the whole country. The 'dark, satanic mills' which horrified Blake were puny affairs compared with the vast factories which sprang up after his death, and Cobbett's 'great wen' of London was not much more than a pimple compared with what it is today. So great, in fact, were the changes which began to take place in the latter half of the eighteenth century with the coming of steam, and therefore of industry and mass-production, that we may well suppose that future historians will alter the customary divisions of history, extend the Middle Ages to about 1770, and realize that Modern History really begins at about that point.

From 1770 onwards the whole face of England began to change

A rapid series of inventions made a sudden demand for labour and brought people flocking into the new industrial areas, mainly on or near the coal-fields, and led to the creation of slums with all the horrors of overcrowding, high infant mortality, lack of sanitation, outbreaks of cholera. and so on. The new towns quickly broke down the age-long contact with the soil which almost all Englishmen had hitherto enjoyed. A new class was now being created, a class knowing little or nothing of country life and the ways of nature, being totally confined within the walls of factories or the shadows of narrow streets. Into these great factories men, women and children were absorbed in the desperate struggle for existence in a world of fierce competition and contempt for the weak. Instead of the old country craftsman, conversant with nature in all her moods and able to turn his hand to anything, there now appeared vast hordes of unskilled labourers, many of them women and even children of five years and upwards, for whom work could be found and so a few pennies added to the family income. With all this went loss of stability, the tearing up of roots which went deep into the past, the disappearance of old customs and the severing of old ties and loyalties. Within a few years England had produced a new phenomenon, the 'industrial area', with all its social and political problems, for an 'industrial area' could very soon become a 'depressed area' if times were bad.

While this was happening in England, Europe was shaken by the sudden explosion of the French Revolution. France, like many other countries, was a land of great opportunity. It was fertile, victorious and wealthy; but it was riddled with inequalities and injustices of which the Church took its full share. Consequently, when the Revolution broke out, the Church was regarded as a natural enemy, and its power and privilege were quickly broken. Tithe was abolished, Church property was confiscated, the religious orders were suppressed, and bishops and parochial clergy lost their independence and became subject to popular control.

The effect of the French Revolution on English thought was to divide the country into two camps. From the first there were some who welcomed it, men who were by no means rebels but who were acutely conscious of the evils from which the world was suffering and were moved by the appeal for Liberty, Equality and Fraternity. The young Wordsworth's cry:

> Bliss was it in that dawn to be alive
> But to be young was very Heaven[1]

was one with which many of his contemporaries would have sympathized and one which the poet himself could still feel in his bones many years later when he revised his poem in the light of further experience and reflection. But from the first there were also those who were stricken with horror at the Revolution and at what it stood for. Edmund Burke's *Reflexions on the Revolution in France* (1791) expressed what many were feeling, and rallied conservative opinion to make a stand against all kinds of insurgence and rebellion.

Thus, from the first, opinion was divided; but the horrors of bloodshed and regicide in France turned many who had at first supported the Revolution into its most vigorous opponents. Reform on doctrinaire lines seemed an excellent thing; but if reform meant mass murder and the rooting up of the foundations of society then let all who cared for civilization and security look to their guns. Thus, in England, the momentary desire for reform in both Church and State, which might have done so much good, was quickly stifled, opinion hardened, and men became suspicious of anything savouring of reform. The Church regarded itself, and was regarded by men like Burke, as one of the greatest barriers against rebellion, and consequently set its face against any kind of interference. The result was that it took a whole generation before the Church seriously began to consider the question, long overdue, of its own desperate need of reform.

Meanwhile big changes were also taking place further afield. During the eighteenth century the S.P.G. had been busy among English settlers and among native Indians and slaves in America and the West Indies. The work had prospered and a number of schools and colleges had been founded. In order that there might be proper leadership and continuity, attempts were made to persuade the English government to appoint bishops; but public opinion at home was not really interested in the well-being of the American colonies, which it regarded mainly as markets for its goods. Consequently neither colonists nor converted natives could be either confirmed or ordained unless they were prepared to make the long, arduous and expensive journey to England for the purpose. The short-sightedness of Parliament brought its own reward, for in 1775 the American War

---

[1] *The Prelude*, Bk. xi, lines 107-8.

of Independence broke out and the thirteen colonies were separated from the Empire to become the United States of America. After the loss of the American colonies further attempts were made by the Church of the west to get the leadership which it so sorely needed, but it was not until 1787 that Charles Inglis was consecrated Bishop of Nova Scotia, though the Scottish bishops had, on their own initiative, consecrated Samuel Seabury as Bishop in America three years previously. Similar difficulties were being experienced in the East, where the East India Company had a large number of chaplains working. But no bishop was appointed in India until 1814.

The attitude of the Church in England to the vast changes which were taking place all over the world was largely one of indifference. The immense social changes which began with the coming of the Industrial Revolution, the political questions raised by the French Revolution, and the international problems created by the expansion of the Empire all contributed to the making of a new age. But the Church in England was in no way prepared to meet these changes. Convocation being virtually dead, there was no meeting-place where policies could be thought out and action prepared. Most of the bishops were prevented, by temperament and by their position, from exercising any real leadership. For the most part they were busy trying to build up family fortunes by the most flagrant place-hunting and nepotism, and lived almost entirely among the upper classes. The death, or even expected death, of a prelate sent a sheaf of letters to the Prime Minister from men hoping for preferment. 'I think it my duty to acquaint your Grace', wrote Dr. Thomas Newton to the Duke of Newcastle in 1761, 'that the Archbishop of York lies a-dying, and, as all here think, cannot possibly live beyond to-morrow morning, if so long: upon this occasion of two vacancies, I beg, I hope, I trust your Grace's kindness and goodness will be shown to one who has long solicited your favour.'[1] Newton was only doing what every ambitious clergyman of his generation thought the most natural thing in the world. Preferment meant wealth and position and the entry into smart society, so smart in some cases that the Hon. Frederick Cornwallis, Archbishop of Canterbury, incurred some censure for the extravagance of his establishment at Lambeth, where

[1] J. H. Overton and F. Relton, *The English Church from the Accession of George I to the End of the Eighteenth Century* (1906), p. 160. Newton was successful, for in the general shuffle which took place on the death of the archbishop, he was appointed as Bishop of Bristol.

balls and routs were held to the great distress of sober-minded and modest churchmen.

The complacency and worldliness of the bishops and superior clergy, their concern with their own advancement and that of their families, their sensitivity to their privileges and their prestige, left the Church without any real spiritual leadership at a time when such leadership was sorely needed. In the end the Church was saved not by its natural leaders but by a handful of individuals who dedicated themselves and all that they had to the salvation of society. The greatest of these was John Wesley.

ii. *John Wesley*

John Wesley, the fifteenth of the nineteen children which Susannah Wesley bore to her husband, the Rector of Epworth, was born in 1703. He was educated at Christ Church, Oxford, and in 1726 became a fellow and classical tutor of Lincoln College. While at Oxford he joined a group of friends calling themselves 'Methodists', earnest young men who sought to regulate their lives according to strict standards of discipline. They read together and prayed together, observed every rubric of the Prayer Book, communicated weekly, were regular in all matters of worship, and generally strove to order their lives in such a way that they might serve as a protest against the slackness and indifference of society as they found it in the university.

In 1736 John Wesley, attracted by the claims of the new colony of Georgia, which had recently been founded by General Oglethorpe, decided to offer his services there as chaplain. While on the boat he made his first acquaintance with the Moravians and was much impressed by their sincerity and courage. Arrived in Georgia he threw himself with great earnestness and vigour into his work, trying to reproduce among the British settlers the type of closely organized religion which he and his fellow Methodists had practised at Oxford. He adhered in all things strictly to the letter of the Prayer Book, celebrated weekly, baptized children by total immersion, and imposed days of fasting. He tried also to extend his work beyond the sphere of the settlers and to convert some of the natives. After two years, however, it was becoming clear that Georgia was not to be the scene of his life's work. His fearless and impulsive nature was not appreciated by the British colony; opposition was aroused; and, in 1738, John Wesley returned to England a disappointed man.

Arrived in London he again made friends with the Moravians, and it was while worshipping with them that he underwent that spiritual experience, on May 24, 1738, which he always regarded as his conversion. A preacher was expounding the doctrine of Justification by Faith when Wesley began to feel things happening to him. 'I felt my heart strangely warmed', he wrote. 'I felt I did trust in Christ, Christ alone for salvation; and an assurance was given me that He had taken away my sins, even mine, and saved me from the law of sin and death; and then I testified openly to all there what I now first felt in my heart.'[1] Wesley had been a priest of the Church for several years, but he always regarded this as the great turning-point of his life and the real beginning of his ministry.

By this time his friend George Whitefield and one or two others had begun wandering about the country preaching to all and sundry, and Wesley decided to adopt the same kind of ministry. Taking 'the world as his parish' he now began, at the age of thirty-five, to travel on horse-back at the rate of several thousand miles a year up and down England, Scotland, Ireland and Wales, preaching often three or four times a day. This he maintained for fifty-two years, and it has been estimated from his *Journal* that during this time he covered 225,000 miles and preached 40,000 sermons. The physical strain of this on a body not naturally strong must have been immense, but the mind and will were so powerful that all bodily infirmity or fatigue was forgotten. In addition to the travelling and preaching, Wesley found time for endless talks and interviews, for the organization of societies all over the country, for reading and for writing. His published works fill thirty-two volumes, many of them written while he rode his mare with a loose rein, or in a few hours snatched between sermons.

His *Journal* gives a fascinating picture of his life. It shows the tireless energy of the man, the complete absorption in the work, the sense of dedication, of urgency which drove him on in all weathers and often in the midst of hostile crowds in order that he might deliver the message which God had entrusted to him. 'After preaching at five' he wrote on March 22 1752, 'I returned [from Wednesbury] to Birmingham. Many were much afraid of my preaching in

[1] J. H. Overton, *John Wesley* (1891), p. 61.

the street, expecting I know not what mischief to be done. Vain fear! I saw not one person behave amiss, while I declared, "There is joy in heaven over one sinner that repenteth". At one I preached at Tipton-green, to a large congregation, though the wind was ready to cut us in two; and about five to a much larger, at Wednesbury; where, in spite of all the wiles of Satan, and the cunning and craftiness of men, the plain, genuine Gospel runs and is glorified.' The entry is typical of hundreds in the *Journal* as this lonely figure rode fearlessly on with the fire of evangelistic zeal always burning in his heart. And everywhere he went crowds flocked to hear him. Indeed, to attract and hold together a crowd of two or three thousand miners at five o'clock on a winter's morning in the open air to listen to a sermon of anything up to two hours on the subject of Justification by Faith is no mean achievement. And Wesley did something of that kind nearly every day.

From 1738 to 1742 Wesley's main work lay in London and Bristol and the places which he passed through on his constant journeys between these two places. But from then onwards he began to journey farther afield, to the Midlands, to Yorkshire and Lancashire, to Newcastle and on into Scotland. Up and down the country he went without any kind of rest or relaxation, preaching, arguing, consoling, disputing, in season and out of season. Often he met with opposition and, within a few months of his 'conversion', there was no pulpit in London open to him. The clergy were often jealous and hostile, and stirred up gangs of ruffians to overthrow his meetings. At his own village of Epworth he was refused permission to preach in the church, so he preached on his father's tombstone in the churchyard every day for a week. Hooligans often set upon him, tore his clothes and knocked him about. Stones were flung at him. Once a mad bull was driven into the crowd while he was preaching. But in spite of minor injuries he always escaped, and was able to continue his work.

As he journeyed about the country, groups of supporters began to form themselves in the towns, and Wesley soon realized that these groups ought to be organized into societies. A methodist 'Society' was defined as 'a company of men having the form and seeking the power of godliness, united in order to pray together, to receive the word of exhortation, and to watch over one another in love, that they may help each other to work out their salvation'. These societies soon began to acquire premises for their meetings, one of the most famous being the old foundry in Windmill Street, London. Here services were held and sermons preached; here also the specific religious exercises of the 'Wesleyans' were held—Class Meetings for the imposition of discipline on erring members; Watch-nights or nights of prayer; Band Meetings in groups according to age, sex or occupation; Penitents' Meetings; Quarterly Meetings and so on. The next step was to appoint men to supervise these meetings, and in 1744 an Annual Conference was founded. But all these were meant not as rivals to the worship and organization of the parish churches but to supplement what the clergy were so inadequately doing.

Another piece of organization was the foundation in 1748 of a school at Kingswood, Bristol. Wesley drew up all the rules for the school. It was to be for boarders only. There were to be no games and no holidays. Much time was to be devoted to prayer and to the hearing of sermons. No food was to be eaten on Fridays until after 3 P.M. Here, as everywhere, John Wesley's word was law. He expected complete obedience from all his people. No one resisted him for long.

Wesley never allowed his meetings to clash with the hours of divine service (though not all his followers were so loyal or so self-controlled) for Wesley was a churchman through and through. To the very end of his life he implored his followers not to desert the Church. 'Ye yourselves were at first called in the Church of England,' he told them, 'and though ye have and will have a thousand temptations to leave it, and set up for yourselves, regard them not; be Church of England men still; do not cast away the peculiar glory which God hath put upon you and frustrate the design of Providence, the very end for which God hath raised you up.' But, as the years went by, the movement grew so big and gathered so much momentum that the slender ties which held it to the Church were broken, and the Wesleyans as a whole drifted away into separatism.

The problem became really pressing by about the year 1760. By this time Wesley's lay-preachers were beginning to clamour for ordination. A regular and frequent participation in the Holy Communion had always been one of the marks of Methodism, but how was this to be achieved if the parochial clergy were content with only quarterly celebrations? Wesley's own loyalty to the Church restrained him from taking upon himself to ordain men, though a Greek Bishop of Arcadia who was in England was roped in to ordain

a man whom the English prelates were steadily refusing to accept.
Meanwhile the Wesleyan movement had spread to America where
it made great and rapid progress among the settlers. Here again the
problem of ordination was acute, since there were no bishops on that
side of the Atlantic at all. Repeated attempts were made to get John
Wesley to take the law into his own hands and appoint one of his
own men as bishop for the Church in America. Eventually, in 1784,
Wesley gave way. Feeling very deeply the spiritual hunger of the
colonists and the fact that the Church at home consistently refused
to help them, he appointed two of his men, Dr. Coke and Francis
Asbury, as 'joint superintendents' and two others as 'elders' to administer the Sacraments to the Wesleyans in America. Such a thing
would not have happened in England, but Wesley defended himself
on the grounds that he was not in any way interfering with the rights
of the English episcopate. 'I violate no order', he said, 'and invade
no man's right by appointing and sending labourers into the harvest.'
Charles Wesley was deeply shocked. 'Before you have quite broken
down the bridge', he wrote to John, 'stop and consider.' But John
had got the bit between his teeth. In 1785 he 'ordained' some men
for work in Scotland and finally three in England. From now onwards complete separation was only a matter of time.

John Wesley died in 1791 having maintained his vigour almost to
the end. On his eighty-fifth birthday he wrote in his diary his rules
for health, which include rising each day at 4 A.M., preaching at 5 and
travelling at least 4500 miles a year. This he had been doing con-
sistently for fifty years, borne on by his intense conviction that his
every action was under the immediate direction of God. Never was
there a man more dedicated to the preaching of the Gospel. He had
complete and absolute faith and trust in God, a faith which made him
wholly indifferent to dangers which might well have caused others to
falter. He had no thought of self. Self-indulgence, even in its mildest
forms was utterly unknown to him. All that he cared for was the
conversion of souls; for this end he put everything else out of his life,
which largely explains why his marriage was never a success. And
behind it all was his sense of responsibility, of urgency, of compul-
sion, driving him on from place to place. In his sermon-book he is
said to have written Baxter's words:

> I preach as never sure to preach again,
> And as a dying man to dying men

and these words were the motto of his life. His every sermon was preached with such earnestness that it might well have been the last that he would ever preach or his congregation ever hear. And in this lay the secret of his success. At a time when the sermons in the parish churches were often cold and dull, Welsey was preaching with intense conviction to crowds which sometimes numbered as many as 20,000 people; and at a time when the Church as a whole seemed indifferent to the fate of the masses, Wesley was bringing them hope and confidence. He taught them that someone cared for them. He taught them where joy and peace might be found. He brought them the love of God.[1]

iii. *The Early Evangelicals*

The peripatetic ministry of John Wesley was part of a great movement of the Spirit which was affecting the Church in many ways. The 'Evangelical Revival', as it has since been called, began as a protest against two things—the frivolity and dissipation of society in the latter part of the seventeenth century, and the meagre theology and frank worldliness of the Hanoverian Church. The Evangelicals were, therefore, puritanical in their dislike of such things as theatres, cards, dancing, and certain types of literature. They were not particularly interested in scholarship, which they mostly regarded with some suspicion as endangering true religion. They were fundamentalists in their attitude towards the Bible, using (in spite of Locke's warning) individual verses torn from their contexts to support their beliefs. In theology they were divided, some being Calvinists, who believed in the predestination of the elect, while others believed equally firmly in free will and salvation open to all who accepted Christ. Above all, the Evangelicals were earnest and single-minded. In an easy-going age they stood for discipline. Their lives were governed by their creed, and all their energies were directed to the presentation to their generation of the claims of religion.

At first the Evangelicals worked through the Church with no idea

---

[1] The literature connected with John Wesley is very great. See his *Journal* (various editions) and his *Letters* (ed. J. Telford, 8 vols., 1931); also R. Southey, *Life of Wesley* (1820), J. H. Overton, *John Wesley* (1891), G. E. Harrison, *Son to Susannah* (1937), M. Piette, *John Wesley in the Evolution of Protestantism* (tr. J. B. Howard, 1937) and R. A. Knox, *Enthusiasm* (1950), chaps. xviii-xxi.

of going outside the parochial system. They found many of the clergy preaching very poor stuff—the unheroic morality of the Age of Enlightenment—and decided that this was not the Gospel. So they began a new type of preaching altogether. Man, they said, is not the noble creature that some would call him; he is fallen and totally depraved. He is therefore in need of salvation, and salvation is through Christ alone and dependent upon faith. The acceptance, by faith, of Christ as saviour was called 'conversion', and this conversion normally took place quite suddenly at a moment which would be remembered and treasured for the rest of one's life. But conversion was not the end. It led on naturally to sanctification and growth in grace. This the believer found through prayer, through Bible-study, through sermons and, to some extent, through the sacraments. But the Evangelicals had little sense of the Church and its authority. To them it was the individual soul which counted above all else.

The main object of the evangelical clergy was to deliver their message to as many people as possible, whether in church or out of it. They were, indeed, men on fire with their message. They had something vital to say, and many of them developed almost hypnotic powers in the saying of it. A sermon by one of the great Evangelicals was often accompanied by strange occurrences as members of the congregation dropped down in a dead faint or cried out to heaven. When John Wesley was preaching at Stroud in 1765 'a young man dropped down and violently cried to God. . . . A young gentleman cried out "I am damned" and fell to the ground. A second did so quickly after and was much convulsed, and yet quite sensible.'[1] 'I observed', wrote Wesley after addressing the children at Whitby, 'one little maid in particular who heaved and strove for some time till at length she was constrained to yield and broke out into strong cries and tears.'[2] Even more remarkable were the scenes when John Berridge was preaching at Everton. On one occasion 'the text was "Having a form of godliness, but denying the power thereof". When the power of religion began to be spoke of, the presence of God really filled the place. And while poor sinners felt the sentence of death in their souls what sounds of distress did I hear! The greatest number of those who cried or fell were men; but some women, and several children, felt the power of the same almighty Spirit, and seemed just sinking into hell. This occasioned a mixture of various sounds, some

[1] J. Wesley, *Journal* for March 18, 1765.   [2] *Ibid.* June 17, 1770.

shrieking, some roaring aloud. The most general was a loud breathing, like that of people half strangled and gasping for life. And indeed almost all the cries were like those of human creatures dying in bitter anguish. Great numbers wept without any noise; others fell down as dead; some sinking in silence, some with extreme noise and violent agitation. I stood on the pew-seat, as did a young man in the opposite pew, an able-bodied, fresh, healthy countryman. But in a moment, while he seemed to think of nothing less, down he dropped with a violence inconceivable. The adjoining pews seemed shook with his fall. I heard afterward the stamping of his feet, ready to break the boards, as he lay in strong convulsions at the bottom of the pew. ... Among the children who felt the arrows of the Almighty, I saw a sturdy boy, about eight years old, who roared above his fellows, and seemed, in his agony, to struggle with the strength of a grown man. His face was red as scarlet; and almost all on whom God laid his hand turned either very red, or almost black.'[1]

From about 1738 onwards there were, up and down the country, an increasing number of clergy who threw themselves into this movement and were supported by a large body of sympathetic laity. Of the clergy the most distinguished was George Whitefield, at first Wesley's greatest friend, then his most formidable rival, and finally his most determined theological opponent. Whitefield had not enjoyed the religious upbringing which the Wesleys had received at Epworth. He was the son of a publican at Gloucester, but made his way to Pembroke College, Oxford, as a servitor. Here he met the Wesleys and soon after began his preaching. He rapidly acquired great homiletic power and was able to hold an audience rapt for long periods. His powers of description and narrative were so great that once when describing a blind man, deserted by his dog, and approaching a precipice, Lord Chesterfield could not refrain from crying out aloud: 'Good God; he is gone!' But apart from his great preaching powers Whitefield had little to recommend him. He suffered from an inferiority complex, and was touchy and difficult. Impulsive, censorious, and dogmatic, he found it almost impossible to live at peace with his fellow-men.

At first Wesley and Whitefield worked closely together, but it was almost inevitable that they should differ before long, and in 1739 the

[1] From the report of an eye-witness, transcribed by John Wesley into his *Journal* on May 28, 1759.

beginnings of conflict appeared. The issue was a theological one, for Whitefield was a Calvinist believing passionately in predestination, while Wesley was what was then called an Arminian believing in free salvation for all men. Each was profoundly convinced that he was right and that he owed his assurance to the direct inspiration of God. There was therefore no possibility of their reaching any kind of doctrinal agreement, and neither was of the type which can agree to differ. A split in the Evangelical movement therefore took place which led to deep divisions and bitter quarrels for many years to come.[1]

John Wesley was warmly supported by his brother Charles and the saintly Fletcher of Madeley. Charles Wesley, though a less forceful character than John, had considerable influence over his brother. It was Charles who tried to hold John in check, to keep him loyal to the Church, and to act as his interpreter and defender against his critics and enemies. The movement, therefore, owes a great deal to Charles Wesley for his work behind the scenes. But outwardly he is best remembered as the poet, the writer of many of the hymns which the Evangelicals learned to love and sing, and which have passed into the devotional treasury of the Church. Charles Wesley is said to have written 6500 hymns which would mean writing at the rate of one a day for nearly eighteen years. Among them are such favourites as 'Jesu, lover of my soul' (which caused considerable distress when first published), 'Let saints on earth in concert sing' and 'Love divine'.

John Fletcher, Vicar of Madeley in Shropshire, was the saint of the movement. He was one of the few parish priests who really appreciated what John Wesley was trying to do. Fletcher was a man of peculiar simplicity and integrity, a holy and humble man of heart who loved and served his people with great devotion. It is said that when Voltaire was challenged to mention a character as perfect as Christ he immediately gave the name of John Fletcher of Madeley.[2]

Fletcher was, like the Wesley brothers, an Arminian; but most of the great Evangelicals were in the opposite camp of the Calvinists. Whitefield was their acknowledged leader, but he had many disciples. Augustus Toplady (1740–78), though a gentle and pious parish priest, was capable of extraordinary bitterness in controversy. He is chiefly remembered today as the author of the hymn 'Rock of ages',

---

[1] For Whitefield see L. Tyerman, *Life of George Whitefield*, 2 vols. (1876).
[2] J. H. Overton and F. Relton, *The English Church from the Accession of George I to the end of the Eighteenth Century*, p. 87.

20

but in his own day he was regarded as a fanatical Calvinist with a power of expressing his feelings in the strongest language. His tracts against John Wesley, whom he describes as 'that hog in armour', are couched in the language of personal invective of a high order and did much to embitter the controversy.

A less violent but no less determined partisan was that remarkable woman, Selina, Countess of Huntingdon (1709–91). Realizing that the Evangelical Revival was affecting the lives mainly of the poor, she tried to extend it towards those of her own class. To this end she devoted all her time, energy and fortune. She gathered in her drawing-room large numbers of the rich and aristocratic, not for cards or dancing, but to hear one of the great evangelical preachers like Whitefield. As the work grew, she raised money to build chapels where such congregations could assemble and sermons be preached. Crowds of distinguished men visited her chapels—heads of noble families, politicians, men of letters, leaders of all kinds. Even bishops were smuggled in and hidden behind curtains. Furthermore she founded, at Trevecca in Wales, a college for the training of ministers who might serve either as evangelical clergymen in the Church of England or in any other protestant Church. Over the chapels, which came to be known as 'Lady Huntingdon's Connexion', and over the college, Selina herself presided with the authority of a pope. She appointed and dismissed the ministers, arranged what services should be held, and ruled all with a rod of iron. Few of the Evangelicals failed to submit to her authority, but John Wesley never quite succumbed, and John Berridge preserved a power of standing up for himself which does him credit. 'You threaten me, madam, like a pope', he wrote, 'not like a mother in Israel'; and 'my instructions, you know, must come from the Lamb, not from the Lamb's wife, though she is a tight woman.'[2]

While the Countess was busy with her chapels and her college, the quiet country town of Olney in Buckinghamshire became the home of two remarkable men who made it a real centre of evangelical zeal. One of these, John Newton (1725–1807), was one of the few Evangelicals who could preach about sin from close personal experience. He had gone to sea as a boy of eleven and, as he grew up, he had got into bad company and had lived a rollicking life on sea and ashore.

[1] See T. Wright, *A. M. Toplady* (1911).
[2] *The Life and Times of Selina, Countess of Huntingdon*, by a member of the Houses of Shirley and Hastings (1840), i, p. 324; ii, p. 20.

Then had come, in 1748, the sudden conversion and the settling down to a respectable life ashore at Liverpool, where he associated with the best evangelical clergymen. After being turned down by at least two bishops he was finally ordained by the Bishop of Lincoln and appointed to a curacy at Olney with the modest stipend of £60 a year. He remained at Olney until 1780 when he became Vicar of St. Mary Woolnoth in the city of London. Newton had known sin and degradation and was able to talk to sinners in a way which his brethren, with their pious and sheltered upbringing, could never imitate. His sincerity was as clear as the day, and his lack of 'clericalism' made him a powerful advocate with the laity. Like many of the Evangelicals Newton wrote a number of hymns. Few of them reach great heights, but 'Glorious things of thee are spoken' is a great hymn of worship, and 'How sweet the name of Jesus sounds' expresses evangelical piety at its best.[1]

Newton attracted to Olney that gentle soul, William Cowper (1731–1800). Before his coming to Olney in 1768 Cowper had had a sad and melancholy life with intermittent bouts of extreme misery and despair amounting to the loss of his reason. He lived at Olney for eighteen years, the calmest and happiest years of his life, though there were times when he was still haunted by the conviction that he was eternally damned. At Olney Cowper took to the writing of poetry, in which he found great solace. His peculiar genius, combined with his own sad experiences, produced a style of poetry which fitted closely with the doctrinal and devotional teaching of the Evangelicals. 'O for a closer walk with God' or 'There is a fountain filled with blood' are typical evangelical hymns—subjective, pious, and intimate—and they won for Cowper a high place among the 'sweet singers of Israel'.[2]

Other Evangelicals were scattered up and down the country. William Romaine (1714–95), who was one of the most scholarly of their number, worked mainly in London. His preaching attracted large crowds of poor people to St. George's, Hanover Square, to the great disgust of the fashionable congregation who normally worshipped there.[3] Meanwhile at Everton in Bedfordshire John Berridge

---

[1] See *Works of John Newton*, with memoir by R. Cecil (1827) and B. Martin, *John Newton* (1950).
[2] See Lord David Cecil, *The Stricken Deer; or the Life of Cowper* (1929) and N. Nicholson, *William Cowper* (1950).
[3] See *Works of William Romaine*, with a Life by W. B. Cadogan (1809).

(1716–93) was drawing vast crowds by his amazing sermons. The son of a Nottinghamshire farmer he had already been inducted to his first living when he passed through the experience of 'conversion'. 'The scales', he said, 'fell from my eyes'; and he then devoted himself to the preaching of the Calvinistic gospel, first in churches and later in the open air or in barns, with the startling results which have already been noticed.[1] Farther north, in the West Riding of Yorkshire, Henry Venn (1724–97) was carrying the gospel to the mill-workers of the dales. The son of a High Church rector with Jacobite ancestors, he became an Evangelical in 1759 and was appointed Vicar of Huddersfield. Here he preached with such vigour that his parishioners affectionately referred to him as 't'owd trumpet'. But he wore himself out, and, after twelve years, retired to the country parish of Yelling, near Cambridge, where he began to influence some of the young men from the university, including Charles Simeon.[2]

The effects of all this preaching soon began to make themselves felt in the country. People whose lives had been dissolute became pious and respectable citizens. Men began to take an interest in the condition of the poor and in the question of the slave-trade. Gambling became less common, savage sports were discouraged, even dress became more sober as gentlemen left off their swords and adopted sober black coats in place of the brighter colours which had been worn. A wave of seriousness and earnestness spread through the country, putting a stop to some of the grosser forms of pleasure. Above all, Sabbatarianism became both fashionable and popular, to the despair of foreigners like Francois de Rochefoucauld who sighed: 'Is there in the world anything so wearisome as the English Sunday?'[3] It was one of the most lasting gifts of the Evangelicals.

iv. *The High Church Party*

The impact of the Evangelical Revival on a somewhat drowsy Church had made people think. Here was something vital, sincere, successful, devout and genuine. But it had obvious defects. It was defective in its doctrine of the Church and ministry and, as such, was

---

[1] Cf. C. H. Smyth, *Simeon and Church Order* (1940), chap. iv.
[2] See J. and H. Venn, *The Life and a Selection from the Letters of the Rev. H. Venn* (1834).
[3] F. de Rochefoucauld, *A Frenchman in England, 1784*, tr. S. C. Roberts (1933).

bound, sooner or later, to come into conflict with authority. Early in the movement Samuel Wesley had written of his brother John: 'I am not afraid that the Church will excommunicate him (discipline is at too low an ebb for that) but that he will excommunicate the Church'. Indeed, a drift away from the Church was almost inevitable. New wine of such explosive quality could scarcely be held in the worn-out, old bottles of the Establishment. A few tried it—men like the Wesleys, Venn and Fletcher—but they were attempting the impossible. Separation was only a matter of time. As has been said: 'It is purely a modern notion that the Wesleyan movement ever was, or ever was intended to be, except by Wesley, a Church movement'.[1] But it made men think. Here was true religion going outside the Church: how could true religion be made to grow *within* the Church?

Among those driven to reconsider the nature of churchmanship was a small group of intelligent men, lay and clerical, each of whom contributed something towards steadying men's minds and reminding them of what was at stake. The oldest member of this group was William Jones (1726–1800), curate of Nayland in Suffolk, who, amid a considerable output of theological and scientific material, wrote an interesting *Essay on the Church*. His friend and biographer, William Stevens (1732–1807), was a London merchant, rich and prosperous. A strong supporter of the religious societies, he gave large sums of money towards the promotion of church work and in 1773 wrote *An Essay on the Nature and Constitution of the Christian Church*. A rather younger man, Charles Daubeny, Archdeacon of Salisbury, came also from a mercantile family. He was a writer of extreme energy and conviction. Rigidly orthodox and unrestrainedly outspoken in his language, he made many enemies. But he was devoted to the Church and spent much money on it. His *Guide to the Church* (1798) was a spirited defence of High Church principles against Dissent on one side and Romanism on the other. A fourth member, Thomas Sikes (1767–1834), buried himself in Northamptonshire as vicar of the country parish of Guilsborough. But, remote though he was, his house became a place of pilgrimage for all who were concerned about the future of religion in England. For Sikes was curiously far-seeing. 'Wherever I go about the country', he wrote, 'I

---

[1] J. H. Overton and F. Relton, *The English Church from the Accession of George I to the end of the Eighteenth Century*, p. 75.

see amongst the clergy a number of very amiable and estimable men, many of them much in earnest and wishing to do good. But I have observed one universal want in their teaching: the uniform suppression of one great truth. There is no account given anywhere, so far as I can see, of the one Holy Catholic Church. . . . The doctrine is of the last importance and the principles it involves of immense power; and some day, not far distant, it will judicially have its reprisals. . . . We now hear not a breath about the Church; by and bye those who live to see it will hear of nothing else.'[1]

Sikes's prophecy was fulfilled with the coming of the Oxford Movement a generation or so later; but meanwhile those who cared about the Church were doing their utmost to see that it was not forgotten. Daubeny writes like the prospectus for an Insurance Company: 'We hesitate not to say that there is absolute security in the Church for every sound member of it; and that we know of no security out of it', while Jones wrote with almost equal confidence: 'We see that the promises of God are confined to the ordinances of the Church and that there can be no assurance of salvation without them'. Daubeny did not hesitate to say that those who lived outside the Church were 'living without God, and consequently without hope', while Jones asked the question: 'If we are out of the Church, how can we be saved?'

These four writers were all closely involved in the clash of religious forces in England. Meanwhile, a detached observer was watching the play from the other side of the Irish Sea—Alexander Knox (1757–1831), a cultivated layman of poor health who lived very quietly in Dublin, but who read and thought deeply. Knox liked to describe himself as 'a primitive Churchman, prizing in our system, most cordially, what it has retained from Christian antiquity, as well as what it has gained from the good sense of the Reformers'. In this he is very much in the succession of the Caroline Divines and an important link between them and the Tractarians. He had not much respect for Daubeny whom he described as a 'High Church bigot', but a great admiration for John Wesley, 'my venerable old friend', with whom he corresponded regularly. He admired the zeal of the Methodists and the vigour of their preaching, which he contrasted with 'the dry details of meagre morality which are pronounced from

[1] See E. B. Pusey, *Letter to the Archbishop of Canterbury* (1842) and H. P. Liddon, *Life of Pusey* (1893), i, pp. 257–8.

most parochial pulpits'; but he grieved at the growing breach between them and the Church.

Living in Ireland, Knox had opportunities of studying the Church of Rome at close quarters. 'The Romish Church', he wrote, 'is like a garden overrun with weeds; but there are in this garden some old fruit trees which bear fruit of extraordinary mellowness.' And again: 'Viewed from without nothing could be more uncouth or revolting; but, under that rubbish, must be all the rich results of a providential training of Christ's mystical Kingdom for fourteen centuries'. But, though Knox could be appreciative of Rome it was to the Church of England that he gave his full allegiance, as unswerving as it was rational. 'In sober, solid verity', he wrote, 'there never was, except where God Himself was pleased to act personally, so good-natured and delightfully wise a system as that of the Church of England. . . . No Church on earth has more intrinsic excellence.' And he realized its true nature. 'I am in the habit', he said, 'of maintaining that [the Church of England] is not Protestant, but a reformed portion of the Church Catholic.'

Knox here was writing to his friend John Jebb, Bishop of Limerick, who, in his *Sermons on Subjects chiefly practical* (1814) set out to 'exhibit more clearly the agreement between the English Church and the Catholic, Apostolic Church of ancient times'. He then argues, as Knox had taught him to do, that the Bible alone is not a sufficient guide, but must be supplemented by 'Catholic tradition'. Twenty years later John Henry Newman in the *Tracts for the Times* took up the task just where Alexander Knox and John Jebb had laid it down.[1]

v. *The Liberals*

The Evangelicals were a strong and well-organized movement of remarkable vigour; the High Church party a mere handful of detached and mostly obscure individuals. Besides these there were a good many men of liberal opinions, scattered up and down the country, who were making their voices heard. To them what was needed was not Enthusiasm, nor Ecclesiasticism, but Reform— credal, liturgical and institutional.

[1] See *The Remains of Alexander Knox*, 4 vols. (1834) and J. Jebb, *Thirty Years' Correspondence with Alexander Knox*, 2 vols. (1834).

The liberals were not altogether happy about the forms of subscription imposed upon ordinands and incumbents, and in 1766
Archdeacon Francis Blackburne published his book, *The Confessional*,
which pleaded for reform. This was followed, in 1771, by a meeting
of like-minded friends at the Feathers' Tavern in the Strand and the
drawing-up of a petition to Parliament to allow clergy to interpret
the Bible in their own way and not to be bound by creeds and formularies. 250 signatures to the petition were obtained, but it was rejected
by the House of Commons after a powerful speech by Edmund
Burke against it.

In the following year an attempt was also made to revise the Prayer
Book in accordance with more liberal ideas. Services were to be
shortened, private baptism was to be abolished, and various minor
alterations made; but this also proved abortive.

Meanwhile attention was being turned to the question of Christian
unity. The exclusiveness of the established Church, and the consequent disabilities of nonconformists, caused a good deal of distress to
liberal-minded thinkers. In spite of the general toleration shown by
the Whig government, the Clarendon Code had never been repealed,
though dissenters had, from 1727 onwards, been to some extent
accommodated by a series of Acts of Indemnity. In 1773 a *Bill for the
Relief of Protestant Dissenters* was introduced into the House, but was
not passed. Five years later, a somewhat similar bill for the relief of
Roman Catholics was actually carried; but it led to such serious rioting, first in Scotland and then in London, that it had to be withdrawn. Feeling ran high. Lord George Gordon excited the mob with
cries of 'No Popery', a Protestant Association was formed, Roman
Catholic chapels were pillaged and burnt, and for several days London
was in the hands of the mob. The time was not yet ripe for Catholic
Emancipation. Indeed the anti-Catholic feeling so strengthened the
protestant party that in 1779 an *Act for the Relief of Dissenters* was
passed, though still without the repeal of the Test and Corporation
Acts, as many had hoped.

Then came the French Revolution. At first it was thought that
Dissenters were potential revolutionaries, and in 1791 Joseph Priest-
ley's house in Birmingham was destroyed with all his books and
scientific apparatus. In 1790 Charles James Fox introduced a bill for
the repeal of the Test and Corporation Acts, but it was thrown out,
largely through the influence of Burke. Meanwhile, the arrival in

England of a number of French exiles, mainly clergy, caused a wave of sympathy towards Romanism which found expression in an *Act for the Relief of Roman Catholics* (1791) whereby they were admitted to the legal profession, granted toleration for schools and places of worship, and relieved from taking the oath of supremacy.

Outside the political sphere there was a fairly general desire for reform and for greater liberty. The established Church appeared to many as hidebound in its theology, antiquated in its laws and intolerant in its attitude towards other Christians. The Methodists, on the other hand, were regarded as insufferably puritanical and extravagant. What was needed was reform; but reform was slow in coming.

Among those who felt most strongly about reform was Beilby Porteous (1731–1808) who spent the last twenty-one years of his life as Bishop of London. His parents came from Virginia, and Porteous always carried about with him a breath of the New World. He was born in York, educated at Cambridge, was Rector of Lambeth and Bishop of Chester, from which he was translated to London in 1787. Porteous was essentially a reformer, who encouraged Wilberforce in his fight against the Slave Trade, supported the newly founded Sunday Schools, and used his position as a bishop to try and bring new life into the parishes and galvanize the clergy into greater activity. Meanwhile, in the theological sphere, William Paley (1743–1805) was busy in his northern parishes writing first his *Horae Paulinae* (1790) and then his *View of the Evidences of Christianity* (1794) which was an attempt to defend the Christian faith against critics like Hume and Gibbon, the latter of whom had already been attacked by Richard Watson (1737–1816) in his *Apology for Christianity* in 1776. Watson was himself not a very striking example of Christian zeal, for though Bishop of Llandaff for over twenty years he took little interest in his diocese but spent most of his time on the shores of Windermere. But though conforming to the habits of the age in some ways, Watson was, in others, in advance of his time, a forerunner of the liberal movement of the nineteenth century.

NOTE ON BOOKS

MOST of the books mentioned above on p. 289 apply to this chapter. Reference should also be made to J. Hunt, *Religious Thoughts in England from the Reformation to the end of the last Century*, 3 vols. (1870–73) and to S. C.

CHAPTER XVIII

FROM WESLEY TO KEBLE
(1791–1833)

i. *The Later Evangelicals*

At the death of John Wesley in 1791 there were said to be nearly 70,000 Methodists in Great Britain and Ireland, with a further 60,000 in America.[1] These were all people who had definitely enrolled themselves in the Society and had accepted its discipline. Many thousands more had heard Wesley preach, and had come, to some extent, under his influence or that of one of his followers. Wesley himself had always hoped that his movement would remain within the Church of England; but almost from the start it had become obvious to discerning minds that separation was only a matter of time. The rift had begun with the places of worship built by the Countess of Huntingdon which, from 1781 onwards, had been registered as dissenting chapels since they would not accept the authority of the established Church. John Wesley's 'ordinations' had widened the breach; and, from the time of his death, Wesleyanism rapidly broke away into a separate religious denomination. Had the problem been wisely handled from the start, had the bishops been in a position, and of sufficient wisdom and charity, to guide the movement along the right lines, it is possible that John Wesley's dream of a great spiritual revival within the Church might have been realized. But the fact that the Convocations were in abeyance, that the parochial clergy were often jealous of their more successful rivals, that the French Revolution had made people suspicious of anything that seemed unconventional or irregular, all helped towards creating a schism.

Towards the Evangelicals who remained within the Church a good deal of hostility was shown by their fellow Churchmen. They were often laughed at and misunderstood; sometimes they were mobbed in the streets or driven out of their churches. Bishop Herbert Marsh of Peterborough tried to prevent evangelical clergy from getting livings

---

[1] R. A. Knox, *Enthusiasm* (1950), p. 427.

in his diocese by requiring them to answer certain questions which no Evangelical could possibly answer to the bishop's satisfaction, and no Evangelical was raised to the episcopate until the appointment of Henry Ryder to Gloucester in 1815. But though public opinion was against them, they were not without their advocates. Bishop Marsh's 87 Questions provoked Sydney Smith to a vigorous outburst in defence of the poor curate. 'How any man of Purple, Palaces and Preferment', he wrote, 'can let himself loose against this poor working man of God, we are at a loss to conceive—a learned man in a hovel, with sermons and saucepans, lexicons and bacon, Hebrew books and ragged children—good and patient—a comforter and a preacher . . . [yet he] is not good enough for Bishop Marsh, but is pushed out in the street with his wife and children, and his little furniture, to surrender his honour, his faith, his conscience and his learning—or starve!'[1]

But though the Evangelicals, both clergy and laity, were often misunderstood and sneered at, their devotion and disinterested goodness gradually broke down all opposition. For the best of the Evangelicals were men of the highest character. They lived exemplary lives and were wholly given to the service of God and man. 'Every hour and every shilling for God' was the motto on which their lives were lived, and they voluntarily accepted strict self-discipline in an age which was by nature easy-going and self-indulgent.

Being in a minority, Evangelicals tended to form themselves into groups in certain centres. At Cambridge the outstanding figure was that of Charles Simeon (1759–1836). He was born and brought up in the High Church tradition, but while an undergraduate at King's College, Cambridge, he passed through a spiritual experience which turned him into a convinced Evangelical. In those days it was customary to enforce attendance at the Holy Communion upon all undergraduates as a necessary qualification for a degree. Simeon was suddenly struck with a sense of his unworthiness to receive the Sacrament—'conscience told me that Satan was as fit to go there as I', he wrote—and after some weeks of spiritual anguish he decided to join the evangelical party. That was in Lent 1779. Three years later he was ordained and appointed perpetual curate of Holy Trinity Church in Cambridge. His appointment immediately aroused much opposition, the churchwardens and many of the parishioners doing their utmost

[1] S. Smith, *Works* (4th ed. 1848), ii, pp. 283-4.

to hinder him in his ministry. The church was locked against him, pew-owners shut up their pews and neither occupied them themselves nor allowed others to sit in them. Simeon was often mobbed and assaulted in the streets on his way from King's to the church. But gradually he wore down the enemy. His devotion to duty, his learning, his courage, his zeal, began to influence both town and university, and before long he was by far the greatest power in Cambridge. 'As for Simeon', wrote Macaulay, 'if you knew what his authority and influence were, and how they extended from Cambridge to the most remote corners of England, you would allow that his real sway over the Church was far greater than that of any primate.'[1]

Compared with most of the Evangelicals Simeon was a staunch churchman, loving the Church and its services with a devotion which did much to strengthen the bonds between those influenced by the religious revival and those who looked upon it with some misgivings. He was most anxious that the new movement should act as a leaven within the Church and that it should conform to Church principles and discipline. To this end he raised money for the purchase of advowsons in order that properly instructed evangelical incumbents might be appointed to important livings instead of leaving the work to itinerant preachers. Thus came into being the Simeon Trust which, by 1836, had the patronage of twenty-one livings, mostly in places of growing importance like Derby and Cheltenham.[2]

In his younger days Simeon had been greatly influenced by Henry Venn who had left Huddersfield to become Rector of Yelling, a village some fifteen miles from Cambridge. Within the university his closest friend was Isaac Milner (1750–1820), President of Queens' and Dean of Carlisle, 'a sort of Evangelical Dr. Johnson',[3] learned, massive, argumentative, a great preacher and conversationalist. Simeon had also, at Magdalene, an exact contemporary in William Farish (1759–1837), Professor of Chemistry in the University and Vicar of S. Giles which he made a centre of 'Gospel-preaching' second only to Holy Trinity.

Another small group of Evangelicals formed itself in Somerset under the leadership of Hannah More (1745–1833). Before her 'conversion' Hannah More had lived much in the world of literature and

[1] G. O. Trevelyan, *Life of Lord Macaulay* (1878), i, p. 67.
[2] See *Memoirs of the Life of the Rev. C. Simeon*, ed. W. Carus (1847); C. H. Smyth, *Simeon and Church Order* (1940); H. C. G. Moule, *Charles Simeon* (1892; new ed. 1948).
[3] J. H. Overton, *The English Church in the Nineteenth Century, 1800-33* (1894), p. 61.

the stage, and had acquired considerable gifts as a writer which she devoted entirely to the service of religion. One of her early works, *Thoughts on the Importance of the Manners of the Great to General Society* (1788) showed up the sins of Society and urged upon those born to rank and power a proper sense of responsibility. From this time onwards she wrote many books and tracts, some of which were addressed to the rich and some to the poor. The latter appear, to modern eyes, intolerably condescending, but they were in accordance with the ideas of the time. When famine struck the West Country, Hannah More encouraged her wealthy friends to do something to help those suffering from starvation, but she addressed the poor in the following terms: 'We trust the poor in general, especially those who are well instructed, have received what has been done for them as a matter of favour, not of right—if so, then some kindness will, I doubt not, always be extended to them whenever it shall please God so to afflict the land.'[1] But Hannah More and her friends did more for the poor than give them moral lectures. They distributed Bibles and started classes in which people might be taught to read them. They founded clubs, dispensed charity and wrote tracts, Hannah More starting a series of *Cheap Repository Tracts* of which more than two million copies were sold in the first year.[2]

Meanwhile the most famous of all evangelical groups was forming at Clapham. The centre of this community was the parish church under a son of old Henry Venn, John Venn, who was rector there from 1792 to 1813. Most of the members of the 'Clapham Sect', however, were laymen, distinguished men in various walks of life, who devoted much of their time and substance to religious and philanthropic work. Perhaps the most remarkable man in this society was William Wilberforce, a Member of Parliament and a man of some wealth. He had joined the Evangelicals because they seemed to him to be the only party in the Church which had any life or zest in it. Wilberforce, like Hannah More and the Countess of Huntingdon, was deeply concerned at the lack of real religion among the people of his own class, and, in 1797, published a *Practical View of the Prevailing Religious Systems of Professed Christians in the Higher and Middle Classes in this Country contrasted with Real Christianity*. This

---

[1] Quoted in S. C. Carpenter, *Church and People, 1789–1889* (1933), p. 43.
[2] See W. Roberts, *Memoirs of the Life and Correspondence of Mrs. Hannah More*, 2 vols. (1834) and M. G. Jones, *Hannah More* (1952).

book, which preached the gospel of seriousness and responsibility, became very popular and did much to influence those whom its author had in mind. But Wilberforce will always be remembered chiefly, not as a writer of religious literature, but as the leader of the anti-slavery movement, that great corporate effort of the Clapham Sect and its friends which aroused first the hostility and then the praise of the country.[1]

Other members of the Clapham Sect were Henry Thornton, a banker and politician who worked closely with Wilberforce in the campaign against the slave-trade; Zachary Macaulay, father of the historian and a business man of great organizing ability; James Stephen, a lawyer; and Lord Teignmouth, an ex-Governor-General of India. These and others who gathered around the church of the Holy Trinity, Clapham, formed a group of serious-minded men, mostly of considerable wealth and position. They were devoted to their Church and used their money, their influence, and their ability in supporting all kinds of missionary and philanthropic enterprise. The great religious revival of the eighteenth century was now to find expression in the practical Christianity of the nineteenth.

ii. *Practical Christianity*

Evangelicalism, in its early stages, had been essentially a personal affair, an appeal to the individual to repent and accept justification through faith in Christ. It was closely bound up with the experience of 'conversion' in which the soul passed through certain well-defined stages—the crushing sense of sin and defilement, the discovery of salvation through the blood of Christ, and finally the assurance of pardon and the joy that comes with it. The Evangelical was not much interested in ecclesiastical authority nor in the idea of sacramental incorporation into the Body of Christ. But, in place of this, he acquired, with the passage of time, a sense of social responsibility which turned his attention to the evils of the world and to the needs of the weak, the ignorant and the exploited.

In the eyes of the Evangelicals, especially those at Clapham, there was nothing so offensive as the Slave Trade. For many years English traders had been engaged in the transport of slaves from Africa to the

[1] See R. Coupland, *Wilberforce* (new ed. 1945).

plantations in North America. The usual route was to go from England to Africa with supplies of cheap cotton goods which were there bartered for slaves. These were shipped across to America and sold to the planters, and the ships then returned to England with raw cotton, sugar and tobacco. This trade had proved profitable, and large numbers of negroes were annually taken from their native soil to serve as slaves on the other side of the Atlantic.[1] The conditions in the slave ships were often very terrible, men and women being herded together in the greatest possible discomfort; and many died in the course of making the famous 'Middle Passage'.

But the slave trade was supported by many powerful groups—merchants, shippers and planters. The English mills were as dependent upon it as the West Indian plantations. Much wealth was coming into the country as a result of slave labour on the plantations, and slave labour demanded a regular supply of negroes. Many people in England turned a blind eye to the evils of the system and comforted themselves with the thought of British prosperity and progress.

But to a small minority of more sensitive souls the whole system was a crime against humanity and a sin against God. The first to denounce the slave trade had been the Quakers. Then Granville Sharp (1735–1813) had tried to organize public opinion against it by forming the Abolition Society, and Thomas Clarkson (1760–1846), a man of great courage and determination, had risked his life many times in collecting evidence of the terrible conditions in which the trade was carried on. But it was Wilberforce and his friend Thomas Fowell Buxton and the men at Clapham, who finally achieved the victory. They knew well the magnitude of the task—the fierce opposition of 'vested interests' and the inertia and complacency of public opinion. They had only one weapon with which to fight—and that was righteousness, the appeal to the conscience. The success of Wilberforce and his friends shows what religious and moral conviction can do even against the heaviest odds. They spared no effort to arouse public opinion against the slave trade. They spoke in Parliament, organized public meetings, collected subscriptions, and issued pamphlets. They studied the art of propaganda, even going to the extent of having anti-slavery slogans painted on their soup-plates, so that as their guests ate their soup they would gradually discern the words: 'Abolish all slavery' or would find a picture of a negro, with the

[1] In 1771, for example, 50,000 slaves were thus transported.

words: 'A man and a brother'. No one was allowed to forget the campaign which they were waging or the evil thing which they were trying to put right. At the end of a three and a half hours' speech in the House of Commons in 1789 Wilberforce cried: 'And, sir, when we think of Eternity and of the future consequences of all human conduct, what is there in this life that should make any man contradict the dictates of his conscience, the principles of justice and the laws of God'.[1] Victory came on February 23, 1807, when, as the result of many years of unremitting labour, Wilberforce carried the House with him and persuaded them, by 283 votes to 16, to declare the Slave Trade illegal. In 1833 all slavery was abolished throughout the British dominions.

The fight against the Slave Trade is the most famous of the many good works of the Evangelicals. But there was also much else going on. The anti-slavery campaign had aroused interest in the spiritual condition of the West African negroes, among whom little missionary work had yet been done. It was largely to meet this need that the Church Missionary Society was launched at a public meeting in London presided over by John Venn in 1799. The Society was to be evangelical and wholly missionary. It was an Anglican society, intended to be within the Church, but it kept in friendly intercourse with other protestant missionary societies, for its chief end was to preach the Gospel rather than to extend the Church.[2] At first no English missionaries could be found to go out to West Africa, and the Society had to employ a party of German Lutherans, all of whom, with their wives and children, perished on the River Pongas in 1807. In 1815, however, a Norwich solicitor, Edward Bickersteth, offered his services, was ordained, and became the real founder of Anglican missionary endeavour in West Africa.[3]

The Evangelicals also turned their attention to missionary work in India. Henry Martyn, at Simeon's suggestion, had gone out to India in 1805, but the difficulties had been great. India was largely governed by the East India Company which was apprehensive of any kind of religious disturbance in the country. In spite, therefore, of Lord Teignmouth's attempts to get an Anglican mission started, it was not until 1813 that an East India Bill was passed allowing the

[1] R. Coupland, *Wilberforce* (new ed. 1945), p. 104.
[2] It has been said that the S.P.G. was really the Church Missionary Society and the C.M.S. the Society for the Propagation of the Gospel.
[3] See E. Stock, *A History of the Church Missionary Society*, 4 vols. (1899).

Church to go ahead with a proper organization. In the following year T. F. Middleton, a London vicar of the most respectable kind, went out as Bishop of Calcutta, where he worked for seven years against great odds. But the foundations were laid, in spite of apathy and opposition.[1]

The year which saw the foundation of the C.M.S (1799) saw also the beginning of the Religious Tract Society to bring cheap religious literature to the masses. Hannah More had started this with her *Cheap Repository Tracts*, the sale of which had shown how great the demand was. The new Society was unsectarian and evangelical, its first secretary being a Welsh Baptist; but its success was immediate. Legh Richmond's tract, *Dairyman's Daughter*, which was one of the most popular of its publications, sold over four million copies and was translated into 19 languages.[2]

More necessary, however, than tracts were cheap copies of the Bible. Attempts had been made for some time to print a cheap Bible in Welsh, but the cost of production had been too high. In 1804, therefore, a further society, again on interdenominational lines, was founded—the British and Foreign Bible Society—to provide cheap Bibles in the Authorized Version 'without note or comment' in the languages of all those countries and tribes where protestant missionary work was in progress.[3]

So far, the pioneers in the field of missionary and philanthropic work had been the Evangelicals. But this is not to say that the High Church party was inactive. While the Clapham Sect was forming on the Surrey side, a group of churchmen was gathering round the old parish church of Hackney. The most conspicuous of the High Churchmen, who formed what was sometimes known as the 'Hackney Phalanx', was Joshua Watson (1771–1855), a devout London merchant as anxious as any of the Evangelicals to spend his time and money for God. Watson devoted himself to all causes connected with the propagation of the Christian faith and the education of people in Church principles. Not only did he support all the main societies such as S.P.G. and S.P.C.K., the Sons of the Clergy, the Additional Curates' Society and the National Society, but we find him paying for cheap

---

[1] See E. Chatterton, *A History of the Church of England in India* (1924).
[2] See W. Jones, *Jubilee Memorial of the Religious Tract Society* (1850).
[3] See W. Canton, *History of the British and Foreign Bible Society*, 4 vols. (1904). All or part of the Bible has now (1952) been translated into over a thousand languages, 808 by the British and Foreign Bible Society.

reprints of the Fathers for Greek Christians, endowing libraries in Iceland, redeeming labourer's clothes from pawn-shops, building churches and supplying ornaments for them.[1] Watson's brother was Rector of Hackney and his close friend H. H. Norris, Rector of South Hackney, and there was a small circle of like-minded men associated with them.

One of the causes which the 'Hackney Phalanx' had very much at heart was that of Christian education. They did much to set forward the work of S.P.C.K., the main educational agency in the Church, and, in 1811, formed the 'National Society for the Education of the Poor in the Principles of the Established Church throughout England and Wales'. Within two years the National Society had 40,000 children on its books.[2]

Another cause which owes much to the North London group was that of church building. The rapid growth of the towns was fast outrunning the accommodation of the churches, and unless new churches were quickly built there was a danger of people being enticed away to the dissenting chapels. John Bowdler was the prime mover in the agitation for more churches. As a result of a petition which he organized, the sympathy of the Government was aroused, and in 1818 the Church Building Society was founded with large subscriptions from the king and others. The largest gift was that of a million pounds by the Government in 1818 as a thanksgiving for victory at Waterloo, followed by another half million in 1824. But generous though these grants from public funds were, the society depended much on private subscriptions, and it is reckoned that between 1818 and 1833 over six million pounds was spent on the building of new churches. As it was no good having new churches unless there were clergy to minister in them, yet more societies came into being, the Church Pastoral Aid Society in 1836 and the Additional Curates' Society in the following year.

The period between the death of John Wesley and the beginnings of the Oxford Movement was, therefore, one of great activity in many spheres. Conscious of the need for reform, of new opportunities and new responsibilities, of new fields for Christian endeavour opening up in all parts of the world, men were getting together in groups to contribute the best that they had to give for the causes

---

[1] See E. Churton, *Memoir of Joshua Watson*, 2 vols. (1861), and A. B. Webster, *Joshua Watson* (1954).

[2] See below, p. 325.

which to them were of the greatest moment. It was essentially the age of the 'society', the expression of religious enterprise through the committee-room and the subscription list. But whether at Clapham, Hackney, or elsewhere, the zeal of the reformers drew its inspiration and strength from the worship and sermons of the parish churches.

iii. Education and Religious Thought

The Industrial Revolution had given men a new conception of power, but the French Revolution had shown what can happen when power gets into the wrong hands. The world was startled and alarmed. Here in England new industrial areas were coming into being where large masses of people were crowded together in conditions which were often brutal and degrading. Unless steps were taken to civilize the masses there was no knowing what horrors might be in store. The place to begin was with the children.

In the eighteenth century the public and grammar schools catered for the more intelligent boys, the charity schools for a limited number of orphans, foundlings and children of the poor. In the country there were a good many small village schools in which children were taught by the clergy, and there were some private schools and 'dame schools' scattered about the land. But with the coming of the big industries, children were rushed into the mills and mines where they worked for such long hours that there was little time left for education. It was to meet this problem that, in 1780, Robert Raikes of Gloucester started Sunday Schools in that city where children could come, on the day of rest, and receive the elements of a Christian education. The movement spread into other towns, and for a time met a real need, though the hours were really too short and the spaces between them too long to allow of much progress being made.

Early in the nineteenth century public opinion became more conscious of the need for greater educational facilities, and in 1807 Samuel Whitbread introduced into the House of Commons a bill to allow schools to be supported out of the rates, as they were in Scotland. The bill passed in the Commons but was thrown out by the more conservative House of Lords which still wished to keep all education in the hands of the clergy. It was not, therefore, until 1833 that the first grant of public money to education was made, by which time considerable progress in elementary education had been made by voluntary societies.

In village schools, where numbers were small and methods primitive, it was possible for the clergy to do the work without much assistance. But with the growth of the towns it was obvious that large numbers of teachers would be needed and at considerable expense. It was to solve this problem of providing teachers on very little money that Dr. Andrew Bell, an army chaplain in Madras in 1789, hit on the idea of 'pupil-teachers' whereby the older scholars devoted much of their time to instructing the younger ones. By this method Bell claimed that one adult could deal adequately with at least a thousand children. A few years later Joseph Lancaster, a young Quaker, started a school in London in which he independently evolved the same system. Both systems flourished, and large numbers of schools were founded in various parts of England on this model.

Between Bell and Lancaster considerable hostility sprang up. At first it was due partly to mere rivalry and partly to a strain of jealousy, each claiming to be the inventor of the system though, in fact, it had been known in France for some years. But, unfortunately, the quarrel soon got involved with the question of religion. Bell, as an Anglican priest, was for Church teaching and the Catechism, while Lancaster, as a Quaker, believed in non-sectarian teaching of what he called 'general Christian principles and them only'. From the start, therefore, of general elementary education two rival systems grew up side by side—church schools and undenominational schools. Each side was well organized, the Royal Lancasterian Society (later, the British and Foreign School Society) being founded in 1808 and the National Society in 1811. Each was determined not to give way on the religious issue. Each had its supporters. The 'dual system' in education had been born.

Both societies achieved considerable success, but even so they were able to reach only a small proportion of the children. Accurate figures are impossible to obtain, but it is doubtful whether as much as 20 per cent of the children of England were receiving any kind of education by 1833 when the first government grant was made of £20,000 to be divided equally between the two rival societies.[1]

[1] Cf. J. L. and B. Hammond, *The Bleak Age* (Pelican ed. 1947), pp. 152-3, and E. L. Woodward, *The Age of Reform, 1815-1870*, p. 459 n.

The Industrial Revolution was also producing a new class, the prosperous manufacturer anxious to give his sons a better education than he himself had enjoyed. In country districts there were many excellent grammar schools—such as the old school at Hawkshead where Wordsworth was educated and where a limited number of boys could be taken as boarders—but many parents aspired higher than this and sent their sons to one or other of the public schools. Though their reputation was high, many of these schools had little to boast of. They tended to be old-fashioned and reactionary. Discipline was slack and the teaching unimaginative. There were no organized games, and boys worked off their animal spirits mainly in fighting each other.[1] Religious exercises were often very perfunctorily carried out; and, in schools which had no chapels of their own, the boys were generally herded together in a gallery in the local parish church on Sunday mornings. At some schools, when the Eucharist was celebrated only members of the sixth form were allowed to communicate.[2]

There was, therefore, great need of reform; and the man who did most to set that reform in motion was Thomas Arnold (1795–1842). Arnold went to Rugby as headmaster in 1828. He found it a full and flourishing school but greatly in need of reform. With 'unhasting, unresting diligence' he set himself to change the whole tone of the school so that the attainment of sound learning and the building up of Christian character should become the aim and object of both masters and boys. 'Every pupil was made to feel that there was work for him to do—that his happiness as well as his duty lay in doing that work well.'[3] Good, intelligent education firmly and deeply rooted in the Christian faith was Arnold's ideal, and he spared himself no pains in working for it. With such fervour did he work that, in spite of an annual holiday at his beloved Fox How in Westmorland, he wore himself out, and died at the early age of 46. But in his fourteen years at Rugby Arnold was able to show what a public school should be, and, as another great headmaster has said, 'his work for the schools stands unchallenged and unchallengeable'.[4]

---

[1] Hence Wellington's remark about the Battle of Waterloo being won on the playing fields of Eton. He was not thinking of cricket and football!
[2] See C. H. Smyth, *Simeon and Church Order* (1940), chap. ii.
[3] Cf. B. Willey, *Nineteenth Century Studies* (1949), p. 53.
[4] Spencer Leeson, *Christian Education* (1947), p. 108. See A. P. Stanley, *Life and Correspondence of Thomas Arnold*, 2 vols. (1844).

The ancient universities of Oxford and Cambridge were also sadly in need of reform. Governed by ancient statutes, they were closed to all but members of the Church of England. At Oxford, matriculation included subscription to the Thirty-nine Articles, and at Cambridge no dissenter could take a degree. Daily attendance at college chapel was compulsory, and all fellows of colleges were required to be in Holy Orders and celibate. Thus there hung over the universities an air of medievalism and exclusiveness which was out of keeping with the new age. Moreover, although reforms had been going on in some colleges—notably at Oriel, Oxford—the teaching was singularly un-imaginative, the statutes sadly out of date, and the general life of the students undisciplined and crude. Gunning's *Reminiscences of Cambridge from 1780* give a melancholy but fascinating picture of the life of the university in its unreformed days.

As a protest against the ecclesiastical exclusiveness of Oxford and Cambridge the undenominational University College, London, with no faculty of theology and no religious tests was founded in 1828. It was an attempt to start a new type of higher education free from the trammels of ecclesiasticism. The Church's reply to 'the godless institution in Gower Street' was the foundation of King's College in the Strand, also in 1829, and of Durham University in 1832, the latter being largely endowed out of the surplus revenues of the Dean and Chapter.

University College, London, with its secularism and freedom, was much in spirit with the new age. The revolutionaries in France had preached Liberty, and Liberty had encouraged Liberalism. There was now a good deal of doubt in many men's minds about the so-called 'Christian verities'. New knowledge was beginning to be dissemin-ated, not only among the educated but also among the masses, by the Society for Promoting the Diffusion of Useful Knowledge in *Penny Magazines* and other kinds of cheap literature. Soon men were beginning to wonder whether the teaching of the Church were really true or not. Was Christianity perhaps only a legend which had served mankind in the days of ignorance, but which ought now to be jettisoned in the age of science?

The Church's first reaction to this was to defend itself and its teaching by further 'evidences'. Archbishop Whately of Dublin re-plied to criticisms of the truth of the Gospels by a skit casting doubts on the existence of Napoleon whom everyone knew to have been very much alive; and many Christian writers rushed to the defence of orthodoxy, among them William Van Mildert and J. B. Sumner. The old arguments, however, were not of much value; and, apart from these, the Church was not in any position to meet the attacks of clever men. There were few really good scholars at the universities and such as there were were classicists rather than theologians; the bishops as a whole were mainly concerned with more mundane things; and the only really active part of the Church, the Evangelicals, were interested either in philanthropy and good works or in the dry details of Calvinism and the theology of Baptismal Regeneration. There was a small trickle of pious literature like Reginald Heber's hymns and John Keble's *Christian Year*, and a certain amount of writing on the interpretation of prophecy; but neither of these was of much avail in fighting the armies of infidelity.

Meanwhile a further danger arose, a new assault upon the faith, not from unbelievers but from the theologians themselves. About 1800 Herbert Marsh began to introduce into England the ideas of German scholars on the criticism of the Bible, and in 1828 E. B. Pusey published his *Inquiry into German Rationalism*. Being staunch Churchmen these two men were probably unconscious of the perils which they ran in creating doubts about the infallibility of the Bible, but unconsciously they were opening the gates to ideas which were to cause the Church much trouble in later years.

Those who did most to rescue Christian thought in this hour of danger, and to give it new vitality, were not the theologians but the poets, especially Wordsworth and Coleridge. Each of these men had at first welcomed the French Revolution and what it stood for, and each had afterwards become shocked by the course which it had taken. Wordsworth, in his revolutionary days, had for a time absorbed the rationalistic teaching of William Godwin, but he turned against this to a conviction of the reality of the feelings and of the imagination, to a study of nature and of man in his simplicity, and to a contemplation of his own experience which led him to a deep and abiding faith. Coleridge, the 'Inquiring Spirit' as he called himself, for a time lost his faith altogether and then found it again. After such an experience he was not interested in conventional Christian evidences. '*Evidences* of Christianity!' he cried, 'I am weary of the word. Make a man feel the *want* of it; rouse him, if you can, to the self-knowledge of his *need* of it, and you may safely trust it to its own

Evidence.'[1] Religion was not a thing that could be proved or disproved; it was within man. No man could therefore be argued into faith; he must act as if he believed, and the rest would follow.

So much for the attack on the truth of Christianity. Coleridge then went on to discuss the infallibility of the Bible in his *Letters on the Inspiration of the Scriptures*. He found that, to most Englishmen, the Bible was 'a theological text-book and rule of faith composed by Almighty God and dictated by Him verbatim to the inspired writers'.[2] Against such a fundamentalist attitude Coleridge fought. He was not worried about the details of Old Testament history, nor with the so-called inconsistencies, inaccuracies and incredibilities of the Bible. What interested him was religion—not the type which worships the Bible ('Bibliolatry' he called it) but that which finds God in Christ in the pages of Scripture and worships Him there.

By 1833 only the first mutterings could be heard of the intellectual storms which were to break over Europe—the battles over scientific agnosticism and Biblical infallibility. But the drums were beginning to beat and the weapons were being forged. The Church had a hard fight, but that it won through in the end was largely due to the work of thinkers like Wordsworth and Coleridge who could see the problem from a detached angle. 'The Church of the future', it has been said, 'was largely being moulded, not at Lambeth and Bishopthorpe, but at Rydal Mount and Highgate, by men who little dreamed that they were doing anything of the kind.'[3]

iv. *The Church and Reform*

The idea of reform was very much in the air in the 1820's and there were few institutions so much in need of reform as the Church. But opinion on the subject of church reform was divided. To some the Church was a mass of corruption and injustice and ready for a complete overhaul. Some of its own members were its most severe critics. 'The Church as it now stands', wrote Thomas Arnold in 1832, 'no human power can save', and many of his fellow-churchmen would have shared in this melancholy view. Even more harsh criticism

---

[1] *Aids to Reflection* (Bohn ed.), p. 272.
[2] B. Willey, *Nineteenth Century Studies* (1949), p. 39.
[3] J. H. Overton, *The English Church in the Nineteenth Century, 1800-33* (1894), p. 212.

came from outside where popular feeling was increasingly anti-clerical. Bishops were burnt in effigy, the palace at Bristol was destroyed by the mob, and crowds cheered when a speaker proposed that Canterbury Cathedral should be turned into stables for the cavalry. Politicians kept telling the Church that she must put her own house in order, and implied that unless she did so it would be done for her by others. But little was done; for, while some clamoured for reform, others saw in the Church a bulwark against revolution and chaos and were afraid to start on reforms which might lead further than was anticipated. Meanwhile, most of the bishops were of the old school, well established on their large incomes and unwilling to surrender their rights or to face the problems which large-scale reform would create. Consequently, reforms long overdue were postponed, and inequalities and obsolete methods allowed to continue.

Some inroads were, however, made by the State on the exclusiveness which the Church enjoyed. Since the days of the Clarendon Code the Church of England had had a virtual monopoly in the country. The Test and Corporation Acts still in theory touched the nonconformists whose numbers were now greatly increased by the secession of the Wesleyans. In fact these acts were so little observed that their repeal in 1828 made very little difference. But the removal of these restrictions was an important step forward. It meant the abandonment once and for all of the theory of Hooker and the Elizabethan Settlement that Church and State were really one, and that those who chose to withdraw from the national Church did so at their own risk and could hardly complain if they lost some of their privileges. From now onwards it came to be an accepted thing that a man could be a perfectly good citizen without belonging to the Church of England, or indeed to any Church at all.

The repeal of the Test and Corporation Acts inevitably raised the question of the Roman Catholics whose numbers were now being swelled by the large influx of Irish labourers attracted to the new industrial areas. Some relief had been given to Roman Catholics in the eighteenth century,[1] but fear of Rome still lay in men's hearts. It was one thing to grant toleration to British nonconformists, whose loyalty and good citizenship no one could doubt; it was quite another thing to give privileges to people owing allegiance to a foreign power

[1] See above, pp. 312-13.

and frankly hostile to the Anglican Church. But, in spite of the dangers, public opinion became increasingly in favour of emancipation. The Evangelicals were, in theory at any rate, in favour of toleration, and Sydney Smith's *Letters on Catholics from Peter Plymley* in 1807-8 made a strong appeal for justice and common sense. Twenty years later, in 1829, the *Catholic Emancipation Bill* was passed and Roman Catholics now became eligible for Parliament. Another milestone had been passed on the road to toleration.[1]

Sydney Smith (1771-1845) was always ready to take up the cause of the downtrodden or neglected. A publicist rather than a churchman, he had been ordained of necessity rather than of choice and always regretted that it had been his lot. He disliked parish life and kept away from his flock as much as he reasonably could. He was a recognized wit in London society where he was admired for the brilliance of his conversation and the charm of his manner. But he was more than just a hero of society. Under the wit and repartee was a very real concern for the poor and the weak and the oppressed. His passionate pleas that toleration might be shown towards Roman Catholics, humanity to chimney-boys and justice to poor curates show where his heart really lay.[2]

If Sydney Smith's zeal for reform came principally from the emotions, that of Thomas Arnold came from the mind. Arnold was deeply distressed at the state of the Church. 'When I think of the Church', he wrote, 'I could sit down and pine and die.' Faced with this despair he set himself to think out paths of reform, especially in the relationship between Church and State. His experiences at Rugby had shown him, in miniature, what a Christian society might be. The school was a unity in which there existed law and order, fellowship, a common purpose, and a sense that each individual, from the headmaster down to the smallest boy, had his part to play towards the welfare of the whole. Above all, the life of the school was impregnated with Christian faith and morality. Why then, asked Arnold, could not the nations be organized on the same lines? Thus there came to him the vision of a truly Christian State in which all would work together for the common good. In this happy and idyllic society no distinction would be drawn between sacred and secular, for religion would be worked into every activity of life. In such a community there could

---

[1] See B. Ward, *The Eve of Catholic Emancipation*, 3 vols. (1911-12).
[2] See Hesketh Pearson, *The Smith of Smiths* (1934).

only be one Church, and Arnold proposed the creation of a truly national Church in which all sincere Christians could be united, though he found it impossible, for various reasons, to extend the invitation to Roman Catholics, Quakers and Unitarians. All this, worked out in considerable detail, Arnold published in 1833 in his *Principles of Church Reform*, but it failed to win much support. The Evangelicals regarded religion as too personal an affair to be mixed up with politics, and the High Church party, now on the eve of its great revival, had other ideas of what the Church should be. Arnold was an optimist and a visionary. In the small world of a public school he was able to realize his ambitions and see his dreams come true; but the nation was too complicated an affair to be so easily moulded to the ideas of one man. Church reform was, indeed, on its way; but not at all the kind of reform which Arnold had in mind.

v. *The Church on the Eve of the Oxford Movement*

The changes which had taken place in the sixteenth century had introduced a number of reforms into the life of the Church but had left many old evils undisturbed. The chief of these was the inequitable distribution of the Church's wealth. The number of parochial clergy in the early years of the nineteenth century was probably about 16,000 while the total income of the Church was reckoned at £7,000,000. This sum, if fairly distributed, would have been enough to provide each man with a reasonable living; but in fact the division of the Church's income was so inequitable that a few favoured individuals were in enjoyment of considerable fortunes while many of the clergy were in want. The Bishop of Winchester, for example, was supposed to have an income of £50,000 a year, and Bishop Sparke of Ely in 1830 was drawing nearly £30,000 for himself, while his two sons and a son-in-law received about £4000 each. Archbishop Moore died in 1805 leaving over a million pounds, and most bishops were able, out of their large stipends, to endow their families handsomely. On the other hand it was reckoned that out of the 4000 curates in England about half received less than £60 a year and were hard put to it to make both ends meet.

The sense of grievance which these inequalities aroused was further aggravated by the evils of pluralism and nepotism. By this time not only the positions of power in the Church but also the richest livings were almost all in the hands of a few families and were therefore the rewards not of ability but of birth. For those born in the purple there was every prospect of rapid preferment and increasing prosperity, but for the humbler member of society a poor curacy or an ill-paid benefice was the best that he could hope for.

Many of the injustices which survived in the Church were exposed in two books, *The Black Book, or Corruption Unmasked* in 1820–23, and *The Extraordinary Black Book* in 1831. These books contained bitter attacks not only on the Church but on 'privilege' generally, especially where large sums of public money were being paid to people who did very little in return. Though much of their evidence is drawn from parliamentary papers and other unimpeachable sources, the authors of these books were undisguised propagandists, anxious to make out a good case for reform and to stir up indignation against obsolete customs. They certainly contributed towards the general unpopularity of the Church which was common in certain circles. Dr. Arnold was not the only one who thought that the Church was doomed. Joseph Hume, speaking in the House of Commons, advised young men that it was useless their being ordained, and expressed a hope that 'these foolish ordinations' would terminate. If, however, young men persisted in anything so absurd he warned them that they could not expect any kind of compensation when the Church fell, as it undoubtedly would.[1]

Among intellectuals and reformers there was considerable criticism of the Church, and much of it was justified. With the honourable exception of men like Charles Blomfield[2] at Chester and Samuel Horsley at St. Asaph, the bishops as a whole took their duties lightly and found plenty of time to enjoy the good things which their affluence provided. The parochial clergy differed enormously. There were a few really devoted parish priests like Edward Stanley at Alderley, and a large number of simple men who carried out their modest duties with reasonable efficiency. Parson Woodforde at Weston Longueville was probably typical of many. He lived the comfortable life of a small country squire, took the necessary services on Sundays, visited where there was sickness, and spent his evenings playing cards or dining with his neighbours. The clergy portrayed in the novels of

---

[1] J. H. Overton, *The English Church in the Nineteenth Century, 1800–33* (1894), p. 12.
[2] See below, pp. 357–8.

Jane Austen were either social climbers, like Mr. Collins, or sons of
the landed gentry, who were appointed to family livings by their
fathers and were able to combine the pleasures of a country gentleman
with the duties, more or less conscientiously performed, of a clergyman. Edmund Bertram in *Mansfield Park* rather surprised his friends
by announcing his intention of living in his parish, for absenteeism
was still regarded as quite normal, three-fifths of the clergy in 1827
being non-resident.[1]

With absenteeism and a general slackness and indifference in
Church life it is no wonder that many churches were allowed to fall
into decay. The country churches were used so little, and the means
of heating them when used so inadequate, that dampness often got
in. Broken windows and loose tiles were often left unattended, dry
and wet rot got into the timbers and floor-boards, books and furnishings became mildewed and musty. On the other hand, in the towns,
where populations were increasing and there was more active church
life, there was a good deal of activity in building new churches.
Churches built in the earlier part of the eighteenth century like S.
Martin's-in-the-Fields had been designed in the classical style, but
from about 1750 onwards it became customary to imitate medieval
styles of architecture. From that time most new churches were
more or less 'Gothic' in appearance, vast sums of money being
spent in erecting sham medieval structures often with little taste or
imagination.

It was still customary to administer the Holy Communion only
quarterly, though some clergy had an extra celebration on Good
Friday. These 'Sacrament Sundays' were well observed in country
parishes and large crowds attended.[2] There was a move, however,
towards rather more frequent celebrations, the Bishop of Bath and
Wells writing rather cautiously to his clergy in 1825 and saying:
'The Sacrament administered *monthly* would, believe me, produce a
sensible amelioration in the feelings and habits of your parishioners;
and this blessed effect would more than repay you for any additional
labour'.[3]

At the usual Sunday services of Morning or Evening Prayer a

---

[1] 6120 out of 10,533; *Extraordinary Black Book*, p. 33 from Parliamentary Paper
No. 471, Session of 1830.
[2] *E.g.* at Llanfyllin, in 1806, out of a village population of not more than 500, about
250 attended at the Easter Communion. Wickham Legg, *op. cit.* p. 40.
[3] G. H. Law, *Charge to Clergy of Bath and Wells*, in *Pamphleteer*, xxvi (1826), p. 427.

battle was now being waged over the question of Hymnody versus Psalmody. The Evangelicals had greatly stimulated the use of hymns as an alternative to the metrical psalms, and many hymns had been written for this purpose. Apart from the two Wesleys and William Cowper the chief hymn-writers were James Montgomery the Moravian and Thomas Kelly. Rowland Hill, working on the principle that the devil should not have all the good tunes, wrote hymns suitable to be sung to popular airs, such as

> When Jesus first, at Heaven's command,
> Descended from His azure throne

to be sung to 'Rule, Britannia'. It was this kind of thing which roused the disgust of the advocates of psalmody, who claimed that they sang only the words of Holy Scripture whereas the hymn-writers could introduce into divine worship any kind of heresy or nonsense.

In the end it was the hymn-writers who triumphed. The metrical versions, even when sung to better tunes such as 'Rockingham', were too much limited in scope, and found it impossible to hold their own against the more popular and more sing-able hymns which were appearing in such large numbers. The battle was really won with the posthumous appearance in 1827 of Reginald Heber's *Hymns written and adapted to the weekly Church Services of the Year*. Heber, who has been called 'the creator of the modern Church hymn-book',[1] set himself to compile an anthology of the best hymns, ancient and modern, to illustrate the teaching of the Church and to fit into the Church's Year. From this time onwards the singing of hymns became popular in all kinds of churches, some of the best of the old metrical psalms (such as 'All people that on earth do dwell') being incorporated into the new collections. Meanwhile a revival of liturgical interests began with the publication, in 1832, of William Palmer's *Origines Liturgicae*, a scholarly study of the origins of the English Prayer Book.

This period also saw the spread of more intelligent ideas about the nature of the Church. For long the Church had been looked on, by the majority of its members, as little more than a department of State, the religious aspect of the national life. Gradually people were beginning to realize that this was not enough, that the Church was

[1] W. H. Frere in *Hymns Ancient and Modern, Historical Edition* (1909), p. xcviii.

a divine institution coming down from Christ Himself, that its authority was not given to it by the State but had been handed down from generation to generation through the Apostolic Succession, that it had a life of its own and must therefore be free from external control if it was to carry out its responsibilities.

These ideas had been germinating in the minds of more thoughtful people when a crisis occurred which raised the whole question of the relationship between Church and State. In England the established Church still represented much the largest part of the population, and it was therefore reasonable that it should continue to levy tithe and church-rates, even on the small minority who dissented from it. In Ireland, however, things were very different. Here the vast majority of those who were obliged to pay tithe were Roman Catholics, who were naturally aggrieved at having to support a Church which they believed to be schismatic. There was, therefore, considerable resentment against the large sums of money which the Church in Ireland demanded, and a good many landlords refused to pay and even offered violence to those whose job it was to collect the tax. In order to lessen the burden on the tithe-payer, Lord Althorp introduced a bill into Parliament in February 1833, to save £60,000 of church money in Ireland by reducing the number of bishoprics from 22 to 12, a reasonable suggestion in view of the smallness and poverty of most Irish sees.

But the proposal was fiercely attacked on a matter of principle. Here was a secular body claiming to interfere with the rights of the Church, and the whole question of 'Church and State' came to the fore. There was much argument and discussion, and on July 14 John Keble preached a sermon before the Judges of Assize at Oxford on the subject of 'National Apostasy'.[1] The sermon did not cause much stir at the time, but it started men thinking, especially a group of Oxford dons who set themselves to arouse their fellow men to a true sense of what Churchmanship means and involves. The 'Oxford Movement' had begun.

[1] The sermon is printed in Keble's *Sermons Academical and Occasional* (1847).

NOTE ON BOOKS

FOR the social background see J. L. and Barbara Hammond, *The Bleak Age* (Pelican ed. 1947). F. Warre Cornish, *The English Church in the Nineteenth Century*, vol. i (1910) covers this period, and to it should be added J. H. Overton, *The English Church in the Nineteenth Century, 1800–33* (1894) and J. Hunt, *Religious Thought in England in the Nineteenth Century* (1896). Basil Willey's *Nineteenth Century Studies* (1949) are illuminating on a number of subjects. For the later Evangelicals see G. R. Balleine, *A History of the Evangelical Party in the Church of England* (new ed. 1933), C. H. Smyth, *Simeon and Church Order* (1940) and R. Rudolf, *Clapham and the Clapham Sect* (1927). J. Woodforde, *The Diary of a Country Parson*, ed. J. B. Beresford, 5 vols. (1924–31) and abridged in the *World's Classics*, one vol. (1949) is full of interest. See also E. R. Norman, *Church and Society in England, 1770–1970* (1976).

CHAPTER XIX

THE OXFORD MOVEMENT AND AFTER
(1833–1854)

i. *Tracts for the Times*

THE Reform Act of 1832 opened a new era in the social and political life of England. Everyone now began thinking in terms of 'abuses' and 'reforms', for there were many institutions as much in need of reform as the House of Commons, among them the Church. But there are two ways in which an organism like the Church can be reformed—from within and from without. Some people thought that the only legitimate and lasting kind of reform was that which would come from within, from better ideas of the nature of the Church, greater self-confidence in its divine institution and mission, deeper consciousness of its spiritual authority. Others thought of church reform in more practical terms, by Acts of Parliament, by the clearing away of abuses, and by decrees and mandates imposed from without. Neither method of reform by itself would have got very far. It was, in fact, by the urge for reform both from within and from without that the Church made such great progress during the nineteenth century.

The first movement came from without with the passing of the Irish Church Bill which led to John Keble's Assize Sermon at Oxford. But it was this sermon which also raised the question of reform from within by dealing with the nature and authority of the Church. Keble called his sermon 'National Apostasy', by which he meant that Christian statesmen were allowing themselves to be led away by public opinion into acts which were disloyal to the Church. He spoke in bitter terms of 'the fashionable liberality of this generation' and pleaded that the Church was entitled to respect, not as a national institution, but as an instrument of the divine will. For laymen to interfere with the pastoral authority of the bishops, 'the Successors of the Apostles', was grievous sin; and a nation which fell into grievous sin could not ask for the protection of God. Keble therefore set on foot an investigation into the nature of the Church which was the real beginning of the Oxford Movement. No wonder that Newman wrote many years later: 'I have ever considered and kept the day [of the sermon] as the start of the religious movement of 1833'.[1]

Oxford at this time was the chief centre of Anglican theological thought and study; and though in some ways it was conservative and remote from life, in others it was well aware of what was happening in the world. Oriel was the most progressive of the colleges, containing, among its fellows, some of the most interesting men of their generation. Among them was a group, calling themselves the 'Noetics', who were liberal in outlook, quick to challenge authority, critical of party men whether High Church or Evangelical, self-assured, provocative, stimulating. The leaders of these were Edward Copleston the Provost, Blanco White, a Spaniard and formerly a priest in the Roman Church, and Richard Whately, noisy, self-assertive and dogmatic.[2] The fellows of Oriel regarded themselves as the intelligentsia of Oxford. But they were prepared to think and to make others think. If it was true, as was said at the time, that the Common Room at Oriel 'stank of logic', at least it was a place where ideas were being formed and young men trained to use their minds.

Among the younger men were four who were to play a leading part in the movement for church reform. First, there was John Keble himself (1792–1866), a true child of the Caroline divines and disciple of Hooker. Keble was Professor of Poetry, with a noble and saintly character which eventually took him away from Oxford to serve as curate to his aged father in a Cotswold village.[3] Secondly, there was Richard Hurrell Froude (1803–36), full of gaiety and exuberance, belonging to the world of poetry and imagination rather than to that of theology. Froude was much interested in French thought, and exerted a great influence on his fellows at Oxford until his early death, from tuberculosis, at the age of thirty-three.[4] Thirdly, there was Edward Bouverie Pusey (1800–82), Regius Professor of Hebrew, a great scholar and recluse and the very opposite of Froude in every way.[5] Finally, there was John Henry Newman (1801–90), the most

---

[1] J. H. Newman, Apologia pro Vita sua (1892 ed.), p. 35.

[2] Whately was also very dressy. Although a clergyman, he wore a pea-green coat, white waistcoat, stone-coloured shorts, flesh-coloured silk stockings, and powdered his hair; see J. W. Burgon, The Lives of Twelve Good Men (1888), i, p. 385.

[3] See J. T. Coleridge, A Memoir of the Rev. J. Keble, 2 vols. (1869) and G. Battiscombe, John Keble: a Study in Limitations (1963).

[4] See his Remains, 4 vols. (1838–9).

[5] See H. P. Liddon and others, Life of E. B. Pusey, 4 vols. (1893–97).

able of them all, with a dynamic personality which dominated the movement for twelve years. Newman came from a world very different from the Tory squirearchy which produced so many of his colleagues. He was brought up an Evangelical, and at the age of fifteen had experienced a sudden conversion, of the reality of which he never had any doubt. He consequently never quite understood the High Church views of his friends. On the eve of the Oxford Movement Newman had been on a journey to the Mediterranean, where he had become conscious of a strong sense of vocation and mission. There was, in his nature, an element of fierceness and determination which quickly made him the leader of the group.[1]

The Assize Sermon was preached in July and soon led to action being taken. It soon appeared that there were two lines of thought among those anxious for reform from within, the one static and conservative, the other dynamic and radical. The 'static' group was, on the whole, defensive. Taking as its model the Church of the Caroline Divines, it wanted to rally the country to a better sense of churchmanship and get back some of the solid learning and holiness of the school of Hooker and Andrewes. In the summer of 1833 a group of men met at Hadleigh Rectory to consider what they should do. The party included H. J. Rose (1795–1838), a Cambridge man who had for some time been talking and writing about the Church,[2] R. H. Froude, William Palmer, an antiquarian and liturgist, author of Origines Liturgicae[3] and A. P. Percival. This group planned a league for the defence of the Church and considered drawing up a Churchman's Manual which should set before laymen a high standard of Christian duty.

While the Hadleigh party was considering a defensive policy a small group at Oxford were planning a much more aggressive campaign, the chief weapon of which was to be a series of Tracts for the Times which were to rally all loyal churchmen and infuse new life into the Church. The first tract appeared in September 1833 and was entitled 'Thoughts on the Ministerial Commission respectfully addressed to the Clergy'. It was a passionate plea for the clergy to unite

[1] The literature on Newman is considerable. Among the most important works are his Apologia pro Vita sua (1864), and W. Ward's Life of J. H. Newman, 2 vols. (1912). Among more modern works are Meriol Trevor, Newman: Light in Winter (1962) and Newman: The Pillar of the Cloud (1962) and C. S. Dessain, John Henry Newman (1966).
[2] See the essay by J. W. Burgon in Lives of Twelve Good Men (1888), vol. i.
[3] See above, p. 335.

in defence of their holy office in the Apostolic Succession. Men, it said, 'have been deluded into a notion that present palpable useful-ness, produceable results, acceptableness to your flocks, that these and such like are the tests of your Divine commission. Enlighten them in this matter. Exalt our Holy Fathers, the Bishops, as the Representa-tives of the Apostles, and the Angels of the Churches; and magnify your office, as being ordained by them to take part in their Ministry.' Tract No. 2 was entitled 'The Catholic Church' and the third 'Thoughts on Alterations in the Liturgy'. These three tracts all ap-peared in September 1833 and were all written by Newman, though largely under the inspiration of Froude. By the end of the year twenty tracts had appeared, by Newman, Keble and Froude and including one, much longer than the rest, by Pusey on 'Fasting'. These tracts were printed cheaply and distributed in large numbers to the par-ochial clergy by supporters of the movement, some of whom rode about the country calling at vicarages and trying to convert their occupants.

In 1834 thirty more tracts appeared, the most important of which were two by Newman (Nos. 38 and 41) on the Church of England as the *Via Media*. Earlier (in Tract 20) Newman had written 'Popery must be destroyed: it cannot be reformed', and he was still anti-Roman in his thought. In his tracts on the Church of England he claimed that it was truly and purely catholic, based on the customs of the Apostolic Church and the teaching of the Fathers, and cor-rupted neither by Romanism nor by protestantism. With these tracts the movement got well into its stride and attracted more recruits. Pusey, who hitherto had stood somewhat aloof, now threw in his weight and influence and, as Newman said, 'he was able to give a name, a form, and a personality to what was without him a sort of mob'. Others who identified themselves with the movement were H. E. Manning (1808–92), Archdeacon of Chichester, and Charles Marriott (1811–58). The tracts now became more learned and more lengthy and included collections of extracts from the Fathers or from the Anglican writers of the seventeenth century.

At this point much was being said about the Church as a Branch of the Catholic Church pursuing a *Via Media* between Rome and protestantism. This theory had many supporters, but there was a small minority, led by Froude, who had no faith in it at all. The whole theory smelt of compromise and caution when they, the more fiery spirits, were crying out for courage and conviction. Froude died in 1836, but already he had begun to shake the faith of some of the party in the *Via Media*. The publication of his *Remains* in 1838-39 split the party into two. If Froude had lived, it is hard to see how he could have remained within the Church of England. His outlook was essentially medieval and he had the utmost dislike of the Reformers. The *Remains* caused something of a sensation. Newman began to lose all faith in the *Via Media*, and W. G. Ward, one of the most outspoken of the party, began to lose faith in the Anglican Church itself. Thus by 1839 the party was really more or less divided into three groups. There were the old conservatives, led by Keble, disliking controversy and longing to restore the devotion and godliness of the Caroline Church; there was the party, now under the leadership of Pusey which clung tenaciously to the doctrine of the *Via Media*; and there was a group of progressives, growing increasingly doubtful of the validity of the Anglican position. Newman was now being dragged more and more into this camp.

Meanwhile the *Tracts for the Times* had made a great stir in the country. Some welcomed them and were thrilled and inspired by their teaching; but many were horrified and indignant. The strict Evangelicals were appalled at their alleged Romanism, their extravagant views of the Church and of the priesthood, and their attitude towards the Reformation. The worldly minded were disgusted by tracts on fasting and all this talk about stirring up the Church to a greater sense of responsibility. So long as the Church provided them with good livings it was best left alone.

At Oxford, the centre of the movement, feeling ran very high. In addition to the Evangelicals and the secularists there was also a strong movement of liberal thought under the leadership of R. D. Hampden (1793-1868). A subject on which the university was very much divided at this time was that of the religious tests and the admission of dissenters to the university, and in 1834 Hampden had come down heavily on the liberal side by his *Observations on Religious Dissent*. This ran directly counter to the teaching of even the mildest Tractarians and caused much distress. Two years later Lord Melbourne rewarded Hampden by appointing him Regius Professor of Divinity, an appointment which horrified the Tractarians who attacked it bitterly, while Thomas Arnold rushed to the defence of liberalism by a counter-attack on the Tractarians in an article called 'The Oxford

Malignants'. In 1837 further controversy was stirred up by the Evangelicals' proposal to erect, in Oxford, a memorial to the three reformers, Cranmer, Latimer and Ridley, who had suffered martyrdom there in 1555–56. That such public recognition should be given to the work of the Reformers was distasteful to a school of thought which was anxious to belittle the Reformation and emphasize the catholicity of the Church of England; and Newman, Keble and Pusey, in spite of their loyalty to the university, felt themselves bound to oppose it.

While the opponents of the Tractarians were busy gathering their forces, the High Church party were full of energy and zeal. Newman, who was now Vicar of St. Mary's in Oxford, was attracting large crowds to his four-o'clock sermons on Sunday afternoons, sermons which are among the greatest in the history of English preaching. Articles by Tractarian writers were appearing regularly in the *British Magazine* and the *British Critic*, and from 1838 onwards scholars were busy translating patristic writings which they published in the *Library of the Fathers*. In 1839 a college for training ordination candidates in the principles of the movement was opened at Chichester under the supervision of Manning and with Charles Marriott as Principal. The party was active, imaginative and determined.

But there was much opposition. By 1839 not only the University of Oxford but the whole Church was feeling the bitterness of controversy as it had not felt it for many years. In the first Tract Newman had said: 'CHOOSE YOUR SIDE. To remain neuter much longer will be itself to take a part. *Choose* your side; since side you shortly must, with one or other party, even though you do nothing.' It was a direct appeal to party-spirit and a call to strife. This call had not been unheeded. Strife there was, growing daily as the Tractarians became more provocative and more challenging. Everyone now was talking about the Tracts and about the policy which they represented. It was, indeed, difficult for any man to remain neutral.

ii. *Tract 90 and the Secession*

To the rank and file of the Church, clergy and laity alike, the Tractarians appeared as enemies of protestant truth. Fear of Rome was deep-seated in the English mind. Men believed that there was a clear dividing-line between catholics and protestants. They might have been a little puzzled to know where to put the Eastern Orthodox Church, but of that they knew little. In the world which they knew everyone was either a catholic or a protestant, and all members of the Church of England were among the latter. The ordinary man could not, therefore, understand all this talk about a *Via Media* and about the Church of England being catholic rather than protestant. Such language was shocking and dangerous and ought to be suppressed. No good could possibly come from playing with the 'Scarlet Woman'.

To more sensitive minds the problem of catholicism was confusing. If the *Anglicana Ecclesia* was in fact the catholic Church in England what was the position of the Romanists, now becoming more active and influential since the passing of the Emancipation Act in 1829? Newman at this stage was convinced that the Church of Rome was corrupt, that it had introduced doctrines and practices which were no part of the traditions of the Primitive Church in which he had such deep faith, and that Rome had no more claim to catholicity than had the Church of England. But various forces were acting on Newman's mind. In 1839 N. P. S. Wiseman, a half-Irish and half-Spanish Roman Catholic priest, was sent to England and began publishing articles on the Donatist schism, suggesting that the Church of England was schismatic in just the same way that the Donatists had been pronounced schismatic in the fourth century. Newman was deeply impressed by this line of thought. Then again a small group of radical thinkers among the Tractarians, including W. G. Ward and F. W. Faber were becoming attracted, not, like Froude, to medieval Rome, the Church out of which the Anglican Church had emerged, but to the Rome of the Counter-Reformation and to post-Tridentine theology and practice. Newman was not, at first, impressed by this. The Church of Rome, he was convinced, had wandered far from the customs of the Primitive Church and, in so doing, had erred from catholic simplicity. But at this point he was introduced to the doctrine of 'Development'. Christ had promised that the Holy Spirit should guide the Church into all truth. The Primitive Church did not know the whole truth; this was revealed only slowly in the course of history. It was not the Primitive Church that should be taken as the model, but that Church which showed most signs of holiness, of being the true Body of Christ. From that moment Newman began to look on

Rome with new eyes. What if her wandering had led her not away from catholic simplicity but on into wider fields of divine truth?

Meanwhile there remained the problem of the Church of England. Writers like Newman might make out a better case for Rome than men had thought possible, but that did not in the least affect the protestantism of the Anglican Church. That was safeguarded by the Thirty-nine Articles, the standard to which every ordinand and even every student at the ancient universities must subscribe. To Newman and his friends, anxious to show that the formularies of the Church of England were entirely in harmony with the main stream of catholic doctrine, the Articles might well present a stumbling-block. Newman therefore set his mind to work on them, and produced, in February 1841, Tract 90, 'Remarks on Certain Passages in the Thirty-Nine Articles'.[1] In this remarkable pamphlet Newman deals with fourteen of the Articles, especially those which appear to be most anti-Roman. With remarkable acumen he demonstrates that what the Articles in fact do, is not to condemn the official teaching of catholicism but certain extravagances which have grown up in the Church of Rome. Thus Article 22 does not condemn 'purgatory, pardons, worshipping and adoration, as well of images as of relics' but only 'the Romish doctrine' of these things; and Article 31 does not disallow the doctrine of the Sacrifice of the Mass but that of the 'sacrifices of Masses' which is a Roman error. Much of the tract is no doubt special pleading unworthy of a great mind;[2] but as a well-deserved jolt to complacency and convention the tract was justified. It certainly roused a storm. At Oxford, writes Dean Church, it was met 'not with argument but with panic and wrath'.[3] Bishops said publicly that they would not trust Mr. Newman with their purses. There were loud cries of 'Popery' and 'Antichrist is at the door'. By many the tract was regarded as indecent and offensive. Joshua Watson, rather acutely, thought that it should have been written in Latin.

Protest was inevitable. Four Oxford tutors, including A. C. Tait, a future Archbishop of Canterbury, sent a letter of protest to *The Times*, while the heads of houses at Oxford met and condemned the tract. So did Richard Bagot, the Bishop of Oxford, who extracted

---

[1] Extracts in H. Bettenson, *Documents of the Christian Church*, pp. 435-40.
[2] Brilioth calls it 'a very melancholy document. It shows how a really great man can become little in a false and ambiguous position.' (*The Anglican Revival* (1925), p. 155).   [3] R. W. Church, *The Oxford Movement* (1891), p. 290.

from Newman a promise that no more tracts should be written. How far Tract 90 was acceptable to the more moderate men in the movement it is difficult to say. Hitherto Tractarians had always proclaimed the loyalty of the party to the Church of England, but from this point onwards the difficulty of convincing their critics became more acute. To many the Tractarians were little better than traitors.

After Tract 90 there is no doubt that opinion hardened against the party. This was shown by three events at Oxford. The first was the defeat of Isaac Williams in the election of a Professor of Poetry in spite of his qualifications. Williams had caused some dismay by writing a tract on 'Reserve in Communicating Religious Knowledge'. The second event was an attempt to prevent another Tractarian, a Mr. Macmullen, from taking his B.D. The third was the attack on Pusey, and his suspension from all preaching in Oxford for two years, as the result of a sermon at Christ Church in which he claimed that it was consistent with the teaching of the Church of England to hold that the Eucharist was a commemorative sacrifice. Further trouble was caused by the failure of the Tractarians to support a plan in 1841 for uniting the protestants in the Holy Land by establishing a bishopric of Jerusalem to be held alternately by an Anglican and a Lutheran.

After the uproar occasioned by the publication of Tract 90 Newman retired more and more from public life. He lived mostly at Littlemore, a few miles out of Oxford, where he built a chapel and library and gathered a small community who lived together a semi-monastic life. He was absorbed now by the thought of Holiness as the only mark of the true Church, and began to study the lives of the English saints. By 1843 he was feeling very strongly the pull of Rome, and in September he felt that he must resign the benefice of St. Mary's since he was fast losing faith in the Church of England.[1]

Pusey now became the leader of the movement in Oxford. Nothing could shake his loyalty to the Church of England, not even the bitter and ignorant diatribes of his opponents. Supported by Charles Marriott, J. B. Mozley and others, he fought a hard battle for unity and sanity against opponents on both sides, those who were opposed to the whole movement and those within the party who were trying to drag them all over to Rome. Ward was now busy exalting Rome and all her ways. His *Ideal of a Christian Church* (1844) was intended

Cf. *Apologia* (1892 ed.), p. 186.

to show how Rome triumphantly achieves the ideal while the Church of England falls hopelessly short. The book could not fail to be condemned by the University and Ward was deprived of his degrees. In September 1845 he and his newly wed wife were received into the Church of Rome. By this time Newman's mind was made up. On October 8 he wrote to a friend: 'I am this night expecting Father Dominic the Passionist. . . . He does not know of my intention; but I mean to ask of him admission into the One Fold of Christ.'[1] So passed from her ranks one of the greatest minds which the Church of England has ever produced, and his departure marks the end of a chapter in the history of the Anglican revival. A few followed their leader; but the majority in the movement stood fast in the faith of their fathers under the wise and firm leadership of Pusey. After many years of tension and strife Oxford could now settle down to other things; 'the nightmare which had oppressed Oxford for fifteen years'[2] was over. But the tracts and their writers and supporters left their mark not only on the University but on the Church as a whole, on its theology, its worship, its whole life. Ideas had been planted which in time were to transform the whole face of the Anglican Communion at home and overseas. The Church could never be the same again.

iii. *The Progress of Reform*

The effect of the tractarian teaching had been to put new life and new self-confidence into the Church. Only thus could any real revival and reform come about. But meanwhile another kind of reform was taking place, not from within but from without, not at Oxford but at Westminster, not by tracts but by acts. Proposals for Church reform were first made by Lord Henley in 1832. As a result of the debates which ensued, a body was set up in 1835, called the Ecclesiastical Commissioners and consisting of the two archbishops, three bishops and four laymen. The commission soon met and made drastic proposals for church reform. They recommended a complete redistribution of the finances of the bishoprics so that there should be much more equality and therefore less temptation to a bishop to seek translation. They suggested also the creation of two new sees in the now

---

[1] *Apologia*, pp. 234-5.   [2] Mark Pattison, *Memoirs* (1885), p. 236.

heavily populated areas of Yorkshire and Lancashire. In the following year they issued plans for a complete overhaul of cathedral chapters. Instead of a large number of endowed canonries which were held by non-resident clergy holding other preferment, they proposed that enough money should be set aside at each cathedral for the endowment of a dean and four residentiaries. Other canonries were to be honorary, and the money thus saved was to go to augment poor livings. The commissioners worked rapidly and ruthlessly. In 1836 the new diocese of Ripon was created,[1] and the diocese of Manchester followed in 1847. In 1837 the Ecclesiastical Commissioners became a permanent body with large powers over the finances of the Church.

Parliament dealt also with other questions relating to church finance, especially tithe and rates. Tithe was, for many clergy the main source of income; but in many ways the whole system was most unsatisfactory. It was disliked by the tithe-payers, especially those who were Roman Catholics or dissenters, and saw no reason why they should be obliged to support the established Church. It was disliked also by the clergy, who never knew just what their incomes would be, and resented having to bargain with their parishioners. For many years there had been a tendency to commute tithe to a cash payment, but each incumbent had made his own arrangements with the tithe-payers. In 1836 Parliament passed a *Tithe Act* which made commutation compulsory and based the amount on a Tithe Rent charge which was fixed by the price of corn.

Church rates had been levied for many years, mainly for the up-keep of the fabric of the church, since the laity had always been held responsible for the nave while the rector looked after the chancel. Here again nonconformists of all kinds felt that they had a grievance. Why, they asked, should they be obliged to support a building which they never entered, when they had their own places of worship to keep up? Various attempts, therefore, were made to circumvent the tax—in Leeds, for example, the dissenters came in vast numbers to the annual Vestry and elected some of their own persuasion as church-wardens in order that church rates might be kept down.[2] But even though the amount might be small, the principle remained a grievance; and in 1837 a case at Braintree was started which dragged on

[1] There had been a diocese of Ripon in the seventh century but it had been absorbed into the diocese of York.
[2] W. R. W. Stephens, *Life of W. F. Hook* (1878), i, pp. 373-7.

for sixteen years. Many bills were introduced into the House of Commons, but none proved workable. The question was finally settled by Mr. Gladstone's bill of 1868, when compulsory church rates were finally abolished. As a result of this bill the responsibility for the upkeep of all parish churches now falls on the regular worshippers, and even they are under no obligation to pay.

Another matter which engaged the attention of Parliament during the 1830's was that of the church courts. In 1830 a commission was appointed to enquire into the working of the ecclesiastical courts. This committee reported in 1832 and recommended the abolition of the old Court of Delegates (which had been established in 1534) and the transference of appeals to the Privy Council which included in its membership a number of bishops. This was done; but in 1833 the final court of appeal was moved again to the Judicial Committee of the Privy Council, a body consisting only of laymen. This was much resented by churchmen, who objected to the hearing of ecclesiastical causes, especially those which raised matters of doctrine, by a purely lay tribunal. In 1840, therefore, an amendment was made saying that if an appeal is sent up from a consistory court every archbishop or bishop who is a Privy Councillor may join the Judicial Committee, and one must always be present. This concession to clerical opinion was largely withdrawn in 1876 when the bishops were made only assessors, leaving the actual verdict entirely in the hands of laymen.

With so much happening in both Church and State, so many problems, so much controversy, it is no wonder that the Church was beginning to feel the need for the revival of its own meeting-ground. Convocation had not met, except formally, since 1717, and there were still many who feared a revival. Many bishops thought that they and they alone among the clergy should have any say in the Church's affairs, the proper place for which was the House of Lords. Others were afraid that gatherings of the clergy in Convocation would lead to greater clericalism and were jealous for the rights of the laity. But there were a few who pleaded most earnestly for a revival of these ancient institutions, among whom were Henry Hoare, a London banker, who founded the 'Convocation Society' in 1851, and Bishop Samuel Wilberforce. Parliament on the whole was, at first, opposed to the scheme; but the pressure brought to bear by its supporters was so strong that in 1852 Lord Derby felt himself obliged to advise the queen to allow Convocation to meet. The machinery was therefore put in motion and the Southern province met in Convocation in 1854 and the Northern in 1861. From then onwards Convocation met regularly and became one of the most important functions of the Church.

One of the most pressing problems with which the Church had to deal at this time was that of Education. In 1833 the first grant of public money for purposes of education had been made, but there were as yet no State schools, and the money was administered by the two societies representing the Church and the dissenters. Many people still thought that education was a matter for the clergy alone. With the expansion of the schools some form of financial support from the State was reasonable; but responsibility still lay with the voluntary societies, and churchmen were determined to resist any interference with the right of the Church to teach its own doctrines. The nonconformists, on the other hand, who were finding the raising of money for their schools more difficult, were more sympathetic towards State interference. They were not so much interested in the teaching of any specific doctrine, but were satisfied with simple Bible lessons of an undogmatic kind. There were, thus, two different traditions and two quite different types of school when the State began to pay serious attention to the question of the education of the poor.

In 1839 an Education Committee of the Privy Council was set up, out of which grew the Ministry of Education. In the same year school inspectors were appointed, but their powers were much restricted. As far as church schools were concerned they were allowed to make suitable enquiries, but their reports, having been sent first to the Board, were afterwards sent on to the archbishops. The Church therefore was still keeping a very tight hand on its schools and its liberties. But, with the steady growth of population in the towns, old systems and ideas were beginning to crumble. Neither the National Society nor the British Schools Society could keep pace with the growing need for education, and in 1843 Lord Ashley (afterwards Earl of Shaftesbury) estimated that less than half the children in the country were receiving any kind of daily instruction. The dangers of this were obvious. Ignorance led to crime and revolution. More schools must be built: more children must be educated. But as soon as plans for more schools were made, trouble began over the religious question. The country as a whole still regarded religion as a vital factor in education, and Joseph Hume's suggestion in 1843, of providing purely secular schools met with very little support. Yet no kind of agreement over the religious issue was in sight. Bishop Blomfield had declared in 1838 that no system of national compulsory education would be tolerable which should not be in conformity with the principles of the Church of England and worked by its instrumentality.[1] In the face of such intransigence the two rival societies could only multiply their efforts to provide more schools of their own persuasion. 'Religion', said Sir James Graham sadly, 'the keystone of education, is, in this country, the bar to its progress.'[2]

Meanwhile the Church had started a number of training colleges to provide qualified teachers for her schools. One of the first of these was St. Mark's, Chelsea (1841) and many diocesan colleges were founded about the same time. Most of the students were aged about fifteen and came from the working classes. Care was taken to see that they were not educated 'above their station'.

iv. *Divided Opinions*

If the Church at the beginning of the nineteenth century had been somnolent, by the 1840's it was very much awake and full of life and activity. Opinion was much divided and vigorously expressed on a variety of subjects of which the most important were Ritualism, Liberalism and Socialism.

The Oxford Movement had begun within the University of Oxford and had been of interest mainly to dons and scholars. It had not much contact with ordinary parish life, nor did it immediately affect the rank and file of the clergy, except in so far as they read the Tracts and took sides in the controversy. In its early days it was essentially intellectual and academic, a movement of thought and of doctrine; but when it began to spread from the university to the parishes it was inevitable that the doctrines for which the Tractarians stood should begin to influence such things as the appearance of the churches and the nature of the worship offered in them. The original Tractarians had been conservative in all outward observances. Keble and Newman celebrated in surplice and hood and at the north end of the

---

[1] F. W. Cornish, *A History of the English Church in the Nineteenth Century* (1910), i, p. 200.   [2] Spencer Leeson, *Christian Education* (1947), p. 68.

altar. They adopted none of the marks of later Anglo-Catholicism such as candles on the altar, wafers and vestments. They preached in black gowns in accordance with the custom of the day.

But though these men were apparently satisfied with the liturgical standards of the day, they were teaching a doctrine of the Eucharist and of the Real Presence which demanded a greater reverence for the altar and for all that surrounds it. Men now began to study the past and to reintroduce customs and garments which had died out in the sixteenth century. The Oxford Architectural Society was founded in 1838, followed next year by the Cambridge Camden Society which, in 1841, began to publish a magazine called *The Ecclesiologist* devoted to the study of worship and its setting. Soon changes began to be made in the appearance of the churches and in ritual and ceremonial. At first all this was very much suspected, largely through ignorance of what it was all about. The natural fear was that it would lead to the revival of Roman customs, which the reformers had got rid of, and would thus undermine the protestant principles of the English Church. But, in spite of criticism and opposition, changes began to take place.

In 1840 W. J. E. Bennett[1] was appointed to the parish church of S. Paul's, Knightsbridge. Bennett was a disciple of the new movement and soon began to make changes at the church. He introduced lighted candles on the altar, the intoning of the services, and a surpliced choir. Not content with this he began to preach in a surplice instead of a black gown, and to adopt the eastward position at the altar. Such changes in old customs led to wild criticism and abuse, and Blomfield, the Bishop of London, was asked to intervene. Blomfield was not naturally sympathetic towards the 'Ritualists' (as they came to be called), but he had a great respect for law and order. Bennett and his friends were not the only people who were breaking the law. It was just as much a breach of the rubrics to neglect to say the daily offices as it was to light candles on the altar. The bishop, therefore, adopted a judicious attitude and censured both sides in so far as they disobeyed the clear directions of the Prayer Book.[2] Encouraged by this, the movement went ahead. In 1850 a new church was built by Bennett—S. Barnabas, Pimlico—in a very poor district, and was consecrated by Blomfield in person. At S. Barnabas cere-

[1] See F. Bennett, *The Story of W. J. E. Bennett* (1909).
[2] C. J. Blomfield, *A Charge to the Clergy of London, 1842*, p. 30.

monial was more elaborate than at Knightsbridge; and, before long, riots began, services were interrupted and damage to property was done. It was a bad year for the Ritualists since it coincided with the setting up of a Roman Catholic hierarchy in England and a wave of what can almost be described as 'hysteria'.[1] Lord John Russell wrote a violent and insolent letter to the Bishop of Durham complaining not only of the papal aggression but of those 'unworthy sons of the Church of England' who were 'leading their flocks, step by step, to the very verge of the precipice' by 'the mummeries of superstition'.[2] Even Blomfield complained that in many churches the services were becoming 'almost *histrionic*'.[3]

Meanwhile, in other parts of the country, things were moving in the same way. In 1845 a new church in Leeds, S. Saviour's, had been built by Pusey at his own expense. It immediately introduced certain unfamiliar and therefore suspicious practices. It was administered by a group of clergy who lived on almost monastic lines. A Midnight Mass was celebrated in 1848, and daily Mass introduced in the following year. Confession was widely taught and practised and many other things hitherto regarded as purely Roman. The Bishop of Ripon described the parish as 'a plague-spot in my diocese'; Hook, the Vicar of Leeds was desperately worried about it; even Pusey was disheartened and fearful. The fact that of the first fifteen clergy to serve the Church, nine had gone over to Rome by 1851 showed that there were grounds for apprehension. In the south of England G. R. Prynne, Vicar of S. Peter's, Plymouth, 1845–1903, was scandalizing the protestant party by hearing confessions and introducing nuns into his parish.

Ritualism, however, was not the only question which was troubling the Church. To many minds the greatest danger lay not in changes of worship but in the undermining of the faith of the Church through the dissemination of liberal thought. The Oxford Movement, in its early stages, had been an acknowledged protest against liberalism; but, to the liberals, the Tractarians seemed retrograde and far too much interested in dogmatism, sacerdotalism and medievalism. Dr. Arnold thought the Tractarians 'a very bad party' which was more likely to wreck the Church than revive it.

---

[1] See, for example, the pages of *Punch* for this year.
[2] Lord John Russell, *Letter to the Bishop of Durham* quoted in F. W. Cornish, *A History of the English Church in the Nineteenth Century*, i, pp. 346–7.
[3] C. J. Blomfield, *A Charge to the Clergy of London, 1850*, p. 51.

More formidable was Dr. R. D. Hampden (1793–1868) whose theology had all along been open to some criticism. Hampden had actually been condemned by the University of Oxford in 1836 and 1842, but he continued to occupy the chair of Regius Professor of Divinity until his appointment by Lord John Russell to the bishopric of Hereford in 1847. The Church as a whole—Tractarian and evangelical—was shocked by this appointment, and even liberals thought it an unnecessarily provocative act. But it was difficult for the chapter at Hereford to withstand the wishes of the crown, and Hampden was duly consecrated and enthroned.

In the same year much confusion was caused by the notorious Gorham case. G. C. Gorham (1787–1857), a Cambridge evangelical, was, in 1847, appointed to the living of Brampford Speke near Exeter. Phillpotts, the Bishop of Exeter at that time, was a Tractarian who disliked Gorham's views so much that, before accepting him, he subjected him to a series of examinations, lasting altogether for 38 hours, mainly in the theological questions of Baptismal Regeneration and Prevenient Grace. As a result of these interviews, Phillpotts refused to institute Gorham on the grounds that he held doctrines which were not in keeping with the teaching of the Church of England. Gorham brought an action in the Court of Arches in 1848 and lost it. He then appealed to the Judicial Committee of the Privy Council which reversed the former verdict and pronounced in favour of Gorham. This was a great shock not only to the Tractarians but to all who believed in the authority and independence of the Church. Here was a decision on a purely doctrinal question being made by a lay tribunal. The whole country was stirred by this; a war of pamphlets broke out; and Manning and a few others were so disgusted with the Church of England that they went over to Rome.[1]

If Hampden was the leader of liberal thought at Oxford the leader at Cambridge was Connop Thirlwall (1797–1875), a man of great learning and of a most acute mind. He had been trained as a barrister, but was ordained and lived for some years at Cambridge until 1834 when he quarrelled with the Master of Trinity over the questions of compulsory chapel and the admission of dissenters to the university. In 1840 he became Bishop of S. David's, which he held until his death in 1875.[2]

[1] See J. C. S. Nias, *Gorham and the Bishop of Exeter* (1951).
[2] See J. C. Thirlwall, *Connop Thirlwall* (1936).

Meanwhile, at the newly founded University of London, Frederick Denison Maurice (1805–72) was making a name for himself as an independent and courageous thinker. He had been brought up a Unitarian, but had entered the Church of England and had been ordained. Coming from a nonconformist background, he was very anxious to explain the teaching of the Church to his friends outside it, but in so doing he said things which, to some minds, were open to criticism. For example, he wrote that Revelation did not mean the direct intervention of God, but the unveiling of the nature of God by degrees as man was able to accept it. He also touched on the extremely controversial question of Eternal Punishment, declaring that this referred not to *everlasting* punishment but to punishment in eternity. Maurice became Professor of Theology at King's College, London, in 1846; but his teaching was regarded as too rationalistic, pantheistic and anti-dogmatic for the authorities, and in 1853 he was deprived of his appointment. His influence, however, continued, and most modern theology is in some way indebted to Maurice's clear and courageous thinking.[1]

For there were big battles ahead. Lyell's *Principles of Geology* in 1830 had begun to cast doubt upon the inerrancy of the Biblical story of creation. Then came the results of the work of German critics who were pulling the Bible to pieces. Men began to feel that the ground was shifting beneath their feet. Old landmarks were beginning to disappear, old certainties to be assailed. It was not the enemy from without who was the most formidable, it was the enemy working within the faith. 'I cannot but think', said Blomfield in 1850, 'that we have more to apprehend from the theology of Germany than from that of Rome.'[2]

The third problem with which the Church was faced was that of the great cities and the Church's responsibility for the appalling conditions in which so many of her children lived. The Evangelicals were essentially practical and philanthropic. They believed in Societies and Acts of Parliament, and did their best to bring relief to those suffering from poverty and injustice. The Tractarians approached the problem from a different angle. They were more theological and eschatological. Their answer to the problem was the Church—good priests

---

[1] See F. Maurice, *Life of F. D. Maurice*, 2 vols. (1884); C. F. G. Masterman, *F. D. Maurice* (1907); H. G. Wood, *Frederick Denison Maurice* (1950); A. M. Ramsey, *F. D. Maurice and the Conflicts of Theology* (1951).
[2] C. J. Blomfield, *A Charge to the Clergy of London, 1850*, p. 58.

working in slum parishes to bring new hope to the oppressed. Meanwhile a small group of thinkers under the leadership of Maurice was evolving a new method. In 1837 Maurice published his book *The Kingdom of Christ, or Letters to a Quaker concerning the Principles, Conceptions and Ordinances of the Catholic Church*. Christ, he said, came to establish not a religious sect or a new society but a kingdom. It was his will that this kingdom should embrace all men, and that the whole world should be brought under the rule of Christ. In such a kingdom there could be no class-distinctions, no rich and poor, no oppressor and oppressed. It envisaged a world in which the law of Christ governed all men. This book was the foundation-stone of what came to be called 'Christian Socialism'.

Maurice was assisted in his work by J. M. Ludlow (1821–1911), a lawyer who had lived in France and studied the French revolutionary movements, and by Charles Kingsley (1819–75) a country parson who did much to popularize the ideas of the new movement by novels such as *Yeast* (1848) and *Alton Locke* (1850).[1] These three, with other helpers, plunged into the radical politics of the day. They held meetings with Chartist workmen, played an active part in the Trade Union movement, founded a Society for Promoting Working Men's Associations, interested themselves in legislation, education and sanitation. They preached many sermons, and published a series of 'tracts for the times' to explain the religious significance of the revolutionary movements which were taking place and to declare the message of the Christian Church in the hour of crisis. *Politics for the People, Tracts on Christian Socialism, The Christian Socialist* were the titles of some of these pamphlets.

Naturally the movement was very much criticized by Tory churchmen. To them the idea of a 'Christian Socialist' was a contradiction in terms. But Maurice was thrilled with his task and with the name which they had chosen; 'it will commit us at once', he said, 'to the conflict we must engage in sooner or later with the unsocial Christians and the un-Christian Socialists'. So the work of christianizing the Socialists and socializing Christianity went on, bringing a new language and a new outlook into theology and discussion. The fact that the revolutions in England have, on the whole, gone so smoothly is partly due to the courageous work of the early Christian Socialists.

[1] See *Charles Kingsley: Letters and Memories of his Life*, ed. by his wife, 2 vols. (1891).

v. *Diocese and Parish*

By 1850 big changes were taking place in diocese and parish. In the towns there was much greater vigour and zeal, and even in the country strenuous efforts were being made to revive the life of the Church after the quiescence of the Georgian era. But there were still large masses of the population who were mostly uninterested in what the Churches were trying to do for them. Many of these were in the big cities which were now growing so rapidly and where living conditions for the poor were so bad. It is often said that the Church at some time lost the support of the working classes, but the fact is that it never had it. The census of 1851 revealed the fact that about 21 per cent of the whole population of England and Wales attended Anglican churches, that 8.7 per cent were Methodists and 1.7 per cent Roman Catholics. The writer of the report complained bitterly of the indifference of the 'labouring myriads'. Secularism, he said, was the creed of masses of skilled and unskilled labourers, of 'hosts of minor shopkeepers and Sunday traders, and of the miserable denizens of courts and crowded alleys'.

Some of the bishops were concerned about this, but not all. There were still a few prelates of the old school who regarded a bishopric as the natural reward for political work and were content with the kind of standards which they had inherited from the past. Among such was George Murray, grandson of a Duke of Atholl, Bishop of Rochester 1827–60 and the last bishop to wear a wig in the House of Lords. William Howley (London 1813–28, Canterbury 1828–48) allowed himself to be enthroned by proxy, but kept up considerable estate at Lambeth, where he was said to cross the courtyard of the palace from the chapel to Mrs. Howley's lodgings preceded by men bearing torches.[1] There were others of this kind; but the race was fast dying out. The work of the Ecclesiastical Commissioners took away some of the attractions of preferment.

Meanwhile there was growing up a new type of bishop of whom the most notable examples are Blomfield, Stanley and Wilberforce. C. J. Blomfield (1786–1857) was the son of a schoolmaster at Bury St. Edmund's. From an early age he devoted himself to Church re-

---

[1] Ollard, Crosse and Bond, *Dictionary of English Church History* (1948), p. 297.

form and soon became well known. In 1824 he was made Bishop of Chester, a diocese which in those days included the whole of Lancashire as well as Cheshire. Blomfield found much in need of reform. Vast cities were springing into being with far too few churches and schools. In the country districts many of the clergy had little sense of their high calling and spent much of their time in drinking and hunting. Blomfield, with indefatigable energy, set himself to visit and reform the whole of his vast diocese. In 1828 he was translated to London, where immense problems faced him. Again there was a rapidly increasing population and a great shortage of churches. Many of the London churches were held by men who had little conception of pastoral responsibility and no desire for reform. Blomfield came among them like a tornado. According to Sydney Smith, he suffered from 'an ungovernable passion for business' and he never spared himself in working for reform in both Church and State. During his time, nearly 200 new churches were dedicated in London, besides many schools. During those twenty-eight critical years Blomfield's tenure of the see of London was of supreme importance. His liberal outlook, his love of justice, his courage and independence, his complete dedication of himself to his work set an example from which the Church as a whole drew great inspiration.[1]

Edward Stanley (1779-1849) was instituted to the family living of Alderley in Cheshire in 1805 at the age of 26. He immediately showed himself to be an excellent priest, devoting himself for the next thirty-two years to his parish. In 1837 he was appointed Bishop of Norwich, a diocese which had a bad reputation for laxity and irregularity. Stanley did much to restore the life of the Church in East Anglia. He had no great industrial areas to administer, but a very large number of country parishes served often by clergy with very low standards of behaviour. The bishop instituted rural deans, with whose help he kept in close touch with his clergy. He did much to restore parsonages and build schools. He supported the societies which were working to improve the morals of the villagers. He took great care over the examination of ordinands and greatly increased the number of confirmations.[2]

Samuel Wilberforce (1805-73) was a son of William Wilberforce. He was therefore brought up an old-fashioned Evangelical, but at Oriel he came under the influence of the Tractarians. At the age of

---

[1] See A. Blomfield, *A Memoir of C. J. Blomfield*, 2 vols. (1863).
[2] See A. P. Stanley, *Memoirs of Edward and Catherine Stanley* (1879).

40 he became Bishop of Oxford, being translated to Winchester twenty-four years later. Wilberforce has been called 'the remodeller of the episcopate'.[1] He was filled with energy and devotion beyond that of most men. Nothing was too small to engage his attention. He went everywhere and saw everything. Under his leadership not only did the two dioceses of Oxford and Winchester receive great inspiration, but the whole conception of the work of a bishop underwent a change. Modern bishops, in danger of being overwhelmed by administrative detail, may have little cause to bless Bishop Wilberforce; but, in an age which had for too long been content with easy-going standards, some such example was needed. Among the many good works which Wilberforce supported were the introduction of parochial missions, the establishment of religious communities, and the foundation of the theological college at Cuddesdon.[2]

Besides these outstanding men there were many other devoted and hard-working bishops. There were also many parish priests who were busy transforming the parochial life of the country. The greatest of these was W. F. Hook (1798–1875) who became Vicar of Leeds in 1837. At this time Leeds, in the centre of the woollen industry, was growing rapidly; but Church life was at a low ebb. Hook was a friend of the Tractarians and, as such, suspect before he set foot in Leeds. He found the parish bitterly divided, largely controlled by dissenting churchwardens who were elected only to keep down church rates and oppose any changes in worship. Into this quarrelsome and hard-headed community Hook arrived with lofty ideas of what the Church should be and of how worship should be conducted. The story of the next twenty-two years is the story of how he gradually overcame opposition and won the respect and even the love of his parishioners. 'I do not oppose Dissenters by disputations and wrangling', he said, 'but I seek to exhibit to the world the Church in her beauty. Let the services of the Church be properly performed and right-minded people will soon learn to love her.'[3] He rebuilt the parish church and introduced a surpliced choir and full cathedral services. He worked incredibly hard; took an interest in all that went on in the city; preached five times a week; supported and advised the clergy throughout the city; conducted a vast correspondence, and yet found time for literary and historical work.

---

[1] J. W. Burgon, *Lives of Twelve Good Men*, chap. v.

[2] A. R. Ashwell and R. G. Wilberforce, *The Life of Samuel Wilberforce*, 3 vols. (1880).

[3] W. R. W. Stephens, *Life of W. F. Hook* (1878), i, p. 405.

There were few of Hook's calibre; but up and down the country were a number of interesting men bringing new ideas into parish life. Among the Evangelicals there was William Champneys who became Vicar of Whitechapel in the same year that Hook went to Leeds. Champneys found himself in a parish of 33,000 people, many of them among the poorest in the country. He devoted himself to their well-being. He opened the first Ragged School in London; he founded a Provident Society, a shoe-blacks' brigade, a refuge and industrial school for boys, and many other organizations, in all of which his strong evangelical faith was preached. Meanwhile, among the High Churchmen there were many who were prepared to work for very little money, in the most unhealthy areas, and often against fierce opposition, in order to teach the catholic faith and win men for the Church. Bryan King at S. George's in the East, and Alexander Mackonochie at S. Alban's, Holborn, were among many of this type.

Of quite a different type was F. W. Robertson (1816–53) who, after an undistinguished career, was appointed in 1847 as incumbent of Trinity Chapel, Brighton, which, by his preaching, he soon made one of the most famous churches in the country. Robertson was not a party man. He thought out his message and delivered it lucidly and fearlessly to his crowded congregations. After his early death at the age of 37 five volumes of his sermons were printed. Many of them are among the classics of English pulpit oratory.[1]

Of yet another type was that remarkable but eccentric Cornish priest, R. S. Hawker of Morwenstow. Hawker was neither High, Broad nor Low Church.[2] His interests were with the Eastern Church which he held to be the mother of Cornish Christianity. For many years he devoted himself to his little parish, full of smugglers, wreckers and poachers. His church was full of activity and colour. He wore a cope, alb and scarlet gloves both at Mattins and the Eucharist (believing this to be in accordance with Eastern customs);[3] he introduced the custom of Harvest Thanksgivings; he revived synods for his rural deanery. He studied Cornish customs and lore, and wrote a considerable amount of poetry. For forty-one years, from 1834 to 1875, he devoted himself to his church and his parish, a strange, whimsical creature on the rock-bound Cornish coast.

---

[1] See Stopford A. Brooke, *Life and Letters of F. W. Robertson* (1865).

[2] He had no faith in Conversion, which he called 'a spasm of the ganglions' (S. Baring-Gould, *R. S. Hawker* (1876), p. 190).

[3] His dress was always very eccentric. On the day of his wedding in London he wore a claret-coloured clerical coat, a blue fisherman's jersey, wading-boots up to the hips and a pink hat without a brim.

NOTE ON BOOKS

FOR the general church history of this period see F. Warre Cornish, *A History of the English Church in the Nineteenth Century*, 2 vols. (1910), S. C. Carpenter, *Church and People: 1789–1889* (1933), and O. Chadwick, *The Victorian Church*, vol. i (1966). The literature on the Oxford Movement is very large, but the following are the most important: R. W. Church, *The Oxford Movement* (1891), Y. Brilioth, *The Anglican Revival* (1925), Christopher Dawson, *The Spirit of the Oxford Movement* (1933), C. C. J. Webb, *Religious Thought in the Oxford Movement* (1928) and, of course, J. H. Newman's autobiography, *Apologia pro Vita sua* (new ed. 1892). See also D. Newsome, *The Parting of Friends* (1966). For the reformers see W. L. Mathieson, *English Church Reform, 1815–1840* (1923) and C. E. Raven, *Christian Socialism, 1848–54* (1920).

CHAPTER XX

THE MID-VICTORIANS
(1854–1882)

i. Changes in Church Life

'IT is not only in Barchester', said Mr. Slope, 'that a new man is carrying out new measures and carting away the useless rubbish of centuries. The same thing is going on throughout the country. Work is now required from every man who receives wages; and they who have to superintend the doing of the work, and the paying of wages, are bound to see that this rule is carried out. New men, Mr. Harding, are now needed, and are now forthcoming in the church, as well as in other professions.'[1] Mr. Slope was right. The mid-Victorian era saw a great revival of church life. It has been justly called 'the period of Self-consciousness'.[2] Under tractarian and evangelical influence the Church was becoming far more conscious of its nature and of its responsibilities. Clergy became more active and efficient; parochial work was better planned and organized; new societies, guilds, fellowships and associations were formed.[3]

Perhaps the most noticeable changes were those in the appearance of the churches and in the nature of the worship conducted within them. A new word had been coined—'Ecclesiology', the science of church-building and decoration—and most churches were in some way altered to bring them into line with the new movement. Naturally the High Church party were most active in this. Teaching about the importance of the Eucharist and the Real Presence led to attempts to beautify the sanctuaries and surround the altar with works of art. Much attention was given to symbolism and to the production of what was called 'sacramentality'. There was a vast output of ecclesiastical furniture such as choir stalls, litany desks, and lecterns. Windows were filled with highly coloured glass; walls were covered with

---

[1] Anthony Trollope, *Barchester Towers* (1857), chap. xii.
[2] Addleshaw and Etchells, *The Architectural Setting of Anglican Worship* (1948), p. 203.
[3] The change is noticeable in the works of Dickens. In the earlier novels the Church obviously counts for very little; but, in the later, clergy of real character appear such as Mr. Milvey in *Our Mutual Friend* (1864) and Mr. Crisparkle in *Edwin Drood* (1870).

stencilled designs; ornaments appeared on all sides; acres of damask and embroidery, and tons of brass and marble were carried into the churches; new floors were put down, steps were raised, old woodwork was destroyed. Scarcely a church in England escaped the attention of the Victorian 'reformers'.

With the changes in the appearance of the churches came changes in the conduct of worship. A new party appeared, 'the Ritualists', who caused much distress by introducing vestments and customs which most people thought had gone for ever at the Reformation. It was not long before priests began to appear in chasubles or copes, to introduce into the services such things as tapers and incense, and even to hold services which they took straight from the Roman books of devotion. Not many churches went as far as this; but in quite moderate parishes crosses and candles were introduced, while chancels were filled with surpliced choirs who began singing the services in a much more elaborate way. Dr. Hook led the way with the choir at Leeds Parish Church in 1841. 'My whole heart', he said, 'is set on this business; I mean to give any money for singers, and then I shall go and beg and preach.'[1] Other churches followed the lead, so that in time the surpliced choir, which at first was regarded as an outrage, became the normal thing in even the smallest churches.

To assist such choirs much attention was being paid to church music. The Oxford Movement had revived an interest in Latin and Greek hymns and various translations were published, including E. Caswell's *Lyra Catholica* (1849) and J. M. Neale's *Hymnal Noted* (1852–4) and *Hymns of the Eastern Church* (1862). Others, like Miss Catherine Winkworth, were enriching English hymnody by translations from the German. Many of the Tractarians had written hymns, especially Keble, Newman and F. W. Faber. H. F. Lyte contributed a number of hymns of which a few, such as 'Abide with me' became extremely popular. Mrs. Alexander's *Hymns for Little Children* (1848) showed real genius in the art of the simple hymn full of sound doctrine.[2] For the accompaniment of these hymns, good tunes were being composed by such men as W. Crotch and Sir John Goss.

With the production of vast numbers of hymns—both original poems and translations—there was, by the middle of the century, a

---

[1] W. R. W. Stephens, *Life of W. F. Hook*, ii, p. 124. An earlier attempt to introduce a paid choir into Leeds Parish Church had been a failure.

[2] *E.g.* 'Once in royal David's city' and 'There is a green hill far away'.

bewildering supply of material. In 1857 a small meeting of experts was called together and a committee formed to consider the production of a really good hymn-book. As a result of their deliberations a small volume of 138 hymns was put out in 1859. In the following year this was enlarged to 273 hymns and the volume published with the title of *Hymns Ancient and Modern*. In 1861 a musical edition was published, and in 1868 the number of hymns was raised to 386. The book soon proved popular, and remained for many years the most widely used hymn-book in the country.[1]

With the changes both in the appearance of the churches and in the worship went also new ideas of the priest and his work. The Rev. E. Monroe, writing a handbook for the clergy of this period, said: 'the clergyman's is a life, not a profession . . . a clergyman must live only for his people'.[2] He then goes on to plead for greater devotion to duty by systematic and unflagging visiting, for daily prayers in church at 5 A.M. if necessary, for a weekly Eucharist, for the observance of Lent and Advent, and for more ceremonial. J. H. Blunt in his *Directorium Pastorale* (1864) defends, at some length, the practice of sacramental confession. This was now beginning to be widely used in some town churches, though in the teeth of much opposition. In 1858 Alfred Poole, the curate of S. Barnabas, Pimlico, was deprived of his curacy by Bishop Tait for refusing to give up the practice of hearing confessions. There was much misunderstanding. Blomfield, in 1842, had described 'auricular confession' as 'the source of unspeakable abominations'.[3] Some of the clergy, however, claimed (and with some justice) that the Book of Common Prayer clearly envisages the practice of confessions being heard in certain cases and invests the priest with the right to pronounce, or withhold, absolution. The custom, therefore, grew in spite of opposition; and in 1877 a handbook for confessors, called *The Priest in Absolution*, was privately printed and widely circulated. Some years before this a book called *The Priest's Prayer Book, with a Brief Pontifical* had been published containing the Hour Services, Prayers while vesting, *Secreta* for use in the Holy Communion, and offices for the blessing of candles, ashes and palms, for washing the altar, and for the consecration of holy oil. The popularity of this book shows how widespread was the

---

[1] See the essay by W. H. Frere in *Hymns Ancient and Modern, Historical Edition* (1909).   [2] E. Monroe, *Parochial Work* (2nd. ed. 1851).

[3] C. J. Blomfield, *A Charge to the Clergy of London, 1842*, p. 57.

demand for forms of service which a previous generation would have shuddered at.

The ritualistic movement arose out of the theology of the Tractarians who had laid much emphasis on the Eucharist and on the doctrine of the Real Presence. This inevitably led to a desire not only for more frequent celebrations of the Holy Communion but also to the wish to surround the altar with all that was bright and glorious, and to conduct the service with greater ceremonial. This was not the habit of the early Tractarians. They provided the theology, but were uninterested in externals. 'Do tell us what a cope is', said Pusey, when the subject of vestments was being discussed. But when the Oxford Movement spread out from the University and began to make itself felt in the slum parishes of the great cities, then began the introduction of ceremonial and church ornaments which led to endless strife and misunderstanding.

The innovators began modestly enough, their early ventures going no further than intoning prayers, wearing the surplice instead of a black gown in the pulpit, adopting the eastward position and placing lighted candles on the altar. In 1850 J. M. Neale began to wear the eucharistic vestments, and the custom was introduced at S. George's mission in London in 1857. By this time much opposition had been aroused. Most of the bishops strongly objected to such innovations and they found plenty of support among the laity in all classes of society. Yet it was difficult to take any legal action against the ritualists since they claimed that they were merely carrying out the directions demanded by the Ornaments Rubric. Vestments, they argued, far from being illegal were, in fact, the only legal form of dress at the Holy Communion; and the same applied to the eastward position. But the agitators were not satisfied with this; and, in default of legal redress, stirred up gangs of ruffians to break up services in the ritualistic churches and to destroy their ornaments. Such action merely encouraged the High Church party to go further. Incense now began to be used, confessional-boxes were erected, holy water was sprinkled on the congregation, the Stations of the Cross were hung on the walls, and altars became increasingly 'Roman' in appearance. In much of this they were tactless and hasty.

In 1854 legal action against the ritualists began in earnest when Liddell, the Vicar of S. Paul's Knightsbridge, was accused of introducing into his church various ornaments, such as an altar cross and a credence table, for which he had no legal authority. When the case went against him he appealed to the Privy Council who declared that crosses were lawful so long as they were not put on the Holy Table, and allowed the use of a credence table. As an *obiter dictum* they said that eucharistic vestments must be regarded as legal. This was a great encouragement to the ritualists; but two years later they had to face a formidable antagonist in A. C. Tait, who became Bishop of London in that year.

In 1860 those who were fighting for the Ornaments Rubric and for reform in worship banded themselves together in a society which they called the English Church Union. Five years later an opposition body, the Church Association, was formed with the avowed object of fighting ritualism by means of legal action. The bishops were very much divided. A debate on vestments in the Convocation of Canterbury in 1866 led to much argument but little agreement. Lord Shaftesbury, as a strict Evangelical, was appalled at what he regarded as breaches of the law, and introduced various bills into Parliament to put an end to them. All of these failed because wiser men realized that this was a question which could not be solved by legislation. But in default of legislation the Church Association fell back on the weapon of prosecution.

In 1867 a Mr. Martin brought an action against the Rev. A. H. Mackonochie, the Vicar of S. Alban's, Holborn. Mackonochie was an advanced and uncompromising ritualist; but he was also a saint, entirely given to his people whom he loved and served with peculiar devotion. He was accused of a number of illegal practices including the elevation of the Host, and the use of lighted candles, incense and the mixed chalice. The judgment of the Court of Arches was that candles and the mixed chalice could not be regarded as illegal, but this was reversed on an appeal being made to the Privy Council. As a result, Mackonochie was suspended for three months, a spiritual penalty being thus inflicted by a secular court.[1] In 1869 a somewhat similar case was brought against John Purchas, perpetual curate of S. James's, Brighton.

The whole issue was now becoming so confused, and such vast sums were being spent in litigation, that, in 1867, a Ritual

---

[1] See E. F. Russell (ed.), *A. H. Mackonochie* (1890) for a full account.

Commission was appointed to go into the whole matter. As a result of their deliberations a *Public Worship Regulation Act* was passed in 1874. It dealt almost entirely with procedure and did not attempt to solve the almost insoluble problem of what was legal and what was not. But, as a result of this Act, further pressure was brought to bear on the recalcitrant clergy, some of whom actually found themselves being sent to prison for contempt of court.

Meanwhile, outside the parochial system, a rebirth of the Religious Orders was taking place. As early as 1839 Pusey had pleaded for the institution of Sisters of Charity to work among the poor. Hook, as a parish priest, was consulted; but he was doubtful whether they would do much good in Leeds. He thought he would get on better with 'an elderly matron' and some other good women. Pusey, however, was much interested in the revival of the religious life, and had the satisfaction of receiving the vows of a Miss Hughes and of his own daughter Lucy in 1841. In 1845 two women started a community in London 'for the relief of distress wherever it may be found', and in 1848 Miss Sellon founded a house for Sisters of Mercy at Plymouth. These devoted women set up a school for sailor-boys, a home for old seamen, an industrial school, a cheap lodging-house, a ragged school, a home for destitute children and a soup-kitchen. Pusey was spiritual director of the community which carried on with its noble and self-sacrificing work in the face of most ungenerous and ignorant criticism and abuse. Other women were beginning to take up the question of 'Penitentiary' or 'Rescue' work. In 1849 Mrs. Tennant founded at Clewer a House of Mercy where prostitutes could be housed and brought under Christian influence. In the same year the Community of S. Mary was started at Wantage, and in 1854 the Community of S. Margaret at East Grinstead. All of these met with much opposition, but the courageous work of sisters in the towns during the cholera epidemic of 1849 did much to commend them to the world.

Communities for men came later than those for women. Newman at Littlemore had gathered together a kind of small community, but no vows were taken. The pioneer in the revival of the religious life among men was J. L. Lyne who, under the name of Father Ignatius, started a Benedictine house in Suffolk in 1863 which he moved to Llanthony in Wales in 1870. Fr. Ignatius was a most saintly man, but the experiment was never a great success. Meanwhile, in 1866, R. M.

Benson, Vicar of Cowley, had founded the Society of S. John the Evangelist in his own parish; and, in the last part of the century, a number of new orders were founded—the Order of S. Paul in 1886; the Society of the Sacred Mission, which began in London in 1891 and later moved to Kelham; the Community of the Resurrection, which finally found its home at Mirfield, in 1892; and the Society of the Divine Compassion in 1894.

ii. *Education*

By the middle of the nineteenth century England was far behind many other countries in its educational facilities. The growth of population, especially in the great cities, had presented a new challenge; but so far little had been done to meet it. The rock on which all plans for educational advance foundered was that of the teaching of religion. For centuries education had been the monopoly of the Church, which had provided the schools and used them for the teaching of the Christian faith by means of the church catechism. But the voluntary schools could not cope with the vast numbers in the towns, and by 1850 it was reckoned that not more than one-third of the nation's children were receiving any kind of regular schooling. The State was now making an annual grant to the voluntary societies and demanding certain privileges in exchange; but as yet no attempt had been made to provide state schools independent of the churches. Meanwhile the religious bodies were making great efforts to raise enough money to build and run more schools; but they were finding the task beyond their means as society became more and more conscious of the need for universal elementary education. Sooner or later the State was bound to step in if the need was ever to be adequately met.

At this period it cost about thirty shillings a year to educate a child. Of this, about a third was paid by the Government, a third by the voluntary societies and a third by the parents. Many of the church schools were very well run, notably that organized by the Rev. R. Dawes at King's Somborne in Hampshire which had a very high reputation. Many, however, were very inadequate, depending much

upon the skill and enthusiasm of the local incumbent. In the towns
the schools were often overcrowded and understaffed.

The *Reform Act* of 1867 added another million voters to the
register, and people became more and more concerned about education since many of those now entitled to vote were illiterate and
ignorant. As Robert Lowe said, 'We must educate our masters'.
Consequently, in 1870, Mr. W. E. Forster introduced a bill, the purpose of which was to build enough schools for every child to have
a place. No attempt was made to interfere with the existing schools,
but only to fill in the gaps by a number of new schools which were
to be under the Board of Education and to be financed partly by fees,
partly by the Government and partly out of the rates. From now
onwards there were, therefore, two types of school—those 'provided' by the State and the 'non-provided' schools of which by far
the greatest number belonged to the Church of England, but a few
were in the hands of the nonconformists and the Roman Catholics.
In the non-provided schools teachers were appointed by a board of
managers, and the religious instruction continued to be that of the
Church to which the school belonged. Since this caused some distress
in single-school areas a 'conscience clause' was inserted, whereby no
child could be compelled to attend worship or to learn the catechism
in any school if the parents objected in writing. Later in the debate
the 'Cowper Temple clause' was added, abolishing all denominational teaching in provided schools.

There was some opposition to the bill. Many of the nonconformists thought that the bill gave too much power to the Church. They
wanted to abolish the 'dual system' in favour of a universal system
of elementary education with simple Christian teaching but exclud-
ing all denominational formulae. The country, however, was not yet
ready for that. The Church was in a strong position, with a large
number of schools, especially in the villages, and new ones constantly being built. The bill, therefore, went through Parliament, and
the new 'board schools' came into being. By 1882 it was reckoned
that there were about two million children in the voluntary schools
and one million in those belonging to the State. By this year the
school accommodation had become big enough to allow of a bill to
make attendance at school compulsory for all children between the
ages of five and ten. In 1891 elementary education was made free.[1]

[1] See J. W. Adamson, *English Education, 1789–1902* (1930).

The public schools and grammar schools continued to flourish during this period. The manufacturing class were making a good deal of money, and were anxious to give their children the best education possible. A number of new proprietory schools, therefore, came into being about this time—*e.g.* Radley in 1847, Wellington in 1853, and Clifton and Malvern in 1862. At most of these schools there was a strong church atmosphere. The headmaster was often in Holy Orders as were also several members of the staff. The chapel played an important part in the life of the school. Confirmation was administered almost as a matter of course, and many of the boys were taught to read the New Testament in Greek. Most of the grammar schools were also church foundations, with boards of governors in which the clerical element predominated. As a result of the Taunton Commission in 1864–67, such schools were thrown open to boys who were not Anglicans and a 'conscience clause' was adopted to ensure religious freedom.

For boys living in or near a town the grammar schools were invaluable, but there remained a section of society who were too far away from a good day-school and unable to afford the high fees of the public schools—£200 a year at Harrow, £130 at Rugby, and so on. It was largely to help this class that Nathaniel Woodard (1811–1891), curate-in-charge of New Shoreham in Sussex, opened a school there in 1847. At first it was a day-school, meeting in his own house. The fees were very low and the masters were paid very little. But the school achieved an immediate success, due very largely to the self-sacrificing work of the staff who were content to do their work for such slender rewards. Woodard, however, was not satisfied with a day-school. He had visions of a whole series of boarding-schools, graded according to the financial ability of the parents, but all designed to serve the children of the great 'middle class', by giving them a good education firmly based on church principles. In 1848 the school at Shoreham became a boarding-school and a second school was opened two years later at Hurstpierpoint. In 1857 the Shoreham school moved across the Adur to Lancing, and a third school was started at Shoreham but moved in 1870 to Ardingly. Woodard was a most successful organizer, and raised vast sums to build and endow his schools. As time went on, more schools were built in different parts of the country.

While big changes were taking place in the schools, the universities of Oxford and Cambridge continued to enforce religious tests demanding of all graduates subscription to the Thirty-nine Articles. This monopoly of the older universities was much resented by a growing section of the community, but little was done. A Royal Commission enquired into the state of the universities in 1850, and drew attention to various reforms which were needed; but it was not allowed to touch the question of religious tests. From 1862 onwards, several petitions for the abolition of the tests were presented, and several bills introduced into Parliament; but they all failed. Eventually, in 1871 Gladstone made it a government issue and carried a bill for abolishing all religious tests at Oxford, Cambridge and Durham. The act caused great distress to many old-fashioned university men; but many saw that it was inevitable. It meant the end of church monopoly in higher education, but it was the saving of the universities.

Meanwhile attempts were being made to bring the fruits of scholarship to the working classes. In 1848 the Christian Socialists, under Maurice's inspiration, started evening classes in London. All the teachers were unpaid, but many of them were the leading scholars of the day who willingly gave their services in this way. In 1854 Maurice became Principal of the Working Men's College in Red Lion Square, having been recently dismissed from his chair at King's College. Classes were held every evening at the College, Maurice lecturing on S. John, Ruskin on Art, J. S. Brewer on History, and other scholars on their various subjects. A number of lecturers from King's College were glad to be able to show their sympathy with Maurice by coming to help him in his self-sacrificing work.

Church teaching was also being disseminated by means of the press. The Record was founded as early as 1828 to publicize the views of the more extreme Evangelicals. It was often very outspoken and exercised considerable influence. In 1846 the older Tractarians founded the Guardian, and in 1863 some active members of the High Church party founded the Church Times. All of these were national newspapers with a wide circulation. Local church news now began to be circulated by means of the parish magazine which made its first appearance at Derby in 1859.[1] Church views could also be presented to people in fiction. Reference has already been made to Kingsley's

---

[1] L. E. Elliott-Binns, Religion in the Victorian Era (1936), p. 333.

novels written to support the Christian Socialists.[1] In the 1850's
Charlotte Yonge (1823–1901) was doing the same for the Tractarians. She was herself a child of the Oxford Movement and a close
personal friend of Keble. Most of her novels, from *The Heir of Red-
clyffe* (1853) onwards, were written to give a picture of a society
deeply influenced by tractarian teaching, and most of her profits were
devoted to the support of church work overseas.

In the more specialized sphere of educating men for the priesthood
several colleges came into existence in the middle of the nineteenth
century. Chichester had been founded in 1839 and Wells followed in
the next year. S. Aidan's, Birkenhead, came into existence in 1846,
Cuddesdon in 1854, Wycliffe Hall in 1877 and the two Cambridge
colleges of Ridley Hall and the Clergy Training School (afterwards
known as Westcott House) in 1880 and 1881. Apart from the theological colleges a number of men received their training from private
tutors. Of these the most famous were C. J. Vaughan (1816–97) who,
first as Vicar of Doncaster and later as Master of the Temple and
finally Dean of Llandaff, gathered together a number of students who
came to be known as 'Vaughan's doves'; and J. B. Lightfoot (1828–
1889), Bishop of Durham, who did the same at Auckland Castle. As
a result of the more careful training of men for ordination, whether
in the colleges or under the inspiration of such men as Vaughan and
Lightfoot, young men went to their parishes far better prepared and
with much higher standards, both devotional and practical, of the life
and work of a priest.

iii. *Religion and Science*

The years after the Oxford Movement were years of great confusion and alarm. Outside the Church the dominant philosophy was
that of the Utilitarians, led by Jeremy Bentham, John Stuart Mill and
George Grote, who were inclined to regard the Church as the source
of all evil and the chief obstacle in the way of progress. There was
thus a good deal of criticism of the Church, and a growing feeling
that religion was out of date and would have no place in the 'new
Jerusalem' of science and progress which lay just round the corner.

[1] See above, p. 356.

In the face of this, the Church clung to its sources of authority—the Evangelicals to the Bible, the Anglo-Catholics to the Church, and the Liberals to their belief in the wholeness and impregnability of truth.

Few churchmen, if any, doubted the inerrancy of the Bible. The Scriptures were the 'Word of God', and could not therefore contain statements which were not true. All religious people accepted as true the accounts of Creation, or the story of the Flood, or the ages of the patriarchs. Many were far more intimate with the history of Israel than with the history of their own country, and felt as close to Abraham, Isaac, Jacob and a host of other characters as they did to their own friends and relatives. Moreover the Bible was thought to be equally true in all its details. It was just as much true that Creation took place in six days as it was that Christ was the Son of God, while to doubt that Joshua made the sun stand still was as bad as to doubt the truth of the Resurrection. On this all schools of thought agreed—High, Low and Broad.

But already events were beginning to take place which would shake this confidence in the infallibility of the Scriptures and lead to a very different approach to the Bible. Reference has already been made to the publication, in 1830, of Lyell's *Principles of Geology*,[1] which showed clearly from the study of the rocks that 'creation' was a much older and much slower process than would appear from the Bible narrative. Far from being completed in six days, the creation of the world as we know it was a process which covered many millions of years. In 1844 Lyell's work was carried further by Robert Chambers' book called *Vestiges of the Natural History of Creation*; but the greatest shock came in 1859 with the publication of Charles Darwin's *Origin of Species*. Darwin was a most humble man and an earnest seeker after truth, but his book caused the utmost consternation. Here was propounded a theory which completely abandoned the idea of the creation of separate species 'after their kind', and showed, from a mass of evidence collected from all parts of the world, that in fact 'species' had originated by natural selection, by adaptation to environment, and by gradual evolution. Twelve years later, in 1871, Darwin, in *The Descent of Man*, went even further, setting out with much cogency the theory that man, far from being 'made in the image of God', was only a highly developed species

[1] See above, p. 355.

of the anthropoid apes.

All this came as a fearful shock to the religious world. Not only did it cut across the Bible account of Creation, but it showed the workings of nature as a gradual and inevitable process of Evolution in which there was little room for the miraculous. As Newman said, the new scientific thought 'increased vastly the territory of the natural at the expense of the supernatural'.[1] Everything now seemed threatened; not only Creation and the Fall, but the Incarnation and even the Love of God. The world was not under the control of a God of love, but of relentless and cruel forces which gave survival to the fittest and allowed the weak to perish. Nature was 'red in tooth and claw' or, as a French philosopher remarked, 'Life is summed up in the conjugation of the verb *manger*, "Je mange, tu manges, il mange", or its terrible correlative, "Je suis mangé . . ."'. How could a God of Love design so hideous a universe in which everything preyed on its neighbour and only the strongest could survive?

Everywhere there was consternation and dismay. The clergy as a whole tended to panic. They saw the ground cut from under their feet. Not only their Bible-teaching, but their ideas of the universe as God's handiwork, and even their conception of the nature of God himself, needed a complete overhaul. Many misunderstood what Darwin and the scientists were trying to say, regarding them as the enemies of religion whereas in fact they were humble seekers after truth. Many rushed headlong into print or made wild statements which contributed nothing to the cause of understanding, even so experienced a man as Disraeli saying to the Oxford Diocesan Society in 1864: 'The question is this—Is man an ape or an angel? My lord, I am on the side of the angels', a remark which was greeted with tumultuous applause. Only a few theologians kept their heads, among them F. J. A. Hort who, as a trained scientist, thought Darwin unanswerable, and Charles Kingsley, who thought all ordinands should read some science.

The low ebb to which theology had sunk made a cleavage inevitable between the old teaching and the new. Divisions quickly appeared between those who stood by the Bible and those who accepted the conclusions of the scientists. A few scientists were churchmen and believers—some, like Philip Gosse, trying to reconcile Genesis and

[1] J. H. Newman, *Apologia*, p. 335.

geology by saying that God created the world with the fossils already in the rocks[1]—but many of them were dogmatic and self-assured. Things were happening so rapidly, and the results of applied science were so obvious and so beneficial, that it is not surprising if the scientists began to think that they held the key to all the problems of life. Evolution, and its partner Progress, took possession of the field. Even morals were affected, for Herbert Spencer's *Data of Ethics* (1879) suggested that standards of right and wrong might be regarded as evolutionary rather than as absolute and imperative.

Faced with so much doubt and opposition, the orthodox believers stood firmly behind their Bibles, only to discover that an attack was being launched against them, not from the front but from the rear, not by scientific 'agnostics' but by the theologians themselves. Much attention was now being paid to the study of archaeology and to the historicity not so much of the *Book of Genesis* but of the whole of the Old and New Testaments. As early as 1829 H. H. Milman (1791–1868) had caused some distress by his *History of the Jews*, which treated them as any other eastern tribe and referred to Abraham as 'an Arab sheikh'. Meanwhile in Germany and elsewhere, similar enquiries were being made into the life of Christ. In 1835 Strauss published his *Leben Jesu*, which was translated into English by George Eliot in 1846. This book glossed over the miracles of the Virgin Birth, Resurrection and Ascension of Christ, declaring that, though they were of eternal significance they need not be regarded as historically true. Strauss's work never had a very wide circulation in England; but Renan's sentimental *Vie de Jésus* (1863) and J. R. Seeley's *Ecce Homo* (1865) both laid much emphasis on the humanity of Christ, and regarded the miraculous elements in the Gospel story as of little importance.

Meanwhile the critics were at work on the text of the Bible, and were beginning to cast doubts on the generally accepted views of the authorship of the Pentateuch and of many of the Epistles, and on the dates of the Gospels. The centre of this work was in Germany, especially at Tübingen; but there were many scholars in England who were closely following what was being done abroad and found themselves much in agreement with many of the theories now being propounded. In order to present their views to the public a group of seven Oxford scholars of liberal outlook banded together to produce

[1] P. H. Gosse, *Omphalos, an attempt to untie the geological knot* (1857).

a book called *Essays and Reviews* in 1860, the year after Darwin's *Origin of Species*. The book came as a bombshell. Six of the writers were clergymen, one was head of a college, two were professors and one was a headmaster. By far the most startling essay was that by Benjamin Jowett, 'On the Interpretation of Scripture', in which he urged people 'to read Scripture like any other book'.[1] Phrases such as this struck terror into the hearts of the orthodox. Here was a man holding office as an ordained clergyman of the Church of England who yet appeared to be attacking the very foundations of the Christian faith.

As soon as *Essays and Reviews* had been read and digested, the bishops met at Fulham and drew up a letter expressing their disapproval, while Convocation pressed for synodical action against the writers. This was not done; but several bishops took up the matter and instituted legal proceedings against the writers, Rowland Williams being condemned by the Court of Arches for heresy. A protest against the book was signed by 11,000 clergy and 137,000 laity, and Samuel Wilberforce continued to press for censure, until, in 1864, after debates in both houses of Convocation, the book was solemnly condemned. Yet it has been calculated that 'four fifths of the actual contents of the book has since been digested into the system of the Church'.[2]

Much of the indignation aroused by *Essays and Reviews* was due to the fact that the writers were mainly clergymen bound by their ordination vows and the Thirty-nine Articles. Much greater dismay was therefore created when even more radical views were found to be held and propagated by no less a person than a bishop. In 1853 the diocese of Natal in South Africa had been created, and J. W. Colenso (1814–83), a well-known Cambridge mathematician, had been appointed as its first bishop. Colenso published a *Commentary on Romans* in 1861, and followed it up by an *Introduction to the Pentateuch and the Book of Joshua* in 1862. In this he devoted much space to elaborate mathematical calculations, measurements and statistics which drove him to the conclusion that many statements in the early books of the Old Testament could not be regarded as historically accurate. This led him on to further and more general statements, such as: 'The Bible itself is not God's word; but assuredly God's word will be heard in the Bible', or 'The ordinary knowledge of Christ was no-

[1] *Essays and Reviews* (1860), p. 338.
[2] S. C. Carpenter, *Church and People, 1789–1889* (1933), p. 508.

thing more than that of any educated Jew of his age'. Statements of this kind caused great distress, and Colenso was censured by the English bishops and deposed and afterwards excommunicated by the Bishop of Cape Town in 1866. But owing to legal difficulties much confusion resulted, and Colenso was regarded by many as rightful Bishop of Natal even after the appointment of his successor in 1869. He died in 1883.[1]

With bishops and professors of divinity going over into the camp of those who were regarded as the enemies of the faith, it was no wonder that the ordinary layman was perplexed. Many found their faith sorely tried; and some, like Matthew Arnold, gave up orthodox Christianity as 'a fond but beautiful dream'. Others began to take up some strange cult such as Theosophy, Spiritualism or Christian Science.

The men who did most to hold things together at a time of great confusion and difficulty were the Cambridge scholars—Lightfoot, Westcott and Hort. They were big enough scholars to have no fear of a scientific study of the Bible, especially of the text of the New Testament. They were also strong churchmen and excellent historians as well as theologians. It was these men who brought the study of the Bible on to a new level—devout, reverent and fearless. Calmly accepting what was indisputable of the conclusions of the archaeologists and biblical critics, they guided scholarship into new channels and did much towards bridging the gulf between science and religion and between faith and criticism.

iv. *The Church and Social Problems*

The year 1854 saw the end of the first phase of Christian Socialism. Maurice fell into considerable despair in the 1860's, living in the midst of 'a triumphant commercialism, surrounded by a new race of confident scientists and optimistic Positivists on the one hand, and a new class of prosperous capitalists and their ever less discontented because more secure employees on the other'.[2] There was some cause for national optimism. England at this time was at the height of her prosperity; large fortunes were being made; and few were aware that much of this prosperity was due to sweated labour and terrible factory

---

[1] See G. W. Cox, *Life of J. W. Colenso*, 2 vols. (1888)
[2] M. Reckitt, *Maurice to Temple* (1947), p. 96.

conditions.

The Church as a whole joined in the prosperity. Many clergy belonged to the families of industrialists and had considerable private incomes to supplement their stipends. Even those who had to depend entirely upon their benefices were probably a good deal better off than they thought or than their successors are today.[1] The Church also had reason to be optimistic. It counted for a good deal in the social and political life of the day. Congregations were generally good, and there was much interest in religion and desire for Christian civilization in spite of what the Utilitarians and Darwinians were saying.

Meanwhile there remained in the cities the vast crowds, most of whom lived and worked under shocking conditions. There were various ways in which the Church attempted to do something to alleviate their distress. There was, first, the way of Lord Shaftesbury and the reformers, who, inspired by intense feelings for the sufferings of the poor, fought for better conditions by means of commissions, reports and bills of every kind—Lunacy Bills, Lodging House Bills, Chimney Sweep Bills, Sanitation Bills and many others.[2] Secondly, there was the way of those who went to live among the poor—the slum clergy and sisters, who made their homes in the darkest and dingiest areas in order to bring new hope and comfort into lives which were sordid and drab. C. F. Lowder at S. George's-in-the-East,[3] and R. W. R. Dolling at Portsmouth[4] were among many who identified themselves with the poor and devoted themselves to their service. A slightly different experiment was that of Samuel Barnett, who went to Whitechapel in 1873 and there founded a settlement the object of which was to bring culture to the east end and show one half of London how the other half lived.[5] The third way was that of moral reform. The dreary surroundings of slum streets tempted people to find relief in drink or vice, while the gin-shops provided opportunities to get 'drunk for a penny: dead drunk for two-pence'.

[1] See the interesting note 'A Family Budget: the Crawleys of Hogglestock', in W. K. L. Clarke, *Eighteenth Century Piety* (1944), pp. 156-8.

[2] See J. L. and Barbara Hammond, *Lord Shaftesbury* (1923).

[3] See C. F. Lowder, *Twenty-one Years in S. George's Mission* (1877), and M. Trench, *Charles Lowder* (1881).

[4] See R. W. R. Dolling, *Ten Years in a Portsmouth Slum* (1896), and C. E. Osborne, *Life of Dolling* (1903).

[5] See Mrs. Barnett, *Canon Barnett, his Life and Letters*, 2 vols. (1918).

Drink, which had been the besetting sin of the gentry in the eighteenth century, was now the besetting sin of the poor, and the Church joined in the cause of 'temperance' by means of the Band of Hope (1847) and the Church of England Total Abstinence Society (1862). Nor did it shrink from tackling the even more difficult problem of vice. The first 'Moral Welfare' work was done by the sisterhoods at Clewer and Wantage and by the Church Penitentiary Association (1852); but the outstanding figure of the movement was that of Josephine Butler (1828-1906) who began her gallant work in Liverpool in 1866 and continued it for forty years in the face of the utmost opposition and misunderstanding.[1] It was to help young men to keep up a high moral standard that a small group of drapers' apprentices in London in 1844 founded a society which they called the Young Men's Christian Association and which spread rapidly and became, in due course, a world-wide institution.

While various groups and individuals were thus engaged in 'ambulance work', trying to succour and help those who suffered from a social system which was in many ways selfish and cruel, the Christian Socialists were working on the system itself and were interested not so much in the results of poverty as in the causes of it. The Church Congress of 1873 devoted much time to a discussion of the Church's attitude towards strikes and labour, and was told that 'a strike may be perfectly legitimate' and asked 'Can we conceive of S. James or S. Paul taking the side of the upper classes against the lower?'[2] This kind of talk was symptomatic of a new feeling, a feeling which was vividly expressed in the episcopate of James Fraser at Manchester (1870-85). Fraser has been described as 'the Citizen-Bishop, the lawn-sleeved citizen, the prince and leader in every movement of civic progress, civic elevation, civic righteousness'.[3] He was so much trusted by all classes that in 1874, in a dispute between the master-painters and their men, he was invited to act as arbiter, and his decision was accepted. Fraser's zeal for justice and righteousness so inspired the hearts of the Lancashire people that, after his death, a statue was erected to his memory, by public subscription, in the middle of Manchester.

[1] See G. W. and L. A. Johnson, *Josephine Butler: an Autobiographical Memoir* (1911).
[2] *Report of Church Congress*, 1873, pp. 30, 31.
[3] J. W. Diggle, *The Lancashire Life of Bishop Fraser* (1889), p. 22. See also T. Hughes, *James Fraser, Second Bishop of Manchester* (1887).

Meanwhile there was, among the clergy, a more revolutionary party which identified itself with the depressed classes and adopted both the phraseology and the tactics of the more radical Socialists. In this party were found men like Thomas Hancock and Stewart Headlam. Hancock loved to describe the *Magnificat* as 'the Hymn of the Social Revolution' and published sermons with startling titles such as 'The Banner of Christ in the hands of the Socialists'. Headlam, a born rebel, became curate of Bethnal Green in 1877 and founded there the Guild of S. Matthew with the purpose of 'justifying God to the people'. He identified Christianity with Socialism, and threw himself with such zest into every movement for better social conditions that he did not shrink from violence if no other way could be found. Thus, while 'ambulance work' of various kinds was going on, there were also some who were trying to get to the very root of the social *malaise* and find some means for its cure.

v. *Legislation and Organization*

During the middle years of Victoria's reign Parliament was obliged to devote a good deal of time to ecclesiastical affairs. Changes were taking place rapidly, and the Church was constantly being faced with new problems which it was powerless to solve. The fact of the Establishment gave considerable authority to Parliament, which was very much aware of its rights and duties as the guardian of the Church. By far the majority of Members were churchmen, and, as such, interested in ecclesiastical politics and problems. So was the queen, who played a considerable part in the affairs of the Church, especially in the matter of appointments.

One of the subjects to which Parliament devoted much attention was that of Church Discipline. The decay of episcopal authority, and the growth of liturgical and other kinds of lawlessness, presented serious disciplinary problems. The first attempt to deal with these was in the *Church Discipline Act* of 1840. This Act instituted legal tests of orthodoxy and obliged all clergy to 'assent and consent' to the Book of Common Prayer and to subscribe to the Thirty-nine Articles of Religion. From now onwards clergy could be brought into court for teaching doctrine not in accordance with the accepted formulas of the Church. It also now became an offence if an incumbent failed to hold the necessary services in his church or used un-authorized ritual or ceremonial. On receiving a complaint the bishop might issue a commission to examine a defaulter who, as a result, could be sentenced to suspension or deprivation.

After this, various attempts were made by Lord Shaftesbury and others to introduce further legislation to control the growth of ritualism, but nothing came of them until the Royal Commission on Ritual was appointed in 1867. When the Commission had fin-ished its work a new bill was prepared and passed in 1874 as the *Public Worship Regulation Act*. The debates on the bill aroused much interest. The bill was introduced by Archbishop Tait, who spoke of the terrible expense of time and money in litigation which was ruin-ing the true spiritual work of the Church. He realized that Parliament could not go into much detail about the legality of every kind of innovation, but pleaded for a simple method of exercising discipline. The bill was opposed by Shaftesbury, who thought it gave too much power to the bishops; but it passed the House of Lords and was sent down to the Commons. Here the protestant cause was loudly cham-pioned by Sir William Harcourt, but Gladstone left his woods at Hawarden to make a special journey to Westminster where he paid a warm tribute to the Oxford Movement and spoke in favour of liberty and variety in public worship. In spite of this the bill passed. It deals with alterations or additions to the fabric or ornaments of a church and with failure to observe the directions of the Book of Common Prayer. Complaint might now be made by the archdeacon, the churchwardens or any three parishioners, but the bishop might veto proceedings if he considered the complaint frivolous. If action were taken, the clergyman was to be tried by a judge appointed for the Provincial Courts of Canterbury and York. Refusal to accept the decision of the judge now meant contempt of court which could be punished by imprisonment.

The third act was the *Clergy Discipline Act* of 1892 which dealt mainly with clergy guilty of certain crimes such as treason, felony, grave misdemeanour, adultery and immorality. It did not raise the question of ecclesiastical lawlessness.[1]

Every year ecclesiastical legislation came before Parliament, and a series of acts was passed dealing with many details of church life.

---

[1] For these three Acts see H. W. Cripps, *The Law relating to the Church and Clergy* (18th edition, ed. K. M. Macmorran, 1937), pp. 36–66.

There were Tithe Acts, Burial Acts, Church Building Acts, Marriage Acts, Benefices Acts, Bishoprics Acts, New Parishes Acts and many others. But while in England the questions were mainly financial, disciplinary or administrative, in Ireland the chief problem was that of the establishment of the Irish Church. The Irish Church, which was part of the Anglican communion, was naturally very unpopular in a country composed mainly of Roman Catholics. For some years a campaign for the disestablishment of the Irish Church had been carried on by Roman Catholics and Irish nationalists who felt it an anomaly that special privileges should be accorded to a Church which represented only a small minority of the people. Gladstone took up the cause of Irish Disestablishment in 1868, working at the problem with his usual energy and determination. His diary for this year has the following entry: 'Dec. 24. At night went to work on draft of Irish Church measure, feeling the impulse. Dec. 25. Christmas Day. Worked much on Irish Church *abozzo*. Finished it at night.'[1] Gladstone introduced his bill in March 1869 by which time he had become Prime Minister. The debate was both loud and long. Gladstone fought hard for disestablishment; but the queen, as a good protestant, was opposed to a measure which she thought would give more power to the Roman Catholics, and she made her wishes known. All kinds of political, national, racial and ecclesiastical prejudices and opinions were dragged into the dispute, but in the end the bill passed and the Irish Church was disestablished and disendowed though remaining in full communion with the Church of England. Burgon's description of this as 'the nation's formal rejection of God:'[2] would appear to need some justification, but it shows how strong opinions were at the time.[3]

With so many problems to be discussed, the Convocations, which had started again in the southern province in 1854 and in the northern in 1861, were kept busy. The situation, however, was not very satisfactory, partly because there were two separate and independent Convocations and partly because there was no representation of the laity. Bishop Wilberforce in 1869 tried to get the two Convocations

1 J. Morley, *Life of Gladstone* (1903), ii, p. 259.
2 Article on J. W. Burgon in *Dictionary of National Biography*.
3 See J. Morley, *Life of Gladstone*, ii, pp. 257-80; F. W. Cornish, *A History of the English Church in the Nineteenth Century*, ii, pp. 288-310. The Church in Wales was disestablished by Act of Parliament passed in 1914, but it did not come into force until March 31, 1920, on which day four dioceses were cut off from the province of Canterbury to form the Church in Wales.

to meet more often in joint session; but nothing much was done. Various attempts were also made to create a House of Laity to be attached to each Convocation so that the opinions of laymen might be obtained on controversial questions. After some discussion these came into being in 1885.

In the meanwhile an opportunity for general debate on ecclesiastical matters had been provided by the creation of the Church Congress. The first meeting was held at Cambridge in 1861 to discuss church rates, division of sees, incomes of the clergy and co-operation between clergy and laity. Next year they met at Oxford, and thereafter annually in some large town. Large numbers attended each year to join in, or listen to, the debates. Full reports of the speeches were published and widely read. The Congress had no legislative power, but it became a useful opportunity for the exchange of ideas, and the Church as a whole was bound to respect its opinions.[1]

One of the most popular subjects at early Church Congresses was that of the division of sees. The subject was raised at the first meeting in 1861 when the Hon. C. Lindsay asked for 130 new bishops in England and Wales. The figure was, of course, much too high; but there was general agreement on the need for division of some of the larger sees. The High Church party supported it, having visions of what a father-in-God should be and realizing that this could hardly be achieved in a vast diocese. Others supported it in the cause of greater efficiency. The chief opponents were among members of Parliament who dreaded the appearance of more bishops in the House of Lords. Suggestions were therefore made of suffragans and coadjutors, and it was in this way that the first move was made. Suffragan bishops had been appointed in Henry VIII's reign, but the office had lapsed. It was revived by the creation of the suffragan sees of Dover and Nottingham in 1870, followed by Guildford in 1874, Bedford in 1879 and Colchester in 1882. In 1877 a new bishopric of Truro was created by the division of the diocese of Exeter into two, and St. Albans followed in the same year. Soon afterwards came four new sees in the northern province—Liverpool (1880), Newcastle (1882), Southwell (1884) and Wakefield (1888).

But while England was slow to increase its episcopate, a vast and

---

[1] Another method of giving the laity a chance to join in church debates was the creation of the diocesan conference for clergy and laity. Such a gathering was first held at Salisbury in 1871.

rapid increase was going on overseas. In 1800 there were but three dioceses overseas—Connecticut, Nova Scotia and Quebec. By 1835 only four more had been added; but by 1854 there were thirty, and by 1882 the number had risen to seventy-two. This was due to the great expansion of missionary work in the middle of the nineteenth century. In Africa the explorations of David Livingstone from 1841 to 1856 had done much to open up the continent and pave the way for later missionaries. In 1857 Livingstone had addressed a meeting at Cambridge which led to the foundation of a new missionary society, the Universities' Mission to Central Africa.[1] In West Africa missionary work had developed rapidly, and those who believed that the future lay with a native ministry were much encouraged by the consecration of the ex-slave, Samuel Crowther, as Bishop of the Niger Territories in 1864. In South Africa the chief architect of the Church was Robert Gray (1809–72) under whom the single diocese of Cape Town grew into a province of seven sees.[2] In India work had been steadily proceeding on the firm foundations laid by Daniel Wilson, Bishop of Calcutta, 1832–58. Here, too, the universities made their special contribution, Cambridge starting its Mission to Delhi in 1851 and Oxford the Mission to Calcutta in 1879. In China the Anglican Church was late in the field, the chief missionary work being done by the China Inland Mission; but a diocese had been formed at Victoria (Hong Kong) in 1849 and a second followed in 1872. In Australia and New Zealand the rapid development of the countries, by means of large-scale emigration and the gold-mines, had presented the Church with great problems, but these had been largely met by the wisdom and energy of such men as W. G. Broughton in Australia and G. A. Selwyn in New Zealand. In Melanesia, John Coleridge Pateson, after many years' work among the islanders, was murdered at Nukapu in the Santa Cruz Islands in 1871. Canada presented problems similar to those in the antipodes; but these were tackled with great vigour by pioneers like Bishop Bompas, who lived for forty years, from 1865 to 1905, mostly in or near the Arctic Circle.[3]

[1] See G. H. Wilson, *The History of the U.M.C.A.* (1936).
[2] See C. Gray, *Life of Robert Gray*, 2 vols. (1876) and A. Brooke, *Robert Gray* (1947).
[3] On the expansion of the Church see K. S. Latourette, *A History of the Expansion of Christianity*, vols. v–vi (1945), J. McL. Campbell, *Christian History in the Making* (1946) and H. G. G. Herklots, *Frontiers of the Church* (1961).

The vast and rapid expansion of the Church overseas presented many problems which the Church at home was in no position to solve. It was to create some opportunity for meeting and discussion that the Church in Canada asked, in 1865, for a General Council to be held in England. Many of the bishops in England were doubtful of the wisdom of this, fearing that such a council might interfere with the authority and prestige of Convocation. However, invitations were sent out and about 70 bishops from all over the world met at Lambeth in September 1867. There was some debate on the Colenso controversy and other matters, and the Conference closed in December, though by this time many of the bishops had gone home. An attempt to repeat the experiment in 1872 failed, but in 1878 the second Lambeth Conference was held. This was more successful. A hundred bishops attended, and valuable discussions were held on such subjects as the unity of the Anglican communion, modern forms of infidelity, and the condition, progress and needs of the Church. So valuable were the discussions, and so important the opportunity for bishops from lonely dioceses to meet other bishops, that it was resolved to hold such a conference at regular intervals. Since then the Lambeth Conference has grown in size and significance and now plays a very important part in the life of the Church.[1]

The second Lambeth Conference owed much to the wisdom and leadership of Archbishop Tait (1811–82). Brought up a Scottish Presbyterian, he was confirmed while a student at Oxford, and shortly afterwards ordained. He progressed rapidly, was made Dean of Carlisle in 1849, Bishop of London in 1856 and Archbishop of Canterbury in 1868. Tait has been called 'the most remarkable prelate that had sat on the throne of Canterbury since the Reformation'.[2] This is perhaps an exaggeration; but there is no doubt of Tait's greatness as an archbishop. He was a statesman rather than a churchman, with a profound understanding of the layman's point of view. This meant that his opinion on many matters was sought and respected by men in all kinds of prominent positions. Tait was, by nature and upbringing, an Evangelical, but there was a bigness about him which made him much more than a party man. To some extent he failed to understand what the Tractarians and their successors were trying to do;

[1] See The Six Lambeth Conferences, 1867–1920 (1929).
[2] F. W. Cornish, A History of the English Church in the Nineteenth Century, ii, p. 347.

but he had a burning zeal for the Gospel, and a wish to see the Church going out to proclaim the Good News in all parts of the world. By the time of his death in 1882 the Church counted for much in the life of the nation and the Archbishop of Canterbury had become a figure of great national importance.[1]

vi. Sister Churches

When the Census of England was held in 1851 an attempt was made to discover the religious affiliation of the population. Of the eighteen million people then living in the country, it was estimated that about four million attended Anglican churches, one and a half million were Methodists of one kind or another, 800,000 were Independents, 600,000 were Baptists, and 300,000 were Roman Catholics.[2]

The separation of the Methodists from the Church of England after the death of John Wesley came fairly quickly. Methodism consisted at first of a loosely-knit body of societies; but these gradually grew into an organised Church. Church order, Church organisation and Church consciousness were all part of this movement. From 1818 onwards Methodist ministers might be addressed as 'Reverend', and in 1836 an ordination service with the laying on of hands made its first appearance. John Wesley had himself appointed a Conference of 100 ministers to direct the affairs of the Society, and this body soon began to exercise considerable power. But, in so doing, it ran into some difficulty, as many of the local societies were very conscious of their independence. The question arose with some acrimony in 1827 when the trustees of the Brunswick Chapel in Leeds decided to install an organ. The District Meeting, thinking that organs were popish instruments, forbade them to do so. The trustees appealed to the Conference, which overruled the decision of the district.

This incident was, perhaps, only petty; but it raised the whole issue as to where power lay; and it was on this issue that the movement was deeply divided during a large part of the nineteenth century. In the earlier years Jabez Bunting, who was four times

---

[1] See R. T. Davidson and W. Benham, *Life of A. C. Tait*, 2 vols. (1891).
[2] *Census of Great Britain, 1851. Religious Worship, England and Wales. Report and Tables* (1853), pp. clxxviii–ix.

President, fought hard to keep all power in the hands of the ministers who formed the Conference and not to allow the laity to have any say in the government of the Church. This autocratic and clerical policy was one of the causes of division—the Primitive Methodists hiving off in 1812 and the Bible Christians a few years later. Then, after a number of expulsions in 1849, further divisions took place, with the result that, by 1853, there were at least seven different, and independent, Methodist Churches in England. In 1857 a number of these came together to form the United Methodist Church.

In spite of all this, Methodism was, by 1850, a powerful influence in the country. It was essentially a middle-class movement which did its best work in the suburbs and watering-places, where large chapels were built. It provided a friendly kind of worship, unconstrained by formularies and liturgies, and with much emphasis on hymn-singing and preaching. In early years Methodism had been strongly sacramental in its worship, but this gradually died out, especially after the introduction of high-church practices in the Anglican churches. In the cities Central Halls were built where popular preachers attracted large crowds. At the same time, Methodists were very active in country areas, where much use was made of local preachers (known at first as 'brothers in the smock-frock'). All this meant that, by the end of the century, Methodism had become a force to be reckoned with.

They were also much concerned in politics, mostly of a Liberal kind, and were active in promoting social reforms of every description. The Primitive Methodists threw themselves into the work of the Trade Union movement, some of whose meetings are still described as 'chapels'. But, in spite of their hopes, Methodism never made a great impression on the very poor. The large and forbidding chapels were too respectable to attract the very poor who remained largely remote from all organised religion.[1]

It was, in fact, an ex-Methodist, William Booth, who succeeded where others had failed. Booth and his wife, Catherine, were out-and-out revivalists who found it impossible to work with any existing religious body. So in 1865 they put up a tent in Whitechapel

[1] See *A New History of Methodism*, ed. W. J. Townsend, H. B. Workman and G. Eayers, 2 vols. (1909); R. E. Davies, *Methodism* (1963); and R. F. Wearmouth's two books—*Methodism and the Working-class Movements of England, 1800–1850* (1937), and *Methodism and the Struggle of the Working Classes, 1850–1900* (1954).

and launched a mission to the 'Heathen of our own Country.' The Booths were determined to go among the very poorest with the Gospel of Salvation and to do it in such a way that the poor would be converted. Churches and chapels were, to most of them, far too respectable to welcome people who had only rags in which to come.

Booth ran his campaign on military lines. In 1878 he adopted the title of 'general', and put his followers into uniform. He expected to have complete control over his Salvation Army and to be given unquestioning obedience by his soldiers. On such terms he led them into battle against sin and vice, facing obloquy and violence. Many of them, both men and women, were assaulted and hustled every time they went out. But their courage was remarkable.

Sudden conversion was the message of the Salvationists, and everything was devoted to this end. Booth was not interested in parliamentary legislation or social reform. As his wife said: 'Christ came to save the world, not to civilize it'. So, at first, the Army confined itself to preaching. But later, largely as a result of William Booth's book, *In Darkest England and the Way Out* (1890), they became more interested in relief work. They now began to provide cheap meals (Food for the Million), Homes for discharged prisoners, Night Shelters for the homeless, and even Farm Colonies both at home and abroad.

The existing religious communities found it difficult to know what to think about the Salvation Army. All admired its zeal, and Archbishop Benson actually formed a small committee of prominent Anglicans—himself, Westcott, Lightfoot and Randall Davidson— to discuss the possibility of incorporating it into the Church of England. Cardinal Manning also praised its work among the poor. But Booth was far too much of an individualist to be able to work with other organizations, and the Salvation Army continued its evangelistic work among the poor all over the world.[1]

The next largest group to the Methodists in the religious survey were the Independents or Congregationalists.[2] Unlike Methodism, which is essentially 'connexional', Congregationalism is based on the absolute autonomy of each local community. But the movement found that it needed some kind of concerted action, and in 1832 a Congregational Union of England and Wales was created, though it

[1] See R. Sandall, *The History of the Salvation Army*, 3 vols. (1947-55)
[2] See above, pp. 239-40 .

was made clear that its purpose was to advise and not to legislate. Compared with the other Free Churches, Congregationalism claimed to be a more academic and intellectual movement, and it certainly produced some notable scholars. But it also had a keen social conscience which showed itself in the setting up of the London Missionary Society and of the London Congregational Union, the purpose of which was to interest the richer congregations in the needs of the poor. In 1883 three Congregational ministers produced a book called *The Bitter Cry of Outcast London*, which described in some detail the terrible conditions in which people were living in the slums, and called for parliamentary action.[1]

The Baptists had always been very independent, both of the other nonconformist Churches, and even of each other.[2] Nevertheless, in 1813 a Baptist Union was founded on much the same principles as the Congregational Union. But Baptists were very conscious of the fact that they stood for a theological principle—that of 'believer's baptism' which separated them from all other evangelical Churches. Like the Methodists, they were not themselves united, as they had a smaller group, known as 'Strict and Particular Baptists', who remained outside the union.

Baptists have never achieved in England anything like the success which they have had in some parts of the United States, where they are the largest single denomination. But they came to be a well-organized Church in England with its own Theological Colleges and with a large number of imposing buildings in the towns. The Baptist Church grew fairly quickly as a result of what is called the Second Evangelical Revival which took place in the 1860's, and it produced some of the most eminent preachers and largest audiences in the land. Charles Spurgeon, who came to London in 1854, soon drew enormous congregations to hear his sermons. In 1861 the crowds were so great that Spurgeon caused a vast building to be erected, known as the Metropolitan Tabernacle with seating for 3,600. Alexander Maclaren had a somewhat similar ministry for fifty years in Manchester, and John Clifford in London.[3]

In view of the vast number of Irish who came to England in the

---

[1] R. W. Dale, *History of English Congregationalism* (1907); A. Peel, *These Hundred Years* (1931).

[2] See above, p. 247 .

[3] A. C. Underwood, *A History of the English Baptists* (1947); E. A. Payne, *The Baptist Union: a Short History* (1959).

first half of the nineteenth century it is, perhaps, surprising to find the attendance at church of Roman Catholics in 1853 so meagre— only 1.7 per cent of the whole population. But the fact is that, apart from the Irish immigrants, the number of Roman Catholics in England was still very small.

After the Gordon Riots in 1780[1] Roman Catholicism declined in England, and by the end of the eighteenth century had reached a low ebb. But as the new century progressed numbers increased. Antipathy died down; there was a general feeling of tolerance; and Roman Catholics began to enter a little more into the social life of the country. Then, in 1829, came the Catholic Relief Bill which removed most of the restrictions from which Roman Catholics were suffering; gave them the vote, and allowed them to sit in Parliament and to hold most kinds of public office.

By this time the Irish immigration was well under way. With the growth of industry and the need for cheap labour in the towns, Irish peasants began to come over in large numbers, especially to London and to the western ports such as Liverpool and Bristol.[2] They were brought over at a cost of two shillings per head, spending three days and three nights on the open decks of cargo boats. As they swarmed into the cities they had to take such accommodation as they could find. The result was gross overcrowding, poverty, dirt and disease. After the potato famine in Ireland in 1846 the number of immigrants increased very rapidly, making confusion even greater. In order to minister to these people, many of whom spoke no English, Irish priests also came in considerable numbers, thus creating in the cities whole colonies of Irish Roman Catholics for whom churches and schools had to be built.

By the middle of the century there were three classes of Roman Catholics in England. There were the old Catholic families, proud of their inheritance and of the fortitude of their ancestors in the face of persecution and intolerance. Then there was this vast inroad of poverty-stricken Irish. Finally there were the converts, mostly from Anglicanism, many of whom had little contact with either of the other classes but who were zealous in their support of anything which would favour the Roman Catholic Church in England and give it greater power and prestige.

[1] See above, p. 312.
[2] In 1821 there were said to be 12,000 in Liverpool; in 1832, 60,000; and in 1840, 80,000 (D. Mathew, *Catholicism in England* (1948), p. 184).

The Roman Catholics were at this time being taught by Nicholas Wiseman, with the support of a convert called George Spencer, that their task was to lead England back once more into communion with the Holy See. As part of this campaign Pius IX, in 1850, issued Letters Apostolic restoring the English hierarchy and appointed Wiseman as Archbishop of Westminster with twelve suffragan sees. This pronouncement was accompanied by a Pastoral Letter which Wiseman issued from Rome and which was couched in the most triumphant terms. The letter was intended for the English Catholics, but it soon got into the press and aroused much anger and indignation. The outcry against 'papal aggression' was loud and prolonged, and Parliament actually passed a bill in 1851 imposing a fine of £100 on any Roman Catholic bishop who dared to use a title conferred on him by the pope.[1]

From now onwards there were parallel episcopates in England and a sudden increase in the building of churches and schools by Roman Catholics and in the publicity given to their activities. A note of aggressiveness now entered into all their work. The Catholic community felt that they had been charged with the responsibility of 'converting' the English people, and were prepared to give time, money and energy to this task. In this they were led by a succession of able and determined men. Wiseman, who was Cardinal Archbishop of Westminster from 1850 to 1865, was flamboyant in his way of life, rigid in his beliefs and exotic in his devotions. His contemporary, Bernard Ullathorne (Bishop of Birmingham, 1850–88), was just the opposite—a simple countryman and a Tory of the old school, who, while the last rites were actually being said over his dying body, suddenly opened his eyes and said: 'The devil's an ass', and then died. Wiseman was followed at Westminster by his closest friend, H. E. Manning, a convert from the Church of England, a great administrator, a convinced supporter of Pius IX on the question of Papal Infallibility, and a man wholly devoted to the cause of the conversion of the English people.

The 'papal aggression' from the middle of the century onwards did much to reawaken the feelings of suspicion and intolerance which had died down during the earlier part of the century. The zeal with which the Roman Catholic Church set about its task; the policy of the Vatican over mixed marriages; the decrees about

[1] The act was never enforced, and, twenty years later, it was repealed.

the Immaculate Conception (1854) and of Infallibility (1870); the repudiation of Anglican orders (1896); the natural antipathy between Irish and English, and the general tone of superiority which some of the more belligerent Roman Catholics assumed, all helped to stir up feelings of hostility and rancour. In such an atmosphere there was little hope of co-operation or even of normal contact, and many devout Evangelicals refused to regard Roman Catholics as even Christians. Writing many years later of his early years towards the end of the nineteenth century, W. R. Matthews says: 'the prevailing opinion of the religious people whom I knew and loved was that Roman Catholic worship is idolatry, and that it was better to be an Atheist than a Papist'.[1]

[1] W. R. Matthews, *Memories and Meanings* (1970), p. 27. For a history of the Roman Catholics in England, see D. Mathew, *Catholicism in England* (2nd ed. 1948) and *The English Catholics 1850–1950*, ed. G. A. Beck (1950).

NOTE ON BOOKS

In addition to those already mentioned in previous chapters see L. E. Elliott-Binns, *Religion in the Victorian Era* (1936) and V. F. Storr, *The Development of English Theology in the Nineteenth Century* (1913). The later history of the Tractarians will be found in W. J. Sparrow Simpson, *The History of the Anglo-Catholic Revival from 1845* (1932) and C. P. S. Clarke, *The Oxford Movement and After* (1932). For the history of education in the nineteenth century the best book is J. W. Adamson, *English Education, 1789–1902* (1930). The Christian Socialist movement is described in G. C. Binyon, *The Christian Socialist Movement in England* (1931) and in Maurice Reckitt, *Maurice to Temple* (1947), and the expansion of the Church in J. McLeod Campbell, *Christian History in the Making* (1946) and in H. G. G. Herklots, *Frontiers of the Church* (1961). R. T. Davidson and W. Benham's *Life of A. C. Tait*, 2 vols. (1891) is the most important biography of this period of church history but see also D. L. Edwards, *Leaders of the Church of England, 1828–1944* (1971). An interesting picture of church life in the country will be found in W. Plomer, *Kilvert's Diary, 1870–9*, 3 vols. (1938–40). *The Church of England, 1815–1948* (ed. R. P. Flindall, 1972) is an excellent collection of documents to illustrate the history of the Church throughout this period.

CHAPTER XXI

THE·TURN OF THE CENTURY
(1882-1914)

i. *Church and Nation*

In spite of the attacks of a handful of rationalists and the doubts of a few scientists, mid-Victorian England was fundamentally religious. People went to church on Sundays and said their prayers and read their Bibles at home. In many houses of the upper classes 'family prayers' were held each morning—the family sitting or kneeling at one side and the servants at the other side of the long dining-room table already laid for an ample breakfast. In the country the parish church was still very much the centre of village life, the parson sharing with the squire in the responsibilities of leadership of the community. In the towns the suburban churches were well filled with large and attentive congregations, and even in the slums many churches and chapels were active and influential among the vast crowds, so many of whom had lost touch with organized religion.

But if mid-Victorian England was fundamentally religious it was also fundamentally protestant. The teaching of the Tractarians was only just beginning to take effect, and the reforms and innovations of the ritualists were acceptable only to a few devotees. Meanwhile the great majority of English people were solidly evangelical. Worship meant attendance at Morning or Evening Prayer on Sundays, and many people followed the example of Queen Victoria and the Prince Consort in receiving the Holy Communion only twice a year. Much attention was paid to sermons and Bible-reading, for it was by these means that a man learnt what was his duty. Duty counted for a great deal in Victorian life and thought and was always to be placed before pleasure, which so often led into dangers and temptations. For the churchman of those days had in him a streak of puritanism which showed itself nowhere more clearly than in his views of Sunday observance. On this day no sport or pleasure was approved of, not even the reading of serious literature other than sermons or the Bible. Mid-Victorian religion was, therefore, essentially respectable, closely bound up with morality and duty, a matter of good behaviour, piety and righteousness. To many people the Ten Commandments counted for a good deal more than the Apostles' Creed.

However, towards the end of Victoria's long reign changes were beginning to take place. More and more people now began to be affected by the new thought which made religion look a little out of date, too closely tied to belief in old legends and myths which science had now proved false. Puritanism was also beginning to lose its hold on society, partly under the good-natured and easy-going example of the Prince of Wales, who entertained his friends on Sundays and enjoyed his cards and his racing. Even the old standards of decency and respectability began to be challenged by the 'decadent' writers of the 'naughty nineties' like Oscar Wilde and his circle. All of which had its effect on church-attendance, which now began to fall rather sharply. Charles Booth's survey of London life in 1897–1900 revealed no more than twenty per cent of the population attending any church or chapel, and comparisons with earlier estimates showed that the decline was greatest in the Anglican churches. Outside London things were better, especially in country towns and villages.

With the death of Queen Victoria in 1901 a new age began. Restraints, taboos and conventions which had been maintained by her strong influence now began to disappear, and life looked very different under the leadership of a man who mixed a good deal with the fast set and enjoyed the pleasures of life. Yet old habits die slowly, and if there were some who exploited the greater freedom which had been given to them, there were still many of more conservative temperament who clung to the old ways of life.

The prestige of the Anglican Church in this period was high. Tait had built up a great position for himself as Archbishop of Canterbury and was regarded as a serious statesman. His successor, E. W. Benson (1829–96), was less interested in political and national affairs, but was a stronger churchman than Tait and made much of his office as head of the Anglican Community throughout the world.[1] Frederick Temple (1821–1902) who followed him in 1896 had but a short pontificate,[2] but his successor Randall Davidson (1848–1930), who occupied the see of Canterbury from 1903 to 1928, did much to raise

[1] See A. C. Benson, *Life of E. W. Benson*, 2 vols. (1899).
[2] See E. G. Sandford and others, *Memoirs of Archbishop Temple*, 2 vols. (1906).

the prestige of the primacy and made himself a very considerable force in the life of the nation[1]. Among other bishops of this period there were some great scholars like William Stubbs, Mandell Creighton, B. F. Westcott and John Wordsworth; pastors and evangelists like Edward King and A. F. Winnington-Ingram, and great leaders like Charles Gore and Walsham How among the High Churchmen and A. W. Thorold and H. E. Ryle among the Evangelicals. There were also scholarly deans like C. J. Vaughan at Llandaff and Armitage Robinson at Westminster, assisted often by learned and able canons, of whom the most notable was Henry Scott Holland, whose sermons at S. Paul's attracted vast crowds. Meanwhile in both town and country parishes there were a great many well educated 'English gentlemen in Holy Orders' who worked hard and conscientiously among their flocks and made their parsonages real centres of Christian life.

In the political world the most important fact of this period was the rise of the Labour Party and its growing power. Some churchmen, from the days of Kingsley and Maurice, had taken a keen interest in this, and had supported it in various ways. From 1877 onwards the Guild of S. Matthew, under Stewart Headlam's leadership, was in the forefront of any movement for pressing the claims of the oppressed. Riots, marches of unemployed, even expeditions for breaking the windows of West-end clubs were often led by the curate of Bethnal Green. But the Church as a whole took a quieter course. Many were, of course, antagonistic to radicalism in all forms; but the remarkable thing is the sympathy which so many showed with Socialist idealism and the identification of so many of the clergy with the Labour movement. The contributors to the volume of theological essays known as *Lux Mundi* in 1889[2] were all more or less socialistic at heart and intended that the book should help to justify Christian Socialism to the thinking public. Out of the interest thus aroused grew the Christian Social Union with Westcott as President and Gore and Scott Holland as leaders. This was a very different method of approach from that of Stewart Headlam and his followers. It was more academic and restrained; it worked by books and articles rather than by marches and demonstrations; but it was inspired by a passionate belief in the Incarnation and therefore in a desire to work for the brotherhood of man and justice to all God's creatures.

[1] See G. K. A. Bell, *Randall Davidson*, 2 vols. (1935).   [2] See below, p. 397.

To these men Socialism seemed the only Christian way of government. Westcott expressed the ideals of the movement when he addressed the Church Congress in 1890. 'Individualism and Socialism', he said, 'correspond with opposite views of humanity. . . . Individualism regards humanity as made up of disconnected and warring atoms: Socialism regards it as an organic whole . . . The method of Socialism is co-operation: the method of Individualism is competition. . . . The aim of Socialism is fulfilment of service: the aim of Individualism is the attainment of some personal advantage, riches or place or favour.'

Westcott was a man of immense reputation as a scholar and administrator and his influence gave great weight to the Christian Social Union. When the Lambeth Conference met in 1908 a committee was formed to consider 'the Moral Witness of the Church in Relation to the Democratic Ideal', and a resolution was passed by the whole synod saying that 'this Conference recognizes the ideals of brotherhood which underlie the democratic movement of this century, and . . . calls upon the Church to show sympathy with the movement in so far as it strives to procure just treatment for all and a real opportunity of living a true human life'. A further resolution declared that 'the social mission and social principles of Christianity should be given a more prominent place in the study and teaching of the Church' and urged upon Christians recognition of the moral responsibility of investments and the importance of a just wage.[1]

But though the Christian Social Union did much for the Church by giving it new ideas and arousing interest in the social responsibilities of its members, it was too 'churchy' and middle-class to appeal much to the Labour leaders, whether they were artisans or intellectuals like Sidney Webb and Bernard Shaw. An attempt to form a Church Socialist League in 1906 with the slogan 'Christianity is the religion of which Socialism is the practice' never came to much. But the work of Maurice and the Christian Socialists, carried on by the Christian Social Union and others, did much for the subsequent peace and strength of England. Abroad, there was a tendency to regard Christianity and Socialism as diametrically opposed. In 1864 the pope had condemned Socialism and declared his antipathy to 'progress, liberalism and modern civilisation'.[2] As a result, continental

---

[1] The Five Lambeth Conferences (1920), pp. 327-8.
[2] In the encyclical, Quanta cura, to which was attached the Syllabus of Errors; cf. F. Nielson, The History of the Papacy in the XIXth Century (1906), ii, pp. 258-69.

Socialism tended to be anti-clerical. But it was not so in England. The early support given by churchmen to radical leaders showed that the Church cared about such things as equality and the removal of injustices, and was not only concerned with philanthropy and what was wrongly described as 'charity'.

ii. *The Work of the Scholars*

In 1882 Westcott published his commentary on *S. John*, which was typical of the work of the Cambridge theologians at this time— scholarly, simple and devout. It was the age of the Revised Version, of which the New Testament was published in 1881 and the Old Testament in 1885, of Westcott and Hort's Greek Testament (1881) and of H. B. Swete's edition of the Septuagint (1887).

Meanwhile, at Oxford a group of younger scholars were working on the theology of the Incarnation and, in 1889, published a volume of essays, under the editorship of Charles Gore, with the title *Lux Mundi, a Series of Studies in the Religion of the Incarnation*. All of the contributors had been to some extent influenced both by the Tractarians and by the Christian Socialists. They had also accepted and digested the results of biblical scholarship and enquiry and were, therefore, well qualified to lead the theological discussion into new channels. Of the twelve essays the most controversial was that by Gore himself on 'The Holy Spirit and Inspiration', which was bound to deal with the question of the authority of the Bible. Gore spoke of the Bible as a means of grace and a vehicle for spiritual truth. He laid much emphasis on the Church as the guardian of truth, and pointed out that the Bible was written by the Church for church people. But he made no attempt to preach the doctrine of infallibility.

All this was very shocking to the older generation. Liddon was terribly upset by *Lux Mundi* (as a previous generation had been upset by *Essays and Reviews*), and tried to raise a public protest. But in this he failed. Things had moved since 1860, and there were few left now to take up the cause of biblical inerrancy.

Meanwhile biblical criticism continued to make steady progress. J. B. Lightfoot had set a high standard with his commentaries on some of the Pauline epistles, published from 1865 onwards and with his edition of the writings of the Apostolic Fathers. In 1891 S. R.

Driver of Oxford published his *Introduction to the Literature of the Old Testament*. This accepted the main conclusions of textual and literary criticism which now became part of the stock-in-trade of preachers and teachers. What Driver did for the Old Testament, F. C. Burkitt was doing for the New Testament, bringing to the general reader the results of the labours of specialists. At the turn of the century James Hastings edited a *Dictionary of the Bible* (5 vols., 1898–1904) which became a standard work of reference and has largely replaced the *Encyclopedia Biblica* (4 vols., 1899–1903) edited by the eccentric T. K. Cheyne.

By 1900 all serious scholars had accepted without hesitation the main conclusions of biblical criticism. Fundamentalism was now confined to a group of extreme Evangelicals and nonconformists, who clung to the Bible in its literal sense as the final authority which could not be touched, and to the Roman Catholics who were bound by the decree of Leo XIII stating that 'all the books which the Church receives as sacred and canonical are written wholly and entirely, with all their parts, at the dictation of the Holy Ghost; and . . . it is impossible that God Himself, the supreme Truth, can utter that which is not true'.[1]

In the early years of the twentieth century the leading question was not that of biblical infallibility, but of Christology. In 1901 appeared an English translation of Adolf Harnack's *What is Christianity?* Harnack was by no means a revolutionary but, after carefully examining the evidence, he found himself unable to accept the traditional doctrines of the person of Christ. This book started many people thinking about the most important of all religious questions: 'What think ye of Christ?' How should a modern man, with his knowledge of science and biblical criticism, approach the question of the divinity of Christ, and what is he to make of the miraculous element in his life, especially the Virgin Birth and the Resurrection? In 1907 R. J. Campbell, then a Congregationalist minister, published a book called *The New Theology* in which he suggested that the Incarnation was not unique but only 'the supreme example of God's indwelling'. The divinity of Christ, he held, differed in degree rather than in kind from that of other men; and, two years later, he wrote: 'Christhood is manhood at its highest power'. To less revolutionary minds this was heretical; and Gore, who himself had been criticized

[1] *Dictante Spiritu*, quoted in W. Temple, *Nature, Man and God* (1934), p. 309 n.

for his views in *Lux Mundi*, now appeared as the leader of orthodoxy, replying to Campbell in a book which he called *The New Theology and the Old Religion* (1907).

Much debate now took place on the person of Christ and the Gospel miracles. The more advanced thinkers, including some of the clergy, were now inclined to deny the Virgin Birth and bodily Resurrection of Christ and most of the miraculous element in the Gospels. For those who were paid to teach the faith of the Church the situation was certainly very unsatisfactory. It was clearly wrong that men should lead their congregations in the recitation of beliefs which they themselves did not hold. In 1907 the papacy had condemned modernist thought in very precise terms, but there was little hope of the English bishops taking so firm a line. But the alternative seemed to be a steady drift into heresy and unbelief, and it was no wonder that men like Gore cried out for a stand to be made and an authoritative statement issued of what a loyal churchman might and might not believe.

It was in the midst of this controversy that the 'Modernist' party in the Church of England was born. William Sanday explained what the modernists stood for in a reply to Bishop Gore in 1914: 'I believe,' he wrote, 'I emphatically and hopefully believe, that a sound and right Modernism is really possible; that the Saviour of mankind extends His arms towards the cultivated modern man just as much as He does towards the simple believer. I believe that the cultivated modern man may enter the Church of Christ with his head erect, with some change of language due to difference of times, but all of the nature of reinterpretation of old truths, and without any equivocation at his heart.'[1] This was all true enough, and in some ways represented a noble ideal. The trouble began when the 'changes of language' became changes of doctrine, and men were found to be denying statements which the Church still officially held to be true.

While this was at its height another group of Oxford men, including William Temple, published a collection of essays under the title of *Foundations* (1912). The book was not modernist; but it was critical, and, as such, led to further controversy and attack.[2] That it represented the prevailing thought of the day is shown by the fact

---

[1] W. Sanday, *Bishop Gore's Challenge to Criticism* (1914), pp. 30-31.
[2] E.g. by R. A. Knox in *Some Loose Stones* (1913).

that five of the seven essayists subsequently became bishops.

Turning to less controversial subjects, the period 1882–1914 saw a considerable production of good historical work. In 1882 Stubbs was at the height of his power and industry at Oxford, teaching people how to read and understand the Middle Ages. There was much publication of original texts, including the great collection generally known as the *Rolls Series*, in which many clergy at the universities and in country vicarages took part. In 1884 Stubbs was made Bishop of Chester, a step which largely brought to an end his literary work, but in the same year Mandell Creighton arrived at Cambridge from his Northumberland parish. Stubbs and Creighton stand out as two of the leading historians of the age, but there were many others, of whom a group combined to produce a *History of the English Church* in nine volumes edited by W. R. W. Stephens and W. Hunt. Many clergy were also interested in archaeological and antiquarian pursuits, and contributed to the collections of learned societies and sat on their committees.

The period also saw a great interest in liturgical history. This was a natural outcome of the religious revival which was taking place as a result of the Oxford Movement. It had led, as early as 1839, to the foundation of the 'Cambridge Camden Society', later replaced by the 'S. Paul's Ecclesiological Society'. In 1888 was founded the 'Plainsong and Medieval Music Society', followed in 1891 by the 'Henry Bradshaw Society for editing rare liturgical texts' and in 1898 by the 'Alcuin Club' to encourage 'the practical study of ceremonial, or the arrangement of churches, their furniture, and ornaments, in accordance with the rubrics of the Book of Common Prayer'. It was as a result of the researches of these learned societies that many of the innovations and improvements, both in ritual and ceremonial, during the twentieth century were made.

iii. *Conflict of Parties*

The year 1882 saw the death of two men who had done much for the Church in England—Tait and Pusey. Pusey had joined the Tractarians in the early days and had given much help to the movement. After the secessions in 1845 it was he who became the leader of the party, which he served with great devotion and wisdom for many years. In the dust and heat of battle it was perhaps inevitable that Pusey's name should have been linked with the ritualists, and thus made the object of much hatred and abuse; yet he was staunchly Anglican, and greatly dismayed by the extravagances and disloyalties of some of his own party.

After his death the rival parties—represented by the English Church Union and the Church Association—continued their warfare, and became increasingly bitter and determined. The Church Association had, from the beginning, believed much in the weapon of prosecution, and had had the satisfaction of seeing several law-breakers among the clergy sent to prison. But the effect of this had often been to make martyrs, for there were clearly elements of martyrdom in a priest being punished by a purely secular court for the crime of worshipping in an unfamiliar way.

In 1888, therefore, the Church Association decided to bring about a trial in a purely spiritual court and to choose as its victim one of the most distinguished men in the Church of England—Edward King, the saintly Bishop of Lincoln. In this year a complaint against the bishop was made to the Archbishop of Canterbury, who was called upon to proceed against his fellow bishop for alleged breaches of the law on seven points—by mixing the chalice, adopting the eastward position at the altar, performing the manual acts in such a way as to be invisible to the congregation, allowing the singing of the *Agnus Dei*, taking the ablutions in the sanctuary, placing lighted candles on the altar, and making the sign of the cross in blessing. After much argument and dispute as to whether an archbishop had jurisdiction to try a bishop, the lawyers eventually decided that he had; and the trial opened in London in July 1889, the archbishop being assisted by five bishops, including Temple of London and Stubbs of Oxford. Proceedings continued intermittently until February 1890 when Archbishop Benson retired to consider his judgment. This was given on November 21 when King was declared guilty on the question of the mixed chalice, the manual acts and the sign of the cross, but innocent on the other four charges. The trial had aroused a great deal of interest. Bishop King was greatly beloved in his diocese and throughout the whole Church, and many who strongly disapproved of some of the points on which he was charged were shocked at the attack on so holy a man. King's own loyalty to authority is shown by his acceptance of the verdict and immediate alteration of his habits in order that he might obey the ruling of his archbishop.[1]

The Lincoln Judgment in no way checked the career of the ritual-ists, many of whom were far in advance of the bishop. In the early days they had taken their stand on the law, especially the Ornaments Rubric, and had, in fact, some justification for regarding themselves as the only law-abiding section of the clergy. But things had changed since then. The line which they now took was that the Prayer Book was inadequate and must be supplemented. The only quarry for such supplementary material was Roman forms of devotion, to which they now resorted with increasing frequency. When it was pointed out to them that their ordination vows bound them to the use of the Book of Common Prayer and forbade them to use any other 'except so far as shall be ordered by lawful authority' they replied that, in their case, the 'lawful authority' was that of the Western Church of which both the Roman and Anglican Churches were a part. As a result, a number of the clergy abandoned the Prayer Book altogether and furnished their churches in such a way as to make them indistin-guishable from those of Roman Catholics. Writing of S. Saviour's, Hoxton, it was said that 'except for the fact that the parish was . . . not in actual communion with the Pope, it was completely "Roman-ized". Perpetual Reservation on the High Altar, Benediction, the Rosary, Shrines of the Sacred Heart, of Our Lady of Victories and of S. Joseph, Corpus Christi processions through the streets, the com-plete disuse of the English language, the regular use of the Latin Missal, Rituale, Vesperale, Ritus Servandus, and for the people the "Simple Prayer Book" of the Catholic Truth Society and the West-minster Hymn Book, gradually became the order'.[2]

Against this sort of thing the anti-ritualists began to muster their forces. Believing most passionately in the Church of England as a protestant Church they were genuinely dismayed and appalled at what appeared to be gross disloyalty and an open attack on the Reformation settlement. Their fault lay in the methods whereby they tried to stop it. First they had tried organized hooliganism, but that had failed. Then came prosecution and imprisonment, but that

[1] For an account of the trial, see A. C. Benson, *E. W. Benson*, ii, pp. 319-81, and G. W. E. Russell, *Edward King* (1912), pp. 143-210.
[2] S. C. Carpenter, *A. F. Winnington-Ingram* (1949), pp. 170-71.

had failed also. Now they tried the methods of abuse and of public protest. Sir William Harcourt, the self-constituted hammer of the ritualists, bombarded the bishops and the press with thunderous letters calling the Anglo-Catholics 'bacilli in the Church's system' and demanding the enforcement of the law. Then Mr. John Kensit began the habit of visiting churches where there was considerable ritual and interrupting divine worship by standing up and making a public protest. Neither method achieved any kind of success. The bishops were perfectly aware that something ought to be done; but they were helpless. They issued pronouncements, charges and directions, but no one took much notice of them, and the movement went its way.

By 1904 things were so bad that a Royal Commission on Ritual Matters was appointed 'to inquire into the alleged prevalence of breaches or neglect of the Law relating to the conduct of Divine Service in the Church of England and to the ornaments and fittings of churches; and to consider the existing powers and procedure applicable to such irregularities, and to make such recommendations as may be deemed requisite for dealing with the aforesaid matters'. The Commission was composed of fourteen members, of whom twelve were laymen. It held 118 meetings and interviewed 164 witnesses. Finally it issued a report in which it declared that 'the law of public worship in the Church of England is too narrow for the religious life of the present generation. It needlessly condemns much which a great section of Church people, including many of her most devoted members, value.' The Commission then recommended a revision of the church courts, the condemnation of certain practices (such as Reservation, the service of Benediction and Invocation of Saints), the preparation of a new rubric regulating ornaments and vestments, and the repeal of the *Public Worship Regulation Act*. The initial statement seemed to some to open the door to all kinds of reforms and innovations, and it was important that it should not be taken as a licence for every man to do what he liked. It was, therefore, decided that the question of Prayer Book revision should be taken in hand without delay, in order that relief might be given to tender consciences and that a standard might be set beyond which no loyal churchman should go.

iv. *The World-wide Church*

In the year 1800 *Ecclesia Anglicana* meant the established Church of the people living in England, Wales and Ireland with a handful of Episcopalians in Scotland and a few English people living overseas. By 1900 the whole thing had changed. What had been a national Church had now become universal and supra-national, extending over practically the whole world, and with a number of independent daughter-churches rapidly developing their own special features according to the needs of the race and country which they served.

This was brought about by two movements. In the first place Anglican missionaries during the nineteenth century had shown remarkable courage, endurance, zeal and wisdom. Undeterred by the dangers which lay in their path, from climate, from nature and from hostile men, they had pushed into the jungles of Africa, the wastes of the Arctic, the remotest villages of China or the islands of the Pacific. Many had met with violent deaths or had suffered from disease; but the work had gone on and many conversions had been made. At the very moment when critics in England were gloating over the apparent decline of the Church in their own land the Church overseas was rejoicing in what must have been the most rapid and spectacular advance in the whole of Church history. If, at first, conversions had come slowly, by 1914 they were taking place on a vast scale. In Uganda, for example, whereas in 1890 only 200 baptisms took place, in 1914 there were nearly 100,000. And the same thing was happening in India and to a lesser degree in the Far East. The second factor in the expansion of the Church was the vast number of emigrants who left the British Isles during the nineteenth century, mostly for North America. In the year 1888 it was reckoned that nearly twelve million people had left the United Kingdom during the past 70 years, and that 250,000 were going off each year. Many of these were members of the Anglican Church and swelled the ranks of churchmen in the colonies or elsewhere.

The Church overseas had not only grown in size and numbers, it had grown also in self-confidence and the desire for independence. In places like Jamaica and Ceylon, where the Church was at first established as at home, disestablishment had come, bringing with it greater liberty. Other Churches rightly abandoned anything which suggested a western origin and called themselves 'The Church of India, Burma and Ceylon' or, in Japan, the 'Nippon Sei Ko Kwai'. The daughter-churches also grew in self-assurance by becoming more and more independent of financial help from England and by beginning to build up a native ministry. The consecration of an Indian, V. S. Azariah, as Bishop of Dornakal, in 1912 met with a great deal of criticism from old-fashioned people, but was an important moment in the natural development of the Church as a whole.[1] At the same time the work of the Church overseas was greatly enriched by the development of social, educational and medical work, by translations of the Scriptures and other Christian literature, and by the emergence of local liturgies and local styles of church architecture.

With the phenomenal growth of the Church in the latter part of the nineteenth century the Lambeth Conference became of increasing importance. The Conference which met in 1888 was attended by 145 bishops from all over the world. They met at Lambeth and then separated into twelve committees which sat for a fortnight, after which the whole Conference met together to hear and discuss the reports. Moral problems, Socialism and Reunion played an important part in the agenda, but problems immediately affecting the Church overseas, such as emigration and polygamy, were also dealt with. The next Conference was held in 1897 in order that it might be part of the celebrations of the thirteenth centenary of the landing of S. Augustine in 597. By this time separate provinces in the Church overseas were being formed, and some time had to be devoted to administrative questions. The fifth Lambeth Conference, in 1908, was much the biggest and most important which had so far been held. By this time the bishops as a whole had become far more conscious of what was happening overseas and were anxious to convince their people that a world-wide Church had come into being, and that the Church in China or in South Africa was just as important as the Church in England. 'It can no longer seem necessary', they said, 'to talk apologetically of Missions.' And again: 'There is the splendid hope that from the field of Foreign Missions there will be gathered for the enrichment of the Church's manifold heritage the ample and varied contribution of the special powers and characteristics belonging to the several nations of mankind'.[2] So the Conference boldly

---

[1] See Carol Graham, *Azariah of Dornakal* (1946).
[2] *The Five Lambeth Conferences* (1920), pp. 298, 306.

went ahead to encourage independence and autonomy, the establishment of native episcopates, and the adaptation of services, discipline and organization of the Church to local needs.

The problems connected with the expansion of the Church were so much the most important issue before the bishops in the early years of the twentieth century—so much more important than all the fuss over ritualism which at the time loomed so large—that in the same year as the fifth Lambeth Conference (1908) a great gathering was held in London called the 'Pan-Anglican Congress'. The idea of a Congress as a meeting place for clergy and laity to hear papers and speeches on the great issues before the Church had been familiar to English churchmen since 1861. The Pan-Anglican Congress was like a vast Church Congress, lasting for eight days and attended each day by 17,000 people. The Congress had no legislative power, but was intended to be informative and inspiring. Events were taking place so rapidly that people should be informed of them and aroused to deeper consciousness of the greatness of the Church —great in numbers, great in opportunity. The Reports of the Congress were subsequently published in eight volumes by the S.P.C.K.

Two years later an even larger gathering was held at Edinburgh, the 'World Interdenominational Missionary Conference'. This was the first big attempt at an interdenominational venture; and the proposal met with some opposition from the Anglo-Catholic party, who were naturally cautious of identifying the Church of England with world protestantism. Archbishop Davidson was at first reluctant to attend, but in the end he went; and, by so doing, officially associated the Church with the other constituent bodies. The Conference was called to discuss missionary problems in so far as they affected all Christian Churches, but the main result of the gathering lay not in the sphere of missions but in that of greater understanding between the denominations. It was at Edinburgh in 1910 that the 'Ecumenical Movement' was born. The fact that the various religious bodies were all engaged in a similar kind of work, that they were all facing the same problems and pressures, that there could be no place in the mission field for petty rivalries and jealousies which poisoned the life of the Christian body at home, all this engendered a desire for fellowship and co-operation which broke down old barriers and calmed old hostilities. Thirty years later William Temple said at his enthronization at Canterbury: 'As though in preparation for such a time as this, God has been building up a Christian fellowship which now extends into almost every nation, and binds citizens of them all together in true unity and mutual love. No human agency has planned this. It is the result of the great missionary enterprise of the last hundred and fifty years. Neither the missionaries nor those who sent them out were aiming at the creation of a world-wide fellowship interpenetrating the nations, bridging the gulfs between them, and supplying the promise of a check to their rivalries. The aim for nearly the whole period was to preach the Gospel to as many individuals as could be reached so that those who were won to discipleship should be put in the way of eternal salvation. Almost incidentally the great world-fellowship has arisen; it is the great new fact of our era.'[1]

v. *Towards Christian Unity*

The Edinburgh Conference gave a great impetus to the efforts which were being made towards Christian unity. The difficulties facing every Christian community at home, and the vast opportunities daily opening out abroad, showed up the tragedy of 'our unhappy divisions' and urged men to find some way of healing and unity.

By far the most difficult problem was (and still is) that of the relations between the Anglican and Roman Churches. Early in the eighteenth century Archbishop Wake had attempted some *rapprochement* with the Gallican Church; but nothing had come of it, and no further overtures had been made by either side.[2] But with the coming of the Oxford Movement men had begun to take more interest in other 'branches' of the Catholic Church, especially Rome and the Orthodox Church of the East. The early Tractarians were severe critics of Rome. Newman seriously thought the pope was Anti-Christ, and said so. But later generations looked upon Rome with much more kindly eyes, and introduced much of her theology and devotion into their churches. The so-called 'Roman Aggression' of 1850, led to a number of conversions; English people became much more aware of the power and purpose of Rome than they had been

---

[1] W. Temple, *The Church Looks Forward* (1944), p. 2.
[2] See above, p. 283.

since the days of Elizabeth I, and most people regarded this aggressive policy with horror.

There were, however, a few High Churchmen to whom Rome appeared not so much as a formidable adversary but as a possible friend and ally. Among these was Lord Halifax, whose highest ambition it was to heal the breach between England and Rome. In 1894, while staying at Madeira, he made friends with a French priest, the abbé Portal, whom he soon found to share his hopes and with whom he had many conversations. These were duly reported both to the Pope and to the Archbishop of Canterbury, and for a moment it looked as if they might be the beginnings of closer understanding; but the Roman Catholics in England, under Cardinal Vaughan, were suspicious of any kind of *rapprochement*, and two years later Leo XIII, carried away by the intransigence of his *curia*, published the bull *Apostolicae Curae* in which he declared that 'ordinations performed according to the Anglican rite are utterly invalid and altogether void'.[1] The Anglican bishops replied to the bull in a learned *Responsio* defending the validity of Anglican orders,[2] and, in spite of the unfavourable climate, the Lambeth Conference in 1908 did its best to keep the door open by accepting the statement of its Committee on Reunion that they were 'not unmindful of the fact that there can be no fulfilment of the divine purpose in any scheme of reunion which does not ultimately include the Great Latin Church of the West'.[3]

While some of the Tractarians were taking an interest in the Church of Rome others were making a special study of the Eastern Orthodox Church. In 1850 Mr. William Palmer paid a visit to Russia and subsequently carried on a long correspondence with a Russian layman called Khomiakoff.[4] Little came of this; but good-will between East and West continued to grow. J. M. Neale aroused interest in the Orthodox Church by his translations of hymns and by his historical works,[5] while W. J. Birkbeck did much to interpret Russian Chris-

[1] H. Bettenson, *Documents of the Christian Church*, pp. 382–3. See J. J. Hughes. *Absolutely Null and Utterly Void* (1968).

[2] The *Responsio* will be found in T. A. Lacey, *A Roman Diary and Other Documents* (1910), pp. 354–94. See also Lord Halifax, *Leo XIII and Anglican Orders* (1912).

[3] *The Five Lambeth Conferences*, ed. R. T. Davidson (1920), p. 422.

[4] See W. J. Birkbeck, *Russia and the English Church* (1895).

[5] E.g. *A History of the Holy Eastern Church: General Introduction*, 2 vols. (1850) and *The Patriarchate of Alexandria*, 2 vols. (1847).

tianity to English people.[1] The question was taken up by the Lambeth Conference in 1897 when suggestions were made for a translation of Anglican rites into Greek and Russian, and, in 1906 an Anglican and Eastern Orthodox Churches Union was founded. Interest and sympathy were by now growing so fast that the Lambeth Conference of 1908 had to issue a caution that 'efforts after unity are in no sense furthered by a whittling away of our distinctive position'; but the Conference agreed to allow communicant members of any church of the Orthodox Eastern Communion to receive the Sacrament in Anglican churches if deprived of the ministrations of a priest of their own communion.[2]

Meanwhile, in 1870, a number of Roman Catholics in Austria and elsewhere, finding that they could not accept the decree of Papal Infallibility, had seceded from the Church. They united with a body at Utrecht which had separated from Rome in the seventeenth century (on a purely local issue), and thus the Old Catholic Church was founded. The Lambeth Conference of 1878 began to take an interest in this body, and there was some progress towards a union of the two Churches. This, however, was seriously impeded by the unfortunate incident of the consecration by the Old Catholics of a certain Bishop Mathew in 1908 to work in England. When this problem had been settled, closer understanding became possible; and the two Churches were finally brought into full communion in 1932.[3]

In the seventeenth century England had maintained friendly relations with Lutherans and Calvinists in Europe.[4] These were further developed in the nineteenth century and led, in 1841, to the establishment of a protestant bishopric of Jerusalem, to be financed partly from England and partly from Prussia, and to be held alternately by an Anglican and a Lutheran. This had been fiercely attacked by the Tractarians on the grounds that it completely compromised the specific status of the Church of England as a 'branch' of the Catholic and Apostolic Church, a status to which the Lutheran Church, having lost the apostolic succession, could advance no claim. The scheme fell through after a few years, and no further attempt was made to reopen negotiations with the Lutherans until overtures were made to the Church of Sweden early in the twentieth century.

[1] See A. Riley (ed.), *Birkbeck and the Russian Church* (1917).
[2] *The Five Lambeth Conferences* (1920), p. 423.
[3] See C. B. Moss, *The Old Catholic Movement* (1948).
[4] See above, p. 282.

Meanwhile there was the ever-pressing problem of the Free Churches in England and the Presbyterian Church of Scotland. In the eighteenth and early nineteenth centuries the dissenters were commonly regarded as people who had deserted the established Church of their own free will, but who could always return to the fold if they wished to do so. The Evangelical Revival, however, led to a good deal of co-operation in social work and in interdenominational societies such as the British and Foreign Bible Society. But co-operation was a very different thing from reunion; and though 'home reunion' was discussed regularly in Convocation and in Church Congresses from 1861 onwards, nothing was done. In 1888 the subject was considered at Lambeth and a statement adopted from the General Convention of the American Church giving four essentials upon which the Church must take its stand. These were: the Old and New Testaments, the Nicene Creed, the two Gospel Sacraments, and the Historic Episcopate locally adapted. This statement, slightly revised, came to be known as the 'Lambeth Quadrilateral' and was repeated in 1897 with the statement that 'we believe that we have been Providentially entrusted with our part of the Catholic and Apostolic inheritance bequeathed by our Lord'.[1]

Meanwhile a few individuals tried to get ahead of the official programme of the Church by unauthorized interchange of pulpits and intercommunion. In 1909 Dr. Hensley Henson, at that time a Canon of Westminster, accepted an invitation to preach in a Congregational chapel in Birmingham, and insisted upon doing so in spite of a formal inhibition from the bishop of the diocese.[2] Two years later the Bishop of Hereford invited nonconformists to make their communion in his cathedral on the day of the Coronation. Lord Halifax and the English Church Union made a protest against this, only to be denounced by the bishop as 'sacerdotalists and medievalists'.[3] There was thus considerable difference of opinion, the Evangelicals anxious for all kinds of co-operation while the Anglo-Catholics fought hard for the maintenance of a clear distinction between what was 'catholic' and what was not.

Controversy was then fanned to great heat by the Kikuyu crisis in 1913. In that year a conference was held of all the 'protestant

[1] The Five Lambeth Conferences (1920), pp. 156–61, 247.
[2] H. H. Henson, Retrospect of an Unimportant Life (1942), i, pp. 92–6.
[3] G. K. A. Bell, Randall Davidson (1935), i, p. 635.

missions' in East Africa (including two Anglican bishops) to consider a Scheme of Federation on the basis of the Bible, the Creeds and the Gospel Sacraments. No mention was made of Episcopacy, and the whole plan was hopelessly premature and unofficial. As soon as the plan became known, Frank Weston, Bishop of Zanzibar and a strong Anglo-Catholic, rose up in wrath and sent a strong protest to the Archbishop of Canterbury demanding action against the two bishops whom he himself proceeded to excommunicate. The storm created great excitement in England and was made the occasion for a fine display of partisanship by many who were not directly concerned in the dispute.[1] In the struggle which ensued Archbishop Davidson was almost the only man who kept his head and his temper, and never were his wisdom and strength more needed. The controversy might have dragged on indefinitely had not the whole thing shrunk into insignificance by the outbreak of war in August 1914.[2]

vi. The Church and Education

Elementary education had been made universal and compulsory in 1882. In 1891 it was made free. At this date the voluntary, or non-provided, schools numbered over 14,000 of which by far the majority belonged to the Church of England. But they were in financial difficulties. Standards everywhere were rising, both as regards buildings and equipment and in the quality and training of teachers. The church schools received some aid from the State, but they had to pay their teachers and maintain their buildings. With the abolition of fees in 1891 the church schools suffered greatly, buildings began to fall into disrepair, new equipment could not be bought, and teachers were underpaid.

In 1902 a Conservative Government took up the question of the voluntary schools and decided to give them far more assistance. A bill was therefore passed which put the non-provided schools on the rates, left them to maintain their buildings but otherwise relieved them of all financial responsibility and gave them control of appointments and of religious teaching. The act was much resented by non-

---

[1] E.g. Hensley Henson, who was quite outside those concerned in the dispute, plunged into the fray. 'It was quite apparent from the first', he said, 'that I could not stand outside the conflict' (Retrospect of an Unimportant Life, i, p. 160).

[2] See the account in G. K. A. Bell, Randall Davidson, i, pp. 690-708 and in H. M. Smith, Frank Weston (1926), pp. 145-70.

conformists, secularists and liberals, many of whom disliked the dual system and wished to get rid of voluntary schools altogether. With the return of a Liberal government in 1905 the question was reopened and a new bill prepared by Mr. Augustine Birrell with the intention of reversing the decisions of 1902. Birrell's bill proposed to abolish all church schools, to give the State power to commandeer non-provided schools, to let the Local Education Authorities appoint all teachers, and to solve the problem of religious teaching by allowing only undenominational teaching in the State schools and denominational teaching in schools which had formerly been church schools, on two days of the week only and never by the teachers themselves.

Such a bill, if carried, would have virtually killed all connection between the Church and elementary education, and vigorous opposition was put up against it. Bishop Knox of Manchester organized a vast protest in London, bringing thirty-two trainloads of Lancashire people to join in a march through the West End, in which both the Bishop of London and Lord Halifax took part.[1] In spite of such protests the bill passed the House of Commons, only to be turned down by the Lords. The dual system therefore remained as before, and the Church continued to enjoy the very real privileges of the previous act.

After the abolition of 'religious tests' in 1871 the universities of Oxford and Cambridge underwent considerable change. They ceased to be exclusively 'church' communities, though attendance at the college chapels was still for a time compulsory, and many of the Heads of Houses and other dons were in Holy Orders. When compulsory attendance at chapel began to disappear the initiative in religious matters passed more and more to the students, who formed their own societies, often on party lines. The most successful of the student societies were the Cambridge Intercollegiate Christian Union (1872) and its equivalent at Oxford, which, strictly evangelical in their tenets, included a number of older men but were mainly run by undergraduates.

The latter part of the nineteenth century saw the rise of the new universities. Owen's College, Manchester (1851), the Yorkshire College of Science at Leeds (1874) and the University College at Liverpool (1881) together formed the Victoria University, which divided into three separate bodies in 1903. Sheffield, Bristol, Birmingham and others followed as the demand for higher education steadily grew. None of these universities had any religious tests, and care was taken

<hr>

[1] See E. A. Knox, *Reminiscences of an Octogenarian* (n.d.), pp. 241-5.

to see that religious controversy was, as far as possible, kept well outside. The charter of Liverpool University goes so far as to say that 'no theological teaching shall be given by or under the authority of the University',[1] while in some universities theological books were excluded from the libraries. Manchester, on the other hand, has always had an excellent faculty of theology, and the study of divinity has been introduced into other universities in more recent years. None of the universities provided anything in the way of a chapel, or arranged for any services beyond an occasional 'university sermon'.

The initiative, therefore, for religious activity in the modern universities has always lain with the students, who have formed among their own numbers various religious societies, of which by far the most influential has been the interdenominational Student Christian Movement. This was founded in 1892 with 'a divine mission to the student world in any and every country',[2] and has been so successful that it has been able to keep resident secretaries or chaplains in the universities to organize the work of the movement and to exercise a pastoral oversight over the students. Without the work of the S.C.M. many students in the modern universities would indeed have been as sheep without a shepherd.[3]

In the specialized sphere of post-graduate training for the ministry a new experiment was started in 1899 when a small college was opened at Farnham and the work entrusted to the Rev. B. K. Cunningham. The hostel, which lasted only for fifteen years, was never very large; but the students were carefully selected, and many passed through it who were afterwards leaders in the Church in various ways.[4]

Outside the walls of the universities and colleges considerable efforts were being made to bring the riches of learning to those whose education had been only of the simplest. Inspired partly by the work of F. D. Maurice, evening classes and adult schools of various kinds had flourished during the latter part of the nineteenth century. Then, in 1903, was founded the Workers' Educational Association largely through the vision and energy of Dr. Albert Mansbridge. The W.E.A. immediately received considerable support from the Church, notably by the adherence of William Temple, who, in 1909, became

[1] B. Truscott, *Redbrick University* (1943), p. 172.
[2] R. Lloyd, *The Church of England in the Twentieth Century*, i (1946), p. 179.
[3] See Tissington Tatlow, *The Story of the Student Christian Movement* (1932).
[4] See J. R. H. Moorman, *B. K. Cunningham, a Memoir* (1947), pp. 42-68.

its president. Temple and Mansbridge together gave the W.E.A. an ideal which was something more than merely educational. 'The W.E.A.', it has been said, 'was a sacrament—a sacrament of a passion for knowledge and for brotherhood in the pursuit of knowledge.'[1] Debates on religious matters were banned by the rules of the Association, but a religious interest lay behind much of its work. 'Knowledge', said Mansbridge, 'can serve a man for a time but only worship can bring its service to abiding value. Out of worship springs all that is good in our common life. As a man worships he opens his spirit, and consequently his body and mind, to the things which are infinite and eternal. He stands on the boundaries of known things and gazes into the face of God, and in the highest moments of corporate worship partakes of the Blessed Sacrament of the body and blood of Christ which will sustain him, whatever chances or toils may be set in his life.'[2] It was in this spirit that many who supported the W.E.A. went about their work.

The Church also did much educational work among children. Sunday schools flourished throughout this period, especially in the towns of the industrial north. There were also many out-of-school activities of various kinds which the Church either organized or in which it played a conspicuous part. Boys' and girls' clubs became an almost indispensable adjunct of any urban parish, but especially in the slums where the need was greatest. In 1891 was founded the Church Lads' Brigade, which attracted large numbers of boys and gave them disciplined recreation which they would otherwise have been denied. In 1907 Sir Robert Baden Powell, a hero of the South African War, held an informal camp at Brownsea Island out of which grew what must be regarded as by far the most imaginative and original of all organizations for young people—the Boy Scouts and Girl Guides. The movement was built upon a religious foundation and received much help from church people, both clergy and laity, from the start. With the growth of State primary schools and the advance of municipal secondary schools after 1906 the Church lost much of its control over the education of the young. But what it lost in this way it did its best to make up through voluntary societies and clubs of various kinds which, from now onwards, became an increasingly important feature of parochial life.

[1] F. A. Iremonger, *William Temple* (1948), p. 80.
[2] A. Mansbridge, *The Kingdom of the Mind* (1944), pp. 36-7.

NOTE ON BOOKS

FOR general history see R. C. K. Ensor, *England, 1870–1914* (1936), and, for the history of the Church in England, the following biographies: A. C. Benson, *The Life of E. W. Benson*, 2 vols. (1889), *Memoirs of Archbishop Temple by Seven Friends*, ed. E. G. Sandford, 2 vols. (1906) and G. K. A. Bell, *Randall Davidson*, 2 vols. (1935). For the development of theology see C. C. J. Webb, *A study of Religious Thought in England from 1850* (1933), A. M. Ramsey, *From Gore to Temple* (1960) and J. K. Mozley, *Some Tendencies in British Theology* (1951). For the early twentieth century reference should be made to Roger Lloyd, *The Church of England, 1900–1965* (1966) and to such biographies as G. L. Prestige, *The Life of Charles Gore* (1935), J. G. Lockhart, *Viscount Halifax*, 2 vols. (1935), and E. A. Knox, *Reminiscences of an Octogenarian* (n.d., about 1935). See also *The Six Lambeth Conferences, 1867–1920* (1929) and G. K. A. Bell, *Christian Unity* (1948). For the ecumenical movement see R. Rouse and S. C. Neill, *A History of the Ecumenical Movement, 1517–1948* (2nd ed. 1967).

CHAPTER XXII

THE CHURCH IN WAR AND PEACE
(1914–1945)

i. *The New Age*

THE outbreak of the first World War in 1914 marked the end of one age and the beginning of an era of rapid change. To a world living in security and prosperity the sudden impact of war on a gigantic scale came as a profound shock. For a time all the old values and proportions seemed to be abandoned. Men of normally sober mind were driven into false judgments, while the more emotional were carried away by mass hysteria and alarm.

To the Church the war came as an opportunity and a challenge— an opportunity, because Christianity flourishes more in the soil of adversity than in that of prosperity and ease; a challenge, because war strikes at the very heart of the Christian gospel of love and forgiveness. But the Church in England was ill-prepared for such an occasion. For long it had enjoyed the fruits of Victorian prosperity, and had never contemplated a crisis of this sort. Consequently it lacked both a message and a policy. Many who ought to have devoted themselves to restraining popular feeling were themselves led away by it, thereby giving the impression that they were more concerned with the fate of the British Empire than with that of the Kingdom of God. To others the war appeared as a great crusade, a struggle between good and evil with the tacit assumption that all the good was on one side and all the evil on the other. Winnington-Ingram, the Bishop of London, became one of the most successful recruiting officers in the country, and even so thoughtful a man as Hensley Henson, then Dean of Durham, toured the country appealing for recruits for the army.

On the other hand, many of the Christian leaders were desperately anxious. At Lambeth, Davidson faced the crisis with his usual calm fortitude, but he felt bewildered by the shock. 'Randall *thinking*— THINKING' wrote his wife in her diary;[1] and, indeed, there was much to think about.

[1] G. K. A. Bell, *Randall Davidson*, ii, p. 735.

One of the most difficult problems was to decide where lay the duty of the clergy. Should they enlist like other men and take their part in the great struggle? Henson thought that the younger clergy ought to join up, and Winnington-Ingram offered 'special dispensations' to clergy undertaking combatant service.[1] But wiser heads, like those of Gore and Davidson, said No. The Archbishop wrote: 'By every line of thought which I have pursued I am led to the conclusion . . . that the position of an actual combatant in our Army is incompatible with the position of one who has sought and received Holy Orders.'[2] In the end only a few clergy actually served as combatants, though many acted as chaplains, often in positions of great danger. The chaplain's job was one of peculiar difficulty. These young men had no special training and little experience. Often they made mistakes through lack of wisdom or of guidance, but, on the whole, they served with courage and devotion. A 'School for Chaplains' in France, under the leadership of B. K. Cunningham, was opened in 1917 and did good work in running weekly courses until the end of the war;[3] but a more permanent outcome of the work of the chaplains was the foundation, by P. B. Clayton, of Toc H, an organization which sought to perpetuate among men the sense of comradeship which the war produced.[4]

Meanwhile at home the churches carried on in the face of great difficulties. The anxieties and sufferings which the war engendered led some to deeper seriousness and faith, while others grew more bitter and hostile. It was in order to encourage the former that the National Mission of Repentance and Hope was held in 1916. A big effort was made to rally the people of England, and most of the leading churchmen took part in it. But the results were disappointing. The nation was not favourably disposed towards repentance, and its natural hope was not of that kind which is envisaged by the New Testament writers but rather for personal safety and national victory.

The war was followed by twenty years of uneasy peace. Abroad there was constant anxiety which grew in intensity with the rise of Fascist Italy and Nazi Germany. At home, industrial strife reached its climax in the General Strike of 1926, followed by the slump, mass

[1] G. K. A. Bell, *Randall Davidson*, ii, p. 890; H. H. Henson, *Retrospect of an Unimportant Life*, i, p. 175.
[2] G. K. A. Bell, *Randall Davidson*, ii, p. 739; G. L. Prestige, *Charles Gore* (1935), p. 370.
[3] J. R. H. Moorman, *B. K. Cunningham* (1947), pp. 80–93.
[4] See P. B. Clayton, *Tales of Talbot House* (1920).

unemployment and poverty. It was a generation of rapid change. Heavy taxation and death duties were dissolving the large fortunes of the rich, while rising wages brought greater amenities to the manual workers. Meanwhile the breaking down of old customs and standards went on apace, for example in the collapse of Sabbatarianism and in the increase of divorce.

The Church was now facing a new situation. A large majority of the people were now almost completely out of touch with organized religion, while their children were growing up totally ignorant of the Christian faith. In the parishes the churches were forced to rely more and more upon small groups of devotees who shouldered the burdens of church work and finance with great courage. On the outskirts of the towns new housing estates sprang up with great rapidity, while in the country a steady drift of population to the towns, and increased transport facilities for those who remained, broke up the old rural economy and transformed village life.

The outbreak of the Second World War in 1939 found both nation and Church much better prepared than they had been in 1914. The war was less of a shock, and was faced more calmly and rationally. Compared with 1914 there was much less bitterness, though there were signs of deterioration as the war progressed, especially under the strain of constant bombing of cities. The war brought many problems to the Church. The widespread removal of children and young mothers from the cities in 1939, and again in 1944, largely disorganized parochial life at both the sending and receiving ends. The black-out and the bombing dislocated life in many ways, and many churches were damaged or destroyed. Meanwhile moral standards were further loosened under war conditions, and juvenile delinquency became a serious problem.

As in 1916, efforts were made during the war to touch the conscience of the nation by 'National Days of Prayer' and, later, by 'Religion and Life Weeks', but little permanent good accrued from these efforts. More successful were the efforts made among the better type of soldier by means of 'Moral Leadership Courses' held during the slack periods of the war. Again, many of the old problems which the Church had had to face in 1914 came up again; but the experience of a previous generation was invaluable, and saved the Church from many mistakes.

In these changing years the Church was led by a remarkable group of men. In the 39 years from 1903 to 1942 the see of Canterbury was occupied by two men, both of whom had been brought up as Scottish Presbyterians. Randall Davidson restored the primacy to a position of great prestige in the country, greater than it had had for many years. In his later years his counsel was sought and respected by many of the most prominent men in the land. To him it fell to guide the Church of England through one of the most difficult periods in the history of mankind, and he did it with great skill and patience if without great inspiration. Cosmo Gordon Lang, who succeeded him in 1928, was of a more romantic nature than Davidson, but less shrewd in his judgments. Like Benson before him he did much to establish the position of the primacy in the eyes of the Church, but he was not the great statesman and national leader that Davidson had been. William Temple, who succeeded Lang in 1942, held office for only two years before his sudden death in 1944. Intellectually the most brilliant archbishop since Anselm, Temple had also a remarkable knowledge of affairs and exerted a great influence on contemporary life at many points— political, social, educational and philosophical, as well as ecclesiastical and theological. His early death robbed the Church of a great leader, respected and loved by vast numbers of his fellow-countrymen whether Churchmen or not. 'He was one of us' they said.[1]

ii. *Life and Liberty*

The vast increase in parliamentary business which took place during the nineteenth century meant that very little time could be devoted to ecclesiastical legislation, and necessary reforms were often long delayed. For some time suggestions had been made for better ways of dealing with church affairs, and a body known as the Representative Church Council had been set up to prepare bills which Parliament would be more or less bound to pass. Then came the war, and the rapid changes of opinion, and enthusiasm for reform. Clergy at home and chaplains with the forces were all anxious that, after the war, the Church should go forward with new vigour to reform itself and so be more able to meet the needs of the new world.

In March 1917 a small group of enthusiasts, including William Temple and H. R. L. Sheppard, met in London and discussed ways

[1] See the tributes in F. A. Iremonger, *William Temple* (1948), pp. 627-31.

in which such reforms could be carried out. The outcome of this was the 'Life and Liberty' movement, the declared aim of which was 'to win for the Church the liberty essential to fullness of life'. Temple resigned the rich living of S. James's, Piccadilly, in order to become the first secretary of the movement, and his vigour and zeal aroused much enthusiasm. Randall Davidson, as might be expected, was cautious. He disliked popular movements, and was unmoved by attempts to force him into what he called 'a policy of hustle and push' and by young clergy who told him he ought to 'scream'.[1] He believed more in the Representative Church Council than in 'Life and Liberty', and wanted to go slow until after the war.

As soon as the war was over plans were drawn up for a new system of church government. The basis of the whole scheme was an electoral roll in each parish. Much discussion took place on the question of what qualifications should be demanded for a place on this roll. Gore pleaded vigorously that only communicants should be admitted, and when opinion went against him on this point he resigned the bishopric of Oxford.[2] Eventually it was decided that membership should be extended to such as 'are baptised and declare that they are members of the Church of England and that they do not belong to any religious body which is not in communion with the Church of England'. Having established this wide democratic basis, the bill went on to give legal recognition to a number of representative bodies —the Parochial Church Council, the Ruridecanal Conference, the Diocesan Conference and the National Assembly of the Church of England. The bill embodying these proposals was passed by Parliament in December 1919, and the compilation of an electoral roll, and the setting up of the various representative bodies, became a part of the law of the land.

Since that date much business has been debated in the Church Assembly and a number of measures have been presented to Parliament, most of which have subsequently become law. Much of this business has been concerned with financial affairs—clergy stipends, clergy pensions, money for training for the ministry, for religious education, for church extension, and so forth—for there were many points at which reform was long overdue. The Assembly has had to deal also with questions of patronage and an attempt has been made to

[1] G. K. A. Bell, *Randall Davidson*, ii, pp. 965, 966.
[2] G. L. Prestige, *The Life of Charles Gore*, pp. 422-4.

give the laity some share in the choice of their incumbent. Clerical discipline has also occupied some of the time of the Church Assembly, and in 1947 an act was passed providing new procedure for the trial of clergy accused of 'conduct unbecoming the character of a clerk in Holy Orders, or of serious, persistent, or continuous neglect of duty'. The number of scandalous clergy is nowadays very small, and the number of those grossly incompetent or negligent is not much higher. But where there is neglect or misbehaviour the well-being of the Church demands that there should be amendment, even if it means a breach of the 'parson's freehold'.

Long debates have also been held from time to time on the subject of the relations between Church and State, and a notable report was published in 1935; but little was done. The Prayer Book fiasco of 1927–28[1] raised the question of the liberty of the Church and led to a cry for disestablishment; but no further action was taken.

One effect of the Enabling Act and the machinery which belongs to it has been a great increase in centralization, and Church House in Dean's Yard, Westminster, soon became the ecclesiastical Whitehall, the home of various departments of church government and administration. The danger here is that so much of the life of the Church came to be controlled by boards and committees composed mainly of those living in or near London. The setting up of so much central machinery also necessitated the raising of vast sums of money, almost all of which had to be raised by the parochial clergy.[2]

The 'Life and Liberty' Movement achieved much of what it set out to do, and made the Church much more democratic. The laity became fully represented on all consultative bodies except Convocation and acquired considerable power in church government. The Parochial Church Councils have done much to create a sense of corporate effort and responsibility in the parishes; but the Diocesan Conferences and the National Assembly were never fully representative of the Church, as only those with considerable leisure and money have been able to attend them. But, in a changing world, some such organization was essential if the Church was to play its part; and plans for giving the laity greater responsibility in all matters which affect the life of the Church, under the general title

[1] See below, pp. 427–8.
[2] On the work of the Church Assembly see *The Church Assembly and the Church; a Book of Essays* (1930).

of 'synodical government', were in due course carried out.

iii. *The Ecumenical Movement*

After the 'public rebuff' of the papal bull, *Apostolicae Curae*, in 1896[1] it was some years before any further attempt was made to re-open negotiations between the Church of England and the Church of Rome. But Lord Halifax remained optimistic; and between 1921 and 1925 conversations were held at Malines between an English team consisting of Lord Halifax, Armitage Robinson, W. H. Frere and others, and a group of Roman Catholics under the leadership of Cardinal Mercier. The conversations were friendly, and considerable agreement was reached; but neither side spoke with any real authority and the atmosphere was essentially private and informal. Even so, suspicion was aroused at Rome and, after the death of Cardinal Mercier, further conversations of this kind were officially banned by the pope.[2]

The First War brought the Anglican and Eastern Orthodox Churches more close together, and appeals from Russian and other eastern Christians suffering from persecution and famine received a sympathetic hearing in England. Russian exiles in Paris and London have formed an alliance with Anglicans in the Fellowship of S. Alban and S. Sergius which exists to promote understanding between the two Churches.

The Lambeth Conference of 1920, meeting after the catastrophe of the Great War, had very much on its conscience the disunity of the Christian Church, and issued its 'Appeal to all Christian People'. 'The vision which rises before us', they said, 'is that of a Church, genuinely Catholic, loyal to all Truth, and gathering into its fellowship all who profess and call themselves Christians, within whose visible unity all the treasures of faith and order, bequeathed as a heritage by the past to the present, shall be possessed in common and made serviceable to the whole body of Christ.' The fundamentals of such a Church were declared to be the Scriptures, the two Creeds, the Gospel Sacraments and a ministry possessing 'not only the inward call of the Spirit but also the commission of Christ and the authority of the whole body'.[3]

Ten years before, the great missionary conference at Edinburgh in

---

[1] See above, p. 408.

[2] Lord Halifax, *The Conversations at Malines 1921–1925* (1930).

[3] *Lambeth Conferences, 1867–1930* (1948), pp. 119–24.

1910[1] had laid the foundations of international and interdenominational co-operation in the sphere of world evangelism. Further conferences of a similar kind were held at Jerusalem in 1928[2] and at Tambaram, near Madras, in 1938.[3] Having found a common meeting-ground on missionary problems, and having discovered that conferences of this kind were both possible and valuable, it was natural that attempts should be made to discuss other problems in the same atmosphere of good-will and hope. Thus, largely through the influence and zeal of Nathan Söderblom, Archbishop of Uppsala in Sweden, a conference was held at Stockholm in 1925 to consider the mind and conscience of Christians on the social and economic questions with which the world was faced in the post-war age.[4] Twelve years later a second conference was held, this time at Oxford.[5] Out of these conferences was born the 'Life and Work' movement.

But the fundamental questions which divided Christendom were not practical but theological; and though co-operation could be achieved, there could be no real unity or fellowship so long as these questions were ignored. Thus, in addition to the 'Life and Work' movement, further conferences were held to discuss 'Faith and Order'. The first of these met at Lausanne in 1927 with Headlam and Gore as the Anglican leaders,[6] and the second at Edinburgh in 1937 with Temple as its chairman.[7] As a result of these conferences the World Council of Churches came into being in 1948.

iv. Modernism and Orthodoxy

'We desire', wrote Bernard Shaw in the preface to *Back to Methuselah*, 'to extricate the eternal spirit of religion from the sludgy residue of temporalities and legends that are making belief impos-

---

[1] See above, p. 406.
[2] See *The Christian Life and Message in Relation to Non-Christian Systems; Reports of the Jerusalem meeting, 1928*; 8 vols. (1928).
[3] See *Tambaram Madras Reports*, 7 vols. (1939).
[4] See G. K. A. Bell, *The Stockholm Conference on Life and Work, 1925* (1926).
[5] See *The Churches survey their Task*, ed. J. H. Oldham (1937), followed by 7 vols. of reports (1937–38).
[6] See *Faith and Order: Proceedings of the World Conference, Lausanne, 1927*, ed. H. N. Bate (1927).
[7] See *The Second World Conference on Faith and Order, Edinburgh, 1937*, ed. L. Hodgson (1938).

sible, though they are the stock-in-trade of all the Churches.' These words were quoted with approval by Dr. Major in 1925 as a just statement of the aims of the modernist movement.[1] This movement, in the words of one more closely connected with the Church than Shaw, 'is based upon evolution in science and the critical method in history; and it demands, not that the great truths of the Christian religion shall be given up, but that they shall be considered afresh in the light of growing knowledge, and restated in a way suitable to the intellectual conditions of the age'.[2] During and after the First War 'Modernism' exerted a considerable influence on English religious thought and was well organized for propaganda.

In opposition to the Modernists were those whom they were accustomed to call 'Traditionalists', and a number of skirmishes took place between these two schools of thought. The controversy turned mostly on the miraculous element in the life of Christ, especially the Virgin Birth and physical Resurrection, both of which the Modernists were anxious to deny or explain away. To 'Traditionalists', such as Bishop Gore, it was a scandal that clergy should accept office in the Church while denying some of the truths for which the Church stood. A climax was reached with the appointment of Hensley Henson to the see of Hereford in 1917. Henson was a liberal who believed that the essential doctrines of the Incarnation and Eternal Sovereignty of Christ could be separated from belief in the Virgin Birth and Resurrection, and clung to his position with considerable pugnacity when Davidson tried to persuade him to state more explicitly his acceptance of the creeds. The incident aroused great interest and caused the archbishop much pain; but, in the end, Henson was obliged to give way.[3]

During the First World War Modernism flourished. It was a period of great unsettlement and rapid change. Many had faith in a brave, new world after the war, and wished the Church to adapt its formularies to meet the needs of the coming generations. They believed that the Christian faith, as expressed in the creeds, was archaic and out of sympathy with modern thought, and set themselves, therefore, to produce a new statement of the Christian faith in simple terms of the love of God, and to formulate a basic

---

[1] H. D. A. Major, *English Modernism* (1927), p. 12.
[2] *Ibid.* pp. 9-10. The writer was Percy Gardner.
[3] See the account in G. K. A. Bell, *Randall Davidson*, ii, pp. 851-82; and in H. H. Henson, *Retrospect of an Unimportant Life*, i, pp. 214-70.

creed which, as Dr. Major proudly and naively asserted, 'Romanists, Anglicans, Unitarians and Quakers could all unite in repeating'.[1] Various books were published expressing modernist thought;[2] but the most notable event was the Conference of Modern Churchmen held at Girton College, Cambridge, in 1921 to discuss 'Christ and the Creeds'.[3] The lectures given at this conference, especially that by Hastings Rashdall, showed Modernism in its most vigorous form, and caused a considerable stir in the press and in theological journals.

One effect of the modernist movement was to create a demand among the 'Traditionalists' for a clear statement of what the Church of England really did believe and teach. Such a suggestion had been made at the first Anglo-Catholic Congress in 1920 and was fostered by the 'modernist offensive' at Girton in the following year. In 1922 a memorial, signed by a number of distinguished scholars, was presented to Archbishop Davidson asking for a commission on Christian doctrine. Davidson was at first a little apprehensive, but eventually such a commission was set up, composed of a representative group of theologians under the Chairmanship of William Temple. Their report was published in 1938 under the heading of *Doctrine in the Church of England*.

Reviewing English theology in the first half of the twentieth century it is seen to be conditioned by the outward events which were taking place—the two World Wars, the social revolution, the drift from the Church, the growth of psychology and the ecumenical movement. This led to a desire for synthesis and a weakening of the old hostilities. In the realm of theology and philosophy the outstanding Anglican writers were Temple, W. R. Matthews and Oliver Quick, Temple's *Mens Creatrix* (1917), *Christus Veritas* (1924) and *Nature, Man and God* (1934); Matthews' *God in Christian Thought and Experience* (1930), *Essays in Reconstruction* (1933) and *The Purpose of God* (1935); and Quick's *The Ground of Faith and the Chaos of Thought* (1931), *The Christian Sacraments* (1927) and *Doctrines of the Creed* (1938) have been described as a 'small library of nine volumes [which] would suffice for a very thorough grounding in philosophy and dogmatics'.[4] The temper of these books is thoroughly Anglican

---

[1] H. D. A. Major, *English Modernism*, p. 98.
[2] *E.g.* M. G. Glazebrook, *The Faith of a Modern Churchman* (1918).
[3] The papers read at the Conference were published in *The Modern Churchman* in September 1921.
[4] J. K. Mozley, *Some Tendencies in British Theology* (1951), p. 95.

and is marked by a fear of dogmatism and a sense of constant effort and struggle for truth.

In Biblical studies the critical spirit which marked the earlier years of the twentieth century gave place to an interest in the theology and message of the Scriptures rather than in their literary history. B. H. Streeter's *The Four Gospels* (1926) is one of the last of the old school of thought. The new spirit was expressed in the same year by a volume of essays by a group of theologians, mostly drawn from the liberal Anglo-Catholic school, entitled *Essays Catholic and Critical*. This represented a conscious attempt to direct theological study into new channels. One of the contributors, Sir Edwyn Hoskyns, struck the new note in his essay on 'The Christ of the Synoptic Gospels' in which he declared that the chief problem was not the 'Jesus of History' but 'the relation between the little group of disciples called by Jesus from among the Galilean fishermen and the *Corpus Christi* of S. Paul or the *Civitas Dei* of S. Augustine'.[1] The problem, in fact, is as much 'What think ye of the Church?' as 'What think ye of Christ?' In more recent years, however, the pendulum swung in the opposite direction, and the Scriptures have once again been subjected to close scrutiny in an effort to discover to what extent the primitive and oral traditions about Christ were modified and interpreted in the years before the evangelists actually put pen to paper.

v. *Worship*

One of the most remarkable features of this period was the great improvement in the appearance of the parish churches. Bad Victorian furnishings were gradually replaced, and churches made to look much more 'cared-for' by higher standards of beauty and cleanliness. The same applies to the cathedrals. Here the good work done by Dean Bennett at Chester inspired many cathedral chapters to unlock their doors and welcome the stranger.

Within the churches there was much variety of worship. A few churches had become almost indistinguishable, in appearance and in ceremonial, from those of the Roman communion, while a few might almost pass for Presbyterian or Congregational chapels. Undeterred by episcopal denunciations and legal threats, clergy

[1] *Essays Catholic and Critical*, p. 153.

went on their own individualistic ways, determined to do what they themselves thought best despite the demands of law and obedience.

It was in the hopes of restoring some kind of discipline that Prayer Book revision had been put in hand after the Royal Commission on Ritual Matters in 1904. Revision, however, proved a slow process, and was held up, first by the war and then by the constitutional changes in the Church which took place as a result of the *Enabling Act*. It was not in fact until 1927 that the proposed book was ready to be presented to the Convocations. In the debates which followed, the book was passed by large majorities. A handful of bishops and a few extremists of both kinds opposed it, but the general opinion of the clergy was warmly in its favour. The same was true of the Church Assembly, which passed the book by the comfortable majority of 517 to 133. It was then taken to Parliament, and Randall Davidson introduced it into the House of Lords in December 1927. The debate lasted three days and created considerable public interest, the motion being eventually passed by 241 votes to 88. On the following day it was debated in the House of Commons. Here a small but well-organized group of staunch Evangelicals made a firm stand against the book, and, by stirring up deep-seated protestant prejudices, secured the rejection of the motion by 238 votes to 205.

This was a crisis. The Church had, by large majorities, decided in favour of the book. The House of Lords had agreed to it. Now the House of Commons, composed partly of members who were not Churchmen or even Christians, had rejected it. Was the Church to take such a rebuff lying down? Faced with such a situation it might have been better if the Church had said: 'This is the book which we want and which we propose to use. If the State does not like it, let it prohibit its use. The bishops have proved themselves incapable of arresting lawlessness. Let the State see what it can do.' Instead of that the bishops decided to make certain alterations in the book in the hopes of appeasing its opponents, and then to offer it to Parliament again. The result was that in 1928 the proposed book was rejected again by a rather larger majority.

The new Prayer Book failed for various reasons. One was that there was too much party feeling in the Church. On both sides were men who disliked the new book and fought hard against it. Again, the House of Commons was not the proper place in which to debate either technical points of doctrine or the intimacies of Chris-

tain worship. Thirdly, neither of the archbishops showed much enthusiasm for the book. Davidson 'could not bring himself to believe
that the revision of the Prayer Book was in fact a vital matter to the
Church',[1] and Lang really wanted a restoration of the 1549 book.
As Lang said:'The Prayer Book baby can hardly be said to have had
very satisfactory godparents since one Archbishop did not really
want it at all and the other Archbishop would have preferred something else'.[2]

What was to happen now? The bishops held an emergency meeting at which most of them agreed to allow the use of the 1928 book,
and to try to stop such practices as were not in keeping with either
that book or the book of 1662. As a result, parts of the new book
came to be widely used, especially the occasional offices. But
attempts to use the book to enforce discipline had very little success.

In matters of parochial worship changes took place often as the
result of changing social conditions. Up to the First War there
was a fairly clear distinction in most parishes between those who
worshipped in the morning and those who went to evensong. The
division was based largely upon class distinctions. That disappeared;
and, in its place, there grew up a desire for co-operation, for one
supreme act of corporate worship each Sunday in which all members
of the Body of Christ can take part. This led to the popularity of
the idea of a 'Parish Communion', a celebration of the Eucharist
at some time between 8.30 and 10 A.M., attended by young and
old, and essentially congregational.[3]

The decline of mattins which resulted from this had some effect
on preaching. In previous years the Sunday morning sermon had
often been an event of considerable importance. More emphasis
was now laid upon worship than upon homiletic, and in many
churches there came to be but one weekly sermon in place of two.
Modern ways of life encourage this. Preaching, to be effective,
demands a regular congregation who will listen week by week to
the preacher's message; but 'the mobility of modern society is now
threatening the Protestant pulpit with practical futility'.[4] Modern
sermons, however, though short are not necessarily worse than
those of more leisured days.

[1] G. K. A. Bell, *Randall Davidson*, ii. p, 1356.
[2] J. G. Lockhart, *Cosmo Gordon Lang* (1949), p. 300.
[3] See *The Parish Communion; a Book of Essays*, ed. A. G. Hebert (1937).
[4] H. H. Henson, *The Church of England* (1939), p. 240.

Much was done during these years to improve the quality of church music. In 1922 the Archbishops of Canterbury and York appointed a commission 'to consider and report upon the place of music in the worship of the Church, and in particular the training of church musicians and the education of the clergy in the knowledge of music as a branch of liturgical study'.[1] Following the report of this committee a vigorous drive was made to improve the standards of music in the parish churches. Much encouragement was given to this cause by Dr. Sydney Nicholson who, in 1929, founded the School of English Church Music,[2] to which many parish and other choirs became affiliated.

The administration of the sacraments of Baptism and Confirmation also had much care and attention devoted to it in these years. Early in the century baptism was often administered in a very casual and indiscriminate way in many town churches—'innumerable babies, about twenty at a time; scarcely ever a godparent, the poor babies very imperfectly washed and clothed, a noise like a parrot-house, and a smell beyond description'.[3] In time more trouble came to be taken over christenings, and the public baptism of an infant in the course of Morning or Evening Prayer or at the Holy Communion was introduced into some churches. Similarly, longer periods were devoted to the training of candidates for Confirmation. The great increase in divorce stimulated interest in the Church's responsibility for those who seek the sacrament of Holy Matrimony, and many parish priests started classes for the preparation of those about to be married.

vi. *The Church at Home and Overseas*

It is frequently said, by those whose vision is limited to their immediate surroundings, that the Church is decaying. In fact, taking the Church as a whole, the first part of the twentieth century saw a phenomenal advance, the like of which has never before occurred since the fourth century. As a result of the courage and zeal of the pioneer missionaries of the nineteenth century the Church vastly increased its numbers, especially in India and Africa.

[1] See *Music in Church* (1951), p. v.
[2] Later, the Royal School of Church Music.
[3] Harold Anson, *Looking Forward* (1939), p. 145.

But the early missionaries were not only zealous, they were also far-sighted. From the very beginning they planned and worked for the day when their own corner of the mission-field would become self-supporting, an independent and autonomous unit in the world-wide Church. From 1914 onwards the churches became increasingly self-governing, self-extending and self-supporting. There has been a steady increase in native ministries, native forms of art and architecture, native liturgy and ceremonial.

Yet the link between the overseas Churches and the Church at home remained a strong one. In spite of the growth of provinces, a number of dioceses continued to remain directly under the authority of the Archbishop of Canterbury; and in spite of growing self-sufficiency, many Churches depended upon England both for men and for money. In providing these, great responsibility was shouldered by the missionary societies, the organizations to which so much of the advance of the Church overseas is directly due. When the *Enabling Act* set up a Missionary (or Overseas) Council of the Church Assembly it seemed to threaten the independence of the societies; but no attempt was made to limit their independence or to dictate their policy.

The great opportunities opening out in many parts of the world, and the difficulties and problems left behind by the First War encouraged the Church to make a big effort to impress upon the people of England their responsibility for the welfare of the Church overseas. This was done in 1926 by a series of reports, six in all, known as *The World Call to the Church*. Each report was prepared by experts and endeavoured to show what had been done and what needed doing. The call was sounded in the ears of English churchmen in many ways, notably by campaigns in which students from the universities took a prominent part.

There is probably nothing which has done more to inspire and hold together the Anglican Communion than the Lambeth Conferences which have grown steadily in size and significance since their inauguration in 1867. The Conference of 1920 was a meeting of bishops many of whom had been isolated during the war and were confused and baffled by the problems which beset them in the post-war world. The theme of the Conference was 'Fellowship'. The war had, for a time, destroyed the universal fellowship of mankind; and yet, out of the war, new forms of fellowship had grown up. It was the task of the Church to teach men the true meaning of Christian fellowship. The Church, however, was itself terribly divided. The Conference, therefore, issued its 'Appeal to all Christian People'[1] in the hopes that thereby further steps towards Christian unity might be made possible. The next Conference, in 1930, took for its underlying theme the idea of 'Witness', the natural outcome of the fellowship which the Church was trying to foster.

The Encyclical Letter was written in a tone of some optimism, with the words 'Sursum Corda' as its theme. The subjects discussed included such things as the Christian Doctrine of God, the Church's attitude towards Divorce, problems of race relations and of youth and questions concerning the Healing Ministry and the ministry of women in the church. It also had to give careful thought to the proposed scheme for a united Church in South India which was now under discussion, and resolved that, as soon as the negotiations were completed, the Churches should be encouraged to go ahead.[2] After this there was a gap of eighteen years, during which the Second World War was fought and won, before the Conference met again in 1948.

During this period much thought was given to questions affecting Church and Society. The social revolution and march of industry, the slump and unemployment, the crises leading up to the Second World War and the growth of Communism all provided much material upon which the Christian sociologists could work. After the First World War there was a strong desire to perpetuate in industrial society something of the comradeship which war conditions had created; and in 1919 Prebendary P. T. R. Kirk founded the Industrial Christian Fellowship by the fusion of the 'Navvy Mission' and the Christian Social Union. In the years of poverty and depression which followed the war, the Church showed an interest in the cause of the unemployed, but was unable to do much towards a solution of the problem. The foundation of the Society of S. Francis in 1921 to work among tramps, and the work of Basil Jellicoe and Charles Jenkinson in the field of housing may be regarded as, in different ways, a contribution towards better conditions for the poor. Con-

[1] See above, p. 422. *Lambeth Conferences, 1867–1930* (S.P.C.K. 1948) contains a full report, and cf. G. K. A. Bell, *Randall Davidson*, ii, pp. 1003-15.
[2] *Lambeth Conference, 1930*, p. 51.

ferences on social problems were also held, in particular the Conference on Christian Politics, Economics and Citizenship ('C.O.P.E.C.'), a large gathering of 1500 delegates from many different communions, which assembled at Birmingham under the chairmanship of William Temple in 1924.[1] In 1939, when war broke out again, plans were already being made for a smaller Anglican conference to discuss 'The Life of the Church and the Order of Society'. This met at Malvern in 1941, again under Temple's influence and chairmanship. The treatment of the subject was much more theological and philosophical than earlier conferences, and some of the members found it too difficult; but Temple was able to express the general feeling of the movement in a small book called *Christianity and Social Order* (1942) which was widely read and discussed in the forces and among civilians.

In education this period saw a steady expansion of facilities and opportunities for young and old. During the First War H. A. L. Fisher produced a new *Education Act* in 1918 to extend the normal period of education at each end of childhood by providing nursery schools for the very young and secondary and continuation schools for adolescents. Fisher called a conference to discuss the religious question and would have liked to abolish the dual system in favour of a national system of education; but nothing came of this. The church schools continued to enjoy the privileges granted to them in the act of 1902 which were further acknowledged and safeguarded in the *Education Act* of 1944. According to this measure, schools were now to be described as either 'County' or 'Voluntary', the latter being divided into two categories according to the proportion of the money which they could raise towards bringing them up to the higher standards demanded by modern education. Those which could provide half of the necessary sum were described as 'aided', the rest as 'controlled'. Religious instruction was to be given in all schools, and church children in county schools could be withdrawn to a near-by church for worship and instruction during school hours. In 'aided' voluntary schools denominational teaching could be given as before in non-provided schools, but in 'controlled' schools the teaching must conform to an agreed syllabus. This act has, therefore, done much to safeguard religious instruction and has been

[1] See *The Proceedings of C.O.P.E.C.* (1924) and 12 vols. of *C.O.P.E.C. Commission Reports.*

regarded as, on the whole, beneficial to the Church.[1]

In the rapidly changing conditions of modern life the Church had to be ready to adapt itself to new methods and to devise new means of presenting its message. The development, after the First War, of broadcasting presented the Church with an entirely new opportunity which was readily seized. The B.B.C. was formed in 1922, and early in the following year the Archbishop of Canterbury was approached about the possibility of broadcast sermons and services. The suggestion met with much opposition from those who thought that such services would keep people away from the churches; but, in spite of this, a service was broadcast from S. Martin's-in-the-Fields on the Feast of the Epiphany 1924, and from then onwards such services became a regular feature of radio programmes. Much interest has also been taken in the progress of religious films and drama. Many playwrights, including T. S. Eliot, Christopher Fry and Dorothy Sayers contributed greatly to the development of religious drama, and much encouragement was given to dramatic effort by the Canterbury Festivals, inaugurated by Dr. G. K. A. Bell, and by the work of the Religious Drama Society which helped to raise the standards both of the plays and of their production.

Changing social conditions also deeply affected the life and work of the clergy. Since the days of C. J. Blomfield and Samuel Wilberforce the demands made upon diocesan bishops, and willingly accepted by them, have steadily increased. Gone are the spacious days of London life, of regular attendance at the House of Lords, of comfort and elegance in the episcopal palace. The bishop of today, in spite of the large increase in the number of dioceses,[2] is obliged to be a hard-working and sometimes over-tired man. Committee-meetings both in his own diocese and in London, conferences, interviews, constant travelling and the weight of correspondence make heavy inroads upon a bishop's time. In the 1840's at Lambeth, we are told, 'the general post letters in the morning for the Archbishop and Mrs. Howley were put in a china bowl in the hall. They

---

[1] See Spencer Leeson, *Christian Education*, pp. 222-38.
[2] Ten new dioceses have been created in England since 1914: Chelmsford, Sheffield and St. Edmundsbury and Ispwich in 1914; Coventry in 1918; Bradford in 1920; Leicester and Blackburn in 1926; and Derby, Guildford and Portsmouth in 1927.

were scarcely enough to cover the bottom of it.'[1].At the present time a very large number of letters goes out from Lambeth each day, in addition to private correspondence. Taxation and the fall in the value of money robbed the bishops of any claim to affluence, though Hensley Henson was over-dramatic in stating that within 'the immemorial homes of feudal pride and Erastian pomp . . . financial embarrassment shadows the attenuated hospitality and frugal house-keeping of the diocesan'![2]

Whereas the number of bishops rose during these years, the number of parochial clergy fell. It has been reckoned that in 1914 there were 18,000 clergy at work in the provinces of Canterbury and York; that by 1930 the number had fallen to 16,000, and by 1946 to 15,500.[3] The diminishing number of clergy led inevitably to two things: to a uniting of benefices and to a shortage of assistant curates. Many parishes in which it was customary, before the First War, to have a large staff of curates have now to manage with but one or two assistants; and groups of country parishes, which were formerly served by two or three men, are now under the care of a single incumbent.

NOTE ON BOOKS

Much the best introduction to the church life of this period will be found in the three biographies: G. K. A. Bell, *Randall Davidson*, 2 vols. (1935), J. G. Lockhart, *Cosmo Gordon Lang* (1949) and F. A. Iremonger, *William Temple* (1948). References should also be made to other biographies and autobiographies such as H. H. Henson, *Retrospect of an Unimportant Life*, 3 vols. (1942–50), C. Smyth, *C. F. Garbett, Archbishop of York* (1959), Owen Chadwick, *Hensley Henson* (1983) and R. Jasper, *A. C. Headlam, Life and Letters* (1960). For general church history see Roger Lloyd, *The Church of England, 1900–1965* (1966), G. S. Spinks and others, *Religion in Britain since 1900* (1952) and *Crockford Prefaces: the Editor looks back* (1947). G. K. A. Bell, *Documents on Christian Unity*, 3 vols. (1924, 1930 and 1948) and R. Rouse and S. C. Neill, *A History of the Oecumenical Movement* (1954) are important for the Ecumenical Movement; and J. K. Mozley, *Some Tendencies in British Theology* (1951) and A. M. Ramsey, *From Gore to Temple* (1960) for theological development.

[1] G. K. A. Bell, *Randall Davidson*, 3rd ed. (1952), p. vii.
[2] H. H. Henson. *The Church of England* (1939), p. 145.
[3] Cyril Garbett, *The Claims of the Church of England* (1947), p. 130.

CHAPTER XXIII

THE MODERN CHURCH
(1945-1972)

i. *The Atomic Age*

WHEN the Second World War ended in 1945 the atmosphere was very different from what it had been in 1918. The end of hostilities should have brought a sense of relief and security—no more casualty-lists, no more air-raids, no more shortages. It was, of course, an enormous relief to know that the monstrous evils associated with Nazism and Fascism were now crushed and impotent. But in spite of this there was little sense of security; for, on 6 August 1945, the Japanese city of Hiroshima had been virtually wiped out by a single atomic bomb. This was the first use of an atomic weapon, but no one expected it to be the last. The world soon came to live under the shadow of the 'mushroom cloud', and the question was 'Whose turn will it be next time?' Everyone knew that the bomb dropped on Hiroshima was not the ultimate weapon, and that bigger and infinitely more destructive bombs would be made before long. Terrifying though the prospect was, it was made more alarming by the knowledge that, in time, all the greater nations would be supplied with weapons of this kind, and that it only needed a madman, or a desperado, or even a mistake to let loose powers which could destroy all life and turn the world into a radioactive cinder heap.

It was no wonder, then, that the post-war world lacked the sense of stability and hope which it had experienced in 1918. There was now a feeling of transitoriness, of uncertainty, which aroused discontent and a desire to rebel. Young people growing up in this atmosphere tended to be more than usually critical of authority, and of the structures and standards of the past. This led to student rebellions in many parts of the world, to demonstrations on every possible occasion, to violence and vandalism, or to the silent revolt against 'civilization' and the rules and understandings by which society lived. For, with this sense of instability and revolt went a desire for freedom, for a 'permissive society' in which the individual would be allowed to do what he liked without paying respect to the conventions and moral standards of society.

Meanwhile, big social changes were taking place with the rapid rise in wages and the appearance of the 'affluent society'. Things which had been regarded as far beyond the reach of the weekly wage-earners—cars and caravans, holidays on the Costa Brava, television and every kind of electrical apparatus in the home—became normal. The barriers which had separated the rich from the poor were swept away, together with the class-distinctions which had been so rigid in former years.

Add together the three ingredients of instability, permissiveness and affluence, and you get a very different kind of life from that in which the pre-war generation had grown up. 'Life may not last long, so enjoy it while you can'; 'Live now: pay later'—these were the slogans of the new world, and there was much to make this sort of life possible, aided and abetted by the Welfare State. Parents were no longer under the necessity of denying themselves in order that their children should get a good education, for this was all done out of public money. There was now no need to save for sickness or old age, since the State would take care of you. Cushioned, insured, protected against the harsh winds of ill-fortune, the individual could enjoy himself with little concern for the future, while, at the same time, nursing a grievance against authority and even against the powers which gave him his freedom.

As far as the Church was concerned, most of these changes in the way in which people live had some effect upon her. The mysterious 'They' who stood in the way of progress—whether 'They' meant the bishops, the Church Commissioners, Church House or some Central or Diocesan Board of Finance—had to be criticised, and, if possible, dethroned. Now was the time to advance—to overhaul the machinery of the Church, whether in the parish, the diocese, or the country as a whole, to introduce new methods of worship freed from the archaic language and thought-forms of the past, to organise all aspects of the Church's work with the aid of experts in psychology, ecology and sociology. The post-war age has been, therefore, the age of consultation, of conference and dialogue; and a feeling has grown up that every problem can be satisfactorily solved so long as enough people spend enough time talking about it, and that if clergymen can be enticed away from their draughty vicarages to spend a few days in a centrally-heated conference-house, then the Kingdom of God has undoubtedly been brought a little nearer.

ii. *The Church in the Post-War Era*

The sudden and unexpected death of William Temple in 1944 deprived the Church of its most able and eminent member at a very critical moment. Many people thought that the obvious person to succeed him was George Bell, the Bishop of Chichester, who, far more than any other of the bishops, had stood up for Christian standards during the war; but the Prime Minister was obviously not willing to recommend him for the primacy.[1] The choice fell, therefore, on Geoffrey Fisher who, for the last five years, had been sorting out some of the confusion left behind by his predecessor in the See of London.

Fisher turned out to be a gifted administrator who quickly made up his mind as to what the Church most needed, and did his best to carry out a policy of reform. His immediate task was to get the Church on its feet again after the war and to provide it with an efficient, well-lubricated machinery with which to do its work. He also realised that, with the vast increase in facilities for travel, he could do something to strengthen the ties of the Anglican Communion all over the world. He also cared a great deal about promoting Christian unity. In all this work he had some very able colleagues—notably Garbett at York and Bell at Chichester.

Six years of war had greatly dislocated the life of the Church in England. Most of the larger cities had been heavily bombed, with the consequent destruction of many churches, vicarages and schools. There was the problem of chaplains returning from the armed forces and wanting livings. There was also the difficulty of staffing some of the parishes, since so few men had been ordained during the war. There was also a host of financial problems due to the rapid rise in the cost of living set against the limited resources of the Church. To these questions Archbishop Fisher gave his full attention as he skilfully guided the Church of England—and indeed the whole Anglican Communion—through a stormy sea.

[1] See R. C. D. Jasper, *George Bell: Bishop of Chichester* (1967), pp. 284-7.

The Lambeth Conference, which had not met since 1930, was called together in 1948. As the bishops, drawn together from all parts of the world, sat down in the library of Lambeth Palace, there were signs that the incurable optimism of the episcopate was in no way dimmed by the devastations and bitterness of war. 'The keynote of our message', they said, 'is encouragement to the people of God all the world over. For those who have eyes to see, there are signs that the tide of faith is beginning to come in'; words which, perhaps, some of them may have regretted as time went by. But in the post-war years, despite the fearful dangers which threatened mankind, they felt confident, and they settled down to discuss a variety of topics, from the Christian Doctrine of man to the propriety of ordaining a woman to the priesthood in Hong Kong.

Undoubtedly the most important debate of this Conference was on the question of Christian Unity. The united Church of South India had been inaugurated in the previous year, with the result that four Anglican dioceses had gone out of the Anglican Communion, at any rate for a period of time. The bishops agreed to support this plan, though with some reservations since they were agreed that, in any future schemes, a method of unification of the ministries at the moment of inauguration should be regarded as essential. Unless this was done, they could see no future for the Anglican Communion. 'The first and dominant concern which we would record regarding all schemes for corporate union', they wrote, 'is that the resulting united Church should be such as could be in full communion with all its parent Churches'.[1]

Six years later an Anglican Congress was held at Minneapolis. This was a great gathering of clergy and laity—the first of its kind since 1908[2]—though it could hardly be 'representative' since, of the 42 lay delegates from the Church of England, 15 were wives of clerical delegates and consequently unlikely, as was pointed out, 'to express radical or rebellious opinions in the presence of their husbands'.[3] The summoning of this Congress was an attempt to get all parts of the Anglican Communion to recognise their responsibility to one another, especially to the Churches struggling towards self-sufficiency and independence in the developing countries.

[1] *The Lambeth Conference, 1948*, Pt. II, p. 51.
[2] See above, p. 406.
[3] See P. M. Dawley, *Anglican Congress, 1954: Report and Proceedings.* (1955). Wales was represented only by two clergymen and their respective wives.

The Lambeth Conference of 1958, over which Fisher again presided, made 'Reconciliation' its watchword. The Encyclical Letter, which is written in a curious kind of ecclesiastical jargon, encourages people to read and study the Bible, to support nuclear disarmament, to preach the traditional doctrines of marriage and family life, and to press on with the work of Christian unity with renewed effort. Perhaps the most constructive work of this Conference was in promoting a sense of fellowship among the different parts of the Anglican Communion, and in creating the post of 'executive officer' whose job it would be to travel all over the world, to find out what were the particular needs and difficulties of the Church in each area, and to make these known to the Church as a whole. The first holder of this new office was Stephen Bayne, Bishop of Olympia. It was to promote this sense of 'togetherness' that an Anglican Congress was later held at Toronto in 1963 when the plan for Mutual Responsibility and Interdependence (MRI) was set up.[1]

Meanwhile, on the home front, the councils of the Church were busy trying to bring the Church up to date in a rapidly changing society. With the creation of vast new housing estates on the perimeter of the great cities, the rebuilding of city centres, and the steady depopulation of the villages, some changes in the distribution of the Church's resources, particularly in manpower, were necessary. In order to make this possible, the Church Assembly passed, in 1949, a Pastoral Reorganization Measure which made obligatory the setting up, in each diocese, of a Pastoral Committee which would be responsible for these matters. This naturally led to considerable discussion on what came to be called the 'deployment' of the clergy (which inevitably included the question of how they were to be supported). In 1960 the Church Assembly asked the Central Advisory Council for the Ministry to examine this question and to make recommendations. The Council decided that the first thing was to lay bare the facts of the present situation, and invited Mr. Leslie Paul to produce a thorough sociological survey of the state of the ordained ministry of the Church of England.[2] This led to much discussion and debate, and to the demand for a plan of reform. A commission was therefore set up, under the chairmanship

---

[1] See *Anglican Congress, 1963, Report of Proceedings*, ed. E. R. Fairweather (1963).
[2] Leslie Paul, *The Development and Payment of the Clergy* (1964).

of Canon Fenton Morley, Vicar of Leeds, to make recommendations. The report of this commission was published in 1967[1] and,
in tackling some of the thorny subjects such as the Parson's Freehold
and Private Patronage, turned out to be imaginative and, in some
ways, radical—so much so that it failed to get the full support of the
Church Assembly when it came up for debate.[2]

One of the matters which exercised the mind of Archbishop
Fisher was the chaotic condition of the Church's laws, which had
never undergone any thorough revision since 1604. Fisher found
this, he said, 'the most absorbing and all-embracing topic of my
whole archiepiscopate'.[3] The Canons of 1604, with their antiquated
provisions for a method of Church life which had long disappeared,
were a totally inadequate guide to the problems facing the Church
in the twentieth century.[4] One or two of them had been slightly
amended in 1865, 1887 and 1936; but the time had come when a
new corpus of Canon Law was necessary. A commission had,
therefore, been working on this for some time before it produced
its report, *The Canon Law of the Church of England*, in 1947. This
consists of a masterly historical introduction in the best style of
Anglican scholarship, and a proposed set of 134 Canons. This
inevitably caused long debates in Convocation and elsewhere as
the wording of each Canon was hammered out. Twenty-two years
later, in 1969, the new set of Canons was finally promulged.

Another matter to which Fisher and the consultative bodies of
the Church gave close attention was the financial condition of the
Church and the problem of raising the stipends of the clergy to
keep pace with the rise in the cost of living. In 1945 the average
income of a beneficed clergyman was about £400 a year, though
some received far more, and some a good deal less. Since then,
the stipend of almost every benefice has had to be augmented, with
the result that there is now little variation in the incomes of the
clergy. 'Good livings' and 'bad livings' have, in financial terms,
more or less ceased to exist. In order to carry out this process of

---

[1] *Partners in Ministry: being the Report of the Commission on the Deployment and
Payment of the Clergy* (1967).
[2] *Church Assembly: Report of Proceedings* (Summer Session, 1970), pp. 347-99.
[3] Quoted by E. F. Carpenter in *Cantuar* (1971), p. 491.
[4] E.g. 'Maintenance of Conventicles censured'; 'Loiterers not to be suffered near
the Church in time of Divine Service'; 'The Sacraments not to be refused at the
Hands of Unpreaching Ministers'; 'The Restraint of Double Quarrels'; 'Abuses to
be reformed in Registrars'; and so on.

levelling up, large sums have been handed over each year to the diocesan authorities by the Church Commissioners, who came into being in 1948 as an amalgamation of the Ecclesiastical Commissioners and the trustees of Queen Anne's Bounty. By skillful investment, the Commissioners have greatly increased their income, and have thus been able to make considerable grants not only for the stipends of the clergy, but also for pensions, new vicarages and church buildings on new estates.

Geoffrey Fisher retired in 1961, at the age of 74,[1] and was succeeded by Michael Ramsey, then Archbishop of York, who belonged to the succession of scholarly archbishops who have turned up from time to time, from S. Anselm onwards. If Fisher, the administrator, was suspicious of the theologians, Ramsey, the theologian, was bored by the administrators. But he took over the leadership of the Church at a time when the administrative burden was becoming daily more oppressive. Changes were taking place with increased rapidity, and in an atmosphere of criticism and even of rebelliousness on the part of some of the clergy; the ecumenical movement was running into rough water; and there were financial and constitutional problems enough to daunt the most seasoned executive.

In the government of the Church, the big change was the virtual disappearance of the Convocations, which were by far the most ancient legislative bodies in the country, and the replacement of the Church Assembly and the Diocesan Conferences by the General and Diocesan Synods. This new system of government was introduced in 1969; but how far it has been able to expedite or further delay the work of the Church remains to be seen, though the principle of consultation and co-operation is a sound one if judiciously handled.

Ramsey presided over the Lambeth Conference in 1968 with a mixture of geniality and profundity. The bishops divided their work into three categories concerned with Faith, Ministry and Unity; and they summed up their work in these words: 'God is active in his Church, renewing it so that the Church may more clearly proclaim its faith to the world, more effectively discharge its mission of service to the world, and may recover that unity for which our Lord prayed and without which it cannot be truly

[1] See W. E. Purcell, *Fisher of Lambeth*, (1969), and *The Archbishop Speaks*, a collection of Fisher's addresses and speeches, edited by E. F. Carpenter, (1958).

itself.'[1] At this Conference there were present, for the first time, a group of theologians to act as consultants, and a further group of observers representing Orthodox, Roman Catholic and other Christian communions. The Lambeth Conference of 1978, under the chairmanship of Archbishop Coggan, was held, not at Lambeth, but at Canterbury, and was residential. The general theme was 'Today's Church and Today's World' with special reference to the ministry of bishops.

iii. *The Pastoral Scene*

In spite of the great changes which have affected the lives of English people in the post-war world, the Church of England has clung tenaciously to its ancient system of providing a ministry which is basically parochial, and which gives to a priest pastoral care of an area, the boundaries of which were, perhaps, fixed before the Norman Conquest. But although this has remained the pattern of ministry, the system has been to some extent modified and supplemented to meet the needs of modern man.

One of these modifications has been the union of benefices, especially in rural areas, so that one incumbent now looks after two or more parishes. This has been made necessary, partly because of the enormous rise in the cost of living, and partly because the number of clergy has become less.[2] No one can suppose that this policy is popular, as English people like to have a parson living in their village even if they don't give much support to his activities; but shortages of men and money have made it inevitable.[3]

Another method of dealing with modern problems has been the introduction of Group and Team Ministries. In 1949 an experiment was started in Lincolnshire, where fifteen small country parishes, with twelve churches and a total population of little over a thousand, was made into a single unit with its centre at South Ormsby. With careful planning, it was found that this area could be efficiently cared for by a vicar, two curates and a deaconess where before

---

[1] *The Lambeth Conference, 1968*, p. 25.

[2] In the 1880's the annual number of men ordained annually was about 700. In 1973 there were 377.

[3] It is not, therefore, wholly justifiable to declare that 'There are some bishops and archdeacons who roam the countryside seeking what parishes they may devour', as was written by the Editor of *Crockford's Clerical Directory* in 1955-6.

there had been six full-time and totally independent clergymen.[1] Similar plans were adopted in other places, mainly in very rural districts, but also in at least one down-town area. Meanwhile, on the new housing-estates, a slightly different system arose, known as a Team Ministry. Where a suburban parish had suddenly swollen to abnormal size, or a new town had been built, practice in the past had been to cut it up into separate units, each totally independent of the rest. As an alternative to this, schemes were adopted whereby the parish remained as one, being looked after by a team consisting of a rector, supported by a number of vicars, each having either territorial or specialist responsibilities, but all acting as a single unit with an agreed policy.[2]

In addition to variations in the parochial scene, most dioceses have established a number of clergy to act in some special form of ministry intended either to advise the parish priests about certain aspects of their work, or to bring the Church's mission to those untouched by the parishes. Among the former are advisers in youth work, stewardship, public relations, immigrants, and so forth. Among the latter are enterprises like Industrial Mission, priest-workers, and clergy working full-time in broadcasting, journalism and the like. The creator of any form of industrial mission, in the modern sense of the word, was the Reverend E. R. Wickham who started the mission to industry in Sheffield in 1944.[3]

The falling off in the number of men seeking ordination, and the fact that more and more clergy left the parishes for some kind of specialist work, caused the Church to think very hard about what kind and size of ministry it needed if it was to do its work efficiently and properly. Two suggestions have been put forward: one, the ordination of men to carry out a part-time ministry; the other to ordain a number of women. Already a number of men have been ordained to the priesthood in order to assist the clergy with their liturgical and pastoral duties. These are men who earn their living in some other occupation but who are prepared to give up their spare time to forward the work of the Church.[4]

As far as women are concerned, the Church of England has always been a bit puzzled as to what kind of Women's Ministry it wants.

[1] See A. C. Smith, *The South Ormsby Experiment* (1960).

[2] Both Group and Team Ministries are provided for in the Pastoral Measure (1968), Part ii, cc. 19–21.

[3] For a theological rationale of this kind of ministry, see E. R. Wickham, *Church and People in an Industrial City*, (1957) pp. 214–73.

[4] See R. Denniston, *Part-time Priests?* (1960).

The order of deaconesses was established many years ago, but it has not flourished as much as was expected. Women who wish to give their lives to the Church are naturally reluctant to enter a profession in which there is no prospect of promotion. Curates, when trained, go to livings; but deaconesses tend to stay where they are because no higher form of service is offered. As early as 1935 a report on *The Ministry of Women* was issued, recommending, among other things, that a deaconess should be regarded as in Holy Orders; but it was not until the Lambeth Conference in 1968 that this was agreed upon, and then only by a small majority.[1] Meanwhile, a working party had been set up to consider 'the proper rôle of women within the accredited ministry of the Church in parishes and elsewhere'. Their report (*Women in Ministry: a Study*) recommends that women be given a greater part to play in worship and that they should be brought more closely into the consultative counsels of the Church; but it did not pass any judgment on the question of ordaining women to the priesthood. This subject had, in fact, been considered two years previously in a report called *Women and Holy Orders*, which went carefully into the biblical, theological, psychological, ecumenical and practical problems involved. The report showed that, while some thought that the ordination of women was right and some thought it wrong, there were others who, while accepting the proposal in principle, thought it would be inadvisable or inopportune, especially in view of the ecumenical implications.[2] The question was discussed at Lambeth in 1968 when it was decided that every national or regional Church in the Anglican Communion should give some attention to the matter, but that none of them should act without consulting the Anglican Consultative Council. This Council was, in fact, consulted on this matter at its first meeting at Limuru in Kenya in 1971 when it was decided, by a very narrow majority, that if a bishop decided to ordain women to the priesthood, his action would not be condemned by the Council, nor, it was hoped, by other Churches in the Anglican Communion. A proposal to ordain women to the priesthood was debated in the General Synod of the Church of England in 1979 but was lost by a considerable majority.

[1] Resolution 32(c) declares that 'those made deaconesses by the laying on of hands with appropriate prayers be declared to be within the diaconate'.
[2] See the note by Dr. Alan Richardson in *Women and Holy Orders* (1966), pp. 123–8.

Meanwhile in the parish churches of England considerable changes were taking place in the pattern of worship offered to God on Sundays. In the post-war world it was not long before people began to call for much more modern forms of worship. This began with such things as hymn-tunes and folk-masses in a modern idiom and with the introduction of new translations of the Bible, some of which received official recognition from the Convocations. The *New English Bible*, the first part of which appeared in 1961, was the work of an ecumenical committee first set up in 1947. It was an attempt to produce a translation of the Bible which would 'in some measure succeed in removing a real barrier between a large proportion of our fellow countrymen and the truth of the Holy Scriptures'. The *New English Bible* had an enormous sale but not a wholly favourable reception by the theologians, some of whom thought that by removing some barriers the translators had erected others which were equally, if not more seriously, obscuring the message which the Scriptures were intended to convey. So far as the liturgical use of the Bible is concerned, many churches have preferred the *Revised Standard Version* (1951) with its more conventional flavour, or the *Jerusalem Bible*,[1] with its more dramatic style.

The worship of the Church of England is controlled by Parliament. It was this fact which caused the fiasco of 1928,[2] and, in introducing new forms of worship, the Church Assembly was anxious to avoid a similar confrontation with the House of Commons. The Assembly, therefore, decided, in 1965, to present to Parliament a 'Prayer Book (Alternative and other Services) Measure', the purpose of which was to make it possible for Parliament to give the Church permission to use experimental forms of worship for a limited period. This was a wise move. A liturgy cannot be understood or appreciated merely by reading it through. It needs to be used, and prayed, over a considerable period before judgment can be passed upon it.

With this permission to try out new forms, the Liturgical Commission was asked to draw up experimental forms of Holy Communion. Two forms were produced, known as Series I and Series II, the former keeping fairly closely to a traditional and

---

[1] The English version (1966) is based on the French translation, *La Bible de Jérusalem* (1956).

[2] See above, pp. 427–8.

conventional style of worship, the latter being more simple and congregational. Series I met with little support, but Series II swept the country and came to be used and appreciated by a very large number of congregations, together with new forms of Baptism, Confirmation and other services. But, in spite of the popularity of Series II, the Commission felt that it had not gone far enough and, in due course, produced a Series III in which more modern language is used (e.g. God is addressed as You and not as Thou), and an attempt is made to bring liturgy more into line with modern conceptions of the nature of worship.

With these new forms of service, the pattern of Sunday worship in many churches has changed very rapidly. Whereas in many urban and suburban parishes the public had for a long time been offered Holy Communion at 8.0 A.M., Mattins with a sermon and a good deal of hymn-singing at 11.0, and Evensong at 6.30[1], the more common programme now is a Parish Communion, or Sung Eucharist, in the morning as the only well-attended service of the day. The same is true also, though less commonly, in country areas where habits and customs change more slowly.

One result of this change of programme has been the decline in preaching. Under the old system the clergy were expected to provide, each Sunday, two sermons each lasting about twenty minutes. These weekly addresses, whether mainly expositions of Scripture, proclamations of the Faith, or exhortations to Christian living, were regarded as an essential part of the priest's function as a teacher. But in churches where the Parish Communion is the only service attended by any number of people, among whom are generally some very young children, a sermon, in the generally accepted meaning of the word, is virtually impossible, and has to be replaced by a very short address, delivered sometimes under conditions which do not make for easy concentration on the part of the hearers. To meet this need, some parishes have introduced weekly seminars and discussion groups in order that matters of faith and conduct can be talked about, and the Church's teaching made clear.

With the destruction of churches during the war and the need for new buildings in new towns and housing-estates, a great many buildings have been erected, mostly designed, more or less, to fit

---

[1] But see above, p. 428 for the introduction of the Parish Communion.

in with modern taste and modern methods of worship. The most
striking example of this was the new cathedral at Coventry, designed
by Sir Basil Spence and consecrated in 1962.[1] With this went a
large number of parish churches, chapels and dual-purpose buildings,
in which attempts were made to get away from the traditional
designs, copied from medieval examples, which had been so
popular up to the middle of the twentieth century. The new
churches were mostly designed to meet the changes which were
taking place—one, the growth of eucharistic as against homiletic
forms of worship; the other, the need to make a service such as the
Holy Communion, far more congregational.[2]

Another, and rather unexpected change which has come about
as a result of new forms of worship has been the breakdown in the
old distinctions between 'high' and 'low' which had divided the
Church for so many years. Before these changes came in, the High
Mass held in an Anglo-Catholic church, largely copied from
pre-Vatican Roman Catholic forms, was very different from the
High Mattins with sermon offered in the more evangelical churches.
But now that so many churches have adopted a simple and congregational form of Eucharist as the main (and perhaps the only) form
of service on a Sunday, there is much less difference between them.

With some reduction in the size of congregations (though perhaps
not as striking as is sometimes supposed),[3] many parishes find
considerable difficulty in raising enough money to keep things
going and to fulfil their obligations outside the parish. This has,
naturally, been made more difficult by the sharp fall in the value of
money. It has also been made more burdensome by the abnormal
increase in the central and diocesan machinery of the Church, and,
therefore, of the sum (or Quota) asked for each year from each
parish to meet these needs.

In order to meet these larger demands in addition to their local
expenses, many parishes introduced the principle of Christian
Stewardship. Stewardship campaigns were aimed at making people
accept a greater responsibility for the right expenditure of their

[1] Basil Spence, *Phoenix at Coventry* (1962). See also Roger Lloyd, *The Church of
England, 1900–1965* (1966), pp. 565–70.
[2] Peter Hammond, *Liturgy and Architecture* (1960), pp. 100–136. See also *Sixty
Postwar Churches* (1956).
[3] The number of people attending Holy Communion on Easter Day varied very
little in the years 1900 to 1970, and was, in fact, slightly higher in 1968 than in 1905.
So much for those who talk of the 'good old days' when everyone went to church.

time and money. These campaigns were not just money-making efforts, but were designed to promote Christian principles of sound stewardship, to arouse people's interest in what the Church was doing, and to encourage them to devote what could be regarded as a proper proportion of their time and of their income to God. The methods were those which had been found workable in other places—notably in the U.S.A.—and the results often turned out to be startling. Many congregations have not only relieved anxiety for their own requirements, but have also been able to increase their giving to the work of the Church beyond the boundaries of their own parish.

iv. *The Search for Truth*

The war of 1939–45, like all great wars, left the world in a state of confusion and uncertainty. As in the First World War, the faith of many had been strained. The old-fashioned ideas about God seemed now to be out-dated and incredible. The Christian Church had, therefore, to reconsider its message in what many were calling 'the post-Christian era' and to a world 'in retreat from Christianity'. It was not easy. The Christian teacher had his box of tools—the Bible, the traditional hymns and prayers, the Catechism and the text books—but what help could these be in a world of doubt and perplexity? What had the Church to say? Was there any message which it could give with confidence? What did Christians really believe?

The Church had a number of writers—men like Eric Mascall and Leonard Hodgson—who were able to put the more traditional point of view both clearly and constructively. Good work was also being done in the field of biblical criticism and interpretation and in Church history and patristic studies. But in the world of ideas, of dogmatic and moral theology, Anglican theologians were not able to give assurance and clear direction to a world in considerable confusion and uncertainty. Perhaps this is due to the Englishman's ingrained dislike of dogmatism. 'Outside observers', writes an American critic of the English scene, 'are repeatedly baffled by the seeming neglect of theology, as they understand it, in Anglican quarters'. And again: 'Anglicanism has a deep-seated suspicion of elaborate speculative systems of doctrinal theology'.[1]

---

[1] Robert J. Page: *New Directions in Anglican Theology* (1967), p. 33.

But if Anglicans had tended, in the past, to be cautious and conservative, they could not ignore the new challenges which were coming from abroad, especially from German theologians like Bultmann, Bonhoeffer and Tillich. These were men who realised that the old, traditional ways of presenting the Christian faith had little to offer to modern man, to 'man come of age' as they called him. In a world of science and technology, of urbanisation and the relentless pressures exerted by the mass-media, people could not be expected to accept without question statements about the nature of God or about the needs and duties of man.

Paul Tillich had been publishing important books since 1921, and Rudolf Bultmann since 1925, but it was some years before their ideas spread to this country, and it was not until after the war that their chief works were translated into English. When the ideas of men of this stature came to be more generally known to English theologians, their own thought was bound to be affected. Perhaps the first sign of this was in a book called *Soundings, or Essays Concerning Christian Understanding*, which was published in 1962. This was a collection of eleven essays, rather on the lines of previous volumes such as *Essays and Reviews* and *Foundations*. The title of this new work was intended to convey the impression that the writers of these essays were trying to discover where they were, and what was happening to the Christian faith, rather than to formulate a policy or to offer a solution. 'It is a time', they said, 'for ploughing, not reaping . . . for making soundings, not charts or maps'.[1] *Soundings* was not, therefore, a dogmatic book. It did not attempt to answer the questions which people were asking. What it did was to make sure that questions were not ignored because they were difficult or because the old answers were known to be deficient.[2]

In the year following the publication of *Soundings*, John Robinson, Bishop Suffragan of Woolwich, published a small paper-backed volume called *Honest to God*, which tried to put into popular language the sort of anxieties and uncertainties from which the theologians were suffering. The book had an enormous sale and was translated into many European languages. The fact that over a million copies were sold in the first three years showed that people

[1] Op. cit. p. ix.
[2] See also the book by four Anglican writers called *Objections to Christian Belief* (1963).

were anxiously waiting for someone to say that men of the 1960's needed to look again, and with critical eyes, at the old language and imagery in which the Christian faith had for so long been presented, ruthlessly to throw out what was false or misleading, and to try to see the fundamentals of Christian belief and practice in their essentials. This is what *Honest to God* did; but, in so doing, it inevitably caused a good deal of controversy.[1] Some readers were shocked at the wholesale slaughter of a number of 'sacred cows'; but others rejoiced that a theologian who was also a bishop had the audacity to say things which were bound to be unpopular in some circles.

Honest to God did not say much that was original. It sometimes put up targets in order to enjoy the experience of shooting them down. It contains long quotations, especially from the writings of Tillich and Bonhoeffer, and it makes much use of phrases like 'religionless Christianity' which, in the original German, mean something rather different from what they appear to mean in English. But the book served its purpose in the sense that it made people think—especially those who would otherwise not have bothered to think about Christianity at all, or who would dismiss it as something irrelevant to life today. It helped them also to see that the essentials of the faith can be detached from the phraseology in which so much of what we hear about religion is wrapped,[2] thus clearing the way for a new and more rational approach to the mysteries of the faith.[3]

Robinson's book was perhaps only a small contribution to the whole debate which, in the post-war years, occupied so many of the theologians. Various philosophies lay at the back of all this. Among these was Existentialism, itself a movement of thought rather than a philosophical system. The 'existentialist' theologians borrowed their thought both from Christian thinkers like Kierkegaard and from humanists like Heidegger. The other dominant contemporary philosophy, linguistic analysis, has been used by Austin Farrer in some of his writings, and, most notably,

---

[1] See J. A. T. Robinson and D. L. Edwards, *The Honest to God Debate* (1963).

[2] E.g. in such popular hymns as 'Hail the day which sees him rise, to his throne above the skies'.

[3] For a detailed criticism of *Honest to God*, see E. L. Mascall, *The Secularisation of Christianity* (1965), pp. 106–89, and for a short and lucid exposition of the more traditional view, A. M. Ramsey, *Sacred and Secular* (1965).

by Ian Ramsey in such a book as his *Religious Language* (1957). There was the endless debate between those who believed in a God who loves and acts and those who find such a conception impossible to accept. 'The real disagreement between Christians and humanists', wrote Alan Richardson, 'does not lie in the area of shadowboxing over the question of a metaphysical God, but in the very live issue of whether the inexorable demands of righteousness can be met out of human resources without the aid of an all-ruling and all-loving power by which the blessings of secularization have thus far been precariously attained'.[1] Then, in the 1960's, came, from the United States, the 'Death of God' movement. The most notable writer of this movement, insofar as its effect on the Church of England is concerned, was Paul van Buren, who, starting from certain well-known sayings of Bonhoeffer, endeavoured, on the basis of a somewhat limited understanding of linguistic analysis, to construct a completely secular gospel.

At the same time a move was being made towards a much more radical approach to the sources of the Christian faith, especially the New Testament. Typical of the new thought was Dennis Nineham's commentary on *St Mark*, published in 1963. This, in some ways, did for the Bible what Robinson had done for the Creeds; it challenged the old-fashioned attitude to the Scriptures, casting doubt on many of the most cherished presuppositions of earlier scholars and of ingenuous readers.[2]

In this 'turmoil of the '60's', with some crying 'God is dead', or 'Our image of God must go', or asking 'Is Holy Scripture Christian?', the seeker after the faith might well feel somewhat baffled. But in more recent years things have steadied down a little by the work of men like John Baker in *The Foolishness of God* (1970), Eric Mascall in *The Openness of Being* (1971), and, above all, in the book *The Founder of Christianity* by the Congregational writer, C. H. Dodd.

The doubts and questions and the courageous and unremitting search for truth which lie at the back of all this are part of the world's need for thinkers and theologians who can offer some answer to the world's problems. So much has been taken for granted for so long that it is no wonder if some of the challenges

[1] A. Richardson, *Religion in Contemporary Debate* (1966), p. 47.
[2] E.g. 'The fact is that . . . the Gospels are not themselves "lives" of Jesus, and scarcely provide the basis on which other people can write such "lives";' *The Gospel of St Mark* (1963), p. 35.

sound strange and perhaps even intolerable. Whether man is any more 'of age' in the middle of the twentieth century than he has been before or will be in the years to come is a matter on which historians might well differ. But at least we know that man is a troubled spirit seeking for rest and for a solution of his problems. It is only through challenge and debate that truth can be discovered, and it is only in the truth that man will find satisfaction and repose.

v. *On to Unity*

Speaking on the occasion of his enthronement at Canterbury in 1942, William Temple referred to the ecumenical movement as 'the great new fact of our era'.[1] By this time discussions about the reunion of the Christian Church had been going on for some time,[2] and a number of organizations had been set up to provide meeting points where members of different Churches could discuss their problems. The World Council of Churches did not come into existence until 1948, but, in 1942, a British Council of Churches had been created, bringing together members of sixteen denominations.[3] From this sprang a number of local councils up and down the country.

While Christians in many parts of the world were discussing their plans for reunion, an experiment in Christian unity had actually been launched in South India. For some time Christian Missions in South India had been meeting with encouraging success; but the barrier of disunity acted as a constant check and bewildered those who had no immediate concern with the history of the Western Church. So in 1919 a group of Indian Christians met, and discussions were set on foot with a view to a union of the Anglican Church with other Christian bodies in South India—Presbyterian, Congregational and Methodist. A plan was published in 1929 and received considerable support from the Lambeth Conference of 1930, which expressed its 'strong desire that, as soon as the negotiations are successfully completed, the venture should be made and the union inaugurated'.[4] On September 29, 1947, the Church of South India

---

[1] W. Temple, *The Church looks forward* (1944), pp. 2–3.
[2] See above, pp. 422–3.
[3] *A History of the Ecumenical Movement*, ed. R. Rouse and S. C. Neill (1967), pp. 624–5.
[4] *Report of Conference* (1930), p. 51.

came into existence, and the four Anglican dioceses of Madras, Travancore, Tinevelly and Dornakal ceased to be in communion with the Church of England.[1] Naturally, a venture so bold aroused considerable anxiety and opposition; but the union, although only experimental, met with such success that further unions have subsequently taken place in North India, Pakistan and Ceylon.

Meanwhile, the Church of England was becoming more and more involved in union schemes and proposals in its own country. A new impetus was provided by Archbishop Fisher when he preached before the University of Cambridge on November 3, 1946. In this sermon, which he called 'A Step Forward in Church Relations', the archbishop declared: 'My longing is not yet that we should be *united* with other Churches in this country, but that we should grow to *full communion* with them'. This would mean that there would be no barrier to exchange of ministries and that the orders of all ordained ministers would be accepted by all. This could be done only if each Church were willing to accept episcopacy, since Anglicans could not recognise a non-episcopal ministry. After referring to the abuses of episcopacy in the past, the archbishop said that he hoped the other Churches would agree to 'take episcopacy into their system'.[2]

On the basis of what the primate had said, conversations between the Church of England and representatives of the Evangelical Free Churches in England now began in earnest and led to the publication of a report called *Church Relations in England*, which was issued in 1950 and which dealt with such things as the nature and faith of the Church, Ministry and Sacraments, with special attention being paid to the doctrine of the Eucharist. The next step was to get conversations going between the Church of England and individual Churches with a view to devising schemes of union. The only Church which immediately responded was the Methodist Church,[3] and in due course a commission was appointed to suggest how reunion could be achieved.

The commission issued an Interim Statement in 1958 setting out

---

[1] See B. Sundkler, *Church of South India: the Movement towards Union, 1900–1947*, (1954).

[2] The Archbishop's sermon has been printed several times, e.g. in *The Archbishop Speaks*, ed. E. F. Carpenter (1958), pp. 63–71, and in R. P. Flindall, *The Church of England, 1815–1948: a Documentary History* (1972), pp. 434–40.

[3] G. K. A. Bell, *Documents on Christian Unity, Fourth Series, 1948–57* pp. 66–75.

the problems involved, but without making any specific recommendations. This was followed by a report called *Conversations
between the Church of England and the Methodist Church* issued in 1963
which contained positive proposals for a union in two stages, the
first of which would be a relationship of full communion, to be
achieved by a Service of Reconciliation, and the second to be a
united Church. On these proposals the Anglican members of the
commission were unanimous; but the Methodists were divided,
and four of them now resigned after signing 'A Dissentient View'.
In 1965 another statement was issued, known as *Towards Reconciliation*, which tried to clear up some of the problems and uncertainties
which had arisen out of a study of the Conversations, and which
contained a revised Service of Reconciliation and a draft Ordinal
for the united Church. This was followed, in 1968, by the final
report on which the two Churches would be required to vote.

This led to much debate, to a pamphlet war, to a number of
threats and appeals, and to a general hardening of opinion as the
matter was discussed and voted on by the Church of England during
the next four years. The Scheme had declared that 'it is unthinkable
that either Church will go forward with the Services [of Reconcilia-
tion] unless it is conscious of overwhelming support' (par. 411); and
it was decided, from the start, that nothing less than a 75 per cent
vote in favour could be regarded as sufficient to make the plan work.
Attempts were, therefore, made to discover how much support was
forthcoming. Discussions were held in the Convocations, debates
in the Church Assembly and in Diocesan Conferences, and a
referendum of all the clergy was conducted. When all this had been
done, a joint meeting of the Convocations of Canterbury and York
was held on July 8, 1969, while, on the same day, the Methodist
Conference was meeting at Birmingham. The result of this was
that, while the Conference voted 77 per cent in favour, the Convocations reached only 69 per cent. But the promoters of the Scheme
did not yield. With the advent of Synodical Government, they
asked that the matter should be debated in the newly-formed
Diocesan Synods and in the General Synod, which, unlike the
Convocations, include a House of Laity. So the battle went on for
another three years until a final decision had to be made by the
General Synod. The question was debated at some length on May 3,
1972; but the vote of 65 per cent in favour was actually less than

before, the lowest figure being recorded in the House of Laity (62 per cent). This meant that the 'overwhelming support', on which the Scheme depended, was not forthcoming, and that new methods of uniting the two Churches would have to be sought.

Meanwhile, conversations had been taking place between the Church of England and the Presbyterian Church of Scotland. These began in 1932, but it was not until 1957 that definite suggestions were made for the future relationships of these two Churches. The suggestions contained in the report of the commission did not win the support of the General Assembly of the Church of Scotland, which asked for further clarification on certain points before there could be any progress—e.g. the meaning of unity as distinct from uniformity, of validity as applied to ministerial orders, of Apostolic Succession and of the doctrine of the Eucharist. This led to the appointment of a Council of Fifty being set up to continue the conversations.[1]

Looking further afield, the Church of England had for long been trying to promote good relations with the Orthodox Churches of the East and with the Church in Russia.[2] Discussion between Anglicans and a Pan-Orthodox delegation had been held in London in 1930, and a Joint Anglican-Orthodox Doctrinal Commission had been set up. Attempts were constantly being made to get the Orthodox Churches to recognise Anglican orders; but, except in the Churches of Alexandria and Rumania, these were unsuccessful, the Orthodox Churches taking the line that recognition of orders (and subsequent intercommunion) should not be considered until there is agreement in the faith. This made theological discussion the first requirement, and facilities for this were now provided.

Up to the outbreak of World War II, the Russian Church had remained somewhat detached from what other parts of the Orthodox Church were doing; but the fact that the war brought Russia into such close contact with the West led to her entry into ecumenical affairs. In 1943 Archbishop Garbett of York visited Moscow, and in 1945 the Patriarch of Moscow came to London. These visits helped to create a much more friendly atmosphere, and, in July 1956, a Theological Conference took place in Moscow,

[1] The four points, to which three more were added in 1963, were dealt with in a report, *The Anglican-Presbyterian Conversations* in 1966.

[2] See above, pp. 283-4, 408-9, 422.

attended by twelve Russians and nine Anglicans, under the leadership of Michael Ramsey.[1]

Meanwhile conversations continued with the Churches of the East; but, although these were conducted in a spirit of mutual confidence and trust, little progress was made. Archbishop Fisher's visit to Jerusalem and Constantinople in 1960 helped things forward; so did the Pan-Orthodox Conference at Rhodes in 1964 which unanimously decided to promote doctrinal discussions with Anglicans. Archbishop Ramsey's long experience of dialogue with Orthodoxy, his great love for the Church of the East, and his frequent visits to eastern Patriarchs, have obviously done a great deal to create the kind of climate in which progress may be looked for.[2]

While conversations and discussions were taking place, Professor H. A. Hodges published, in 1955, a pamphlet called *Anglicanism and Orthodoxy: a study in dialectical churchmanship* in which he declared his hope that the Churches of the Anglican Communion would come to be recognised as actual members of the Orthodox family of Churches. Believing that Orthodoxy represented 'the Christian faith in its true and essential form', he hoped that the whole of the Western Church, including Rome, would one day return to ' a sound mind and a healthy life' which, to him, could be found only in the Orthodox Church. The last fifteen years have shown little sign of an agreement between Canterbury and Constantinople; but, in the meanwhile, a new relationship has, quite suddenly, grown up between Canterbury and Rome.

While most of the Christian world had been engaged in consultation and planning for reunion, the Church of Rome had continued to live in what Father Congar called 'a closed citadel'. For many years the Vatican had taken the line that there was only one way of achieving Christian unity, and that was for those who were outside the true Church to come in. As late as 1950, Pius XII, in *Humani generis*, had declared that 'the Mystical Body of Christ and the Catholic Church in communion with Rome are one and the same thing'; and, so long as this attitude was maintained, there was not much hope of dialogue. But when the World Council of Churches

[1] See H. M. Waddams, *The Anglo-Russian Theological Conference, Moscow, 1956* (1958).
[2] V. T. Istavridis, *Orthodoxy and Anglicanism*, trans. Colin Davey (1966), pp. 45–70.

met for the first time at Amsterdam in 1948, Rome sent an observer in the person of Fr Charles Boyer, S.J., and subsequently arranged for two Anglicans, Dr. Prestige and Dom Gregory Dix, to meet a representative of the Vatican in Rome.[1] As a result of this, and of some private conversations with a group of French theologians, a group was formed—part Anglican and part Roman Catholic— to make some theological enquiries into the subjects which divided the two Churches. This group met on a number of occasions between 1950 and 1962, but no record of their meetings was published.

While these discussions were taking place, big changes were happening in the Vatican with the election of John XXIII in 1958 and his announcement in the following year that he intended to summon a Council to consider not only the renewal of the Church but also questions of reunion. It is true that John XXIII, like his predecessors, saw reunion only in terms of a return to the fold of those who had left it;[2] but by this time there was, in the Roman Church, a growing feeling of resentment against the intransigent policy of the past and a growing desire for closer co-operation with the non-Roman Churches.

While preparations for the Council were taking place, Archbishop Fisher decided to go to Rome and pay a visit to the Pope. This, the first visit ever made by an Archbishop of Canterbury since the Reformation, was a real step forward. Although described as 'only a courtesy call' and deliberately played down by the Vatican, this encounter sowed the seeds of a new relationship between the Churches out of which great things have grown.[3]

In 1961 the preparations for the Vatican Council were in full swing, and the Archbishops decided to send Canon Bernard Pawley to Rome to act as a kind of liaison officer between them and the Secretariat for Promoting Christian Unity which had now been set up. Pope John then invited the Archbishop of Canterbury to send to the Council three observers to represent the Anglican Communion throughout the world, and three men were duly appointed—Professor F. C. Grant of New York, Archdeacon Harold de Soysa of Ceylon, and the present writer. Although the

[1] This was J. B. Montini, who later became Pope Paul VI.
[2] See, for example, his encyclical *Ad Petri Cathedram*.
[3] For pre-conciliar work between Anglicans and Roman Catholics see Owen Chadwick's article in *Anglican Initiatives in Christian Unity* (1967), pp. 94–107.

personnel changed from time to time, an Anglican delegation was present throughout the whole of the Council and played no small part in its deliberations.[1] One result of their work was the special recognition afforded to the Anglican Communion in the Decree on Ecumenism which states that 'among those [i.e. the Churches separated from the Holy See] in which some catholic traditions and structures continue to exist, the Anglican Communion occupies a special place'.[2]

Knowing that students and others would now want to know more about the Anglican Communion, an Anglican Centre was set up in Rome in 1966, with a library and opportunities for lectures, seminars and discussions. In the same year, Archbishop Ramsey visited Pope Paul VI. This was a very different affair from Fisher's visit in 1960. On this occasion there was a Solemn Reception of the Archbishop and his party in the Sistine Chapel and a Joint Service next day in St Paul's-without-the-Walls at which was read out a Joint Declaration calling for 'serious dialogue' between the two Churches. This led to the setting up of a Joint Preparatory Commission of ten Anglicans and ten Roman Catholics, drawn from all over the world. The Commission met three times—at Gazzada in Northern Italy, at Huntercombe in England, and at Malta. At the third meeting it produced a report, outlining what it felt was the most hopeful line for future action, and submitted this to the Pope and to the Archbishop of Canterbury.[3] The Preparatory Commission was now replaced by a new Commission, which adopted the title of the Anglican-Roman Catholic International Commission. This held its first meeting at Windsor in January, 1970, when it declared that 'no doubt exists in the minds of any of the members that the final aim of our work is the attainment of full, organic union between our two communions'. At its third meeting, in September 1971, the Commission issued an 'Agreed Statement on Eucharistic Doctrine', which was followed by another Agreed Statement on 'Ministry and Ordination' in 1973, and a third on

---

[1] See *The Second Vatican Council: Studies by eight Anglican Observers*, ed. B. C. Pawley (1967), and John Moorman, *Vatican Observed* (1967).

[2] *De Ecumenismo*, par. 13. The Anglican Church is the only Church, apart from Rome, which is mentioned by name in any of the sixteen decrees of the Council.

[3] The report, although marked 'Strictly Confidential', was published in full in various journals, e.g. in *Herder Correspondence*, Vol. 5, No. 12 (December, 1968).

'Authority in the Church' in 1976.[1]

While the work of the Commission continues, relations between the two Churches in parishes and elsewhere are steadily improving. The long night of suspicion and ignorance is giving way to the dawn of trust and fellowship. Anglicans and Roman Catholics are learning to treat one another with respect as they discover that many preconceived notions as to what their fellow-Christians believed and did were false and uncharitable. It is in this new atmosphere of mutual understanding and toleration that we can cherish the hope of a coming unity of all Christian people in truth and in holiness.

[1] The *Three Agreed Statements* were published together by S.P.C.K. in 1978.

NOTE ON BOOKS

MANY of the books referred to in the note to Chapter XXII apply also to this period. To the biographies should be added R. C. Jasper, *George Bell, Bishop of Chichester* (1967), W. E. Purcell, *Fisher of Lambeth* (1969) and E. W. Kemp, *The Life and Letters of K. E. Kirk, Bishop of Oxford* (1959). For the study of theological thought during this period see D. L. Edwards, *Religion and Change* (1969), R. J. Page, *New Directions in Anglican Theology* (1967), Alan C. Clark and Colin Davey, *Anglican–R.C. Dialogue, the Work of the Preparatory Commission* (1974) and *A.R.C.I.C., the Final Report* (1982), and Alan Richardson, *Religion in Contemporary Debate* (1966). For the history of the ecumenical movement, see G. K. A. Bell, *Documents on Christian Unity, Fourth Series, 1948–57* (1958), H. E. Fey, *The Ecumenical Advance: a History of the Ecumenical Movement*, vol. 2 (1970) and *Anglican Initiatives in Christian Unity* (1967).

ADDITIONAL NOTE ON BOOKS

In addition to the books mentioned in the footnotes and at the end of each chapter as applicable to that particular period, the following will be found of general use.

The standard history of the Church in England is still W. R. W. Stephens and W. Hunt, *A History of the English Church*, 8 vols. in 9 (1899–1910), though much of this now needs revision. The work is gradually being replaced by *An Ecclesiastical History of England*, four volumes of which have so far appeared: viz. M. Deanesly, *The Pre-Conquest Church in England* (1961), Owen Chadwick, *The Victorian Church*, 2 vols. (1966 and 1970) and J. C. Dickinson, *The Later Middle Ages* (1979). To these may be added such works as *Lives of the English Saints* (ed. J. H. Newman, 4 vols. 1844–5 and re-edited by A. W. Hutton, 6 vols. about 1900). W. F. Hook's *Lives of the Archbishops of Canterbury*, 12 vols. (1860–84) forms a general history, as does also E. F. Carpenter's *Cantuar: the Archbishops in their Office* (1971).

For original documents the standard work is H. Gee and W. J. Hardy, *Documents illustrative of English Church History* (1896 etc.), to which should be added A. W. Haddan and W. Stubbs, *Councils and Ecclesiastical Documents relating to Great Britain and Ireland*, 3 vols. in 4 (1869–78) and D. Wilkins, *Concilia Magnae Britanniae*, 4 vols. (1737). The last of these is being brought up to date in *Councils and Synods, with other documents relative to the English Church* under the general editorship of F. M. Powicke, of which Volume II in two parts appeared in 1964. H. Bettenson, *Documents of the Christian Church* (1943) contains much which concerns the Church in England, and R. P. Flindall, *The Church of England, 1815–1948: a Documentary History* (1972) is a very useful collection of modern material. The constitutional history of the Church may be read in F. Makower, *The Constitutional History and Constitution of the Church of England* (1895, reprinted 1960), and in H. M. Gwatkin, *Church and State in England to the death of Queen Anne* (1917).

The following books of reference will also be found useful: the *Dictionary of National Biography; The Oxford Dictionary of the Christian Church*, ed. F. L. Cross (1957); Ollard, Crosse and Bond, *A Dictionary of English Church History* (3rd ed. 1948); and J. Julian, *Dictionary of Hymnology* (revised ed. 1907). A convenient hand-list of the diocesan bishops from the earliest times will be found in *Crockford's Clerical Directory*, and there are more detailed lists in W. Stubbs, *Registrum Sacrum Anglicanum* (2nd ed. 1897) and F. M. Powicke, *Handbook of British Chronology* (1961). For other church dignitaries see Le Neve, *Fasti Ecclesiae Anglicanae* (1716, revised by T. D. Hardy, 3 vols. 1854, and now issued in a new edition in 12 vols. (1963 etc.). A good many medieval episcopal registers have now been published, mainly by the Canterbury and York Society. A list of those still known to exist will be found in A. B. Emden, *A Survey of Dominicans in England* (1967).

INDEX

Aachen, 31-2
Aaron, Martyr, 4 n.
Abbot, Abp. George, 225, 227
Aberdeen, 11
Abingdon, 33; monastery of, 43
Adamites, 248
Additional Curates' Society, 322, 323
Adelphius, Bp., 4
Advertisements of Abp. Parker, 214
Aelfric, 51-2
Africa, slavery in, 319-20; missionary work in, 321, 384, 429
Agricola, 6
Aidan, S., 18, 27
Ailred of Rievaulx, 71, 149
Alban, S., 4
Albert, Prince, 390
Albertus Magnus, 133
Alcuin, 31-2
Alcuin Club, 400
Aldate, S., 9
Alderley, 333, 358
Aldhelm, S., 30
Alexander II, Pope, 55, 59
Alexander, Mrs., 363
Alfred, King, achievement of, 41, 42-3; courage of, 40, 41, 52-3; love of learning of, 41-2; and monastic life, 42; translations by, 42
Alleluia Victory, 6
Allen, William, 206
Alphege, S., 48, 53
Althorp, Lord, 336
America, pilgrims to, 224; colonization of, 267; Bp. Berkeley in, 275; missionary work in, 295-6; War of Independence, 295-6; United States of, 296; Wesleyans in, 301; slavery in, 320
Amiatinus, Codex, 33
Amsterdam, Conference at, 423
Anabaptists, 186, 211
Ancren Riwle, The, 127
Andrewes, Bp. Lancelot, and James I, 223; and the Arminians, 225; writings of, 235; mentioned, 222, 233, 249
Angles, 8, 12, 13
Anglia, East, conversion of, 17; S. Cedd in, 19-20; Congregationalism in, 247; Bp. Stanley in, 358
Anglican Congress, Minneapolis 1954, 438; Toronto 1963, 439
Anglican Consultative Council, 444

Anglican-Roman Catholic Joint Preparatory Commission, 458
Anglican-Roman Catholic International Commission, 458-9
Anglican and Eastern Orthodox Churches' Union, 409
Anglo-Catholics, and the Church, 365-6; Sir W. Harcourt and, 403; and the Ecumenical Movement, 408, 413; Congress of, 425; mentioned, 352
Annates, Conditional Restraint of, 167
Anne, Queen, accession of, 269-70; character of, 270; and Abp. Sharp, 280
Anselm, S., early life of, 64-5; becomes Abp. of Canterbury, 64-5, 66; and the papacy, 65, 66; and Investitures, 65-6; and the monarchy, 66, 74, 75; exile of, 66-7; death of, 67; writings of, 67-8, 84, 134; mentioned, 83, 416
Anthems, 259, 363-4
Apocrypha, The, 223
Apostolicae Curae, 408, 422
Appeal to all Christian People, An, 422, 431
Appeals, Act in Restraint of, 167
Appropriations, 96-7, 142
Aquinas, S. Thomas, 133, 134, 161
Arabic, study of, 150
Aragon, Katharine of, 162, 164-5, 168, 169
Arcadia, Bp. of, 300-301
Archdeacons, origins of, 48; Norman, 62; administration by, 141-2; in eighteenth century, 284
Arches, Court of, 354, 366, 376
Architecture, Saxon, 33-4, 50; Norman, 61, 68; Early English, 89, 147; Gothic, 94, 334; Decorated, 147-8; Perpendicular, 147-8; Restoration, 260
Ardingly College, 370
Arimathea, Joseph of, 3
Aristotle, 133, 275
Arles, Council of, 4
Armada, Spanish, 207, 221
Armagh, diocese of, 8; Archbishops of: *see* S. Patrick; James Ussher
Armenian Church, 284
Arminian Nunnery, The, 236
Arminians, origins of, 225; Puritans and, 227; Laud and, 230; Wesleyan, 305
Army, New Model, 240
Arnold, Matthew, 377